Fish Out of Water

The Newfoundland Saltfish Trade
1814 - 1914

Shannon Ryan

BREAKWATER

Canadian Cataloguing in Publication Data

Ryan, Shannon, 1941-
  Fish out of water : the Newfoundland saltfish trade 1814-1914
Bibliography
Includes index
(Newfoundland history series ; 2
ISSN 0831-117X)
ISBN 0-919519-47-4 (bound) — ISBN 0-919519-90-3 (paper)
1. Fish trade - Newfoundland - History. 2. Fish, Salted - Newfoundland - Economic
aspects. 3. Newfoundland - Commerce - History. 4. Cod-fisheries - Economic
aspects - Newfoundland.
I. Title.
HD9464.C33N48 1985   338.3'72758   C85-099215-X

Breakwater gratefully acknowledges the support of The Canada Council.

The publisher acknowledges the financial contribution of the Cultural Affairs
Division of the Department of Culture, Recreation and Youth, Government of
Newfoundland & Labrador, which has helped make this publication possible.

For Margaret
and
In Memory of Keith

CONTENTS

Key to Abbreviations

B.T.	Board of Trade
c.i.f.	cost, insurance, freight
C.N.S.	Centre for Newfoundland Studies, Memorial University of Newfoundland
C.O.	Colonial Office
cwt	hundredweight or quintal; 112 pounds, avoirdupois
d.	pence (sterling)
D.N.E.	*Dictionary of Newfoundland English*
F.O.	Foreign Office
f.o.b.	free on board
fol.	folio
J.H.A.	*Journal of the House of Assembly*, Newfoundland
lb.	pound, avoirdupois
m	maravedis
MHG	Maritime History Group, Memorial University of Newfoundland
MUN	Memorial University of Newfoundland
P.P.	*British Parliamentary Papers*
r	real de vellon
R.G.	Research Group, National Archives, United States of America
s.	shilling (sterling)
S.P.	*Sessional Papers*, Canada

List of Maps

List of Tables in Text

List of Tables in Appendix

Preface

Newfoundland, in 1814, was at the beginning of a century of political growth and constitutional development within the context of both the British Empire and British North America. The local political leaders who campaigned for Crown Colony status, Representative Government, and finally, Responsible Government, and who led the governments during this century of political evolution were convinced that commercial developments would be enhanced by these constitutional developments. However, although political "progress" had a momentum of its own in nineteenth century Newfoundland the real question was whether the colony could maintain a permanent politically independent existence given its traditional economic and commercial systems. Indeed the extent to which any small country almost wholly dependent on the production and sale of a single product in highly competitive and often unstable international markets can remain politically independent is the question that is central to this book.

The study of Newfoundland's cod fishery was first recommended to me as a possible M.A. thesis topic in the fall of 1968 by the late Dr. Keith Matthews. Keith and Kay and their family had come to Newfoundland in 1967 from Oxford where Keith had just finished his D.Phil. thesis on the Newfoundland-West of England cod fishery. He suggested that I begin where he had left off and in 1971, under his supervision, I completed an M.A. thesis which dealt primarily with the internal developments of Newfoundland's nineteenth century cod fishery. In 1982 I received the Ph.D. degree for my thesis on Newfoundland's saltfish markets, completed under the supervision of Professor Glyn Williams, University of London. This book is a synthesis of both theses and of additional research carried out since 1982. Portions of this book have been published in James Hiller and Peter Neary (eds.), *Newfoundland in the Nineteenth and Twentieth Centuries* (University of Toronto Press, 1980); *Canada's Visual History*, Volume 26; *Acadiensis* (Spring 1983), 34-52; *Newfoundland-Spanish Saltfish Trade: 1814-1914* (St. John's: Harry Cuff Publications, 1983); *Encyclopedia of Newfoundland and Labrador*, Volume II, pp. 144-55; *Horizon Canada*, Volume 1, Number 8, 169-75.

There are several points which I must bring to the readers' attention. The Ph.D. thesis was heavily documented, particularly in the case of many tables where information was often drawn from a considerable number of sources. In order to save space this book sometimes refers the reader to the thesis for more information on the sources. In most cases the thesis, in turn, will direct the reader to the Foreign Office General Correspondence, Public Record Office, England.

Because the Newfoundland cod fishery operated, almost exclusively, using the hundredweight (commonly abbreviated to cwt) of 112 pounds, avoirdupois (50.8 kg), this system of weight measurement has been retained in this book. Consequently, I have converted the different systems of weight including the Castilian quintal, the Portuguese arroba, the Norwegian våg, and the kilogram, for example, into hundredweight at the various conversion rates indicated in the footnotes. This hundredweight was almost universally referred to as a quintal (early spelling, kentall) in Newfoundland parlance.

Many people contributed to the completion of this book but I owe the greatest debt to Keith Matthews. From the time we both agreed in 1968 that I should study the cod fishery up until his sudden and unexpected death in May 1984, he was always eager and willing to listen and ready with advice and suggestions. It is most unfortunate that no more Newfoundland graduate history students will be able to work with this brilliant, courageous, and sensitive academic whose knowledge of Newfoundland history was equalled only by his own commitment to Newfoundland.

Also, I owe a special debt of gratitude to the late Dr. David Alexander, History Department, MUN, who was so generous with his advice and assistance until his death in July 1980.

Among the many other scholars who were most generous with their advice and assistance I must thank the following in particular: Professor Glyn Williams, University of London, who supervised my Ph.D. thesis; Dr. Fred Aldrich, Dean of Graduate Studies, MUN; Dr. Leslie Harris, President, MUN; Mr. G.E. Panting, MHG, MUN; Dr. J.K. Hiller, Head, History Department, MUN; Dr. Gordon Jackson, University of Strathclyde; Mr. Ken Kerr, MUN; Dr. Elliot Leyton, Anthropology Department, MUN; Dr. Peter Neary, University of Western Ontario; Professor Helge Nordvik, University of Bergen; Dr. Patrick O'Flaherty, Head, English Department, MUN; Dr. R.E. Ommer, History Department, MUN; Mr. Greg Palmer, author and historian, London; Dr. Sarah Palmer, University of London; Dr. George Schwarz, History Department, MUN; Dr. Larry Small, Folklore Department, MUN; Professor Trygve Solhaug, Norwegian School of Business, Bergen; Dr. George Story, English Department, MUN; Professor Björn Þorsteinsson, University of Iceland; Dr. William Whiteley, History Department, MUN;

Professor John Widdowson, University of Sheffield; the members of the Imperial and Commonwealth History Seminar (1977-79), Institute of Historical Research, Senate House, University of London; and the members of the Maritime History Group, MUN.

I would like to thank the archivists and staffs of the Public Record Office, the British Library, the Senate House Library (London), the Institute of Historical Research (London), the National Archives (Washington), the University of Oslo Library, the Provincial Archives of Newfoundland and Labrador, the Centre for Newfoundland Studies (MUN), the Newfoundland Provincial Reference and Resource Library, and the Conception Bay Museum (Harbour Grace). Also I would like to thank the late Mr. Martin R. (Mac) Lee who allowed me access to his collection and Dr. Bobbie Robertson, secretary, the Newfoundland Historical Society.

In preparing the illustrations I have made every effort to identify, credit appropriately, and obtain publication rights from copyright holders of the photographs and sketches used in this book. In this respect I would like to thank the photographers, the collectors and the repositories for permission to use their photographs and sketches: Captain George C. Whiteley, Jr., Friendship, Maine, USA; the late Martin R. (Mac) Lee, Placentia, Newfoundland; Mrs. Dale Fitzpatrick and the Newfoundland Book Publishers (1967) Ltd.; Mr. Gordon King, St. John's; Mr. Robert Pitt and the Division of Educational Technology, MUN; Mrs. Gertrude Crosbie, St. John's; Mr. Hal Andrews, St. John's; the Newfoundland Provincial Reference and Resource Library; Mr. Jack Martin, MUN, St. John's; Rev. Don Harvey, MUN, St. John's; Baine Johnston & Co., Ltd.; the MHG, MUN; Dr. Wilfred Wareham, St. John's; Mr. Michael Harrington, MUN, St. John's; and Mrs. Frank Ryan, Harbour Grace, Newfoundland. Secondly, I would like to thank the individuals who examined the illustrations and advised me, to the best of their knowledge, on the identity of copyright holders and/or the accuracy of the captions: Mr. John Andrews, St. John's; Mr. David Davis, Provincial Archivist, St. John's; Captain Morrissey Johnson, M.P., Bonavista-Trinity-Conception; Mr. Tony Murphy, Archivist, PANL; Dr. Patrick O'Flaherty, Head, English Department, MUN; Mrs. Shirley Scarlett, St. John's; and Dr. John Widdowson, Sheffield. (Notice of any errors and/or omissions in this regard will be gratefully received and appropriate corrections made in any subsequent editions.)

In addition I owe a great debt to the Newfoundlanders who so willingly answered my many questions on matters pertaining to local history: Mr. & Mrs. Andrew Short; Mr. Edward Russell (since deceased); Mr. Patrick J. Walsh (since deceased); Mr. John Shannahan, Riverhead,

Harbour Grace; Mr. Joseph Ryan (since deceased), Bay Roberts; Mr. Stephen Hogan (since deceased), Carbonear; Mr. R.J. Connolly, M.A., K.S.G., Harbour Grace; and my father, Bernard Ryan (since deceased), and my mother, Lillian Ryan.

I would also like to thank the administrators of the History Department and Memorial University who helped me to schedule leave during 1977-79 to complete my research in England; Memorial University for assisting with a number of grants; the Social Sciences and Humanities Research Council (formerly Canada Council) for Doctoral grants to help with my Ph.D. research expenses; and the History Department office staff who have been most cooperative and helpful.

Finally, I would like to thank the people who have aided in the physical preparation of this volume: Mr. Geoff Budden, Ms. Cathy Horan, Ms. Willeen Keough, Ms. Kathy Pike, Ms. Linda White and my wife Margaret, who assisted with the proof reading; my sister Brenda who prepared the index; Mr. Jack Martin, MUN, who prepared most of the photographs; Ms. Heather Wareham, Archivist, MHG and Mr. G. Learning, who assisted with the maps; Mrs. Dallas Strange and Mrs. Susan Snook who did the typing; and the management and staff at Breakwater Books.

Introduction

Newfoundland has experienced several traumatic decades in the twentieth century. At the beginning of the Great Depression, it was forced, because of financial difficulties, to give up local responsible government and accept government by a British-appointed commission, which became known as the "Commission of Government." Very little changed in the lives of the people during the following decade but the government bond holders were accommodated and Newfoundland's credit rating maintained. During the early years of the Second World War, an Anglo-American agreement provided for the establishment of American armed forces bases in Newfoundland and employment opportunities rose dramatically. Part of the new prosperity was related to the general increase in government war-time spending but most was the result of the demand for local labour in the construction and maintenance of the American bases. By the thousands, men and women left their traditional jobs and lifestyles in the depressed cod fisheries and assumed positions in various trades and professions at the naval base in Argentia, the airport in Gander, the air force base in Stephenville, and the various bases in St. John's. When the war ended two developments became apparent. Great Britain was anxious to reduce its colonial obligations and Newfoundland's financial situation had improved to the point where local business, professional, and religious leaders could look forward, once again, to assuming responsibility for the government of this dominion. This local movement was centred in St. John's, the capital, which dominated the rest of Newfoundland. However, another local movement which aimed at confederation with Canada, and which had the tacit support of the Canadian and British governments, arose also. This second movement became a well-organized party and promised the electorate immediate financial benefits of old-age pensions and family allowances if they should become Canadians. On the other hand, the party advocating the return to responsible government could promise only the return to a system that had failed to survive the Great Depression. Many of the electorate had personally experienced the results of that failure when the fishery had almost totally collapsed and the unemployed and unemployable were expected to live on the daily allowance of six cents (6¢) given them by the Commission of Government. Despite a historic fear in Newfoundland of union with Canada, the confederate party won the British-supervised referendum and in 1949 Newfoundland became the tenth province of Canada. Not only were there immediate financial benefits to the old and to people with young children but there was also immediate access to employment in the industrial centres of Canada, especially Toronto. Newfoundland's new government attempted to establish light industries, but this effort was largely a failure because it was difficult to compete with mainland Canadian industries. These attempts were followed by others which aimed to develop large industries based on the province's resources of hydro-power, minerals, and timber. To handle some of the province's cod, Newfoundland's most famous resource, the number of fresh-frozen fish plants was increased. Very little was done to encourage the production of saltfish,[1] largely because few in Newfoundland were sufficiently interested. The reputation of the traditional saltfish industry, like the reputation of responsible government, had been practically destroyed among Newfoundlanders during the previous decades. The credibility of both had suffered because of Newfoundland's inability to provide a livelihood and independence for its citizens. Like responsible government, the saltfish industry had been associated with failure ever since the First World War. The post-war depression in the 1920s, the Great Depression, and employment on the armed forces bases, had all conspired against the re-establishment of a substantial saltfish industry. In addition, the Canadian government in Ottawa had no real interest in this industry. Since the new province's saltfish industry was dependent on markets in Spain, Portugal, Italy, Greece, Brazil, and the Caribbean, any efforts to revive it would need the active support and participation of the Department of External Affairs in Ottawa. With its foreign trade limited to the exportation of wheat and to its bilateral trade agreements with the United States, Canada neither had in operation nor desired to create the machinery which was needed to negotiate the sale of saltfish in foreign markets.[2] Newfoundland's traditional markets were not those that purchased Canadian wheat and Canada itself provided no local market. Consequently, the saltfish industry dwindled.

Most of the problems which troubled Newfoundland's saltfish trade in the twentieth century were not unique to that period in the industry's development. They were problems of production and marketing that had existed from the beginning of Newfoundland's history as a colony. In fact, these problems had prevailed throughout the three-hundred-year-old history of the British migratory fishery in Newfoundland waters — an industry which was brought to an end by the Napoleonic wars. By 1814 the problems which had been primarily the concern of the British migratory fishery had become the concern of the Newfoundland resident population.

Newfoundland underwent considerable development between 1814 and 1914. In the former year, Newfoundland was looked upon still, in certain quarters, as the base for a British-centred migratory fishery; by the latter, it was on the threshold of assuming Dominion status. In 1814 the cod fishery was synonymous with Newfoundland, but by 1914 the colony was making a determined effort to exploit alternative resources. In 1814 Newfoundland was very much a part of the new world and was a haven for thousands of immigrants, especially from southern Ireland; by 1914 it had become part of the old world insofar as its emigrants were seeking new opportunities on the American mainland. It was during this period between the Napoleonic War and the First World War that the society which has since become known as "traditional Newfoundland" crystalized.

The history of Newfoundland's development during the period between 1814 and 1914 occupies an important place in the history of Britain's colonial empire. Newfoundland was generally considered to be Britain's oldest colony; it had been the site of Britain's most famous fishery, the West of England-Newfoundland cod fishery; and this fishery had been used for centuries as the major recruitment ground for sailors for the Royal Navy. For these reasons Newfoundland's nineteenth century development did not correspond closely to the developments in Canada, New Zealand, Australia, and the British West Indies. Although the colony's political evolution resembled that of the rest of British North America (later Canada — from which Newfoundland remained completely independent), its economic developments differed. Newfoundland's saltfish was sold in foreign markets along with British goods like woollens, coal, and iron products. Unlike Canada and the British West Indies, which directed most of their trade to the mother country and, later, to the United States of America, Newfoundland's export trade was directed to southern Europe, Brazil, and to one market within the empire, the British Caribbean. Within the British Empire, therefore, Newfoundland's economy was unique. Thus while the production of the colony's saltfish became entirely a local matter after 1814, the actual sale of the product in the markets was practically identical to the trade in other British exports. Newfoundland's saltfish was treated as a British item by the British Foreign Office in general, and by the Consular Service in particular. Because of this, the history of Newfoundland's saltfish trade in the nineteenth century is uniquely part of British trade history, British colonial history, and British colonial commercial history, as well as being the story of Newfoundland's economic development.

This combination of internal, local developments in production and external developments in marketing meant that responsibility for the operation of Newfoundland's saltfish industry was often divided and the forces which influenced the trade were often diverse. From the time the cod was caught and processed by the local fishermen to the time it was purchased and consumed by the poorer classes in the overseas markets, the industry was subject to many local and external factors. Consequently, developments both within Newfoundland and within the market countries together explain why the colony, which became increasingly politically independent during 1814-1914, demonstrated, at the same time, tendencies towards economic decline because of problems in the saltfish industry while world-wide demand for saltfish was increasing.

Newfoundland's history during the period between 1814 and 1914 has been unevenly covered.[3] The older works are politically and constitutionally oriented while some of the later ones have dealt, in part, with the colony's social and economic history.[4] Within both the framework of Newfoundland history and that of the history of the northwest Atlantic cod fishery in general, the colony's cod fishery has received various types of treatment. The most comprehensive work in the general field remains that of Harold A. Innis.[5] In his largest undertaking, he studied that geographical fishing area which stretches "from Cape Cod to Labrador." He gives a detailed description of the origins of the cod fisheries of the European nations and the growth of local fisheries in the region. He paints a panoramic picture of wars, exploitation, colonization, revolution, and capitalism. However, he has little to say about the markets for the codfish. This is the major gap in Innis' work. Ian McDonald studied the rise of the Fishermen's Protective Union after 1908 and examined in great detail the social, economic, and political forces which culminated in its rapid expansion and, later, its equally rapid collapse.[6] David Alexander applied the theory of a common property resource to the Newfoundland cod fishery prior to 1934.[7] He showed that the utilization of the cod fishery by Newfoundland could not, under normal circumstances, stabilize at a point where those involved could expect a reasonable living with the surplus population moving elsewhere or into other activities. This approach to the study of the Newfoundland fishery was a new and intriguing one, for it raised the question of what would have happened had Newfoundland retained the monopoly on the codfish trade which it had briefly held during the Napoleonic War. Presumably, the population dependent on the fishery would have continued to grow until total investment and total income were about the same and the standard of living had declined to a minimum. However, demand would have determined the time frame here, and other factors such as technological developments, war, depression, climatic changes, and the imposition of political controls over the common property resource would be certain to interfere. All of the works which aim mainly to study the Newfoundland cod fishery during the period from 1814 to 1914 have been primarily concerned with production. The availability of local sources combined with the elementary level of research in this field have been the reasons for this. As Grant Head has written, "In regard to Newfoundland in particular, the most obvious and important gap in our knowledge is that of markets for cod."[8] Thus no studies have examined Newfoundland's cod fishery thoroughly with emphasis on both production and marketing during 1814-1914; such an examination is the intention of this study.

This work proposes to examine the colony's saltfish trade during the period between 1814 and 1914 to determine the general trends and developments and their causes. Because the total number of markets located in the three regions concerned — southern Europe, the Caribbean, and Brazil — was considerable and given the hundred-year period covered in this study, it has been necessary to limit the amount of research involved. Therefore, the writer has concentrated on the reports of the British consuls in each of the market ports (the richness of this source will become self-evident) and has had to confine himself, for the most part, to the general developments in these markets. As David Alexander points out: "Variations in the run of ground fish in various parts of the world could generate either gluts or shortages in the markets. A poor curing season could mean that firms were short of high-quality fish for Europe and overloaded with lower grades for the Caribbean."[9] Therefore, specific developments on a monthly, weekly, and daily basis have been largely ignored because of the amount of work and time that such treatment would demand. As Alexander also notes, even "if the prices for complementary items such as olive oil rose, then the demand [for codfish] would be sharply reduced."[10] Therefore, any discussion of codfish vis-à-vis other foods in the various markets has been limited, for the most part, to a brief discussion of the competition from other producers of codfish and, in the case of the Brazilian markets, jerked beef. Consequently, while this study will make every effort to explain the vagaries in the markets, it will concentrate on the more general developments as perceived by the consuls and the Newfoundland exporters. It will also examine the response of the Newfoundland exporters to the market information they were receiving from the consuls but, again, no attempt will be made to examine the specific factors that governed the daily decisions of each firm. Finally, some conclusions regarding the effectiveness of Newfoundland's response to market developments will be drawn.

The actual production and market operations can be briefly stated here, although certain developments occurred throughout the century which will be discussed later. The merchants in the Newfoundland cod fishery generally sold their product through agents in the markets.[11] However, some of the older and bigger firms had their own establishments in the markets as well. One such enterprise was Newman, Hunt and Company of England which had a port wine operation in Oporto and a fishing operation in Newfoundland. (The disappearance of these old English and Jersey firms from the Newfoundland fishery is discussed below.) In the vast majority of cases, the agent arranged for the sale of fish when it arrived at the market or, in some cases, he arranged for the cargo to be forwarded to another market. The agent then arranged for the payment of the fish through a London bank and also arranged for a return cargo to Newfoundland — for example, salt from Spain or rum from Barbados. In other cases, the agent arranged for a freight to another port where a cargo for Newfoundland would be waiting — for example, cotton from Brazil to England, and textiles and fishing equipment from England to Newfoundland. The agents advised the exporters about the condition of the market, although such information was often out of date by the time the exporter's fish arrived. Thus good agents who could make independent decisions were essential. However, immediate problems could not always be solved satisfactorily. Rosemary Ommer quotes from a letter which a Jersey merchant received from his agent in 1771:

> Ten more cargoes of baccalao have arrived...Two of exceeding fine fish from Placentia, two-thirds large of this at 5 dollars...five still remain unsold: the buyers being daily more terrified on [sic] so many arrivals and adverse to engage in small fish. We have advised both Captain DeCaen and Valpy to proceed to Italy but they are alarmed at the quantity they say has gone forward to these markets...we should be glad some of the others would proceed and by their lightening our market, for the present spare us the mortification of submitting to the low terms proposed by the buyers.[12]

The agents' effectiveness was increased in the 1860s by the introduction of the telegraph. The importance of good agents and the expense involved in paying them was, no doubt, a factor which led to the concentration of Newfoundland's export trade in the hands of a relatively small number of big St. John's firms by the early twentieth century.

During the earlier part of the period, the trade was carried on throughout the year, although the month of October was particularly busy, as was the period directly before and during Lent. The exporters were often under pressure to get the season's catch sold before the next became available. Therefore, all fish had to be sold because there was no point in bringing it back to Newfoundland; this meant that heavy losses were not uncommon. As Alexander says, "...so long as saltfish consumption was dominated by the poor, there was a ceiling on price increases, but very little in the way of a floor."[13] The introduction of large steamers into the trade in the latter part of the century changed this pattern of small cargoes exported over a twelve-month period to one of large concentrations of exports in the autumn. In addition, during periods of expansion (and the Napoleonic War period was the last one that has any bearing on this study), new entrepreneurs would often send a relative or colleague to accompany the cargo to market; as their business prospered, they hired agents. Finally, as Ommer points out, exporters, in their efforts to increase sales, often wrote to saltfish importers in various markets.[14] On the whole, one must agree with Alexander that exporters "found it difficult to regulate output in terms of market expectations."[15]

In purely organizational terms, the production of codfish for export was also relatively straightforward, although there were distinct developments throughout the period which are discussed below. The merchants generally supplied the fishermen in advance for the summer fishery and received the fishermen's complete catch in the autumn. Ideally, this catch was sufficient to pay off the debt to the merchant and also pay for the fishermen's winter supplies. The fishermen who fished near their homes around the island were expected to produce a light-salted, hard-dried product referred to as *shore* fish. This cure was unique to Newfoundland (with small quantities produced in Gaspé) and, as Alexander stated, "no competitor had been able exactly to duplicate shore fish, either by natural or artificial drying processes."[16] In 1920 (the first year for which a complete description of the various qualities is available) the Newfoundland shore fish (as opposed to the Labrador-cured product) was sent to the various markets as follows: Spain bought *merchantable prime* (top quality) fish which was thick, yellow or golden in colour, well-split, light-salted, and not too dry. That country also purchased a small quantity of *merchantable number two*, which was slightly inferior to prime. In addition, in the Spanish markets, the fish was purchased in three sizes: twelve to seventeen inches, seventeen to twenty-two inches, and over twenty-two inches. Portugal purchased similar fish, but as small as ten inches in length, well-dried, and of a medium thickness. Also, southern Portugal preferred about two-thirds of its cargoes to be made up of small fish and one-third to be made up of large and medium, while northern Portugal preferred two-thirds large and medium and one-third small. The product consumed in Italy was also classified merchantable prime and number two and was well-dried, but thickness was not important and only two sizes were acceptable: small — twelve to eighteen inches; and large — seventeen to twenty inches. Brazil bought the medium-quality fish, *Madeira*, which was light-salted, well-dried, and hard, and eighteen inches and under in length.[17] The inferior product, *West India*, was sent to the Caribbean. The designations *Madeira* and *West India* referred to the quality, not the market. For example, when merchantable fish was scarce, cargoes of Madeira or West India were sent to Europe; furthermore, sometimes buyers disagreed with the exporters regarding the quality of the product sent out from Newfoundland and downgraded merchantable to Madeira or West India, before agreeing to purchase it. The fish cured on the Labrador coast, where there was less opportunity for natural drying, was more heavily salted and this *Labrador* cure was moister and sold in two qualities, No. 1 and No. 2, to Spain, northern Italy, and Greece.[18] Fish caught on the Grand Banks was sometimes classified as shore and sometimes as Labrador, depending on the curing process. All shipments to Europe were sent in bulk without any packaging, while fish for the Caribbean was packed in casks containing four cwts each and that going to Brazil was packaged in drums and half-drums. (Officially, a drum contained four Portuguese arrobas for a total of 129.517 lbs., avoirdupois, but 128 lbs. was often the weight used by the Newfoundland shippers.) The fishermen caught and cured their fish according to their own expertise and inclinations, and the finished product was a combination of qualities and sizes. In the autumn, the merchant fixed the price of the fisherman's catch, deducted the sum owed, and gave winter supplies for the balance. Often there was very little balance and sometimes merchants were forced to advance further credit — if only to prevent the fishermen from starving or emigrating. Good fishermen were generally overcharged while the merchants were often left with bad debts and bankruptcy. During extended periods of depression, the fishermen emigrated and the merchants went bankrupt. Newman, Hunt and Company, London, summed up the merchants' attitude towards giving credit, and indeed towards the trade itself, when they wrote to their Newfoundland branch, Newman and Company: "...we wish you to understand that our business in Newfoundland is not to buy Fish but to sell goods, and that we only take Fish in payment because the Planters [fishermen] have no money to give us."[19]

In any case, the whole system of production and marketing made it impossible to plan a season's voyage. The fishermen were given very little indication, if any, of the price they could expect to receive for their catch. At the beginning of the fishing season, they only knew the price they had received the previous year, while the merchants' information was often only slightly more up-to-date, and even that could prove to be incorrect by the time the new season's catch began to reach the markets. Even with the improvement in communication following the introduction of the telegraph to the trade, market changes could occur too late in the season for exporters or fishermen to be able to compensate for them. Sometimes, as one Jersey merchant wrote, the trade was a "mere lottery."[20] At the same time, the fishermen were not happy with the situation. Larry Small writes: "Fishermen usually worked from May until September without knowing what price they would receive for their catch. And there was the feeling that men had to literally beg price information from their dealers."[21] Small quotes one informant who was recalling his experiences at the beginning of the twentieth century:

> We shipped fish yesterday [for example]. Any price? No, no price. They [the merchants] been hammering at this ever since last winter about the price a [sic] fish. They blamed the markets last year. We lost three and four dollars on a quintal [112 pounds] a fish last year and they said they blamed the markets. The markets were down.... It wasn't the markets at all, wasn't so bad as that. Wasn't so bad as they predicted, 'twas only a bluff. So you're bluffed from the cradle to the grave, a fisherman is. He got no choice. He got to take what's offered 'n. You go to the store; a man got a pound of potatoes to sell. What's the price? Oh, ten cents a pound. He got a pound of carrots to sell, salt meat, whatever it might be they got a price on it. But a fisherman just got to wait till somebody makes a price. But everything else in the world is sold got a price on it clear [except] a quintal a fish. And a man got to wait till somebody puts a price on it. Why can't a man make a price on his fish so well as the farmer can make a price on a barrel of potatoes?[22]

As will be seen later, the production of a top-quality product — a product which required care — under these conditions was subject to difficulties.

Several facts concerning the period from 1814 to 1914 provide the basis for the questions which are at the core of this study. Although the colony diversified its economy during the early decades of the century (by the utilization of its seal resources), diversification failed in the long term; furthermore, no worthwhile attempts were made to develop local industries that would reduce the dependence on imports. Therefore, without an agricultural base and other easily exploitable resources (except seals) and given the island's harsh climate, Newfoundland's economy was almost completely dependent on the sale of dried salted codfish in unregulated markets — a situation not unlike that faced by some less developed countries today.[23] The St. John's Chamber of Commerce wrote in 1841:

> The resources of Newfoundland are entirely external, and consist alone in her fisheries; she is dependent for almost everything upon foreign importation; nearly all her provisions, both salted and fresh are imported. The great exertions which of late years have been made to introduce agriculture have succeeded in extending it no

farther than to the immediate neighborhood of the fishing settlements, from whence offal fish can be carried for manure; the growth of grain, except oats in small quantities, which when grown are for the most part cut down for fodder, is almost unknown amongst us; and even of potatoes, the only article of human subsistence produced in any quantity, we are forced to depend for large supplies upon England, Ireland, Scotland and the neighboring colonies....[24]

Similarly, a contributor to a newspaper wrote in 1879: "This isolated community have no choice of an occupation, and must pull upon a single line, and fish or die."[25] At the same time, world-wide demand for codfish was increasing, and while other codfish producers responded by increasing production and exportation of this product, Newfoundland did not. Norway, which became Newfoundland's chief competitor, increased its exports of salted dried codfish from an average of 28,732 cwts[26] annually during the five-year period ending in 1819 to an annual average of 991,120 cwts[27] during the five-year period ending in 1914. Newfoundland's exports averaged 944,998 cwts[28] during the former period and rose only to 1,345,633 cwts during the latter. Also, as will be seen, the French and Icelandic fisheries became increasingly competitive later in this period. Furthermore, it must be borne in mind that Newfoundland's population increased from 35,952 in 1814 to 242,619 in 1911, which meant that per capita exports declined from 20.7 cwts to 4.9 cwts.[29] Given the extent of Newfoundland's dependence on the cod fishery and the growth of world consumption and production of codfish, one must examine the colony's inability to avoid a continuous decline in per capita production and its failure to maintain a large share of the growing world markets.

In keeping with the internal and external factors influencing the history of Newfoundland's saltfish trade, research for this book has involved chiefly the examination of local (mainly production-oriented) and British (mainly market-oriented) documents.

The statistical and literary reports prepared by the various Newfoundland government departments and printed as appendices in the *Journals of the House of Assembly of Newfoundland* and the *Blue Books* are indispensable to the study of the colony's general nineteenth-century economic history. These provide information on the local development of the saltfish industry and also contain extensive records of the exportation of Newfoundland's saltfish and its ports of destination. However, there are two major weaknesses in this statistical data. In the first place, exports of fish from Newfoundland's Labrador coast were not listed prior to 1860. Secondly, statistics of exports to European markets were often inaccurate because ships did not always unload their cargoes at the ports to which they had cleared from Newfoundland. In fact, all ships which cleared from the colony for Gibraltar did so to receive orders there for their final destinations. Lisbon, although an important market in its own right, was similarly used by shippers. During periods of severe and sudden market disruptions (as occurred in Spain after 1815, for example) statistics in the Newfoundland records mean very little. After 1906 the Newfoundland Customs Office seems to have been able to gather more accurate statistics of this nature. A somewhat similar situation existed with regard to shipments to Halifax and New York which were re-exported to the Caribbean or Brazil. However, in this case, the problem is much less extensive and important. The records of exports south to the Caribbean, and especially to Brazil, are particularly useful, as will be seen. Despite their limitations, the *Journals* and *Blue Books* are a rich source of information.

Most information concerning the sale of fish, on a general level, in the foreign markets is located in the reports of the British consuls. These reports can be found in the appropriate Foreign Office collections for the earlier part of the period under study and in the British Parliamentary Papers for the later years. Some also turn up in the Board of Trade and Colonial Office collections. Also, a fair number were forwarded from the Foreign Office to the Board of Trade but can only be identified and retrieved with difficulty. Sometimes reports or extracts of reports can be found in other collections and publications. Nevertheless, in whatever form they appear, they provide an invaluable source of basic information on the markets. Also useful in conjunction with the British consular reports are the reports and dispatches from British embassies in the market countries. These tend to concentrate on wider market issues, especially those relating to the national tariff policies. The British consular reports are uneven in value. Some individuals were extremely competent, energetic and well-informed, and wrote very comprehensive reports, while others lacked these qualities and often wrote little or nothing. The majority fell between these two extremes. However, on the whole, these reports are important because of their extensiveness and objectivity. As the British consul in Oporto wrote in 1886:

> ...in my opinion, under the present system of drawing up and circulating Consular Trade Reports, a better general result is obtained than by the corresponding systems followed in other countries. The only reports which can be compared with ours are those sent by the United States' Consuls which I have had an opportunity of perusing for some years past.[30]

Fortunately, the British consuls treated Newfoundland saltfish as a British commodity and, therefore, reported regularly on the trade. Very few records of the Newfoundland exporters have survived because of fires which destroyed the wooden warehouses and office buildings on the waterfront of St. John's. In 1892, when nearly all the business was in the hands of the St. John's exporters, the town's commercial section was almost totally destroyed by fire and, consequently, few older records have survived. However, records from some of the outport firms are available and these have been used. Naturally, a number of other sources concerning the markets have also been used in this study, as will be seen from the references.

The Colonial Office records are the major source of information on the colony's reaction to market developments and the response of the Colonial and Foreign Offices to these reactions. Most other sources depend on these records. In the case of many significant (and sometimes not so significant) documents, copies were enclosed with the Colonial Office correspondence. Thus, petitions from the Newfoundland Commercial Society normally went to the colony's governor, who transmitted them to the Colonial Office for its attention or for further transmittal to the Foreign Office. Replies returned via the same route. Consequently, copies were recorded in the Colonial Office collections. Of course, this source has been supplemented by others.

A number of other sources were useful in different ways. United States consular reports were helpful in examining the developments in the British Caribbean and also useful as a supplement to the British consular records, especially in the case of Spain during the French occupation. *Journals of the House of Assembly of Nova Scotia*, Colonial Office records relating to British North America and the British Caribbean, and *Canadian Sessional Papers* were also quite useful. Finally, a variety of other documents helped to complete the explanation of the international saltfish trade in general and Newfoundland's trade in particular.

There are certain intrinsic difficulties in studying this international trade. One difficulty arises from the fact that saltfish was sometimes re-exported with local produce and consequently cannot be properly identified. There are several instances where this pertains to Newfoundland. Some Newfoundland saltfish was exported to Nova Scotia and the United States. Then Nova Scotia exported saltfish to the United States as well. The United States, Nova Scotia, and Newfoundland exported large quantities of fish to the Caribbean. Similarly, Newfoundland exported some saltfish to Great Britain which in turn was exported to southern markets. Consequently, it is not always possible to identify the origins of some of the saltfish arriving at the markets. Exporting countries during the nineteenth century did not always record the final destination of their exports; instead they recorded only the immediate destination. Norway, the most important example in this case, recorded substantial exports to Great Britain and these quantities cannot be traced with any degree of certainty, although it must be assumed that they were re-exported. Another difficulty is that *saltfish* is not always specifically identified in the records. Fortunately, Newfoundland and Canada clearly identified their product and the Norwegians, Icelanders and Faroese were equally clear about their exports of *klippfisk* as were the French with their exports of *morue séchée et salée*. However, the Americans exported fish which were generally listed as "cod, haddock, hake, pollock — dried, smoked, salted, pickled" and Great Britain's exports of saltfish were apparently recorded generally as "unenumerated" fish. Similarly, markets sometimes recorded imports under various rubrics, including "fish," "salted fish," "cured fish," and "dried fish". Later in the period, the trade in fresh-frozen codfish also created some confusion in the records. Nevertheless, all these problems of re-exportation, and the question of the different species traded, and the different cures concerned, are confined, for the most part, to the periphery of this study. Only in the case of the British records does one wish that clearer distinctions could be made. As will become clearer, the major producers and the major markets were not, on the whole, in any doubt about what they were selling and buying, and while some records are missing, those that remain are generally straightforward.

Although the study of production in Newfoundland's saltfish industry is a clearly defined and logical unit its marketing is a broad and diverse subject. Consequently, organizational problems arise. Newfoundland's political and constitutional history from 1814 to 1914 can be, and has been, studied in chronological units. Its economic history does not lend itself to this approach. In this case, the subject has no natural chronological milestones. Production in the cod fishery experienced decline, stagnation, and then expansion with marked fluctuations. The markets followed patterns different one from another and often different from the overall pattern in the codfish trade. These peculiarities of the subject matter make a strictly chronological approach impossible. Therefore, this study is organized topically. Chapters 1 and 2 cover the internal developments of the cod fishery. Chapter 3 deals with the international saltfish trade while Chapters 4 to 9 examine the individual markets in detail. The conclusion presents the major findings of the study, attempts a synthesis, and provides a reminder that the work is primarily concerned with people: as in the words of Walter Scott, "It's no fish ye're buying — it's men's lives."[31]

CHAPTER 1

Origins and Early History of Newfoundland's Saltfish Industry

The fish that launched thousands of ships from the North Sea to the Mediterranean and had a major influence on maritime developments and trade in the north Atlantic was the cod. Coastal people always consumed it in a fresh state, while the northern Norwegians dried it without salt for export to the Baltic, and other producers with access to salt pickled it. It seems that the English, with access to limited amounts of salt, were the first to develop the light-salted, well-dried product. The almost universal use of cod as a food is evident from the fact that its name became synonymous with the term *fish*. Thus the Norwegians called their salt-free dried cod *tørrfisk* (dried fish or stock fish), while the thirteenth-century English called it *stokfische*.[1] The salted dried cod was at first called *Terranova fisk* by the Norwegians[2] but, later, the term *klippfisk* was adopted. The French referred to cod dried on the shores of St. Pierre and Miquelon as *poisson de côte*,[3] while that cured in Bordeaux and sold in the Mediterranean was often referred to as *lavé*,[4] but their general term for cod was *poisson*.[5] In Newfoundland it was (and is) simply called saltfish. To process the cod into saltfish, it was split along the underside, and the head, offal, and part of the backbone were removed so that the fish lay flat, somewhat like a kippered herring (except that the latter is split along the back). It was then washed, salted in piles (saltbulk), and, later, spread on wooden platforms (flakes) or rocky surfaces to dry. When well dried, it could be stored almost indefinitely. Its keeping qualities and the comparative ease with which it could be transported (unlike bulky barrels of pickled beef and pork, for example) combined to make saltfish a useful and popular source of protein. Its popularity was particularly evident in cities supplied by sea, in areas where people were under a religious obligation to eat fish, particularly during Lent, and amongst crews on tropical voyages such as the Spanish and Portuguese were undertaking. Codfish had always been caught around the coasts of the British Isles, Iceland, Norway and, later, Greenland, but it was the discovery of the vast stocks of this fish off the coast of Newfoundland at the end of the fifteenth century, when Spain and Portugal were acquiring unprecedented wealth, which turned this fishery into an international industry. On the fishing banks near the island of Newfoundland and in the island's coastal waters, the Newfoundland saltfish industry was born.

The island of Newfoundland is roughly triangular in shape and measures about 300 miles on each side. It includes several prominent peninsulas, a number of commodious bays, and a considerable number of good harbours. Forests of fir and spruce, patches of rocky ground, and bog land make up most of the island's surface, and, except for parts of the western interior, there is no land suitable for extensive agriculture. The climate is unstable, affected by the Labrador and Arctic currents, but tends to be cool and wet with a short, though often hot, summer. This combination of brief summer and little arable soil has prevented Newfoundland from developing an agricultural base and consequently the inhabitants have never been able to do more, agriculturally, than utilize small vegetable plots to supplement their diet.

The fishing stocks for which Newfoundland became famous were found in two major localities: the Grand Banks off the island's southeast corner and in the coastal waters. Thus Newfoundland became the centre for a bank or deep-sea fishery and for a coastal or shore fishery. While the bank fishery could be carried out through most of the year the shore fishery was only possible during June, July, and August. The eastern half of the island, because of its proximity to the migrating schools of fish from the Grand Banks, was always the area best suited to the shore fishery, although stocks of fish surrounded the whole island.

It became apparent very early that markets would be found in southern Europe for these new supplies of saltfish. Northern Europe, with its more productive agriculture, was richer in protein, and its superior internal transportation systems were better able to distribute its beef and pork provisions. Furthermore, in northern Europe there were additional supplies of local salt herring and stockfish. Southern Europe, especially Spain and Portugal, needed protein for their coastal cities which were more easily supplied by sea than by the Iberian hinterland. French seaport cities on the Atlantic coast were also potential markets for saltfish from Newfoundland.

At first, the new fishing industry was carried out by migratory fishermen from Spain, Portugal, France, and England, who sailed to Newfoundland for the fishing season, returning in the fall with cargoes of saltfish to be sold in their home markets. Of the four, England had the smallest home market (and consequently the smallest fleet), partly, no doubt, because of its extensive coastline, its own coastal fisheries, and fewer obstacles to overcome in its internal trade. However, several fortuitous events (from England's point of view) occurred during the latter sixteenth century to change this situation.[6] The Huguenot wars in France disrupted its fishery and turned that country into a saltfish importer. Then the Spanish fishing fleet was attacked and destroyed by Bernard Drake in 1585 and the subsequent attempt by Spain to invade England was disastrous for its fleet (and Portugal's, as that country had just come under the Spanish Crown). Although England lost its saltfish markets in France when peace was restored to that country at the beginning of the seventeenth century, it had acquired by then substantial markets in Spain and Portugal (although both these countries continued to carry on a limited fishery in Newfoundland waters until the outbreak of King William's War in 1689). In any case, by the beginning of the seventeenth century, a strong English-Newfoundland fishery had been established which was controlled almost entirely by the West of England.

The West of England fishermen consolidated their gains in the early years of the seventeenth century. The crews built substantial facilities on

Newfoundland's east coast in order to carry out their annual activities. These facilities consisted of stages,[7] flakes, cookrooms, and warehouses. In addition, quantities of tree rinds were needed to cover the fish piles during wet weather. In Newfoundland, where forest regrowth was slow, and often never occurred at all because of soil erosion, these activities resulted in extensive deforestation. Consequently, the property built and provided for the annual fishery became valuable, partly because of the size of some of these *plantations*, but also because more and more time was required each spring to build new premises or rebuild old ones as the dense forests were depleted. As a result, caretakers were left behind to carry out any necessary repairs and have everything ready for an early start the following summer. Of more importance, they ensured that the owner retained control of his premises because, under the traditional practice of the first arrival every spring having first choice of the *fishing rooms*, the builder of a fishing room could lose it the following year if it was unoccupied.[8] These caretakers, plus the occasional deserters from the fishing ships and the remnants of several largely unsuccessful colonization attempts, became the first permanent European residents. Although the fishermen crossed the Atlantic in what were recorded as *fishing* ships, and while it seems likely that in the very early years they fished from the sides of these ships, by now this was no longer the practice. The ships were anchored and the men fished from small boats which, of course, could also be left behind in the care of residents. Almost simultaneously, others became boat owners and hired small crews to fish for them. These men, called *bye boat keepers*, left their boats in Newfoundland during the winter and found transportation for themselves and their crews to and from Newfoundland on the fishing ships. In the autumn, they sold their catch to visiting *sack* (trading) ships or to other fishing ships that were going directly to market. These bye boat keepers were to provide a valuable source of income to the fishing ship owners. By the end of the seventeenth century, the residents, bye boat keepers and fishing ships were all well established. At the same time, there were no rigid divisions. Residents often returned to the West of England for the winter, and bye boat keepers often spent a winter on the island. Similarly, fishing ship captains sometimes remained in Newfoundland to look after that end of their company's trade, and other captains and mates often became bye boat keepers in times of depression. Nevertheless, by the end of the seventeenth century, on the whole, these three groups were distinguishable, with the migratory branches being by far the most important. Meanwhile, the cargoes of saltfish were taken from Newfoundland in late summer each year by sack ships to the rich markets of Spain and Portugal whence salt, wine, olive oil, fruit, and specie were taken to England to pay for the products needed in the fishery and to provide a livelihood for the fishermen and profits for the investors. Briefly then, this comprised the Newfoundland fishery during the seventeenth century.

Throughout the eighteenth century, the saltfish industry and its various segments fluctuated. The resident fishermen prospered in wartime when the migratory fishermen were unable to travel safely across the Atlantic, or avoided the seaports for fear of impressment. These periods brought about an increase in the island's resident population. Between 1710 and 1715, for example, the population increased from 1,400 to more than 4,000 persons and, similarly, between 1750 and 1764 it increased from 8,225 to nearly 16,000.[9] The post-war periods caused severe problems for the residents and usually brought about a decline in their numbers. The migratory fishery, on the other hand, being well supplied with ships, sailors and fishermen released from naval service, always recovered after the wars. This pattern was repeated several times during this century, with the resident fishery gradually becoming stronger, especially after the American Revolutionary War put an end to the easy migration of residents to New England.

By the 1780s the English-Newfoundland saltfish trade had acquired several characteristics. Although West of England firms remained dominant, the Channel Islands had become involved and, latterly, Scottish and Irish firms also. In addition, the independence of the new United States of America resulted in the exclusion of New England ship owners from the Newfoundland-West India saltfish trade. This encouraged some ship owners to move to Newfoundland to take part in this two-way trade. In the meantime, British ships came out to Newfoundland in the spring bringing fishermen and supplies: flour, bread, and fishing equipment from England; salt beef, salt pork, butter, and porter from southern Ireland; and salt and some wine and fruit from southern Europe — sometimes via England. Vegetables and some flour were acquired from the rest of British North America. Beginning in mid-summer, the saltfish was collected from residents and from the migratory crews and brought to markets in Spain, Portugal and the Italian states — in scattered cargoes at first but, by September and October, in increasingly greater numbers. There the company agents or, in the case of larger firms with wine interests in Oporto and southern Spain, the company's local branch handled the sale of the product, receiving bills of exchange drawn on London banks, and arranged for a return cargo to England or to the Newfoundland fishery. In addition, the British West Indies, especially Barbados, had become important markets for the refuse saltfish — the kind that was unsaleable elsewhere. This fish was used by the sugar plantation owners to feed their slave populations. To pay for it they exported sugar, molasses, and rum to the Newfoundland fishery. The trade had adapted to changing conditions before and continued to do so during the eighteenth century as the resident fishery increased in importance.

Meanwhile, there had been also developments involving the ownership and governance of Newfoundland. In the sixteenth century, the fishermen of Spain, Portugal, France, and England had all visited the island. Spain and Portugal had been excluded by the end of the 1500s and control over the island and its waters rested with the English and the French. Both these nations were anxious to encourage their fisheries and they both increased their control over sections of the island during the seventeenth century. The English concentrated their activities on the east coast between Trepassey and Bonavista and their area included the harbours of Ferryland, Brigus, Bay Roberts, Harbour Grace, Carbonear, Trinity, and especially St. John's. Most of their harbours were in Conception and Trinity Bays, and as a result were often blocked with Arctic ice in the spring; but they were well sheltered and close to excellent inshore fishing grounds. The French turned their attention to the south coast, which was along their route up the St. Lawrence River to New France. Their area of concentration was in Placentia Bay, with their headquarters at Placentia. The south coast was nearly always ice-free. At the end of the War of the Spanish Succession in 1713, France agreed to remove its settlers from Newfoundland and received in exchange the liberty for its fishermen to fish on the island's west and north coast between Point Riche and Bonavista. This area which became known as the French Shore was not noted for its fish stocks, nor was it conveniently located vis-à-vis the other French possessions in North America. In 1763 France was forced to give up all its mainland possessions in northern North America to Great Britain and was given in return the small islands of St. Pierre and Miquelon off Newfoundland's south coast as a base for its fishing fleet. It was also at this time that the Labrador coast was placed under the jurisdiction of the British naval governor, who was responsible for patrolling the summer fishery in Newfoundland waters. French fishermen retained the liberty to fish on the French Shore. At the end of the American Revolutionary War, the boundary of this area was adjusted to take into account the fact that English fishermen had occupied during the war the best fishing harbours on the north coast. The north coast boundary was moved back from Bonavista to Cape St. John while the west coast boundary was moved south to Cape Ray. At the same time, England, which had always been very ambivalent about English settlement, ever fearful that residents would compete in the markets with the mother country, was forced to recognize that settlement existed. In 1729 a naval governor was appointed in charge of all components of the English fishery in Newfoundland — resident as well as migratory — during the summer months. Then magistrates, constables, and, later, customs officials were designated. This increase in government brought with it a slight increase in stability and encouraged the further growth of settlement.

Although the migratory fishery was a much more ancient institution and had the active support of the British government, it could not survive the growing competition from the resident fishery. Increased cost of facilities as the forests were depleted, and disruption by wars eventually forced the migratory fishery out of business, especially since the fishing ships found it profitable to supply the residents with their needs in return for their catch. Increasingly, the migratory fishermen found it necessary to remain in Newfoundland year-round. Even before the final effects of the French Revolutionary and Napoleonic Wars could be felt, the end of the migratory fishery was in sight (see Table 1.A,[10] below). A writer in 1790, after pointing out that the migratory fishery had declined between 1788 and 1790 by 148 ships, 600 boats and 3,500 men, wrote:

> Whether this great and rapid reduction of the fishery is to be described [sic] solely to bad markets, or to bad Regulations, I shall not pretend to say. I am sorry, however, to observe, that all the Decked Vessels, and the greater part of the Boats, which had been withdrawn from the Fishery are owned by Merchants and Boatkeepers [bye boat keepers] usually residing in Great Britain, and chiefly in the County of Devon.[11]

TABLE 1.A

Number of Men in the
English-Newfoundland Saltfish Industry:
1784-1795

Year	Men in Fishing Ships	Men in Bye Boats	Resident Men
1784	2,603	2,606	5,106
1785	2,866	2,887	4,604
1786	2,651	5,236	6,190
1787	3,112	3,625	10,185
1788	4,306	2,397[12]	10,794
1789	2,824	-	9,950
1790	1,112	-	8,362
1791	2,255	-	7,585
1792	2,351	-	8,722
1793	1,348	-	6,664
1794	1,894	-	8,036
1795	1,362	-	7,063

The eighteenth century migratory fishery reached its peak in 1788 and declined during the remainder of the century. It had been weakened before the start of the French Revolutionary War, and by the end of the Napoleonic War, it had been eliminated.

The early years of the Napoleonic War[13] were not especially prosperous for the Newfoundland fishery. However, the brief period of peace in 1803, accompanied by the Passenger Act of that same year, which made it cheaper for people to travel to Newfoundland than to other parts of North America, resulted in increased immigration to the island; more than 1,700 people arrived in 1803, followed by 646 in 1804. By this time, the cessation of the migratory fishery had placed the production of saltfish in the hands of the residents so that when the trade did improve, it was the Newfoundland industry, and not that of the West of England, which benefitted.

The American embargo of 1807, followed by the outbreak of the Peninsular War in 1808 and the Anglo-American War in 1812, all contributed to the expansion of the Newfoundland saltfish industry. America's exports to Spain, which had included considerable amounts of saltfish, ceased altogether, and, furthermore, the Spanish junta granted preferential tariff treatment to imports of British goods. Consequently, Newfoundland found itself with a near monopoly on sales of saltfish to Spain and Portugal. Prices rose from an average of 13s. 6d. per cwt (free-on-board) in 1807 to 32s. in 1813. This stimulated capital investment, which led to a growth in production so that saltfish exports, which averaged 674,584 cwts annually during the three-year period from 1806 to 1808, increased to an annual average of 1,059,033 cwts during 1814-1816. At the same time, wages and prices increased. Fish splitters, for example, who had previously earned £30 to £32 per season, were paid as much as £140 for the same work in 1814. Food prices also rose and bread, a major import article which sold for 20s. to 30s. per cwt in 1804, cost from 70s. to 84s. in 1813. However, there was an actual improvement in the standard of living and, as a result, the resident population increased from 21,975 in 1805 to 40,568 in 1815. By the end of the war, Newfoundland had changed from a "fishing ship moored on the Grand Banks" to a firmly established colony. Governor Keats' remark that "...in consequence of the late wars St. John's became the Emporium of the Island and changed its character from a fishery to a considerable commercial town"[14] summarized the situation. This period of growth in the saltfish industry had much more important implications for the island than any similar period during the preceding three centuries.

The Napoleonic War brought major changes to Newfoundland. The migratory fishery ceased because the fishermen found it advantageous to remain on the island, partly to take advantage of the prosperity in the fishery and partly to escape the war; consequently, the fishery became completely residential. The profits were such that tavern owners, clerks, and shopkeepers became buyers and exporters of saltfish. These people formed the basis of a class of local entrepreneurs with no direct connections with British firms. Their existence marked the beginning of the growth of local indigenous firms centred in St. John's and, to a lesser extent, Conception Bay. Thus part of the saltfish export trade was taken over by inhabitants as well. In addition, a spring seal fishery developed[15] as fishermen travelled, increasingly, to the Arctic ice floes to hunt these mammals for their skins and fat. This industry was to become very important to Newfoundland and was to provide the resident fishermen with something they had always lacked — employment to supplement the summer cod fishery and an industry that could make use of the local shipping which was tied up during the winter and spring. The population of over 40,000 people (in 1814) was engaged in the shore fishery in small communities on the east coast, though there were larger concentrations in St. John's and around Conception Bay. This was the period during which Newfoundland emerged as a colony, although formal confirmation of this fact by the British government was withheld for a number of years. The English fishery had become a truly Newfoundland fishery, and for the next one hundred years, the colony would struggle to support itself by this industry.

CHAPTER 2

Structure and Development of the Saltfish Industry: 1814-1914

Newfoundland, during 1814-1914, was dependent on the cod fishery to an extent unmatched by any other major producer. Most fishermen fished in the waters along the coast near their homes, carrying on what has already been described as the shore fishery. Others migrated annually to the Labrador coast, and a lesser number were engaged in the deep-sea or bank fishery. Single lines with baited hooks were universally used at first and remained common in the shore fishery; long lines or bultows were used later in the century, especially in the bank fishery; and the cod trap was introduced into the shore fishery towards the end of the century. Small boats powered by sail and oar were used in the actual fishing, and by 1914 the internal combustion engine was being adopted. The production of saltfish was affected by developments within Newfoundland as well as by developments in the market countries and among competitors.

Production Trends and Developments

Throughout the years 1814-1914, the production of saltfish fluctuated (see Table 2.A,[1] below). During the five-year period ending in 1815, the average annual exportation was 935,450 cwts. With fluctuations, this quantity dropped to 737,805 cwts during the five-year period ending in 1835. This was the bottom of a trough, and by the five-year period ending in 1860 the annual average exportation had increased to 1,236,868 cwts, although there had been short downswings in the early 1850s. A downswing and stagnation followed during the 1860s, but there was an upswing in the early 1870s, and during the five-year period ending in 1875, the average annual exportation was 1,319,138 cwts. Another downswing followed, but during the first half of the 1880s the average annual exportation rose to 1,428,208 cwts. A rapid decline followed which reduced the average annual exportation during the following five years by 284,740 cwts, or 19.9 percent. This was the bottom of the trough and there was a slow but fairly steady expansion which peaked during the five-year period ending in 1910, when

1,529,215 cwts were exported. Finally, this was followed by a decline, and during the four-year period ending in 1914 the average annual exports amounted to 1,306,536 cwts. These fluctuating peaks and troughs, which were part of a rising trend, resemble closely the "...cyclical behaviour in economic activity [that] has generally taken place in the context of a growing economy [as in] the United States and western Europe."[2]

TABLE 2.A

Newfoundland's Saltfish Exports:
1811-1914
(cwts, five-year averages)

Year	cwts	Year	cwts
1811-1815	935,450	1866-1870	1,116,887
1816-1820	883,387	1871-1875	1,319,138
1821-1825	920,607	1876-1880	1,181,777
1826-1830	927,993	1881-1885	1,428,209
1831-1835	737,805	1886-1890	1,143,469
1836-1840	841,525	1891-1895	1,206,368
1841-1845	961,260	1896-1900	1,248,880
1846-1850	980,340	1901-1905	1,301,653
1851-1855	959,126	1906-1910	1,529,215
1855-1860	1,236,868	1911-1914	1,306,536
1861-1865	1,100,119		

This picture of Newfoundland as a "growing economy," however, must be qualified when one examines the colony's population growth and the per capita exportation of its primary product. Newfoundland's population continued to grow during the 1814-1914 period (see Table Introduction.1, Appendix) and that growth was proportionately greater than the increase in saltfish production. As David Alexander points out, a free-access resource which needs a minimum of capital is subject to this kind of development[3] — especially a free-access resource like that involving the shore fishery. (The Labrador cod fishery, which required greater capital investment, and the bank fishery, which was even more expensive to operate, could and did experience contractions to a much greater extent than the shore fishery. Thus the shore fishery could survive adversity more easily.) In fact the shore fishery could be exploited to the point where investment and return were almost identical because the industry was based on a free-access resource and because the fishermen were independent operators who needed very little capital investment. Therefore, although the cod fishery was stagnant, an increasing number of people became dependent on it. This could lead to a situation in which fishermen were barely able to subsist. Since the migration of British fishermen and their families to Newfoundland ceased shortly after the end of the Napoleonic War, the picture presented by Table Introduction 1 is not distorted by the practice evident in earlier periods of fishermen supporting families in Britain. In addition to problems concerning quantity, the colony also faced problems involving price. The value of saltfish varied during the century (see Table 2.1, Appendix). Sometimes it was high, as during the latter Napoleonic War, when top-quality fish brought 32s. per cwt. The price dropped after peace was established in 1815 and it remained low during the following decades. In the 1820s and 1830s the average price was often as low as 10s., actually less in some years, and this remained the case until the 1850s, when a rise in price occurred. In the 1860s low catches led to further increases. Fluctuations followed until the mid 1880s when the price fell with the growth of world production and the decline in the quality of the Newfoundland product. A temporary decrease in world production led to an increase in the price of the colony's saltfish during the early years of the twentieth century. Despite the development of ancillary trades and services the history of Newfoundland's saltfish industry during the period from 1814 to 1914 is best described as fluctuations around a declining trend.

Production Problems: Catch Failures and Inferior Cures

The Newfoundland cod fishery, as has been seen, failed to expand to any worthwhile extent, and one must examine two factors which were often associated with this lack of expansion: periodic catch failures and inferior curing, both of which hindered the production and sale of fish.

Even if one accepts that production was most dependent on market conditions, since good markets meant higher profits which led to increased capital investment and greater production, the actual failure of the fish to appear at certain times in certain places could and often did mean serious losses for the industry in these areas. The cod usually migrated to the waters near shore in early summer, when the shallow water had warmed sufficiently, in pursuit of caplin. Sometimes because of unsatisfactory water temperatures, the fish failed to appear. A glance at various fishery reports[4] can show that practically every year these failures occurred in some parts of Newfoundland and Labrador. Occasionally, however, the fish would be plentiful in all areas in large quantities and big catches would result, as in 1857 and 1874. Also, occasionally, the fish would fail to appear in a number of places and a general catch failure, similar to the one in 1868, would occur. In that year, Captain Parish, in a survey of the south coast of the island and the Labrador coast, discovered that out of the sixty settlements visited, the cod fishery had been good in five, fair in twelve, indifferent in eighteen, and very poor in twenty-five.[5] Thus, while catch failures could be serious for the individual community or region affected, very seldom was it as extensive as in 1868 although even in that year overall production was not seriously affected (see Table Introduction.1, Appendix). Another period of catch failures which had larger lasting results occurred in the mid 1880s and coincided with the expansion of both the Norwegian and French fisheries. These failures brought about an increase in local prices which forced the colony's exporters to compete fiercely with each other in their efforts to send cargoes to markets early and thus avoid the low prices which were endemic later in the season when these markets became glutted with fish from Norway and France as well as Newfoundland. The British consul in Naples described the situation as follows:

> The past season has been more disastrous for British shippers, as with a short fishery in Newfoundland and on the Labrador high prices were paid to the fishermen, and the attempt to obtain corresponding prices on this side [Naples] led to a large increase in the consumption of Norwegian and French cod-fish, and after commencing the season for Labrador cod-fish at the equivalent of about 20s. 6d. per quintal, cost, freight, and insurance, the prices receded to as low as 8s. to 10s. per quintal towards the close of the season....
>
> The imports of British cod-fish during the past year were only about one-third of the total imports whereas in former years the great bulk of the Neapolitan consumption was supplied by British cod-fish, and there is every probability of a further reduction, if not a total extinction, of the consumption of Labrador cod-fish, which is the most prejudiced by the French bounty system. The British Newfoundland merchants have to thank themselves for this reduction, for of late years the quality of Labrador fish has been so inferior, for apparently no attention is paid to the selection of the fish or to the curing of it.[6]

Nevertheless, the important factor here was foreign competition, which kept down the market price and thus reduced Newfoundland's profits and investment.

Also, unlike the Norwegian Lofoten fishery and France's deep-sea fishery the Newfoundland fishery was not disrupted to any great extent by stormy weather. In Newfoundland, storms usually occurred in the winter although gale-force winds were not unknown in the fall. The Labrador coast was more susceptible to damage than the island because fishing establishments at Labrador were more exposed to these winds and fishermen were more likely to be caught at sea returning to their island homes. In 1867 and again in 1885, for example, serious wind storms caused extensive damage and some loss of life on the Labrador coast. However, since most fishermen had already given up their activities for the season the overall effects were minimized. In general, stormy weather was not an important factor in the development of Newfoundland's industry.

As per capita production declined during the century (and catch failure was not a major reason for this), the quality of the fish seems to have declined as well. While this could be considered a market problem, since high prices for good quality could improve the product, it is necessary to look at the Newfoundland end of the operation.

Producing a light-salted, hard-dried fish was an involved process requiring skill, patience, and good weather conditions (plus, of course, a suitable reward). After the fish was landed, its head was removed, it was split open, and the insides were taken out. The major part of the backbone was then severed cleanly and neatly from the rest of the fish. At this stage, the well-handled fish could lie flat and did not have any ragged ends. It was then lightly salted in layers, with about eight to nine hogsheads of salt (one hogshead is equal to 52.5 imperial gallons) for each one hundred quintals.[7] (Labrador and bank fish usually required twelve to thirteen hogsheads for the same quantity of fish.[8]) The fish then remained in this bulk for fifteen to twenty-one days, after which it was washed and allowed to drain.[9] The water content of the fish was then fifty-six percent to fifty-eight percent. Whereas the Norway and Iceland stockfish (without salt) could be dried to a water content of sixteen percent, at which point mold growth became suspended, the lightly-salted Newfoundland product was usually dried to a water content of forty to forty-five percent. When it was intended for the Brazilian markets, the longer journey and warmer climate demanded a lower water content of thirty-eight percent. Saltfish could only be dried when the relative humidity was below seventy-six percent, and the best drying occurred when it was forty-five to fifty-five percent. Cutting points out that this is due to the fact that "the pressure of a saturated salt solution in salt fish lowers its equilibrium water vapour pressure to about 76% relative humidity." Whereas stockfish required cold weather so that the fish could dry before spoiling, thus limiting its production to the colder months, for the best cured Newfoundland fish, a temperature of 60°-80°F (16°-27°C) was necessary, with 75°F (24°C) being preferable. A light wind was also essential. Any number of mistakes could be made during this long process and those mistakes, combined with unfavourable weather conditions, often resulted in a poor-quality fish.

The factors that could cause an inferior cure can be divided into two groups: those over which the fishermen had direct control and those which were beyond his control. It is fairly evident that the former was by far more important; furthermore, one could say that deception and carelessness were probably the most important reasons for a poor-quality product (ignoring market demand for the moment). Carelessness and/or deception were often evident in the manner in which fish was salted. The correct procedure allowed the pickle (the solution formed by the union of the moisture of the fish and the salt) to drain off the fish, but this was sometimes prevented. The result would be a heavier fish with a very white finish that could often deceive the culler who was grading the fish. This fish would deteriorate on a long voyage so that, for example, that which was originally purchased as Madeira would have to be sold at a loss as West India.[10] Newman and Company suffered from this practice and were of the opinion that the fishermen were doing it intentionally.[11] However, whether deliberate or not, the practice seems to have been fairly widespread.[12] Other problems arose from the fishermen's application of too much or too little salt and carelessness in splitting and heading, but these were easily detected and hurt the fishermen as well as the trade. By the 1830s the recovery of the other fish-producing nations and the consequent increased competition caused the Chamber of Commerce to express its concern over the poorly-cured fish being produced at Labrador and to advise the fishermen there to be more careful.[13] During the 1850s Newman and Company became very disturbed about the quality of their fish, which, they claimed, was causing their biggest financial losses.[14] They stated that their fish was not selling in Brazil because of its poor quality and ordered their agents to rectify the situation.[15] This seems to have worked for awhile, for in 1864 the company noted an improvement in the cure.[16] However, quality remained a problem for the Newmans and they stated on many occasions afterwards that it would have to be improved.[17] They blamed both the planters who cured the fish and the agents who bought it.[18] The Chamber of Commerce became concerned again during the depressed 1860s[19] and the Department of Marine and Fisheries (a relatively recent government creation) reported in 1896 and 1897 that the quality problem was serious and was the chief reason for the poor fish sales.[20] In 1909 the same department reported that: "There has been little or no attempt to alter the cure of salt codfish to meet the desires or requirements of the markets generally."[21] The following year, the annual report stated that: "The necessity for a standardization of the cull of fish has been, if anything, more in evidence this season than probably ever before."[22] However, no attempt was made to standardize the cull during the remainder of this period, although some of the major exporters tried to improve their marketing practices in 1911 (as will be discussed later).

The weather was the other major factor involved in obtaining a good cure, but except for isolated seasons, for example, 1894[23] and 1907,[24] it did not cause many problems in the shore fishery. However, the shorter drying season on the Labrador coast was responsible for the generally inferior, or at least cheaper, quality of that fish. In the shore fishery, which comprised by far the largest segment of the cod fishery, the incidence of unsuitable weather conditions was similar to that of catch failures — possible in limited areas or for a limited time but never extensive enough to affect overall production. Many things contributed to the deteriorating cure during the period and, as Job Brothers pointed out, nearly all of them (once again, ignoring market conditions) could be summarized with one word — "carelessness."[25]

Market demand influenced the amount of time, effort, and money that a fisherman could put into his catch, and in this regard, many problems combined against the efforts of the producer. First of all, every exporter had his own cullers and his own standards. These standards were liberal when demand was high and stringent when it was low. In addition to this, the exporters were forced to compete with each other in difficult market conditions (which will be discussed later) and, consequently, no uniform standards were possible. For instance, the agent for Punton and Munn of Harbour Grace, Robert Badcock, who was stationed at Dark Tickle, Labrador, explained to John Munn in 1886 that he would have to be rather liberal in his dealings with the fishermen since a vessel belonging to Ryan and Company had arrived and were offering all the fishermen cash for their produce.[26] Newman and Company had similar problems with competitors on the south coast, as evidenced by their letter books during this period.[27] This company considered strict culling to be an essential practice and the only fair and reliable means of getting a good product and of rewarding the best fishermen.[28] Besides the faults attached to the culling system itself, by the second half of the century, buyers had begun to buy fish at a flat rate without any culling. (This was known as buying *talqual*.) As early as 1852 some fish was purchased talqual on the Labrador coast,[29] but the practice was not prevalent until later in the century. W. Waterman and Company, Fogo, purchased some fish talqual in 1878, 1879, 1800, 1882 and 1883, but the amount was generally only a very small percentage of their total purchases.[30] Grieves and Bremner, Trinity, did not buy any talqual fish until 1886, when they bought some from Labrador, but during 1887-1890, at least, they bought nearly all their Labrador fish as well as some of their bank fish talqual.[31] Similarly, in 1888 John Munn and Company of Harbour Grace purchased 9,000 cwts of bank fish talqual.[32] The Earles in Fogo, however, bought a very insignificant quantity of their fish talqual in 1895 and 1896 and no talqual whatsoever in 1897.[33] Newman and Company refused to buy any fish talqual,[34] but the practice seems to have become fairly common by the 1890s,[35] although it was probably used for the purchase of Labrador fish more than any other. Nicholas Smith claims that the introduction of the steamer for transporting fish to market led to talqual buying[36] as a means of saving time, but it must be noted that Smith is referring to the Labrador fishery — the only one with which he was familiar. He wrote:

> [A proper] method of cure went on [at Labrador] until steamers were introduced to take large cargoes from the coast. John Munn and Co. of Harbour Grace, were the first to load a steamer with fish on Labrador; in the year 1887 they loaded two steamers of 12,000 quintals each at Emily Harbour, Labrador....
>
> The next year Baine Johnston and Co. and Job Bros. and Co., also had steamers chartered to load fish. That was the first of keen competition, each trying to get the first steamer to market, and the agents or supercargoes took fish that was not half made or cured. This was the beginning of bad cargoes in future years and the losing of our markets. The fishermen took advantage of these opportunities by shipping fish after one day's sun, and saving a lot of time and work.[37]

Similarly, in 1907 it was reported:

> In the desire to rush off shipments to market, especially at Labrador, the condition of cure, coupled with the difficulty of careful cull, result in cargoes being sometimes delivered in indifferent condition. The usual complaints from Mediterranean ports of the imports of semi-cured fish from Labrador has [sic] again been in evidence this year. It is hoped that this may cease, as it is bound to have a prejudicial effect on this article of export.
>
> The value of cod greatly depends on its perfect cure. With practically each catcher his own curer, uniformity of cure cannot be looked for. The real remedy must naturally be in the hands of the merchant or shipper, and the improvement can only take place when there is more discrimination shown in the rates of prices for good as compared with indifferent cures; with an enhanced price for the perfectly made fish and a lower value for the imperfect cure, the system of buying commonly known here as "tal qual" being very unfair both to the buyer or seller, and certainly to the good curer.[38]

However, this unfair system continued. While talqual buying was, no doubt, harmful to the industry, it was largely confined to the Labrador fishery. Rather, the general deterioration in cure during the century stemmed from the lack of steadfast standards among the buyers and the problems of consistency from one year to the next, with the fishermen fully aware that if the exporters wanted their fish, they would buy it, and that if the fish was not wanted, any extra effort expended in curing it would be wasted. This led to the real problem — negligent curing. This was a market problem as well as an internal one, since high market prices were not always available for Newfoundland fish; consequently, the island found itself in the ever enlarging spiral of low market prices leading to quality deterioration, which, in turn, led to a further reduction in prices (see Table 2.1, Appendix, for a selected list of saltfish prices).

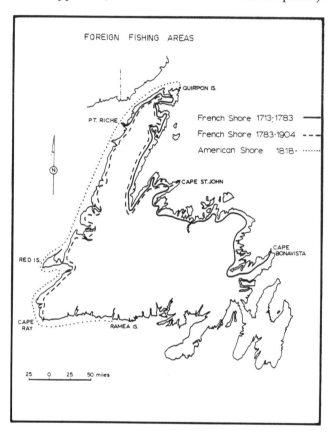

Labrador Cod Fishery

During the Napoleonic War, many fishermen from Newfoundland's northeast coast, particularly Conception Bay, became engaged in a migratory cod fishery on the *North Shore* of the island. This area between Quirpon and Cape St. John — referred to by the French as *Petit Nord* — had always been a part of the traditional *French Shore*. French activity in the area ceased with the outbreak of war and by 1798 schooners shallops from Conception Bay were fishing there and at Labrador.[39] The men and ships participating in this activity were, for the most part, the same ones engaged in the spring seal fishery. This made both industries independent but, at the same time, it made greater economic growth possible in those areas which depended solely on the cod fishery.

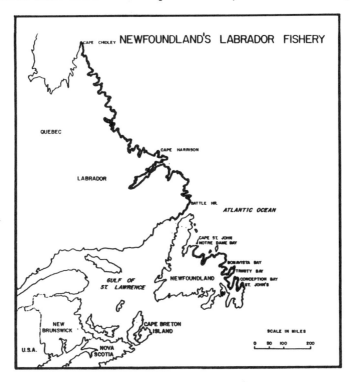

While it is impossible to precisely determine the scope of the early Labrador fishery, it is evident that the later, extensive Labrador fishery grew out of the North Shore fishery. It seems that, in the beginning, vessels would sail to the North Shore and occasionally, if prospects were not favourable, would continue to the Labrador coast in time for the later season farther north. In 1803 (the earliest year for which figures are available) there were forty-seven ships and 435 men engaged in the fishery on the North Shore and by 1811 these numbers had risen to 107 ships and 717 men. Between 1811 and 1815 the number of ships remained constant but the number of men increased to over 1,000.[40] Governor Gower observed in 1806 that the planters from Conception Bay had established a cod fishery north of Cape St. John and he was concerned because he knew they would have to leave the area and proceed to the coast of Labrador once a peace treaty was signed with France.[41] Another source points out that, due to the scarcity of fish around St. John's and Conception Bay, the fishermen went annually to the North Shore for the whole fishing season.[42] While the Labrador fishery was prosecuted to some extent during the war years, the fishery on the North Shore was much more important. In 1834 the newly-elected House of Assembly wrote concerning the French presence in Newfoundland: "The Labrador cod fishery was generally considered to be a precarious venture and most agreed that losing the right to fish at Petit Nord was very unfortunate to the Newfoundland fishermen."[43] Similarly, in that same year, the St. John's Chamber of Commerce wrote:

> That the fishery at Labrador being exceedingly precarious derives its value chiefly from the employment it has given of late years to the Sealing Vessels and men after the termination of the Seal Fishery; and was, as is doubtless known to His Majesty's Government, but little pursued from this Island until by the late treaties which ceded to France and America a right to occupy the part of our shore to which the Sealing Vessels had formerly resorted for the Cod Fishery. His Majesty's subjects were driven from their own Coasts to seek elsewhere new but vastly inferior sources of employment for the Capital and Industry which those treaties so suddenly paralyzed.[44]

Although it could be said that the Labrador fishery had its origin in the Napoleonic War, its expansion resulted from the Treaty of Paris (1814) which returned the North Shore to France.

It is not clear exactly when the North Shore fishery ceased but it did not last long after the restoration of French rights. Governor K.B. Hamilton reported in 1853 that this fishery was concluded in about 1821, when the fishermen "with few exceptions abandoned the fishery and betook themselves to the Labrador."[45] In 1820 Governor C. Hamilton reported that "An unusual number of people...resorted from this Island [to Labrador] when compared with former years."[46] Although the *Abstract of C.O.194 Statistics* records a large number of Newfoundland ships on the North Shore as late as 1827, in view of the governor's remarks just cited and the fact that the French fishermen returned to the area after the war, it is very probable that the Newfoundland fishery of the North Shore had ceased by the early 1820s.

By the late 1820s, the Labrador fishery was a firmly established industry. It consisted of two types of fisheries, besides a small resident fishery. The islanders who journeyed to Labrador and established themselves on shore, catching and curing their fish in one place, became known as stationers, while those who lived on board their ships and moved around to the various fishing grounds were called floaters. The floaters generally brought their fish back to the island to be dried. In the beginning, the fishery developed on the southern part of the Labrador coast, but as the century progressed, the fishermen moved farther north.[47] However, while stationers did not go north of Cape Harrison, the floaters could go as far as Cape Chidley and increasingly did so during the century.

The fishing area was very large — 7,100 square miles, compared with the 4,119 square miles that were used in the Newfoundland shore fishery (excluding the French Shore).[48] Because of the lack of charts, however, it was hazardous and many vessels were lost.[49] As previously noted, the Labrador fishery began later than that of the island and the season was shorter. While the northeastern coast of Newfoundland had a fishing season of about 143 days, that of southern and northern Labrador averaged about eighty-seven and fifty-two days, respectively. It was not unusual for island fishermen to sail to Labrador late in the summer when it appeared that the shore fishery in their locality was going to fail.[50] The late arrival of the fish in Labrador waters and the shortness of the drying season made it difficult to obtain a light-salted, hard-dried product. As early as 1835, the St. John's Chamber of Commerce cautioned that "the people employed curing fish...at Labrador [should] be more careful."[51] The Labrador fishery, besides producing a generally cheaper product, was not considered to be viable on its own. It was, therefore, closely tied to the seal fishery with the same outports, men, and ships involved in both industries. As mentioned earlier, the Chamber of Commerce pointed out that the Labrador fishery derived its value chiefly from the employment it gave the sealing ships and men after the seal fishery.[52] Similarly, although the Labrador cod fishery failed on a number of occasions, it generally took a failure of the seal fishery (during the heyday of the seal and Labrador fisheries), as in 1834, to disturb the Newfoundland business and political community.[53] It is important to realize that from the beginning, the Labrador fishery was not, by itself, generally remunerative and its success depended largely on the seal fishery.

The Labrador fishery increased in both size and importance during the first half of the century. In the 1820s and 1830s about 250 ships, with an average of nine men each, annually sailed from the island to Labrador.[54] The extra-large seal harvests of the 1830s and 1840s were probably instrumental in the expansion of the Labrador fishery during the same period, for in 1848 over 400 registered vessels, besides boats of between ten and thirty tons, were engaged in that branch of the cod fishery.[55]

Although other parts of the northeast coast could and did participate to some extent in the Labrador cod fishery, the industry was dominated by Conception Bay and St. John's, with the vessels from the former outnumbering the vessels from the latter by two or three to one during 1812-1833.[56] Until St. John's captured what remained of both industries near the end of the century, Harbour Grace had probably the most important and largest sealing and Labrador fleets. In 1847 the population of that town was 4,129 (men, women and children), of whom two-thirds

49

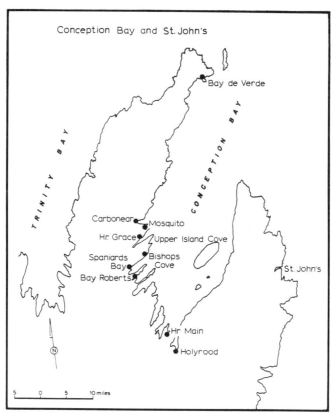

Conception Bay and St. John's

TRINITY BAY

CONCEPTION BAY

Bay de Verde

Carbonear
Mosquito
Hr Grace
Upper Island Cove
Spaniards Bay
Bishops Cove
Bay Roberts
St. John's

Hr Main
Holyrood

N

5 0 5 10 miles

were engaged in or dependent on the cod fishery.[57] One-third of the
latter number lived from the proceeds of the shore fishery in the
neighbourhood, while the remaining two-thirds were dependent on the
Labrador fishery. Approximately 1,800 people in Harbour Grace, then,
were involved in the Labrador fishery. Mosquito (now called Bristol's
Hope), just north of Harbour Grace, had a population of 456, of which
four-fifths, or about 360 people, depended on the Labrador fishery. In
Spaniard's Bay, one-quarter, or approximately 175 people out of a
population of 715, were likewise occupied as were one-third, or about 600,
of the 1,799 people in Bay Roberts. In the area under the jurisdiction
of the Harbour Grace Police Office, approximately 3,135 people (fishermen
and their families) out of the total population of 7,099 were engaged in
the Labrador fishery. Other Conception Bay outports, particularly
Carbonear and Brigus, also carried out a vigorous Labrador fishery (and
seal fishery) and contributed towards Conception Bay's near
monopolization of the industry. Even as late as 1889, when the St. John's
firms had taken over nearly all the fish trade, John Munn and Company

of Harbour Grace shipped 75,150 quintals of dried cod from Labrador out of the company's total shipment of 186,933 quintals[58] and his company was by far the largest exporter of Labrador-cured saltfish at that time. Trinity Bay was also involved in the Labrador fishery but to a lesser extent. It was reported in 1850 that the 4,000 migratory fishermen at Labrador belonged to Conception and Trinity bays,[59] but the evidence shows that the North Shore and seal fisheries practically originated with the Conception Bay fishermen; moreover, the available records on fish collections in Trinity Bay indicate that the shore fishery was much more important in that area.[60] While a small Labrador fishery was prosecuted from the Fogo area, records similar to the ones regarding Trinity indicate that it was only a minor part of the total fishery of that region.[61] However, while Conception Bay remained paramount in the Labrador fishery during the era of the sailing ships and the large seal harvests, St. John's benefitted from the introduction of steam power and eventually captured both the Labrador and seal industries.

Information on various changes within the structure of the Labrador fishery is scarce but the evidence points plainly to the decline of the outports and the expansion of St. John's in this sphere. During 1854-1863, for instance, Job Brothers and Company, St. John's, collected an average of less than 20,000 cwts of Labrador fish annually.[62] During the ten-year period ending in 1882, this firm collected an average of over 45,000 cwts of Labrador fish annually.[63] Since the Labrador fishery certainly did not double production between these dates, it is obvious that this firm increased its share of the Labrador fishery. The situation in Harbour Grace during the second half of the century was indicative of the trends which were current in the Labrador fishery. In 1867, fifty ships from that port were engaged in the seal fishery. Of these, thirty-six took part in the Labrador fishery after the sealing voyage was over, and another fifty-four small vessels went to the Labrador coast as well; hence, ninety ships comprised the Harbour Grace-Labrador fleet of 1867. Meanwhile, most of the fourteen sealing ships which did not sail to the Labrador in June and July went later with supplies and trade goods and were required to transport the saltfish back to Harbour Grace or directly to market. It is unfortunate that more information is not available on the Harbour Grace-Labrador fleet prior to 1867, but it is evident that the fleet declined after the late 1860s.[64] Similarly, although it is rather difficult to ascertain because of incomplete records of the total number of people travelling to Labrador from Harbour Grace and the other ports each summer, it is obvious that in Harbour Grace, there was a very significant decline. During 1867-1870, the first three years for which reasonably complete figures are available, an average of some 4,000 men and women from that outport went to

Labrador each year. By the end of the century, this number had declined considerably. During 1910-1914 an average of 855 people from Harbour Grace travelled to the Labrador fishery annually. As the large sealing vessels were replaced by the St. John's steamer fleet, the average size of the Harbour Grace Labrador vessels declined. John Munn and Company operated two or three large steamers at the seal fishery for a few years prior to the bankruptcy of the company in 1894. The use of these steamers to transport the Harbour Grace stationers to and from their fishing rooms on the Labrador coast enabled this branch of the Harbour Grace-Labrador fishery to survive. After Munn's collapse, this segment of the industry was handled by the St. John's firms, with the colony's capital profiting at the expense of the outport. Yet, although the Conception Bay-Labrador fishery declined, by 1910 the Labrador cod fishery was still more important than the shore fishery in Harbour Main, Port de Grave, Harbour Grace and Carbonear, and the Labrador catch even slightly exceeded the shore catch in Trinity Bay and Bonavista Bay (see Table 2.2, Appendix).

As is the case with information concerning other aspects of the Labrador fishery, data regarding the actual exports of Labrador saltfish are incomplete. Some saltfish was exported directly from the Labrador coast and the remainder was brought back to the island for shipment. Steamers reduced the sailing time across the Atlantic and so brought an increasing proportion of the Labrador saltfish directly to market. This resulted in competition among the companies for the first loads of fish, which led to a deterioration in the product due to the shipment of fish that was not completely cured. Although the amount of fish exported directly from Labrador declined during the 1880s and only recovered slightly during the 1890s,[65] the proportion of fish exported directly from Labrador must have increased in comparison with that shipped via the island. The statistics — the earliest available — for the five-year period 1874-1878 show that nearly 300,000 cwts of fish were exported annually from Labrador, and this quantity increased to about 375,000 cwts annually during the following five-year period, 1879-1883. In the eight-year period ending in 1891, on the other hand, the average annual exports were just a little over 200,000 cwts and there was very little improvement during the remainder of the century, as will be discussed later. There was an increase in exports to more than 200,000 cwts by 1907 followed by a decline with fluctuations during the remainder of the period. While, no doubt, deterioration in the cure was one of the causes for this decline, the failing seal fishery and developments in the saltfish markets[66] were also important contributing factors.

Although this industry had recovered a little by 1891, the recovery was only temporary and the Labrador saltfish industry continued to experience problems. After the commercial crisis of 1894, the St. John's firms curtailed their Labrador dried cod business and it was reported in 1897 that "Bowring, Job, Tessier, Baird, Bennett, Rogerson, Goodfellow, and others" had cut out nearly all their credit to fishermen.[67]

In the early years of the twentieth century, the Labrador saltfish industry continued to fluctuate, but it remained an important component of the total industry. While there is very little statistical evidence relative to the Labrador industry in general, and even less concerning the fish that was caught on the Labrador coast but cured on the island of Newfoundland, whence it was shipped, there is enough information to give some indication of the importance of this branch of the fishery and the downswing which occurred.

It is known that 250,887 cwts were exported directly from the coast in 1906 and that an additional 545,000 cwts of Labrador fish were cured on the island and exported from there.[68] This total of 795,887 cwts of Labrador-produced saltfish comprised 53.7 percent of Newfoundland's total exportation for that year. In 1907, 289,493 cwts of saltfish were shipped directly from Labrador, while an additional 345,000 cwts were brought to the island for curing and shipment.[69] Thus, exports of Labrador saltfish in that year amounted to 634,493 cwts, or 44.62 percent of the colony's total exportation. These quantities were unusually large and this was made clear in the report just cited. During the remainder of the period, it was reported that Labrador exported the following amounts of saltfish from its coasts:[70]

1908 — 288,826 cwts	1912 — 194,995 cwts
1909 — 168,692 cwts	1913 — 111,876 cwts
1910 — 81,368 cwts	1914 — 91,049 cwts
1911 — 161,043 cwts	

No reference was made to the amount brought back to the island for curing and shipment. Nevertheless, the impression given is one of decline in the industry. In 1908 it was reported that "the quantity brought home to be cured was...considerably less than last year, in fact, many schooners returned empty."[71] In 1910 it was estimated that 178,560 cwts of saltfish were brought back to the island from Labrador; this amount, combined with the 81,368 cwts exported from the coast, comprised a total of 259,928 cwts or 17.31 percent of the colony's total production.[72] The following year an official wrote: "Although nearly twice the quantity [of Labrador saltfish] of last season was exported [in 1911], it must be remembered that the year 1910 was one of the worst on record for this coast, and it is evident that this fishery has not yet recovered from the setback occasioned by some of the largest suppliers having, through death and other causes, withdrawn from business."[73]

By the last years of the period under study, it was felt that the Labrador fishery was in a state of decline and that, apart from the problems of quality control which will be discussed separately, this decline was due to the withdrawal of capital from this branch of the fishery. The Department of Marine and Fisheries reported the following in 1914: "To a great extent this [decline in the Labrador cod fishery] is due to the dying out of the large supply firms and the consequent absence of the outfit necessary to procure bait and provide suitable boats and gear."[74] Furthermore, this withdrawal of capital was generally considered to have been caused by a deterioration in the cure and by successful competition from other producing countries. Without elaborating here, one can summarize the general feeling of the Newfoundland government in 1912 by quoting from one of many similar reports:

> The great danger to the disposal of the Labrador catch is due to the ever increasing carelessness with which both fishermen and exporters are permitting the fish to be handled and shipped from the coast.
> In view of the better handling, curing and packing of the Iceland and Norwegian products competing with Labrador, which is yearly becoming more and more noticeable, a policy which permits irregular salting, careless splitting, and dirty shipments is, to say the least, suicidal, and all parties interested should awake to the very serious results of its being permitted to continue.[75]

The Labrador-cured saltfish, which was generally inferior to the shore-cured product, was the more vulnerable to competition.

Nevertheless, the Labrador fishery, during its peak and in conjunction with the seal fishery, provided the Conception Bay-St. John's area and, to a lesser extent, Trinity Bay and points north, with a basis for greater population concentration than could be expected from the shore fishery alone.[76] However, the introduction of steam power enabled St. John's to capture the entire sealing fleet and eventually to take over the stationer traffic to the Labrador fishery. The Labrador floating fleet, operating from the outports, declined in size, average tonnage, and importance with the disappearance of the sailing seal fleets. Towards the end of the century, the floaters began to journey to St. John's for employment in the seal fishery in the spring and were supplied, while at Labrador, by the St. John's businesses. These developments led to the further growth of St. John's and the relative decline of the outports, particularly the large ones in Conception Bay. At the same time, deterioration in cure, combined with market conditions, resulted in a decrease in the sales of Labrador fish which, by this time, caused major problems for the St. John's exporters as well as for the outport fishermen.[77] The Newfoundland economy probably owed its survival after 1815 to the development of the Labrador and seal fisheries, and the decline of these industries contributed greatly to the failures in that economy in the 1890s.

Bank Fishery

As the Labrador fishery declined, it became obvious to both business and government that the bank fishery would have to be developed. This branch of the cod fishery had been one of the first to be prosecuted by the West of England fishermen. It survived the Napoleonic War but remained very weak and finally disappeared in the 1840s. A report in 1907 summarized the early history of the Newfoundland-British bank fishery as follows:

> The connection of this Colony with the Bank Fishery has not been a happy one. Foreign nations saw that this open-sea fishery would be of immense value to them as a source of food and wealth, but of perhaps still greater importance as furnishing real seamen when they should be required to man the national fighting fleet. It was cheaper to pay large bounties to these fishermen than to employ them permanently as seamen in the Royal Navy of France. Several times during the war, however, as for example from 1793 to 1815, British fishermen had a practical monopoly of the Bank Fishery, when prices...reached the highest mark they had ever attained. On the conclusion of peace, when French and American fishermen were able to return to the banks, the bounty system was resumed by their Governments and pushed to such an extent that by 1847 they had

practically forced the Newfoundland fishermen to confine themselves to the inshore fishery. It was reported to the King of France in 1828 that the bounty paid annually at that date was £125,000. In 1848 there were on the banks 360 French vessels of from 150 to 300 tons, with from 16,000 to 17,000 men, furnishing a catch of 1,200,000 cwts. The American fleet was at least as large; and Newfoundland was not represented. The United States was paying a bounty of 20s. a ton, and giving besides a highly protected market. The bounty system kept the vessels of this Colony off the banks till 1876, when a timid experiment was made by fitting out four vessels. In 1877 the number rose to seven vessels; in the following year to ten; and in 1879 to 28 vessels.[78]

As pointed out, the Newfoundland and British bank fisheries had been eliminated by the 1840s, and although the re-establishment of a Newfoundland bank fishery had been suggested as early as 1866,[79] it was not until 1876 that the government initiated a system of bounties to encourage its development.[80] A shipbuilding bounty was also introduced[81] since it was important that both industries be developed simultaneously. The bank fishery expanded and seems to have reached its peak in 1889; it then declined but increased again in the early twentieth century (see Table 2.4, Appendix).

While the bank fishery failed to fully expand, a few places, particularly on the south coast, continued to maintain substantial bank fleets and in 1914, out of a total fleet of 105 vessels, 104 came from this area.[82] The south coast, with its tradition of winter fishing and its ice-free harbours, was in a much better position to adjust to the bank fishery and this area was able to retain moderate-size fleets.

During the period examined here, however, the bank fishery was of less importance than the shore or Labrador fisheries. Newman and Company, for instance, found it very unprofitable and by 1898 would have nothing else to do with it.[83] Marketing the bank fishery's product at a profit — given the expense of the operation — was difficult and contributed to the industry's problems.

Technological Developments

There were several technological developments which had an impact on the saltfish trade, particularly during the second half of the period covered by this study, but, for the most part, they failed, as did governmental and mercantile actions, to deal with the problems of the industry.

The use of bultows (long lines from which hundreds of baited hooks were suspended) was the first major innovation in the traditional hook and line fishery. It required a larger capital investment and was only slowly adopted, but by the 1850s the hook and line fishermen were complaining about its use.[84] Because the application of bultows to the cod fishery required plenty of room to avoid entanglements, its adoption was considerably curtailed in the shore fishery (although it became the favourite method of catching cod in the bank fishery).

In 1866 Captain W.H. Whiteley invented the cod trap.[85] This was a box-like apparatus made from netting with one opening from which another long net extended. Cod moving in schools along the shore in search of caplin were guided into the opening of the trap by the long extended net and they simply milled around until the fishermen came and closed the opening, crowded the cod to one corner near the surface, and dipped them into the boats. No evidence is available to allow one to fully analyze the effects of the cod trap on the fishery, but its use had become quite widespread by the last decade of the nineteenth century because of its applicability to the shore fishery and to the Labrador fishery. The utilization of cod traps may have partly accounted for the increased production of codfish during the last decades of the period covered by this study, although this method required a larger boat and a larger crew than the hook and line fishery and the traps were comparatively expensive. Furthermore, a whale or iceberg could destroy a trap and thus ruin the season for the fishermen or, as was more often the case, the fish would, for some unknown reason, refrain from swimming in its vicinity. Finally, if the trap was productive — and one could be very productive given favourable circumstances — the fishing crew involved experienced a mini-glut and were unable to process the fish properly.

Although the use of the bultow in the bank fishery and the use of the cod trap in the shore and Labrador fisheries may have slowed the decline of the saltfish industry, the decrease in per capita exports was not reversed.

Improvements in communications made a striking advance in the 1860s with the laying of the transatlantic cable and the extension of telegraph lines to many parts of the island. If Newman and Company's reaction to these developments is representative of exporters in general (and there is no reason to think otherwise, although no equivalent records exist for other firms), the merchants recognized the importance of being able to telegraph instructions and information in a matter of hours. Formerly, letters often took months. Newman and Company quickly devised a code book in order to keep their telegrams confidential. Strangely enough, there is no evidence that this communication breakthrough had any noticeable positive result on the saltfish trade. As Small's informant points out, the fishermen continued to remain ignorant of fish prices well into the twentieth century[86] and McDonald, also writing about the early twentieth century, says that

> ...exporters suffered from an almost complete lack of fishery statistics and sources of information concerning the condition of foreign markets, and this defect often led to unnecessary losses brought about by sending fish to overstocked markets. Exporters were not only unaware of total market demand for given markets and how much their local and foreign competitors were shipping, but frequently sent the wrong cures and qualities of fish to markets for which it was not suited, as often out of ignorance as out of a deliberate attempt to 'put one over' on foreign importers.[87]

That there was a communication problem is evident and why this was not rectified after the 1860s is difficult to understand. Although further research is necessary, it appears that Newfoundland's exporters did not learn to take full advantage of the telegraph.

It was also during the 1860s that steam power was introduced into the seal fishery, with effects on that industry, on the Labrador fishery and, consequently, on the outports, particularly in Conception Bay, which have already been discussed. The use of steamers resulted in much larger cargoes of fish being carried to market than ever before, often causing market gluts. This prompted the exporters to compete in order to provide the first shipments in the markets and, consequently, there was a deterioration in cure. As one British consul reported, "It would be far better to return to the old system of sailer cargoes, and eliminate entirely these 'steamer races', which ruin the markets at the beginning of the season, say, in October."[88] While the introduction of steamers was one of the most significant technological developments as far as the saltfish trade was concerned, it brought problems as well as benefits.

There was an overall decline in the per capita production of Newfoundland's saltfish during 1814-1914 and this decline adversely affected the colony's economic health. Most fish was produced as light-salted shore fish but a considerable amount was caught on the Labrador coast and cured somewhat differently. In addition, there was a smaller bank fishery. Although there were some technological developments, there were no revolutionary changes in the industry and the cod was cured in much the same way in 1914 as it had been a century earlier. To handle the exportation of this product, British and indigenous firms with their operations in the outports and in St. John's, respectively, competed for the trade which would eventually be dominated by the capital.

Local Organization of the Trade

Saltfish, whether shore, Labrador or bank, had to be exported in order for the economy, and consequently, the population, to profit from it. Fish was collected, transported to market and sold; supplies and equipment were imported and distributed to the fishermen. However, since the rate of population growth outstripped the rate of growth in production, a given quantity of cod was required to support a larger number of people each year. This led to a shrinking profit margin, which was, to a large extent, responsible for the changes which occurred in the commercial organization of the saltfish industry.

As already indicated, by 1814 Newfoundland's saltfish trade was dominated by British firms, although a few local entrepreneurs had managed to become established in the trade during the post-1808 boom. While the long-established British firms had branch operations or agencies in the foreign markets to handle their fish sales, it is not known how the local Newfoundland exporters were able to make initial contacts in Spain and Portugal. They may have begun by using the captains or other representatives who accompanied the cargoes as agents. Given the high demand for saltfish during 1808-1814 and given the fact that the names of the chief market ports were well known, it should not have been difficult to make contact with buyers. In addition, the local Newfoundland residents who became involved in the fish trade were not entirely ignorant of trade practices. Benjamin Bowring and Charles Ayre, for example, were two men whose businesses prospered and survived the subsequent depression (and who consequently earned reputations as creditable businessmen); the former was in the watch business while the latter had been employed by a British firm in Newfoundland. They set up their own establishments in St. John's, the naval and governmental headquarters and the most important centre of population, business and trade. It was reported at the time that during the war, St. John's "became the Emporium of the Island and changed its character from a fishery to a considerable commercial town."[89] Competition between these indigenous St. John's firms and the large British firms which were established in this port as well as in the outports soon became evident and continued until the last British firm, Newman and Company, withdrew from Newfoundland in 1907.

Major developments occurred in the structure of the fish trade during the century. The traditional relationship between the supplier and the supplied changed as business became more uncertain and a colonial government became more willing to provide poor relief. At the same time, the outport firms experienced difficulties, and during periods of depression, bankruptcies among these firms were much more common than in St. John's. Out of these developments, a new arrangement grew, based on the St. John's merchant, who supplied the small outport merchants who, in turn, supplied the fishermen; this replaced the old, direct merchant-fisherman relationship which disappeared with the decline of the outport firms.

While the saltfish trade stagnated after the peace treaty of 1815, the 1830s were especially unproductive and damaging to the outport firms. Insolvencies among these firms became common, with some of the largest establishments having to declare bankruptcy. For instance, in April of 1831 Christopher Spurrier and Company of Poole declared bankruptcy and their extensive premises at Burin, Oderin, Barren Island and Isle Valen had to be disposed of piecemeal due to the lack of interested buyers.[90] In May of that same year, Hugh William Danson of Bristol was also forced to declare insolvency, and his equally large establishments at Harbour Grace, Holyrood and Bay de Verde had to be sold.[91] This decade witnessed one of the more serious depressions as far as the outport firms were concerned.[92]

Because of the insolvency proceedings of some of the smaller firms at this time, the terms *current supply* and *current supplier* were redefined. Traditionally, the fisherman received his fishing supplies on credit from a merchant and, in the event of a fisherman's bankruptcy, the supplying merchant for that fishing season was considered the current supplier; second only to the servants, whose wages were paid first, the supplying merchant was entitled to full payment for the supplies of that summer, which were referred to as the current supply. Only after the current supplier had been fully paid could other creditors share in the fisherman's estate. In the case of the insolvent estate of William Alexander, merchant at Bonavista,[93] James Stewart and Company claimed full payment for all the goods sold to Alexander for that fishing season. The company pointed out that these goods were used in the fishery and therefore could be designated as current supply. Baine Johnston and Company, another creditor, contended, on the other hand, that the law regarding current supply could not be applied to that case since Alexander, although engaged in the fishery, was also a merchant who supplied other fishermen. The case was decided in favour of Baine Johnston and Company, and the court pointed out that a broad interpretation of this law could be detrimental to the fish trade in the long run, since establishments would be taking smaller risks in advancing credit to other firms and insolvencies would become extremely complex. This case is representative of what was happening in the fish trade at the time. St. John's firms, like that of James Stewart, were moving into the outports and supplying small merchants who, in turn, supplied the local fishermen. Although Stewart lost his bid to be protected under the law of current supply, the St. John's firms had the advantage of having to deal only with small merchants who were much easier to control than individual fishermen.

Other evidence also indicates that the traditional merchant-fisherman relationship, which had always been the bulwark of the large outport merchants, began, for a number of reasons, to break down in the 1830s. A Patrick Hogan wrote in 1882:

> Up to the year 1836 the fisheries of this country were conducted not alone under British law, but also in accordance with certain usages which were adopted from time to time, and which grew with the trade, and were found necessary to its well working. One of these rules was, the current supplier furnished the planter with all requirements necessary for the prosecuting of the voyage, viz., nets, lines, provisions, etc., in return the supplier got the entire voyage, large or small, at current rates. On receipt of which he paid all the wages, bait, boat hire, freight, and gave the planter a moderate supply for the winter, even if he had no work, which he generally had to give him.
>
> In 1836 the merchants, for the first time, refused to pay the wages, falling back on British law, and discarding the usages of the fishery, the planter being in debt after the summer; this was the small end of the wedge that divided, from that day to this, the supplier and supplied; the planter, unable to depend on the supplier, as formerly, for his winter supply, was driven, and has been driven, ever since, to consult the first law of nature, self preservation, and hard to blame him, in the face of a long winter. The wages not being secured to the servants, they declined serving the planters, at sea or on shore, the fishery suffered in consequence, there being no shoremen to cure the fish, as formerly. Women were called in, who pickled the fish, producing an inferior article, which ruined the character of our fish in foreign markets.[94]

This report illustrates several significant developments which were taking place during the 1830s. The merchants discovered that the growing population (40,000 people in 1815, 75,000 in 1836) could no longer be supported by the stagnating cod fishery — it had actually declined in that decade. Also, by that time, the newly-elected House of Assembly was in a position to offer poor relief, and some of the responsibility for the fishermen's welfare which had formerly rested with the merchants was taken over by the colonial government. Hogan also points out that the breakdown in the large planter fishery dates from about that time, and this appears to have been the case. The general insecurity arising out of the cod fishery led to the disappearance of the large planters and the development of small, family enterprises, with the men catching the fish and the wives and children doing the shore work. This apparently resulted in a deterioration in quality. Thus the decade of the 1830s was probably the major turning point in the internal operations of the fish trade.

St. John's continued to extend its control over the outports, to the detriment of the old firms. James Simms, the attorney general, while discussing the decline in certain court cases in the outports, wrote in 1849:

> One great cause that has operated to diminish the utility of these Courts through a long series of years, has been, that in fact they become less required, for at the time when this Species of Court exercised its ambulatory functions under the domination of Surrogate Courts, there might be counted between St. John's and Fortune Bay, throughout the Harbours of the Southern Settlements upwards of thirty mercantile establishments of importing, exporting and supplying Merchants surrounded by their numerous planters, dealers and fishermen — whereas now within these extensive limits there is only one or at most two, such Establishments existing. And in the Northern District beyond Conception Bay, very few of the once great number of such Mercantile houses are now remaining, for St. John's has become, through the process of thirty years, the emporium of the Island, and absorbed to a great extent the supplying of planters and fishermen, where of course they resort spring and fall for supplies and for settlement of accounts.[95]

By 1850, therefore, the trend towards the centralization of commerce in St. John's was obvious.

A clearer picture can be obtained of what was happening in the latter half of the century (although there were only a few old outport firms remaining) because of the availability of more material. An examination of these records reveals the decline of these firms and their reactions to the general situation. Similarly, it can be seen why the St. John's businesses could succeed where the others failed. At the same time, it is possible to study the difficulties that confronted many of the St. John's firms.

By 1865 there had been a severe decline in the number of old outport firms.[96] The big St. John's houses had become heavily involved in the outports. Much of the fish exported from St. John's was brought from the outports by traders, ships belonging to the St. John's firms, or the outport fishermen themselves. While in Twillingate, Fogo, and Greenspond, William Cox and Company of Poole were still taking a large share of the fish being handled by those communities, in Catalina, Trinity, and Hant's Harbour, local business was under the complete control of St. John's and Harbour Grace (Ridley and Sons). In Carbonear, a local firm and a Harbour Grace firm were in control and a sizable quantity of fish was being exported from Harbour Grace and, possibly, St. John's. Two major Harbour Grace firms controlled the business in that district in addition to a large share of the Labrador fishery. Punton and Munn, and Ridley and Sons were not too unlike the St. John's firms themselves in that they carried on business in various parts of the island and Labrador. However, for the most part, they were retail merchants dealing with individual fishermen, while the St. John's merchants carried out only a small part of their business in that manner. St. John's controlled all the business in the districts of Ferryland, St. Mary's, and Placentia Bay and a large share of the south coast business, where the old British firms of Newman and Company, Nicolle and Company, and Degroucy, Renouf and Company were being effectively outmaneuvered.

It was the beginning of the end for the old outport firms. The Slades of Poole were in the process of winding up operations, and only Newman and Company, William Cox and Company, Nicolle and Company, and Degroucy, Renouf and Company remained. The Slades, under various names and combinations of names, had had establishments in Fogo, Trinity Bay, Carbonear and Labrador. The Carbonear business was the first to be sold and was purchased by John Rorke in 1839.[97] In the spring of 1852, Robert Slade, the senior partner of the Fogo-Twillingate complex, began to curtail his business and ceased to extend credit to the dealers, doing business in cash or barter only.[98] In the fall of that year, he tidied up his books by forgiving one-half the amount of each old debt if the other half was paid immediately.[99] In 1861 the Trinity Slades went bankrupt and part of that business was taken over by Walter Grieve and Alexander Bremner of St. John's.[100] It seems that the Fogo establishment was disposed of also around this time, for by 1865 it had ceased to exist, but the Battle Harbour operation continued under the management of the Slades until it was taken over by Baine Johnston and Company, St. John's, in 1871.[101] The Jersey firm of P.W. Nicolle and Company, with its Newfoundland headquarters at Jersey Harbour, Fortune Bay, went bankrupt in 1863, with liabilities amounting to nearly £54,000.[102] It was a very depressed period and all these establishments had difficulties. In 1864 Newman and Company were forced to close their business in Burgeo;[103] although this establishment had been their smallest operation on the south coast, it had always done a fair trade, with forty-four full-time employees in 1859 and three times that number during peak periods.[104] On the northeast coast, William Cox and Company, a Poole firm connected with the Slades, left Newfoundland entirely during the 1860s. They closed their Fogo and Greenspond branches in 1867 and that in Twillingate in 1868,[105] thereby bringing to an end Poole's predominance on that part of the island. One of the biggest insolvencies of this period was the failure of Ridley and Sons in 1870, with liabilities amounting to £250,000.[106] This firm had a major establishment in Harbour Grace, with smaller branches elsewhere, and was one of the largest firms outside St. John's at this time. Meanwhile, P.W. Nicolle and Company's business in Jersey Harbour had been taken over by other members of that Jersey family[107] and operated for a time under the name of Nicolle de Quitteville and Company.[108] This firm sold its Jersey Harbour premises to Degroucy and Company in 1872[109] and its Labrador properties at Forteau Bay and Blanc Sablon to a Philip Simion in 1876.[110] In 1882 Newman and Company pointed out that they and Degroucy were the only two old-style outport firms remaining in Newfoundland.[111] In 1886, when the Jersey bank suspended business, Degroucy and Company were forced to declare insolvency.[112] Newman and Company decided to reduce their establishment in Gaultois in 1897 and in 1899 they offered it for sale for £3,500.[113] This establishment was sold in 1900, and in 1907 their business in Harbour Breton was sold also, thus bringing to an end, after three hundred years, the company's participation in the Newfoundland saltfish trade.[114] The Harbour Grace business of John Munn and Company (the successor to Punton and Munn) was the biggest of the outport firms to survive until the 1890s. That company's bankruptcy in 1894 and Newman and Company's withdrawal from the trade in 1907, marked the climax of St. John's successful struggle to eliminate the independent outport merchant houses and to capture the whole Newfoundland saltfish trade.

During this struggle between the two commercial groups, the outport exporters were extremely antagonistic towards the St. John's businesses. Newman and Company complained on several occasions about the St. John's firms — their cut-throat competition,[115] their glutting of the markets,[116] and their refusal to cooperate with the Newmans.[117] Similarly, William Cox and Company were usually very upset about the competition from St. John's merchants[118] and generally found that "few of them are to be trusted."[119] The adaptation of the St. John's firms to the changing conditions in the trade helped to propel them farther and farther ahead of the old outport firms.

There are a couple of reasons why the St. John's firms were relatively successful. They were under much closer control, having their principal partners (who were quite willing to modify their operations to take advantage of different situations) residing on the island. The outport firms, on the other hand, continued to use agents to operate their establishments. Few of these agents could be expected to devote the time and energy to the business that became increasingly necessary as the profit margin decreased. That Newman and Company survived in Newfoundland for so long can be attributed chiefly to their ruthless efficiency in dealing with their agents, their painstaking scrutiny and careful examination of the account books, and their specific and detailed instructions regarding all matters. When an agent's work was unsatisfactory, he was usually invited to London for a conference and, if necessary, dismissed while there.[120]

St. John's merchant Thomas R. Job made it quite clear how he felt about agents when he wrote: "The business under one's own supervision is hazardous enough nowadays without leaving it to servants."[121] Related to this, of course, was the gradual withdrawal of the St. John's merchants from the actual operation of retail establishments in the outports. For example, Job Brothers and Company ceased the operation of their business in Hant's Harbour in 1864[122] and Baine Johnston and Company closed their Harbour Breton establishment in 1871.[123] This process brought with it a change from the old merchant-fisherman credit relationship to a St. John's merchant-small outport merchant (or trader)-fisherman one. It was much easier for the large firms to control small outport merchants and traders than it was to control thousands of individual fishermen. Once the competition from the old outport firms had disappeared or was no longer serious, the St. John's exporters found that it was more profitable and less risky to concentrate on the wholesale part of the outport trade. This willingness on the part of the St. John's merchants to supply traders, who could go anywhere along the coast trading for fish, was the major complaint of the old outport firms against St. John's establishments.[124] Newman and Company, and others like them, could see no advantage in selling goods at wholesale price to traders and small merchants, who could then compete with their suppliers in the retail trade. To make matters worse for the outport firms, the number of traders increased during periods of high market demand, thereby reducing the profit margin for all concerned, whereas very few traders bothered to operate when markets were poor and prices low, thereby putting pressure on the big firms to buy all the fish and supply all the credit. This whole system was extremely favourable to the St. John's merchants and played havoc with the business of the outport merchants. As a consequence, by 1882 Newman and Company was probably the only remaining establishment that was still operating under the old system.[125] They made a major effort to curtail credit, cutting it off completely in Gaultois in 1898[126] and in Harbour Breton in 1899.[127] It was certainly due to their assiduous vigilance that their company was able to operate for so long and on such a large scale despite very unfavourable conditions. Finally, with their headquarters and shipping located in Newfoundland, the local firms were in a much better position to take advantage of the substantial profits to be made from the lucrative spring seal fishery. The close individual control that was possible in the capital and the willingness of the St. John's merchants to adapt combined to make St. John's the sole commercial centre of the colony by 1900.

Although the St. John's exporters prospered at the expense of the large outport firms, they were by no means able to avoid losses themselves.

In 1864, for example, Thomas Job's father felt that the Job family should study the possibilities of liquidating their firm.[128] However, Job Brothers and Company and, no doubt, the other large St. John's firms made reasonable profits even during the depressed 1860s (see Table 2.B,[129] below, for a rare business account of this period), partly because of the seal fishery. On a total capital employment of £614,500, during the eleven-year period 1861-1871, the company made a profit of £76,525 (including annual dividends of five percent).[130] It is significant that the loss of £9,000 in 1864 is explained by the note, "Seal Voyage very bad." Similarly, after the 1869 entry, which shows a profit of £15,000, there is the explanation, "Nimrod [sealing vessel] very successful," and in 1871, which was the most profitable year for the period, another note reads "Hector and Nimrod [two sealing vessels] both very successful."[131] The outcome of the sealing voyage seems to have been a determining factor in the level of profits attained by the export firms, and the decline in seal production during the 1880s was, no doubt, one of the reasons for the economic problems of the early 1890s. However, the decrease in seal exports was only one of the causes for the failures of that period. The exports of saltfish declined after the mid-1880s and the average and below-average prices heightened the difficulty. The growth in population from approximately 75,000 people in 1836 to over 200,000 by 1891, without a comparable increase in exports and no worthwhile developments in other commercial spheres, resulted in an over-extension of credit and contributed greatly to the business difficulties of the 1890s. In 1893 the firms of P. and L. Tessier and J. and W. Stewart both failed,[132] and in 1894 most of the St. John's exporters (Bowring Brothers was the major exception) were hurt very badly as a result of the suspension of business by the Union Bank

TABLE 2.B

Job Brothers and Company's Account: 1861-1871

Year	Profit £	Loss £	Year	Profit £	Loss £
1861	5,500		1867		14,250
1862	11,000		1868	11,550	
1863	-	-	1869	15,000	
1864		9,000	1870	9,000	
1865	3,000		1871	18,000	
1866		4,000			

and the Commercial Bank. (This event has come to be known as the bank crash of 1894.) Some firms were able to compromise on their debts, such as Baine Johnston and Company, which owed the Union Bank $618,000.[133] Others were forced to liquidate completely, including John Munn and Company and Thorburn and Tessier, which owed the Union Bank $520,000 and $458,000, respectively;[134] and Edward Duder and Company, which owed the Commercial Bank $668,676.[135] On the basis of a superficial examination of the situation, it seems that the economic crisis of 1894 resulted from the problems in the saltfish industry, combined with the decline of the seal fishery and the general lack of diversification in the economy.

Prime Minister Whiteway, whose efforts to industrialize Newfoundland met with opposition from some of the traditional merchants, accused the latter of bringing on the bank crash by withdrawing capital from the saltfish industry.[136] He pointed out that the deaths of John Munn, Arthur Duder and Allan Goodridge (well-known merchants) resulted in a shortage of working capital, owing to large legacies going to their dependents. Furthermore, he accused Charles P. Hunter, Walter Grieve and James Grieve of withdrawing a substantial amount of capital from Baine Johnston and Company, and he blamed Thomas and Robert Job and Stephen Randell for doing the same in the case of Job Brothers and Company. This may have been an important factor, but the writer has not been able to ascertain whether these withdrawals were exceptional. Conversely, the general economic situation of the early 1890s may have precipitated the withdrawal of capital.

Meanwhile, developments in shipping resulted from the introduction of steamers to the seal fishery. The fish trade was quick to make use of these larger, faster, and more reliable ships to send saltfish to market. This changed the nature of the trade because Newfoundland's fish had always been exported in sailing ships in cargoes of about 2,500-4,000 cwts. Sailing ships arrived in foreign ports on an irregular basis which meant that the supply of fish was staggered and the cargoes were small. Now, however, steamers crossed the Atlantic (steam shipping was introduced to the southern European trade before it was introduced to the Brazilian and Caribbean trades) within days, sometimes hours, of each other, especially during September and October. Larger cargoes arriving together created gluts and low prices so the local Newfoundland merchants began to compete with each other in an effort to reach market first and this encouraged the exportation of poorly cured fish and incompletely cured fish as merchants attempted to send early cargoes to market. Shipments of inferior fish (see Production Problems, above) created a market climate conducive to increased competition from other saltfish producers, especially

France and Norway (see below), during the last decades of the nineteenth century.

The Newfoundland exporters responded to the general problems in the saltfish industry through their influence on the government and other activities, but their work in this regard was usually hampered by self-interest. For most of the century, the old, surviving outport firms were usually instrumental in having candidates elected who were favourable to their interests. Newman and Company, for example, was successful in having its candidate elected in 1874, 1878, 1882, and 1885.[137] The introduction of the secret ballot and the election of "radicals" in 1889,[138] however, considerably weakened the Newmans' influences and, as far as can be ascertained, the company stayed out of politics for the remainder of its stay on the island. The business community in St. John's did not restrict exercising their influence to elections. Their displeasure with Whiteway's policies during the early 1880s, for example, prompted them to become directly involved in politics. Opposed to Whiteway's investment in the railway and other non-fishery ventures, the business community felt that government expenditure should instead be channelled into the fisheries. As Thompson points out, "Too much independent labour employed on railways and public works had increased wages in the fishery: at least this was the view...of the St. John's merchants."[139] Hence, in 1885, these merchants were instrumental in having Whiteway and his administration replaced by a pro-merchant administration led by Robert Thorburn.[140] This government actively encouraged the exporters to improve and rationalize fish production but with only limited success; the government party was defeated in the following election in 1889. Besides capitalizing on their power at the polls, the merchants used their local Chamber of Commerce as a vehicle to make formal requests to the government for assistance.

That the merchants of the colony were incapable of working together is clear; the only questions on which they agreed were those that did not make demands on their own operations. The merchants concentrated on requests to the British government for assistance in obtaining lower or preferential tariffs in the markets (with some requests to the colonial government for financial assistance). Petitions were drawn up by the merchants and submitted to the governor. The governor then forwarded those petitions, usually accompanied by his written support, to the Colonial Office. The colonial secretary decided on the action to be taken. If he felt that the matter should be referred to the Foreign Office, the petition was forwarded there, usually accompanied by his note of support. If the Foreign Office decided that further action was inappropriate for some reason, a reply was sent to the Colonial Office to that effect. Usually the

Foreign Office felt it could support the document as it stood and forwarded it to its embassy or consular officials in the market country or countries to which the petition referred, with further instructions that action be taken to facilitate the merchants' request. Replies were received from the embassy or consular officials and relayed back to the merchants via the same chain of communication.

Those areas in which the merchants cooperated concerned external marketing problems. When it came to making changes to their own business operations they were very reluctant, although there were obvious ways in which they could have improved the fish trade. By establishing a marketing board, for instance, they would have guaranteed that all exported fish was uniformly graded. Maybe they should have retrenched during depressions and avoided, to some extent at least, the heavy debts which they incurred during the 1880s and 1890s. Yet, the competition amongst the merchants prevented them from cooperating, and if any serious retrenching had been done, it is quite possible that both the economy and the population would have suffered the consequences. In 1911 the bigger St. John's firms, including Job Brothers, Harvey and Company, and Bowring Brothers, agreed to market their fish in Spain exclusively through George Hawes, an English commodity broker in the Mediterranean markets.[141] As Alexander points out, "This was the nucleus of the organization which eventually assumed marketing responsibility for all Newfoundland's saltfish production."[142] However, that organization did not become operative until the 1930s when local responsible government was suspended and the British-appointed commission of government imposed certain guidelines upon the industry. In the meantime, the acquisition of almost complete control over the colony's saltfish trade by the St. John's merchants created a backlash on the northeast coast. There a fishermen's cooperative was formed, but it experienced a relatively brief and geographically limited success. By and large, by 1914 the *Water Street* merchants of St. John's dominated the industry.

Local Government

Meanwhile, Newfoundland was undergoing political, social, and economic changes. Some of these developments occurred as part of the general growth and political maturation of British North America and had their origins in this arena. Others were peculiar to Newfoundland with its fishing economy, its Irish-Catholic and English-Protestant population, and its history as the site of an international cod fishery.

During the eighteenth century, the senior naval officer in Newfoundland waters was appointed governor over the fishery and inhabitants. He and his officers came to the island annually during the fishing season and his duties included the discouragement of permanent settlement. With the collapse of the migratory fishery and the growth of settlement during the Napoleonic War, the governor's duties became those of a colonial governor and the position became a full-time year-round one. In 1825, under local pressure for political reform, the British government granted Newfoundland the status of a crown colony and appointed a council to assist the governor. Then followed a period of more intense agitation for representative government by St. John's and Conception Bay merchants and the newly-enfranchised Roman Catholics. Both the government and the British firms in the outports were concerned that this would result in the domination of the colony by St. John's and so were somewhat opposed to the proposal. Their arguments against political reform did not convince the new Whig government, and so in 1832 Newfoundland was granted representative government with an elected legislative assembly, an appointed legislative council and a governor and executive council. An Anglican/Tory-Catholic/Liberal deadlock subsequently developed, and the Colonial Office accordingly modified the representative government so that during 1841-48 the legislative assembly was combined with the legislative council to form an amalgamated body. In 1848 that amalgamation was terminated by the Colonial Office and Newfoundland's governmental structure of 1832 was returned. By the 1850s an alliance of Catholics and Methodists had strengthened the Liberal party, enabling them to convince Great Britain to grant the colony responsible government. This alliance collapsed at the beginning of the depressed 1860s, and a re-alignment of forces, still dominated by St. John's (but less dependent upon Conception Bay support), controlled the government throughout that decade. The controversial issue of confederation with Canada split the assembly, and in the 1869 election, the Anti-Confederate Party rose to power. The failure to find a political solution to Newfoundland's economic problems via confederation with Canada prompted most prominent politicians to seek solutions through industrialization.

Because of the new emphasis on industrialization, the decades which followed the 1869 election are noted for the conflicts between those who favoured railroad building and those, generally in the minority, who favoured complete dependence on the fisheries. The comparative success of the former in gaining popular support resulted in the government's developmental policies up to the First World War: railroad building commenced in 1883 when St. John's and Harbour Grace were connected by rail, and by 1896 the trans-island line was completed, with a number of branch lines already built or in the planning stages; an iron ore mine was opened on Bell Island, Conception Bay, in 1895; and a pulp and paper mill was built in Newfoundland's interior between 1905 and 1909 and was serviced by the railroad. Nevertheless the fisheries, though often neglected, as was demonstrated by the rise of the Fishermen's Protective Union beginning in 1908, remained the chief employer: in 1911 the census reported that 43,795 men and 23,245 women were engaged in the fisheries, while only 2,821 men were engaged in lumbering and 2,260 were miners.[143] By 1914 Newfoundland had acquired *Dominion* status and, despite the nagging doubts of many (expressed most vocally by the Fishermen's Protective Union), it was generally felt that the *Dominion's* future success depended upon further industrial development.

In an attempt to reverse the decline in the economy brought on chiefly by the faltering cod fishery, the Newfoundland government embarked on several initiatives which proved, for the most part, rather inadequate. Since France was a major competitor in the saltfish trade, the government made some effort to curtail the French fishery by hampering French activities in Newfoundland's coastal waters and even on the Grand Banks. In addition, bounties were introduced to encourage the various segments of the cod fishery — chiefly shipbuilding and the bank fishery. Efforts were also made to diversify the economy, create a department of fisheries, and introduce a programme to conserve and increase fish stocks. And, finally, new markets were sought, particularly in the United States. Nevertheless, very few benefits resulted from these measures.

The French had been granted the liberty to fish and dry their catch on part of the island's coast in 1763. In 1783 this area, known as the *French Shore*, was defined as that part of the coastline from Cape Ray on the southwest corner of the island, extending north and east to Cape St. John on the northeast coast. (This Anglo-French agreement was reaffirmed in 1815.) All British fishermen were forbidden to interfere with the French fishery in this area, although the French were not allowed to remain on the island during the winter nor to build permanent structures there; nor were they allowed to trespass on any other part of the Newfoundland and Labrador coasts. The French interpreted the treaty as giving them exclusive rights to the French Shore, while the British (and Newfoundlanders) argued that the fishing rights were concurrent. The Newfoundland government could not take any action against the French fishermen on the French Shore, but they became determined that the French would not use any other part of the colony's coast.

Although the British navy had been patrolling the coasts of Newfoundland and Labrador, it was not until the 1850s that the Newfoundland government decided it was necessary to supplement the British service. From the reports of the commanding officers of Her

Majesty's ships, it was obvious that French fishermen were crossing the Straits of Belle Isle to fish on the Labrador side,[144] contrary to the Anglo-French agreement. In 1852 the Newfoundland government appointed four fishery protection officers.[145] Two were ordered to operate along the Labrador coast and in the Straits of Belle Isle, and were provided with a cutter and a schooner for this purpose; one was given a boat to patrol the L'Anse au Loup area; and the fourth was put in charge of Cape St. John. These provisions were successful in keeping the French confined to the terms of their agreement with Britain.

Meanwhile, efforts by the Newfoundland government to acquire exclusive control over the French Shore continued. In 1857, after an abortive attempt to come to an agreement with France over the issue, the British government promised Newfoundland a veto over any further agreement affecting the colony's French Shore. Since France opposed not only the presence of Newfoundland fishermen on the shore, but also any attempts to exploit mineral, agricultural and timber resources in the area, as well as the building of a trans-island railroad, it is obvious why this matter became a major issue during the latter decades of the century. Finally, in 1904 Britain managed, in the Anglo-French treaty of that year, to bring to an end the French presence in the region and the French Shore became an integral part of the colony.

Newfoundland's other attempt to hamper the French fishery involved the passage of the Bait Act in 1888. This act, which was intended to damage the French bank fishery, forbade the sale of bait to the French by Newfoundland residents living on the south coast of the island. It is difficult to measure the extent to which the French bank fishery suffered from this discriminatory legislation, but that it was adversely affected is certain.

The United States of America also attracted considerable attention from the colony's government and fish exporters. The United States bought some Newfoundland saltfish and herring and during 1854-1866 the Reciprocity Treaty between British North America and its southern neighbour allowed for a freer exchange of goods between them. During 1873-1885 the Washington Treaty did likewise. By the early 1890s the Newfoundland government became fascinated by the prospect of regaining access to what appeared to be an attractive and expanding market. Efforts to that end in the 1890s failed because of Canada's objection that its interests would be negatively affected. Early in the twentieth century, new attempts received the support of Great Britain, but in this instance American fishing interests successfully blocked negotiation. Newfoundland had offered its ample supplies of bait to American fishermen and now tried to cut off supplies in hopes of gaining its objective. The United States did not resume discussions and its markets remained protected.

In the meantime, the United States of America had been granted concessions, based on historic usage, to parts of the Newfoundland coast, and these had been reconfirmed in 1818. Although the feelings against the Americans were never as extreme as those against the French, since the former did not claim exclusive fishing rights and were not competitors in the major saltfish markets, Newfoundland in 1904 began to assert its control over waters previously frequented by United States fishermen in search of bait. The problem was referred to the Hague Tribunal and in 1910 a decision was reached which gave Newfoundland control over its coasts and ownership of its bays.

In 1888 the Newfoundland government turned its attention also towards the problem of saltfish production. In that year, a fisheries commission was appointed to study the local problems and to make recommendations. The commission advised that Adolph Nielsen of Norway be hired as superintendent of fisheries. Furthermore, it was suggested that perhaps the fish stocks in the coastal waters could be increased. Neilsen was hired and told "to examine the shores of Conception, Trinity, Placentia and St. Mary's Bay with the view of selecting the most eligible site for a hatchery."[146] He applied himself assiduously to his terms of reference, and within a short while, he was operating a cod hatchery in Dildo, Trinity Bay. During the six-year period ending 31 December 1895, this establishment hatched and planted a total of 832,929,000,000 ova in Trinity Bay.[147] That year it was disclosed that there were numerous reports of an "abundance of cod fish of various sizes...in the head of Trinity Bay, while at that time there were none in either Bonavista or Conception Bay." The cod could be seen "covering the bottom in a thick mass for long distances." Meanwhile, twenty-three lobster hatcheries had been established in 1893 and these operations, by the end of 1895, had hatched and planted 2,610,475,000 lobster ova. There were also reports of an annually increasing yield from this industry due to the massive restocking programme. The work continued during 1896 and 1897, but Nielsen became ill and was forced to return to Norway in January of 1897. The government which followed Robert Thorburn's administration was much less enthusiastic about the project and this, combined with the government's financial difficulties and Nielsen's illness, brought the hatcheries to a close. It is impossible to assess the impact of this programme on the fisheries, but its effectiveness could be questioned at least in the case of the migratory cod. These efforts to increase the catch and lower the cost of production seem to have had very little overall effect on production and exports.

The government's efforts to make the cod fishery a reliable economic base for the colony failed (as did their efforts to bring about diversification of the economy). While it is easy to point out their failures, it is almost impossible to show what could have been done, given the situation and the ethos of the period. Something should have been done, no doubt, about the deteriorating quality of the fish and the cut-throat competition among the exporters, but strict government controls in this area would have been considered very radical moves indeed. Similarly, considering the conventions of the time it is difficult to determine what the government could have done about the withdrawal of large amounts of capital from the island (if indeed such a withdrawal occurred, as Whiteway suggested). However desirable blocking the export of capital might have been, in general, the fewer international trade restrictions, the better for Newfoundland. Also, it is questionable whether additional capital would have been invested in the cod fishery, even if it had been forced to remain in the island and, even if it was so invested, whether this action would necessarily have been economically wise. While the implementation of measures such as these might have helped matters, it is easy to understand why nothing of this nature was done. To the writer's knowledge, even the anti-merchant Whiteway party did not advocate any restraints on the movement of capital, nor were they in favour of greater government direction and control in the saltfish trade. All in all, the efforts of the government, like the efforts of the saltfish exporters, failed to stop the inexorable decline of per capita exports and the general decay of the saltfish industry.

Summary

By 1914 Newfoundland had undergone a century of considerable political development and had achieved a high level of maturity in the international sphere in terms of its relations with France and the United States. Its industrialization programme, however, had been expensive and had had limited success, giving rise to highly capital-intensive industries with comparatively small labour forces, while profits were exported to foreign shareholders. Newfoundland's general economic condition was not good, but neither was it critical. In the fiscal year 1913-1914, the revenue was $3,618,329 and the expenditure $3,920,178 but, partly because of expensive efforts to industrialize, the public debt stood at $30,450,765.27, while total foreign trade amounted to $30,327,000.[148] However, the saltfish industry had been neglected at the local level, although it continued to be the mainstay of the Newfoundland economy.

The saltfish on which Newfoundland's economy was so dependent during the period from 1814 to 1914 was sold in foreign markets. Yet, at the same time, the colony had very little direct influence on these markets. This was the case because, although the colony was forced to purchase from abroad almost all the manufactured goods and food it required, its suppliers generally were not the saltfish markets but, rather, the United Kingdom, the United States, and Canada. (Exceptions to this were southern Europe which traded salt, wine, and fruit and the Caribbean which traded sugar, molasses and rum.) This was one of the significant features which made Newfoundland's situation different from that of Canada and the British West Indies. It is for these reasons, and others which have become apparent in this chapter, that an examination of the factors governing the markets is so important to the study of the Newfoundland saltfish industry.

CHAPTER 3

The International Saltfish Trade: Newfoundland's Competitors

The international saltfish trade was one of the more complex nineteenth century trades and involved a larger number of producing and consuming countries than most others. Within the British Empire, for example, there were several substantial nineteenth century trades in primary or semiprocessed colonial products, but none as complex as Newfoundland's saltfish trade. West Indian sugar was exported to Great Britain, British North America and, later, the United States; Canadian timber, grain and, later, meat were exported to Great Britain; and, by the end of the century, meat and wool from Australia were sold there as well. On the international trade scene, for example, Argentina and the United States exported much of their grain and meat to Great Britain. In fact, Great Britain was a major market for New World products in general and for colonial produce in particular — but not for Newfoundland saltfish.

The international saltfish trade was unusual too in that there was a large number of producing countries and colonies spread around the edge of the North Atlantic. These were New England; Newfoundland, Nova Scotia and Quebec in British North America; Iceland and the Faroe Islands under Denmark; Scotland; Norway; France; and Portugal. The markets were even more diverse and included Brazil, the Caribbean, the United States, Canada, Great Britain, France, southern and Mediterranean Europe, and north Africa. As can be seen, a number of countries both imported and exported saltfish. Then finally, it must be emphasized that the saltfish trade depended on cod stocks found only in particular areas on both sides of the Atlantic: the banks of New England; the banks off Nova Scotia; the famous Grand Banks of Newfoundland and lesser banks off Newfoundland and Labrador; the coastal waters in this general area, but especially the coastal waters of Newfoundland and Labrador; the coastal waters and banks of Iceland, the Shetlands and the Faroese; and, finally, the famous area around the Norwegian Lofoten Islands, and the smaller Finmark region farther north. Nearly all producers fished in their own local waters; however, the French fished partly in

Icelandic but mostly in Newfoundland waters, and the Portuguese, with their tiny fleet, fished the Newfoundland Grand Banks. Thus the international saltfish trade was probably the most truly international of all trades involving a British colony.

During the nineteenth century, the saltfish trade reached its zenith. In 1814, when peace was re-established in Europe and America, the total amount of fish sold in overseas markets was over 1,000,000 cwts; nearly all of this was produced by Newfoundland and exported to Spain, Portugal, Italy and the Caribbean. In 1914 over 4,000,000 cwts were exported[1] and there were a number of major suppliers.

The principal producers and consumers of saltfish during the nineteenth century engaged in a trade that crisscrossed the Atlantic from west to east and from north to south. Norway sold its product in Spain and, later, Portugal and Brazil; France provided for its home market, its Caribbean and north African possessions, Greece, and during the latter part of the century especially, exported to Italy and Spain; Iceland eventually became a major exporter to eastern Spain; Nova Scotia and the United States supplied much of the Caribbean demand, while Quebec sold to Italy and southern Brazil; and the Faroese and Shetland fisheries were heavily dependent on the Spanish markets. As already indicated, Newfoundland exported to Portugal, Spain, Italy, Greece, northern Brazil and the Caribbean. In addition, some Newfoundland fish was also sold to Nova Scotia, the United States and Great Britain. It has been generally assumed that the latter markets re-exported this fish, but this writer is convinced that this was not entirely so. In any case, they were relatively minor markets in the international saltfish trade in general and the Newfoundland trade in particular.

A cursory examination of Newfoundland's principal markets can help explain the demand, in fact the increasing demand, for saltfish. The population growth of the Mediterranean market countries, especially in their coastal cities and provinces, was considerable. Spain's total population almost doubled during the century and totalled over 18,000,000 in 1900; Portugal's more than doubled to over 5,000,000; Italy's rose to almost 33,000,000 by 1901; and Brazil's increased from about 2,500,000 in 1808 to over 17,000,000 at the end of the century. In particular, the coastal cities, which were generally more easily supplied by sea, contained substantial populations. Alicante, Corunna, Malaga, Cadiz and Seville, for example, contained approximately a half million people each in 1900, while Santander and Bilbao contained almost a third of a million, Valencia three-quarters of a million, and Barcelona about a million at this time. Lisbon and Oporto, the chief cities of Portugal, had half a million people between them while Genoa, Naples and Leghorn contained in all over 2,000,000 and Bari and Ancona on the Adriatic coast totalled over 1,000,000. Finally, Pernambuco and Bahia, Newfoundland's two major markets in Brazil, contained well over 3,000,000 people in 1911. Therefore, by the beginning of the twentieth century, the traditional market towns for Newfoundland saltfish, including those that had been lost to competitors, contained about 12,000,000 people. This figure does not include the several hundred thousand potential consumers in Greece, nor the populations of the Caribbean, nor the consumers scattered throughout the United States, Canada, and Great Britain. Neither does it include the consumers in hinterlands, who bought their fish through neighbouring ports. For example, Leghorn was the entrepôt of Tuscany. Consequently, the population of the market countries for saltfish contained a substantial number of potential consumers.

Markets for saltfish were indeed substantial since saltfish was cheaper than most meat and therefore appealed to the poorer classes. Two examples illustrate this. In Naples, a major Mediterranean market, in 1889 (which was not an unusual year) mutton cost twenty to twenty-five cents per kilogram, beef forty to fifty cents, and veal sixty to ninety cents, while saltfish cost only twelve cents (U.S. currency).[2] In Jamaica, which bought cheap fish, the prices of protein-rich food between 1858 and 1864 were as follows: fresh pork — 4d. to 7d. per pound; fresh beef — 4d. to 6d.; salt pork — 6d. to 1s.; salt beef — 6d. to 10d.; and saltfish — 3d. to 6d.[3] Unlike Jamaica, which produced much of its own food, Barbados, another important West Indian market, imported all its protein and there the differences were no doubt greater. The price of saltfish vis-à-vis other protein-rich food was always an important factor in the importation of saltfish.

Finally, it must be borne in mind that markets needed purchasing ability to import saltfish. Portugal and Spain had managed quite easily in this regard prior to losing the bulk of their New World empires in the early nineteenth century. Although conditions changed during this century, these countries, as well as Italy, Greece, Brazil, and the Caribbean, had vigorous import-export trades into which the importation of saltfish fitted. However, before discussing the various saltfish markets which were important to the Newfoundland trade, it is necessary to examine briefly the developments in the saltfish export trade of Newfoundland's competitors.

Canada: Quebec and Nova Scotia

What eventually became the Canadian saltfish industry was, prior to confederation in 1867, two separate British North American fisheries: the Quebec (Gaspé Peninsula) fishery and the Nova Scotian fishery.

Quebec

Quebec's Gaspé Peninsula on the south shore of the St. Lawrence was originally part of the early French fishery. Following the conquest of New France, Channel Island merchants, expanding their Newfoundland operations, established businesses there. In 1777 this area exported 16,000 cwts of saltfish to European markets.[4] Innis states that the Gaspé region profited from the Napoleonic War and its trade was extended to Brazil when markets opened there. During the 1820s this area exported between 22,000 and 27,000 cwts of saltfish. The trade gradually grew, with saltfish being sent to Italy, especially Naples, and to Rio de Janeiro — the latter market becoming the more important one (see Table 3.A,[5] below).

TABLE 3.A

Gaspé's Saltfish Exports: 1875-1895
(cwts)

Year	Naples	Italy (total)	Brazil
1875		36,534	43,246
1876		27,039	57,870
1877		36,447	65,747
1878		-	-
1879		25,816	67,017
1880		29,733	66,393
1881		28,782	88,406
1882		29,396	74,322
1883		29,487	48,530
1884		38,018	55,317
1885		15,271	54,668
1886		18,648	63,043
1887		10,210	73,461
1888		8,655	61,541
1889		7,263	51,005
1890		7,067	63,977
1891	13,222		
1892	14,100		
1893	12,627		
1894	13,383		
1895	10,521		

It is difficult to distinguish Quebec fish from Nova Scotian fish in statistics reported after 1890, because both were listed as Canadian. However, very little Nova Scotian saltfish went to Brazil during the period from 1875 to 1890, except in 1882 and 1888, when 15,730 cwts and 19,550 cwts, respectively, were sold there, and on a few other occasions, when several thousand hundredweight of this product entered the market. Furthermore, it is very likely that even this fish came from Gaspé via Halifax for, as Grant writes, "Halifax, rather than a producing, became a distributing centre for large fish export firms which drew their supplies from Gaspé, Newfoundland and Nova Scotia out-ports."[6] Finally, Governor Davidson of Newfoundland, who knew and understood the saltfish trade, explained in 1914 that Newfoundland fish was imported by northern Brazil and Gaspé fish by the south.[7] This would indicate that the composition of this part of the Canadian saltfish trade had not changed. Consequently, the present writer believes that Quebec continued to be the major supplier of all saltfish entering Brazil from Canada. Canadian exports of saltfish to Brazil increased briefly, but suffered from a depression early in the twentieth century and fluctuated widely (see Table 3.B,[8] below). However, during the five-year period ending in 1914, Canada's

TABLE 3.B

Canada's Saltfish Exports to Brazil:
1891-1914

Year	Cwts	Value $
1891	83,669	409,419
1892	67,341	322,026
1893	-	397,452
1894	-	442,976
1895	-	584,701
1896	113,134	552,084
1897	87,377	359,216
1898	97,067	412,727
1899	89,436	408,536
1900	92,808	427,732
1901	95,740	434,189
1902	88,392	435,037
1903	121,540	616,405
1904	60,934	293,074
1905	72,280	408,342
1906	90,097	611,062
1907	95,632	617,542
1908	115,658	770,353
1909	94,855	528,239
1910	132,138	708,819
1911	143,157	886,304
1912	98,160	640,700
1913	118,858	830,006
1914	96,527	691,313

exports of this product to Brazil averaged 117,786 cwts annually. From what is known of the Norwegian trade to Rio de Janeiro, it appears conclusive that the Gaspé saltfish shared the market with Norway as a junior partner at first, but as very much the senior partner during the last years before the First World War.

Nova Scotia

Nova Scotia's saltfish industry originated in the late eighteenth century. It received its initial boost from the demand for saltfish in the Caribbean following the American Revolutionary War, when American products were barred from the British Caribbean, creating a demand for British North American saltfish in these markets. This demand increased later, during the Napoleonic War, and after this war, Nova Scotia continued to benefit from the exclusion of the Americans from that trade. The Nova Scotian-Caribbean saltfish trade[9] was a substantial part of the international saltfish trade. In the five-year period 1829-34, an annual average of over 142,000 cwts was exported to these markets, and this quantity had increased to an average of over 180,000 cwts annually by 1835-39. The Nova Scotian-Caribbean trade fluctuated during the following decades and by mid-century foreign cargoes were free to enter the Caribbean ports as well. In 1864 and 1865, years for which complete reports are available, Nova Scotia's saltfish exports to the British West Indies stood at over 161,000 and 174,000 cwts, respectively.[10] During the remainder of the century, this trade continued to be substantial (see Table 3.C,[11] below), with exports to the British West Indies averaging almost 260,000 cwts during 1876-90. There was a slow decline up to 1914, when just over 151,000 cwts were exported there.

Nova Scotia also became a major supplier for the foreign West Indies. The colony began to send saltfish to those markets in the 1830s. In 1832, for example, 3,225 cwts were sent to Havana and another 2,004 in 1833. In 1839 Nova Scotia's total exports to the foreign West Indies reached almost 11,000 cwts and the trade continued to expand. In 1851, for example, the colony's total exports of saltfish were valued at £117,288, of which £67,524 worth went to the British West Indies, leaving slightly under £50,000 worth for other markets. The trade continued to grow and in 1864, 106,830 cwts of saltfish were exported from Nova Scotia to the foreign West Indies. In 1865 the statistics were differentiated further, and it was recorded that this British colony sent over 30,000 cwts to the French West Indies and over 54,000 to the Spanish West Indies. Exports to the latter increased throughout the 1870s to about 200,000 cwts annually (see Table 3.C, below), but those to the French West Indies declined during the 1880s following the expansion of the French saltfish trade.[12] Apparently, the

TABLE 3.C

Nova Scotia's Saltfish Exports: 1876-1914
(average cwts)

Years	British West Indies	United States	Spanish West Indies	French West Indies	
1876-80	272,099	59,065	200,149	47,016	
1881-85	254,275	167,457	192,019	39,870	
1886-90	248,366	132,960	192,857	17,669	
1891-99	235,228	114,362	226,639		
1900-05	219,609	159,601	75,069 (Cuba)	79,077	American West Indies
1906-10	196,900	78,056	66,080 (Cuba)	75,010	Puerto Rico
1911-14	183,264	130,286	65,819 (Cuba)	83,263	Puerto Rico

increase in trade was especially noteworthy in Puerto Rico. The British consul reported from there in 1856 that trade had only recently developed with British North America. He wrote that formerly, Puerto Rico had been practically a vassal of the Danish island of St. Thomas, a free port through which most Puerto Rican imports came.[13] Similarly, in 1872 it was reported that "Dry and pickled fish are almost exclusively imported from British North America."[14] However, after the Spanish-American War, Puerto Rico was ceded to the United States, and in 1903 Cuban sugar was granted preferential tariff treatment in the United States. In return, American saltfish received preferential tariff treatment in Cuba. However, Nova Scotia continued to export considerable quantities to Cuba and Puerto Rico. Nova Scotia, therefore, acquired major markets in the Spanish West Indies (Puerto Rico and Cuba).

In the meantime, a considerable quantity of saltfish was exported to the United States. However, it is very likely that much, if not most, of this Nova Scotian saltfish was re-exported to the Caribbean. McFarland blames the Nova Scotian-American saltfish trade for contributing to the problems and eventual decline in the American cod fishery.[15]

Nova Scotia's total production and export of saltfish increased considerably during the latter half of the nineteenth century (see Table 3.D,[16] below) but declined sharply after the 1880s. There was another more gradual decline in the early twentieth century.

TABLE 3.D

Nova Scotia's Exportation of Saltfish: 1869-1913
(cwts, five-year averages)

Years	Cwts
1869-1873	464,686
1874-1878	506,345
1879-1883	616,115
1884-1888	791,044
1889-1893	569,388
1894-1898	557,204
1899-1903	569,309
1904-1908	508,364
1909-1913	486,029

Nova Scotia's foreign saltfish trade was substantial and until the 1880s it was surpassed only by the trades of Newfoundland and Norway. However, it was almost completely dependent on markets which bought the poorest-quality fish at the lowest prices. Furthermore, the Caribbean, especially the British Caribbean, declined in wealth and importance during the nineteenth century, unlike the European and Brazilian markets, where population growth increased the demand for saltfish.

Nevertheless, the combination of Quebec's Gaspé saltfish trade to Brazil and Nova Scotia's trade to the Caribbean assured Canada a major role in the supply of saltfish to these two areas.[17]

The United States of America

The United States of America (before 1783, the British New England colonies) had a long history in the saltfish trade. In the 1620s West of England fishermen settled New England, and within a few years, the area was completely occupied by residents, bringing the English migratory fishery in these waters to an end. Some of the saltfish produced was exported to Spain, but most went to the sugar plantations in the Caribbean. These markets required the cheapest product, which was used primarily to feed the slave populations. Prior to 1783, New England ships also came to Newfoundland to buy cargoes of this poor *West India* fish. The situation changed after the American Revolutionary War, when Newfoundland and the rest of British North America became the chief suppliers of the British Caribbean. However, with the outbreak of war between England and France in 1793, the United States again became an important saltfish supplier to the British West Indies as well as to Spain. While it is impossible to distinguish the amount of Newfoundland-produced saltfish carried by American ships, it is evident that America's fishery increased. Fleets of American fishing ships began to fish on the Labrador coast, for example. During the Napoleonic War, American saltfish exports increased, and in 1807, 473,924 cwts were exported, of which 268,332 cwts went to the Caribbean and 192,981 cwts went to Spain and France, especially to Alicante.[18] With the passage of the Embargo Act in 1807, the American saltfish trade ceased and the fishery itself was curtailed. Later, the Anglo-American War of 1812-14 completed this disruption.

After the war, there were attempts to revive the American saltfish trade with Spain but these failed, presumably because of the chaotic state of the Spanish import trade and the amount of Newfoundland (and, to a lesser extent, Norwegian) fish being offered for sale there. Similarly, the Americans found themselves excluded from the British West Indian trade by British North American producers. America's foreign saltfish trade was reduced and became almost totallly dependent on the foreign West Indian markets. During the thirty-three-year period between 1819 and 1851, an average of over 242,000 cwts was sent there annually.[19] However, American fishermen had a substantial home market and McFarland argues that the opening of the Erie Canal increased this market. He quotes a contemporary source: "New York and Albany markets, which previously required only a few thousand quintals for their annual supply, now afford a demand for nearly 150,000 quintals."[20] It was this extensive home market which continued to support the large American saltfish industry.

The American saltfish industry had grown considerably by the mid-1880s (see Table 3.E,[21] below), with production rising to over 1,000,000 cwts in 1883 and 1884. However, it declined quickly during the

TABLE 3.E

New England's Saltfish Production:
1880-1909

(cwts, five-year averages)

Years	Cwts
1880-1884	874,632
1885-1889	698,464
1890-1894	481,078
1895-1899	465,885
1900-1904	435,312
1905-1909	434,843

following decade and settled at about 450,000 cwts annually during the early twentieth century.

The American saltfish industry experienced several problems, both inherent and imposed. In 1848 the United States import tariff on saltfish was reduced from $1.00 to twenty percent ad valorem per cwt. This encouraged imports from British North America and during the year immediately following this reduction, imports from there rose from just over 1,000 cwts to over 42,000 cwts annually.[22] Imports from British North America during the periods of the Reciprocity Treaty (1854-66) and the Treaty of Washington (1883-85) were also blamed for competing with the locally produced salt cod.[23] Another problem (not unique to America) was the fact that its cod fishery was a deep-sea fishery, involving greater capital investment than that of Newfoundland, for example. McFarland is convinced that the cod fisheries in British North America were, on the whole, prosecuted more cheaply, in terms of both labour and capital investment, than those in the United States.[24] Finally, since the American saltfish industry was dependent largely on its home market, it was vulnerable to competition from other locally produced fish. During the latter nineteenth century, the expansion of the canning process and the development of refrigeration created a demand for cheaper coastal fish like herring, sardines, alewives and shad. In the meantime, the exportation of saltfish from the United States remained restricted — once again, no doubt, because of the competition from British North America. Although a little was exported to the British West Indies after the repeal of the British Navigation Act in 1846, this area was already glutted with fish. Consequently, most American saltfish was sent to the foreign West Indies. By the 1890s total exports amounted to less than 100,000 cwts, and this figure had declined to less than 40,000 cwts by the early years of the twentieth century.[25] After a long and important place in its foreign trade America's saltfish industry was coming to an end.

Norway

The Norwegian cod fishery was an ancient industry which had traditionally concentrated on the production of tørrfisk (stockfish). This product was cured by drying without salt during the cool spring weather and it was exported to the Baltic countries. The practice of producing dried salted cod fish was introduced into Norway by outsiders who wished to take advantage of the southern European demand for this product, and by the late eighteenth century small quantities of Norwegian klippfisk (saltfish) were being sold in Spain. This trade collapsed during the Napoleonic War. However, throughout the nineteenth century, the production and export of klippfisk expanded and Norway soon became a leading exporter (see Table 3.F,[26] below).

TABLE 3.F

Norwegian Saltfish Exports: 1815-1914
(cwts, five-year averages)

Years	Cwts	Years	Cwts
1815-1819	28,733	1865-1869	510,623
1820-1824	59,546	1870-1874	544,761
1825-1829	120,783	1875-1879	794,945
1830-1834	126,134	1880-1884	815,388
1835-1839	193,339	1885-1889	843,921
1840-1844	172,161	1890-1894	1,069,229
1845-1849	224,252	1895-1899	844,713
1850-1854	244,536	1900-1904	653,989
1855-1859	380,945	1905-1909	747,443
1860-1864	362,390	1910-1914	991,120

Beginning with the revival of trade in 1815, most Norwegian saltfish was exported to Bilbao and Barcelona. In 1828, one of the few years for which a breakdown is possible, these two markets each bought over 70,000 cwts of klippfisk out of a total export of just over 158,000 cwts.[27]

As Table 3.F, above, indicates, the export of Norwegian saltfish continued to grow. Meanwhile, Bilbao and Barcelona increased their importation steadily. In 1855, for example, the former imported over 150,000 cwts, while in 1851 the latter imported over 100,000.[28] In addition, Norway increased its exportation to other Spanish ports. By mid-century both Santander and San Sebastian were purchasing Norwegian saltfish and in 1861 the former bought over 51,000 cwts while the latter bought about 17,000.[29]

During the latter part of the century, Norway's exports of saltfish increased dramatically, especially between the early 1860s and early 1890s, when exports trebled to over 1,000,000 cwts annually. Then there was a steep decline followed by a recovery just before the First World War. Bilbao remained an important customer (see Table 3.G,[30] below), as did Barcelona for most of the period. The latter market purchased 98,000 cwts in 1887 and over 100,000 during the 1890s.[31] However, this trade to Barcelona was almost completely displaced by Icelandic saltfish during the early years of the twentieth century. Norway continued to trade with other Spanish ports: Santander bought an average of over 90,000 cwts of saltfish annually during 1886-1889, mostly from Norway, but the port itself was in decline and it imported just over 40,000 cwts during

1909-1912;[32] Corunna imported just under 18,000 cwts during 1883-1894, lesser amounts during the following years, but over 30,000 cwts annually by 1910;[33] and Tarragona was also a market for over 30,000 cwts annually.[34] In addition, Norway managed to develop a new trade with southern Spain. Exports to Alicante averaged just under 20,000 cwts during 1882-1894[35] but then declined. Also, a small amount of Norwegian saltfish was sold in Malaga and Valencia.

TABLE 3.G

**Bilbao's Saltfish Imports from Norway:
1882-1912**
(average cwts)

Years	Cwts
1886-1890 (5 years)	144,132
1891-1895 (5 years)	180,360
1896-1900 (5 years)	155,968
1901-1905 (5 years)	152,860
1906-1912 (7 years)	165,633

Norway also exported saltfish to other markets during the latter half of the century. In 1875 Norwegian saltfish was sold in Naples for the first time, presumably because Newfoundland's production had declined somewhat.[36] This trade increased and the British consul wrote in 1880 that: "The consumption of Gaspe and [Newfoundland] shore fish has been much interfered with by the heavy imports of Norwegian codfish, which has now taken a firm footing in the provincial markets, and, owing to the economy in price, is now preferred by many provincial buyers who had hitherto dealt only in hard-cured British codfish."[37] During the 1886-1895 period, Norway exported over 36,000 cwts annually to this market. This was followed by a decline, but the trade recovered again and in both 1912 and 1913 Naples imported over 60,000 cwts of saltfish from Norway.[38] Some Norwegian klippfisk was also sold in Leghorn, Bari, Palermo and Messina, but it was Genoa that became Norway's principal Italian market. Norway's exports to Genoa increased in the 1880s as Newfoundland's declined. In 1894 over 75,000 cwts of "klippfisk, stockfish, and smoked herring" were imported from Norway[39] and in 1898 over 83,000 cwts of saltfish were imported from this supplier.[40] During the three-year period ending in 1904, Norway's share of this market amounted to over 116,000 cwts of saltfish annually,[41] and according to Vollan, Genoa gradually became the centre of the Norwegian saltfish trade in Italy.[42] Meanwhile, Norway's trade with Portugal also increased dramatically. Exports of the country's saltfish to Oporto rose from just over 40,000 cwts in 1883 to over 200,000 cwts in 1894. This was followed by a decline, after which there was a recovery, so that in 1914 over 150,000 cwts were imported.[43] Similarly, a large amount of Norwegian saltfish was sold in Lisbon, at least by the end of this period. According to Vollan, Portugal bought over thirty percent of Norway's total exports in 1912 and 1913.[44] This suggests that more than 330,000 cwts of Norwegian saltfish were sold in Portugal during these years. In addition, large amounts of Norwegian saltfish were sold in Brazil late in the century. It is difficult to identify the quantities, but 97,500 cwts were sold there in 1906, quantities valued at £218,600 and £211,200 in 1908 and 1909, respectively, and about 200,000 cwts in each of 1912 and 1913.[45] In addition, considerable quantities of Norwegian saltfish were exported to the United Kingdom, presumably for reshipment elsewhere. During the five-year period 1895-1899, for example, just over 300,000 cwts were sold there annually.[46] Finally, some fish was also sent to Cuba. Thus during the nineteenth century Norway continued to dominate the Spanish trade and captured an increasing share of the other international markets as well.

The Norwegian saltfish industry experienced a severe depression around the turn of the century, with exports declining by thirty-nine percent between 1890-94 and 1900-04. The Lofoten fishery declined by over fifty percent between 1895 and 1896 because of extremely bad weather, and this along with other problems beset the industry during the following years. In 1899 the British consul general in Norway wrote:

> ...Both the migration and appearance of fish on the coasts, and the incessant storms, upset all calculations. The year will long be remembered among the fishery population for its abnormally bad profits, and the great loss of life and property.[47]

The following year was no better:

> Taken as a whole the cod fishery was far below average in quantity. In the Lofoten district, poor as the take was in 1898 and 1899, the past year is said to have witnessed the smallest catch ever recorded.[48]

In addition, the scarcity of the cod forced up the price which the merchants paid the fishermen, and this made Norwegian saltfish more expensive and less competitive at the very time that Iceland was enjoying large catches. This probably helps to explain why Icelandic saltfish successfully replaced the Norwegian product in Barcelona. However, the Norwegian fishery recovered and by the beginning of the First World War, Norway was a supplier of saltfish on a level with Newfoundland, with a good potential for further growth.

The reasons why the Norwegian saltfish trade expanded so dramatically during the nineteenth century have not been adequately studied. As recently as 1975, a Norwegian academic explained Norway's post-1814 growth in this area as follows: "Since the New Foundland cod fisheries were disturbed during the war years, the Norwegians were quick to step in to fill the vacuum."[49] In reality, however, Newfoundland's cod fisheries benefitted immensely from the war and were not disturbed in this sense. The reasons for the expansion of the Norwegian saltfish industry must therefore be sought elsewhere. It seems most likely that Norway's saltfish could undersell that of the only major producer — Newfoundland — especially during the immediate post-1815 period. In 1815 Newfoundland had just gone through a period of high inflation with high prices, wages and living standards. On the other hand, Norway's overseas commercial activity had practically ceased with the British blockade beginning in 1807. Businesses went bankrupt and there were very serious financial, economic and even food crises. Derry states that "In many districts the population declined during these 'Hunger Years', which reached a climax in 1812, when the harvest failed and bark bread was the only substitute."[50] With a lower standard of living, Norway was in a position to produce a less expensive product, other factors being equal. In addition, the Norwegian fishing season began earlier and lasted longer than that in Newfoundland. In January, Norwegian fishermen moved to the Lofoten Islands to catch the cod which migrated annually into these coastal waters to spawn. This fishery, the most famous of all in Norway, lasted until April, when the fishermen either returned to their farms or went farther north to fish on the Finmark coast during the summer. The procedure for curing the klippfisk from the Lofotens was also peculiarly Norwegian. The fishermen caught the fish and sold it fresh to merchants from Bergen, Kristiansund and Ålesurd. These merchants sent their collection vessels to the Lofotens to buy the fish from the fishermen, and the ships' captains oversaw the splitting and salting. Unlike Newfoundland fishermen, the Norwegian fishermen were not responsible for curing their own catches; thus Norway's fish was more uniformly salted and dried; and when prices were depressed, the fishermen were not under the same pressure to concentrate on quantity at the expense of quality, which seems to have been the case in Newfoundland on occasion. In 1829, for example, the British ambassador in Madrid reported to the Foreign Office that the Norwegian saltfish was better cured than that from Newfoundland.[51] Similarly, in 1888 the British consul in Naples wrote that "The increase in the consumption of Norwegian codfish is due in part to the care and attention given to the curing and the shipment of the fish."[52] Also, since the Norwegian saltfish was cured and stored at only the three ports mentioned above, transportation costs were low. Newfoundland fish, on the other hand, was produced and stored in hundreds of centres. Furthermore, the general shipping costs of Norwegian fish seem to have been lower. Vollan points out that Spanish ship owners preferred to send their ships to Norway instead of Newfoundland because it was easier and presumably cheaper.[53] Also, the Norwegian economy was much more diversified than that of Newfoundland and this helped to cushion the effects of depressed seasons. Finally, the Norwegian fish trade was strongly supported by the Swedish Foreign Office. It was reported in 1859 for example, that the Swedish-Norwegian consul in Bilbao was actively engaged in the importation of saltfish into that port. Consequently, for a variety of reasons, the exportation of Norwegian saltfish increased during the nineteenth century and Norway became a major partner in the international saltfish trade.

France

After 1815 the French resumed their cod fisheries in Newfoundland waters. Some French fishermen returned to resettle the French islands of St. Pierre and Miquelon off the south coast of Newfoundland, where they engaged in a local coastal fishery similar to the inshore fishery carried out by the residents of Newfoundland. With the return of a French fleet to the French Shore of Newfoundland, the annual migratory summer fishery on Newfoundland's west and north coasts was re-established. Yet another French fleet engaged once again in the bank fishery on the Grand Banks of Newfoundland, travelling to the French Shore or St. Pierre for water and bait.

In order to maintain a supply of sailors who could be drafted into the navy and in order to satisfy the fishing interests of the French Atlantic ports, especially Bordeaux in the late eighteenth century, France had established a system of financial support for its Newfoundland fisheries. At first, this bounty system was not intended to stimulate the foreign saltfish trade because France had its own home markets, both in Europe and the Caribbean; therefore the saltfish trade was not viewed as a way of earning foreign exchange. (Later in the nineteenth century this position was to change.) This extensive system of bounties was unique to France's cod fishery. In 1851 the system of bounties was extensively revised (see Table 3.H,[54] below) to encourage not only the training of seamen, but also the exportation of fish to foreign markets. This does not seem to have had much immediate impact because the export of French saltfish actually declined after the 1840s and remained depressed until the 1880s (see Table 3.I,[55] below). There was a spurt of growth in the saltfish industry in the

TABLE 3.H

French Bounty System: 1851

Bounties Paid to Support the French Fishery

Per man, for those outfitted for the fishery on the Newfoundland coast, St. Pierre and Miquelon, and the Grand Bank	50 francs
Per man for the fishery in the Iceland seas, without drying fish	50 francs
Per man, on the Grand Bank, without drying fish	30 francs
Per man, on the Dogger Bank, without drying fish	15 francs

Bounties on Exported Fish (per Metric Quintal)

Dry codfish, of French catch, exported directly from the coast of Newfoundland, St. Pierre or Miquelon; or warehoused in France and exported to the French colonies or to transatlantic ports having a French consul	20 francs
Dry codfish, not warehoused, exported from French ports	16 francs
Dry codfish carried directly from fishing regions to ports of France, Portugal, and Spain, or to other foreign ports in the Mediterranean	16 francs
Dry codfish carried directly to ports of France, and thence to Sardinia and Algeria	12 francs

1880s, partly as a result of the increased use of bultows in place of handlines.[56] This growth faltered in the early 1890s, but recovered again and even expanded during the years just before the First World War.

Although there were other important explanations for the growth of the French saltfish trade — such as France's new rail links with Spain and Portugal — there is common agreement among contemporary observers that the system of bounties allowed France to become and remain an important saltfish exporter. The British consul in Naples recognized the potential strength of the French saltfish trade when he wrote in 1886:

> The heavy drawback paid by the French Government enables shippers of French codfish to oppose a most serious competition to British curers, and particularly to soft cured fish as Labrador...[because the French shippers can]...send the overplus fish to foreign markets...at a very low price, as they receive on fish landed

TABLE 3.I

France's Saltfish Exports: 1825-1914
(cwts, five-year averages)

Years	Italy	Spain	Grand Total
1825-1829			113,182
1830-1834			102,813
1835-1839			137,514
1840-1844			158,707
1845-1849			151,564
1850-1854			116,173
1855-1859			138,513
1860-1864			73,979
1865-1869			52,075
1870-1874	34,947	2,871	80,152
1875-1879	36,658	3,439	73,478
1880-1884	39,110	59,639	149,073
1885-1889	87,218	167,730	320,644
1890-1894	65,461	63,882	216,883
1895-1899	106,340	124,922	339,245
1900-1904	105,792	213,609	380,104
1905-1909	138,701	71,538	315,603
1910-1914	154,427	86,697	398,691

at Leghorn 16 fr. per 100 kilos., equal to 6s. 6d. per English quintal, and on that landed at Genoa and Naples 12 fr. equal to 4s. 10d. per English quintal.

In former years French codfish was not imported to Naples, or if so, in very small quantities when Labrador fish was scarce or dear; but with the stimulus given to French shippers the importation of French codfish of last year's [1885] catch to this market amounted to above 10,600 quintals, whilst from this year's catch a similar quantity has already been imported, and further large arrivals are expected.

This leads to a corresponding decrease in the consumption of Labrador codfish, and although the catch on the Labrador coast this year [1886] was a small one, the average price for Labrador codfish has not exceeded 14s. per quintal (cost, freight, and insurance), whereas in former years, under about similar circumstances, 16s. to 18s. per quintal (cost, freight, and insurance) was usually paid for this quality.

The price of 14s. for Labrador could correspond to 18s. 10d. per quintal for French codfish landed at Naples or Genoa, and to £1.0.6 on codfish landed at Leghorn, and with so heavy a difference in favour of French shippers it is difficult to understand how Canadian [sic] shippers can be expected to compete.[57]

There were numerous similar reports, especially concerning the Italian ports. For example, in 1901 the British consul in Naples wrote:

> ...It is the French fish that causes the greatest trouble, for being dried at Cette, Bordeaux and Marseilles, it is imported weekly from the last named port to Naples as required, and the high bounty which is given by the French Government on their fish when exported handicaps British fish, and especially the Labrador cure. Both cures [i.e. French and Labrador] being soft, are consumed in the same market, namely, the city of Naples and its immediate neighbourhood. The other qualities are consumed in the province.[58]

As illustrated above, Naples had become a major market for French saltfish by the end of the nineteenth century. By 1911-13 that port was importing over 52,000 cwts of the French product annually.[59]

By the mid-1880s France was also exporting saltfish to Leghorn — 25,000 cwts in 1885 and over 85,000 in 1889.[60] The trade declined after 1889, but recovered to over 88,000 cwts in 1896 and over 100,000 cwts in 1897. During the next five years, the amount remained steady and averaged just over 82,000 cwts annually.[61] Although statistical evidence is not readily available for later years, it was reported in 1910 that *bounty-fed* French saltfish was being imported in increasing quantities.[62] One of the contemporary explanations for this was the fact that the French export bounty was higher for fish going to Leghorn than for fish going to either Naples or Genoa. It was reported that exports to Leghorn were subsidized at the rate of 16 fr. per 100 kilograms, while those going to the other two ports were subsidized at the rate of 11 and 14 fr., respectively.[63]

While Genoa had always bought some French saltfish, trade expanded in the last quarter of the century. In 1874, 27,000 cwts were imported into Genoa from France and the quantity averaged under 29,000 cwts during 1876-84.[64] While statistical evidence is incomplete because imports by rail were not recorded, the literary evidence suggests that France became an important supplier of saltfish to this market by the mid-1880s. The British consul wrote in 1885 that "It is a fact much to be regretted that year by year French cured fish are supplanting ours [Newfoundland] in the market...."[65] Nevertheless, it does not seem that Genoa became as important to the French saltfish trade as Leghorn or Naples.

In the meantime, France also exported considerable amounts of saltfish to Spain. It was reported in 1887 that Cadiz "still continues to be supplied almost wholly by French fish," chiefly because it was subsidized by the French government to such an extent that it could be sold at a profit for 10s. to 12s. per fifty kilograms, while Labrador sold for 15s. and Newfoundland shore-cured for 19s to 20s.[66] French saltfish was sold in Bilbao as well, and an average of almost 25,000 cwts was imported annually during 1886-89; an average of over 31,000 cwts during 1899-1903; and 26,000 and 19,000 cwts, respectively, in 1909 and 1910.[67] In 1886, 6,000 cwts of French saltfish were exported to Alicante and exports to that port averaged over 9,000 cwts annually during the following three years. They then declined, and rose again to an average of almost 29,000 cwts annually during 1899-1901; however, after this period of growth they declined completely.[68] A small quantity of French saltfish was sold to Barcelona as well. On the whole, it is difficult to document exports of French saltfish to Spain during the period under study; however, the evidence that is available suggests that the quantities were considerable, particularly after the mid-1880s.

Probably because of a series of catch failures, the export of French saltfish declined during the early years of the twentieth century. The British consul in Bordeaux described the 1905 fishing season as follows:

> French owners had reason to complain once more of the very bad results of their Newfoundland fishery in 1905 which were worse than in 1904, itself a bad year. The better part of the cod vessels from Fécamp, Granville and St. Malo returned with half cargoes and unloaded at their own ports, their produce being subsequently despatched by rail or coasting vessel to the markets of La Rochelle and Bordeaux [to be cured for final sale or export]. The Cancale fleet alone, which is described as the élite of French cod fishing, met with fair success at Newfoundland and these preferred to discharge at La Rochelle, where delivery is said to be more economical and convenient than at Bordeaux.
>
> During the last three years Bordeaux has suffered from a marked decentralisation of the codfish trade, of which it used formerly to hold a monopoly. The change is attributed to various causes, such as reduced railway tariffs favouring despatch from other French ports and to the establishment of cod curing factories in the north of France. The chief cause, however, is undoubtedly, the bad state of the fishery, which naturally induces owners of vessels with only half cargoes to dispose of them at reduced prices in their own ports rather than to incur the heavy expense of taking insignificant catches as far as Bordeaux. It is generally held that Bordeaux will recover its old position in this respect as soon as the Newfoundland catch returns to even average proportions.[69]

This decline of the French saltfish industry was widespread. The Bordeaux fishery fell off steadily from over 418,000 cwts exported in 1901 to just over 121,000 cwts in 1905. Similarly, the St. Pierre fishery declined steadily from over 475,000 cwts exported in 1900 to just over 241,000 cwts in 1905. Finally, Marseilles exports declined from about 154,000 cwts in 1902 to 71,000 cwts in 1904.[70] Thus Bordeaux saltfish exports declined by over seventy percent and the other two by about fifty percent.

The British consul in St. Pierre described the rise and fall of the saltfish industry on the islands of St. Pierre and Miquelon:

> Looking back...I find that 1886 was a record year with an export of 45,556 English tons [911,120 cwts].... In 1885, although only 41,154 tons [823,300 cwts] were exported, the value amounted to £300,000 and £400,000 worth, and the prosperity of the colony [St. Pierre] appeared secure; but since 1900 cod has gradually but surely become scarcer. In 1902, a good year 21,930,370 kilos. [431,360 cwts] were caught by local vessels or an average of 1,945 cwts. per schooner. With 1903 the poor season commenced. In that year the catch was only at the rate of 983 cwts. per vessel, and in 1904 it fell to 825 cwts.[71]

Woodhouse thought that there were two reasons for the decline in the St. Pierre fishery — scarcity of fish and a lack of bait. The first was an act of nature but the latter was the result of Newfoundland legislation prohibiting the sale of bait to the French fishermen. Another reason for the decline of the St. Pierre fishery, however, was the decision by the French fleet to cease using the island as a depot. This decision had been made because St. Pierre could no longer provide bait supplies. The St. Pierre schooner fleet declined steadily from 208 vessels in 1902 to only twenty-eight in 1913,[72] although the small inshore fishery continued to survive.

The fishing fleet from France did not suffer the same fate as St. Pierre's schooner fleet. After the depression, the Grand Bank fishery from France recovered. In 1906 the French introduced steam trawlers into their deep-sea fishery and this was a major technological breakthrough, not least of all because it eliminated the traditional dependence on bait. The British consul in Bordeaux wrote: "The fair success obtained by the steam trawlers belonging to the ports of Dunkirk, Gravelines, and Boulogne, has made it difficult for sailing vessels to compete with their old-fashioned line fishery."[73] This recovery continued and was reflected in the increased exportation of saltfish from Bordeaux to foreign markets in the Mediterranean, which rose from less than 120,000 cwts in 1907 to over 390,000 cwts in 1910. However, once again this trade declined steeply to just over 141,000 cwts in 1913.[74] In the meantime, the use of steam trawlers in the French bank fishery increased and in 1909 France had thirty of these ships on the Grand Banks, while all of British North America had only two.[75]

The place of the French in the international saltfish trade was very significant, beginning in the 1880s. There was an increased demand for the French product, partly because of quality problems with the similar Labrador-cured from Newfoundland and partly because the French subsidy made this fish cheaper. However, Newfoundland's prohibition of bait sales to the French after 1888 adversely affected the French fishery and reduced the importance of their depot and base in St. Pierre. At the same time, it must be remembered that the French fisheries were most dependent on their home markets: the foreign trade never involved a big proportion of the catch, it did in the Newfoundland, Norwegian and Icelandic fisheries. Consequently, French exports were likely to fluctuate much more widely than the exports of the other major producers because in time of low catches, the natural tendency was to supply the home markets first. In fact, if one examines the annual export figures for the French saltfish trade, one can see the considerable deviation from the mean. For example, total exports declined from over 480,000 cwts in 1902 to just over 142,000 cwts in 1906, rose to almost 650,000 cwts in 1910 and declined again to less than 240,000 cwts in 1914.

At the same time that French saltfish was becoming more important to the international trade, the French cod fisheries in Newfoundland waters were undergoing a remarkable transformation. The migratory fishery on the French Shore continued to decline until France agreed in 1904 to give up its traditional rights on that coast. The St. Pierre schooner fishery declined as well, leaving only a small inshore fishery carried out by the small resident population. Finally, the fleet of sailing bank ships dependent upon the use of baited bultows was being replaced by steam trawlers during the years before the war. These adaptations and the necessary capital investment were possible because of the large, guaranteed, and well-protected home market.

Iceland

Iceland was one of the less important saltfish producers and exporters of the nineteenth century. This island entered the trade in 1787 after the Danish government lifted the trade restrictions which they had imposed on the island earlier.[76] Although Hermannson states that by 1800 "a very considerable traffic in fish was carried from Iceland to Spain and the Mediterranean,"[77] Iceland was a small producer. After the Napoleonic War, Iceland increased its exports of saltfish, which amounted to 85,000 cwts by 1855,[78] with most of the best-quality fish going to Spain and the rest to Denmark (possibly for re-export to the Danish West Indies). The Icelandic fishery grew during the latter part of the century and fish was sent to Italy as well as Spain. In 1897, for example, 60,000 cwts were sold in Genoa.[79] Nevertheless, Spain was probably the most popular destination for Icelandic saltfish; some fish went to Bilbao[80] but most was sent to Barcelona. In the latter market, Iceland was supplying almost the total demand by the end of the period under study and had completely displaced Norway. During the five-year period 1909-13, Iceland exported an annual average of almost 150,000 cwts of saltfish to this market.[81] By the beginning of the twentieth century, Iceland was exporting a total of between 300,000 and 500,000 cwts of saltfish annually.[82]

Faroe Islands

The Faroe Islands were, like Iceland, under Danish rule during this period and were also engaged in the saltfish trade. This colony's fish was often sold with the Icelandic fish, especially in Bilbao.[83] By the early years of the twentieth century, exports from the Faroe Islands averaged over 100,000 cwts annually.[84]

Scotland

Scotland was also an exporter of saltfish to Bilbao. Throughout the nineteenth century, Scottish fish was sold in that market and by the years before the First World War, the amount of Scottish fish going there had risen to just over 36,000 cwts annually.[85] In addition, it was reported on a few occasions that United Kingdom saltfish was being sold in Malaga.[86] During this same period, on the other hand, the Shetland saltfish trade was declining (see Table 3.J,[87] below). Furthermore, to complicate the documentation the United Kingdom continued to export large quantities of "unenumerated" fish, which may have included saltfish. However, there are no reports of British saltfish being sold in large quantities in any of the traditional markets, with the exception of the instances mentioned above. Consequently, this trade is not considered a major factor in these markets.

TABLE 3.J

Shetland's Saltfish Exports: 1860-1914
(cwts, five-year averages)

Years	Cwts	Years	Cwts
1860-1864	56,800	1890-1894	53,600
1865-1869	66,200	1895-1899	41,600
1870-1874	83,000	1900-1904	18,800
1875-1879	86,000	1905-1909	11,400
1880-1884	63,600	1910-1914	10,400
1885-1889	58,400		

Portugal

In 1836 the Portuguese Government encouraged the formation of a National Fishing Company with its headquarters in Lisbon. Its purposes were to reduce the dependence on imports and to rebuild Portugal's maritime strength. The company attempted to obtain landing and curing rights to part of the Newfoundland coast but failed, and in 1857 it went bankrupt. A number of individual ship owners continued the fishery, but the scale of their operations was not large. In 1900 and 1901 they brought into Lisbon about 25,000 cwts of saltfish each year.[88] The industry was not helped by the ambivalent attitude of the Portuguese government, which, for a long time, did not want to see a reduction in imports of foreign saltfish because they contributed substantially to the tariff revenues. Thus the number of ships that could engage in the Grand Bank cod fishery was restricted to eight, and these were required to use only the port of Lisbon.[89] In 1901 these regulations were removed[90] and the fleet expanded almost immediately to fifteen vessels.[91] This expansion continued for the remainder of the period, and in 1912 the American consul in Oporto reported that in addition to the Lisbon fleet, there were twenty-six vessels, of about 200 tons each, from the Oporto area engaged in this fishery.[92] However, Portugal, on the whole, did not play a large role in the international Newfoundland trade.

Summary

Several general statements must be made at this point. Norway, with its cheaper fish, became a major international saltfish supplier early in the nineteenth century, especially in the Spanish markets. Later in the century, Norway expanded into other European markets at about the same time as the French bounty-supported fishery also expanded. A crisis occurred when all the major fisheries experienced growth during the 1870s and 1880s. For example, Newfoundland's total exportation rose to over 1,400,000 cwts annually during the five-year period ending in 1885; Norway's total exports rose steadily during the 1860s, '70s and '80s, as Table 3.F shows; and French exports rose dramatically during this same period. These three fisheries put severe pressure on the European markets at this time, as shall be seen. Similarly, Nova Scotia (see Table 3.D, above) increased its exports to the Caribbean at the same time, and thus competed directly with Newfoundland in those economically depressed markets. In addition, there were fluctuations in the trade during the following decades, accompanied by the growth of the Icelandic fishery. It is in this context of increasing world production of saltfish that the history of Newfoundland's saltfish markets must be examined.

CHAPTER 4

Spanish Markets

Background

In 1814 Newfoundland's sales of saltfish to Spain probably reached 400,000 cwts — nearly one-half the production for that year and fully one hundred percent of Spain's importation. By 1914 Newfoundland's saltfish markets in Spain had undergone profound changes. Spain's purchases of Newfoundland saltfish dropped to about 80,000 cwts in the mid-1820s — about ten percent of the colony's production. Sales improved and rose briefly to over 300,000 cwts in 1863, but they had nearly ceased by the end of the century. There was, however, a late and partial recovery during the last few years before World War One. In the meantime, Norway had found a market in Spain for an ever-increasing quantity of klippfisk, France had begun sending large shipments there after the 1870s, and Iceland and the Faroe Islands had developed their fisheries on the basis of Spanish demand for their product. Even though Newfoundland's product had monopolized the Spanish markets by 1814 and the colony had developed a highly efficient production and distribution system, the greatest disappointments experienced by Newfoundland in any markets during the century were experienced in Spain. Why Newfoundland should suffer such a fate while others, most notably Norway, thrived is one of the most intriguing questions in the history of the colony's fisheries.

Spain was confronted with massive political and economic problems at the end of the Peninsular War. Its economy was in a state of disorder and expensive reconstruction was needed. In addition, it was immediately faced with wars of independence in the colonies from which much of its wealth was obtained. This loss of government revenue from the colonies was one reason why import tariffs were increased during the early part of the century. In 1820-1825 when the protectionist fever was at its peak and duties were at their height, Spain lost its cocoa interests in Venezuela and Columbia, and its mines in Mexico and Peru.[1]

Vicens Vives divides Spanish foreign trade in the nineteenth century into two periods and its tariff policy into four. He writes that Spanish foreign trade prior to 1854 was noted for its contraction, while it expanded during the latter half of the century. In the development of its tariff structure, Vicens Vives identifies four periods: highly protectionist from 1814 to 1841; moderately so from 1841 to 1869; inclined towards free trade from 1869 to 1891; and protectionist after 1891.[2] It seems that the failure of the protectionist policies to bring about economic growth in the early part of the century led eventually to the later freer trade policies, although the political situation was an important factor as well. Apparently, protectionism in other countries during the 1870s produced a reaction in Spain and, again, protectionist ideas became increasingly popular until the new tariff schedule of 1891 repudiated the previous free trade policies.[3] Needless to add, Spain's individual tariff schedules did not always correspond to her general tariff policies. This will become evident when the Spanish saltfish trade is studied in detail. Furthermore, regional differences caused other deviations from the norm.

Specific information about the state of the Spanish saltfish markets on the regional level during the Peninsular War is practically non-existent. However, as Montgomery, the American consul in Alicante, reported, the importation of saltfish from Newfoundland in British ships was considerable during this period, while the American product was totally excluded.[4] One is left with the impression of rather amorphous markets buying ever-increasing quantities of Newfoundland saltfish at rising prices. There is certainly no doubt that during the period of monopoly of the Spanish markets between 1812 and 1814, Newfoundland supplied more saltfish to Spain than at any time before or after, but precise statistics are not available. When one examines the Spanish markets after the war, three regions of trading activity are readily discernible: north, east, and south. The northern market covered an area from the Portuguese border to France and included such important ports as Corunna, Santander, Bilbao and San Sebastian. The southern markets are a little more difficult to define since they merged with the eastern markets, but generally speaking they extended from the southern Portuguese border to Valencia. This region included the famous ports of Cadiz, Seville, Malaga, Alicante, and Valencia. Finally, the eastern markets were located on the remainder of the coast, dominated by the port of Barcelona.

In order to study the Spanish markets logically, one must examine those factors that are common to the whole country; those that are common to the individual regions; and finally, those that are peculiar to individual ports. To that end, the present writer will examine the Spanish markets in three chronological sections: 1814-1833; 1834-1876; and 1877-1914. Thus the first section will cover the period up to the outbreak of the First Carlist War, which led, among other things, to the end of prohibitive import tariffs on saltfish. The second section will cover the period that followed up to the end of the Second Carlist War, when the more moderate tariff policies terminated. The third section will study the period from 1877 to 1914.

1814-1833

The Spanish War of Independence (known to the British as the Peninsular War) created a perfect opportunity for the expansion of the Newfoundland saltfish industry. The Newfoundland fishery had been experiencing problems since the closure of the Spanish markets to British goods but the new revolutionary government, under the Junta, and later the Regency, agreed to a British proposal that British exports would receive preferential tariff treatment. This agreement allowed British-Newfoundland saltfish to enter Spain under a low tariff, thus excluding other fish — American in this instance — from these markets. Robert Montgomery, the American consul in Alicante, reported in 1810 that American saltfish imports had to pay double the duty charged on the British product.[5] He went on to say that "the Americans bold Competitors with the English in that Article are now drove out of the Market by an unjust decree of the Spanish Government...."[6] Furthermore, he pointed out that the Americans normally sold about 100,000 cwts of saltfish annually in Cadiz and Mediterranean Spain and about 20,000 cwts in northern Atlantic Spain, and that all of this was now being supplied by the British. In all, Spain probably purchased an average of over 400,000 cwts of Newfoundland saltfish annually during the several years prior to 1815.[7] The American saltfish trade in Spain was terminated and Newfoundland enjoyed unprecedented commercial expansion and wealth. Unfortunately for the Newfoundland cod fishery, this situation did not continue after the conclusion of the War of Independence.

The rapid increase in Spanish tariffs that followed the restoration of peace on the Iberian Peninsula in 1814 was the single most important factor that immediately affected the Newfoundland saltfish markets in Spain. In December 1808 Great Britain and Spain had reached a trade agreement whereby Newfoundland saltfish was allowed to enter Spain after paying a nominal tariff of 3s. 8d. per cwt.[8] With the rapid growth in demand and the price of fish rising to over 40s. per cwt, 3s. 8d. represented a very low rate. Almost six years later, in October 1814, Spain unilaterally raised this tariff to the level already charged on non-British saltfish. Allen, the British consul in Corruna, reported in November that the tariff on British saltfish had trebled.[9] The same month, Athy, the British consul in Alicante, made a similar report.[10] He explained that the tariff had risen to the level that had existed in 1796 and applied as well to American and Norwegian saltfish. Athy feared that the American producers would capture the Spanish markets because he felt they could produce saltfish more cheaply than the British could in Newfoundland waters. Of course, he was thinking in terms of a migratory British fishery — something that no longer existed. In addition, there were a number of varying local duties always added to the Royal or national duties. These local charges not only differed from port to port, but were constantly being revised to suit local demands and situations. Because of this difference in local duties the tariff more than doubled in Alicante and tripled in Corunna. In 1817 Colonel Meade, the British consul general in Madrid, submitted a list containing the local and national tariffs — as complete as could be ascertained — that were charged on Newfoundland saltfish per arroba (see Table 4.A,[11] below). From the differences in charges, one can see that it was not entirely coincidental that Newfoundland lost the Barcelona market and retained the one in Alicante. (This will be discussed later.) An examination of Table 4.A illustrates how difficult it is to generalize about Spanish import tariffs during the early nineteenth century. Nevertheless, the approximate tariff charges on a hundredweight of saltfish entering Barcelona in 1817 was 143r 17m, or about 7.2 hard dollars or 36s. — a large sum. In Alicante, on the other hand, the charges on the same amount of fish totalled 62r 11m, or about 3.1 hard dollars or 15s. 7d. Thus, within a very short period Newfoundland saltfish was confronted by rapid and enormous tariff increases in her best markets during a period of general trade depression.

TABLE 4.A

Spain's Tariffs on Saltfish Imports: 1817
(Reales de Vellon and Maravedis per Arroba)

Port	National Duty		Local Duty		Total Duty	
	r	m	r	m	r	m
Barcelona	12	1	20	0	32	1
Valencia	12	1	4	25	16	26
Alicante	12	1	1	30	13	31
Cartagena	12	1	11	18	23	19
Malaga	12	1	10	33	23	0
Seville	12	1	11	0	23	1
Cadiz	12	1	12	17	24	18
Corunna	12	1	11	9	23	10

The British government, fully aware of the trade crisis in Newfoundland, attempted, through the British ambassador in Madrid, to obtain some relief from these high charges, but without success. The Spanish finance minister explained:

On the 17th of December 1808 the Central Junta ordered that English Salt fish should be subject to no higher duties than those which it paid in 1779 — viz — one hundred Maravedis per arroba instead of three hundred and seventy nine Maravedis which it paid in 1808. The distressing situation in which the Nation was at that time was the cause of the granting to the English this favor, which under the circumstances would have been then and now very impolitic and ruinous to the Interests of the State and of the King...[and]...its continuance would occasion an annual loss to the Royal Treasury of eleven Million five hundred and fifty three thousand four hundred fifty-eight Rials in duties....[12]

The Spanish finance minister pointed out that there had been competition in the saltfish trade earlier. He said that in 1792, the last year of peace, 1,579,469 arrobas of saltfish had been imported into Spain, of which 1,074,541 came from British suppliers. He continued:

With that order of the Junta, England had an ample Market in our Ports for the sale of the said Article, and at the same time succeeded in augmenting her own fishery and in annihilating ours. He [sic] subjected us to a complete monopoly, that is to say by supplying us from her hand alone to the exclusion of other Nations to which no such favor was granted, depriving us of the benefit which might be derived in the price from a competition with the rest....

Our liberty and independence cannot be established without revising, amongst other things our Marine, by encouraging its nursery which are the fisheries, by protecting Commerce and giving to Agriculture and the Arts all the extension of a free system enobling all Industry, in as much as in proportion to the quantity which the Nation annually produces, are its wealth and power.[13]

Finally, the minister ended on a note of bitterness by accusing the British of only looking after their own interests and of refusing to give Spanish minerals, brandies and cloths a fair deal under existing British tariffs. The suspicions which lay behind these accusations were to hinder Anglo-Spanish relations for quite some time. The British government even went so far as to order a review of all treaties of commerce with Spain from 1667 to 1783 in order to see if a case existed for demanding that Spain reduce its tariffs on saltfish. After carrying out the desired review, John Hunter, the British consul general in Madrid, replied: "I have examined the Treaties of Commerce with Spain from the year 1667 to 1783 and I do not find in any of them that any Stipulation is made in respect to the duties to be levied in Spain on British Salted Fish."[14] Thus ended Britain's first effort to gain relief for the Newfoundland saltfish industry when faced with a major market crisis.

Not only did the increased tariffs pose a major problem, but the administration of the tariff system — sometimes on the local level, other times on the national level — also added to the expense and inconvenience of the saltfish trade. In 1817 Allen, the British consul in Corunna, reported that all imports of fish and grain were to be weighed and measured ashore instead of on board the vessels. He wrote:

> I beg leave to observe that the greatest part of the salt fish imported into Galicia, Asturias and Santander is from Newfoundland, [and] this novelty [weighing ashore] will diminish said importation and will only injure the trade by lessening it, but also by not obtaining a price for it as before by ten to twenty Reales de Vellon per Galician quintal of 125 lbs.
>
> I have further to state that the Duties on all sorts of salt fish are exhorbitant, that from Newfoundland pays 1496 maravedis per Castilian Quintal of 100 lbs. of 16 ounces. A Spanish hard dollar contains 680 maravedis and a current or exchange dollar 512. The present exchange is 36 pence per Current Dollar, and no allowance is made for inferior qualities, or if it has received any damage for which reason at times fish has been thrown into the sea that was fit to be consumed in the Town and its neighbourhood but was not of a quality that would fetch a price equal to the above mentioned high duties; all other articles when damaged are surveyed and have a deduction of percentage awarded in the value, and the Duties bear the same reduction. Fish and grain have not the same indulgence.[15]

High national and local tariffs, arbitrarily administered, combined to form the predominant obstacle in Newfoundland's sale of saltfish to Spain. Nevertheless, it is essential to appreciate two factors which influenced, and perhaps even determined, the course which these markets were to follow in relation to Newfoundland's saltfish trade. The general political and economic conditions in Spain and their developments throughout the century fixed the parameters within which the trade had to operate. Secondly, the framework thus established was not a uniform one because regional differences in Spain affected all developments, from tragic civil wars to the price of fish.

Bilbao, the principal port of Viscaya and the gateway to the three Basque provinces, was a major market for saltfish and its position was assured by the absence of any real competition from other ports. In addition, it occupied an almost unique position in Spanish trade (like its smaller neighbour, San Sebastian); Royal or national tariffs were not collected in the Basque provinces because of local privileges (fueros) dating back to the Middle Ages.[16] The national customs houses were established in the interior between these provinces and the rest of Spain. With the exception of a brief period during the 'liberal' administration of 1820-1823, when national customs houses were established on the Basque coast,

Bilbao's imports were to remain unhindered by the national tariff until 1842.

In comparison with all the saltfish markets, Bilbao emerged from the war as one of the most important consumers of this product. Dawson, the British consul, reported on the market situation in this port in 1820[17] (see Table 4.B,[18] below). Dawson was interested in illustrating the total consumption and in the state of the competition. From his figures and his impressions and from what is known about the other markets, it is obvious that this market was a large one.

TABLE 4.B

Bilbao's Saltfish Imports
by Place of Origin: 1815-1828
(cwts)

Year	British	American	Norwegian	Duties
1815	85,382	1,420	7,270	3.5% ad valorem
1816	74,155	24,925	11,118	3.5% ad valorem
1817	75,442	30,174	5,980	3.5% ad valorem
1818	61,523	2,541	2,330	3.5% ad valorem
1819	53,914	3,329	11,370	3.5% ad valorem
1820	63,756	4,565	16,630	72r per cwt
1821	28,565	650	12,428	72r per cwt
1822	90,792	1,174	14,720	42r per cwt
1823	45,629	1,357	19,151	42r per cwt
1824	63,230	140	35,612	3.5% ad valorem
1825	53,890	0	35,438	3.5% ad valorem
1826	52,805	118	45,069	3.5% ad valorem
1827	39,517	350	72,081	3.5% ad valorem
1828	35,456	0	70,092	3.5% ad valorem

The collapse of the American saltfish trade in Bilbao was symptomatic of American trade in general and in that port, as well as of the overall commercial health of northern Spain. In 1818 the American consul appointed to Bilbao wrote from Havana, where he had gone to take passage to his consulate:

> ...since my arrival here the accounts which I have received from Bilbao describe that city to be in a most deplorable situation for want of Commerce and indeed Trade of every kind. I have therefore been deterred from returning for the present or until a more favourable change takes place; so as to insure me in my mercantile Profession a comfortable support which the present state of my Country cannot afford me.[19]

Evidently, de Ealo, a Spanish businessman, was acting in his own best interests, and Bilbao commerce was perhaps not as chaotic and depressed as he suggested. Nevertheless, he obviously felt that his business prospects there were poor, and almost two years later he was still in Havana, though still the American consul for Bilbao, a fact that would suggest the American government probably agreed with his general conclusion. Apparently the situation had not improved by 1820 because in that year he wrote again complaining about the stagnation in Bilbao's trade.[20]

Leaving the post vacant until 1824 while de Ealo remained in Havana is indicative of Bilbao's importance to American trade. Finally, in May 1824 de Ealo, who was still the American consul, arrived in Bilbao and his report for that whole year recorded that twenty American ships entered the port with cargoes of cocoa, sugar, hides, oil, tobacco, rice, and sundries.[21] Ten cleared in ballast and the rest with cargoes of wool and iron. American exports of saltfish had been important to Bilbao's trade but had, by now, completely ended, and British fears that the American product would drive out Newfoundland's had not materialized. De Ealo remained in Bilbao for some years and reported annually on the city's American trade, which steadily declined.[22] He reported that only five American ships entered in 1830[23] and in 1832 he returned with his family to Havana and explained that "The depressed state of Commerce in Bilbao made me abandon that area."[24] He was replaced in 1833. Although his reports concern only American ships, combined with his general observations, they do indicate that Bilbao trade was in a depressed state during this period.

Nevertheless, Bilbao did not remain a preserve of the Newfoundland saltfish industry for very long. By the 1820s Norway had acquired a considerable proportion of this trade and in 1827 and 1828 replaced Newfoundland as the major supplier (see Table 4.B, above).

The other market in northern Spain which was important to the Newfoundland saltfish trade during the war was located in the British consular district of Corunna and included Santander, Gijon and Vigo. Naturally this market was outside the duty-free Basque provinces and was subject to the national tariffs. Corunna was one of the first Spanish ports to receive a British consul, Allen, and he was one of the first to complain about the rise in the import tariff on saltfish in 1814.[25] Although he did not report actual quantities, probably because he did not know them, Allen certainly gave the impression that Corunna was a major market for Newfoundland saltfish. Furthermore, he pointed out that the consumption of saltfish generally would decrease because it would be too expensive for transportation into the interior.[26]

While it is not known to what extent imports of saltfish declined immediately after the war, Allen reported a major decline throughout his district in 1819.[27] A complete picture of the Corunna saltfish market was submitted by the British ambassador in Madrid. He described the near collapse of Newfoundland sales in Corunna during 1815-1828 (see Table 4.C,[28] below). Bosanquet gave separate figures for Gijon in 1817 and 1828 (3,455 and 4,749 hundredweight respectively). He pointed out that the Newfoundland saltfish trade in his port ended in 1820, as did the very small American trade. However, the Norwegian klippfisk trade had started and had slowly grown to several hundred cwts by the late 1820s. Apparently, Vigo's imports of saltfish had ceased completely by 1820, and there is no record of any competition in that port. The vice-consular records in Santander were lost in the 1820-1823 political disturbances, but Bosanquet reported that a large trade there in Newfoundland, Gaspé and Arichat saltfish had completely collapsed by 1828.[29] As far as the port of Corunna is concerned, it is significant that after 1821 the British consul began to keep records of the amount of saltfish actually sold, no doubt because now ships were leaving with cargoes of saltfish unsold. It is obvious that after the extremely high import tariff of 1824, the market completely collapsed.[30] Furthermore, according to Bosanquet, the American saltfish trade to this port was practically non-existent: only 403 cwts in 1827. However, although he did not mention which direction the trend was going, if there was a trend, he reported that 13,689 cwts of klippfisk from Norway had entered Corunna during 1815-1828, of which 7,474 were sold.

TABLE 4.C

Corunna's Imports of Newfoundland Saltfish: 1815-1828
(cwts)

Year	Quantity Entered	Quantity Sold
1815	41,698	
1816	21,106	
1817	3,807 [sic]	
1818	13,571	
1819	4,364	
1820	3,956	
1821	6,216	
1822	7,189	3,567
1823	14,869	8,285
1824	3,936	0
1825	3,707	1,539
1826	2,390	217
1827	3,133	3,133
1828	2,632	0

Corruna's importance as a market for Newfoundland saltfish had ceased by the end of the 1820s, although it was to revive for a short while later.

Barcelona was also the centre of a substantial saltfish trade. High tariffs and Norwegian competition seem to have combined to force the Newfoundland product out of this area (see Table 4.D,[31] below). Bosanquet's report attributed Norway's success in this market to the superior care used in drying Norwegian fish.

TABLE 4.D

Barcelona's Saltfish Imports
by Place of Origin: 1815-1828
(cwts)

Year	Newfoundland	Shetland	Norway	Total	Duty (s. & d. per cwt)
1815	26,750		15,900	42,650	10s. 5d.
1816	32,750		33,200	65,950	10s. 5d.
1817	34,200	1,600	9,300	45,100	10s. 5d.
1818	26,700	5,000	30,000	61,700	10s. 5d.
1819	24,330	5,780	16,100	46,210	10s. 5d.
1820	24,060	2,500	21,100	47,660	10s. 5d.
1821	6,418	7,152	13,570	27,140	*11s.3d.
	4,450		7,500	11,950	**13s.9d.
1822	24,175	7,000	30,320	61,495	8s.9d.
1823	10,260	3,200	26,760	40,220	8s. 9d.
1824	14,830	1,050	10,550	26,430	10s. 5d.
1825	870	2,230	13,195	16,295	27s. 1d.
1826	0	0	49,040	49,040	13s 4d.
1827	0	0	39,480	39,480	15s. 5d.
1828	0	0	71,000	71,000	9s. 9d.

*to June
**to December 31

The province of Valencia had always been a market for Newfoundland saltfish. It contained two principal import cities, Valencia and Alicante. Immediately after the war, concern was expressed by the British consul that American saltfish would displace the British,[33] because Alicante had formerly bought a fair amount of the American product.[33] This did not happen (see Table 4.E,[34] below). However, total imports declined considerably, although Newfoundland retained complete dominance in these markets. Furthermore, although the high national import tariff adversely affected imports, and 1824 was an extreme case, Alicante, the

TABLE 4.E

Valencia Province's Saltfish Imports
by Place of Origin: 1815-1828
(cwts)

Year	British Fish from Newfoundland & Labrador			American Fish from United States & Labrador			Grand Total
	Alicante	Valencia	Total	Alicante	Valencia	Total	
1815	73,258	6,750	80,008	5,670	2,240	7,910	87,918
1816	64,545	14,500	79,045	4,120	5,500	9,620	88,665
1817	51,450	24,600	76,050	1,360	4,600	5,960	82,010
1818	30,480	19,000	49,480	1,620	7,800	9,420	58,900
1819	43,200	21,500	64,700	1,200	3,700	4,900	69,600
1820	33,270	18,495	51,765	1,320	0	1,320	53,085
1821	51,300	15,540	66,840	2,350	0	2,350	69,190
1822	46,250	16,300	65,050	4,600	0	4,600	69,650
1823	43,200	24,040	67,240	0	0	0	67,240
1824	4,200	28,370	32,570	0	0	0	32,570
1825	30,500	3,875	34,375	1,320	0	1,320	35,695
1826	32,200	10,465	42,665	2,250	0	2,250	44,915
1827	24,800	6,580	31,380	0	0	0	31,380
1828	12,300	21,230	33,530	0	0	0	33,530

principal port, kept local duties at a minimum, the lowest in the kingdom, and Valencia's were only slightly higher (see Table 4.A, above). This was a significant contrast to Barcelona, where local duties were the highest in the kingdom. As can be seen, the modest American trade ceased altogether in the 1820s while the local trade was severely curtailed, especially after 1823, when the national import tariff rate reached its peak (see Table 4.F,[35] below, for the total duties collected on imports of saltfish). It is immediately apparent that the highest tariffs after 1823 coincided with the sharpest fall in saltfish imports. Since this is consistent with reports from other Spanish markets, there is no doubt that these high tariffs caused the sharp decline in imports. Furthermore, the decline in the Newfoundland-Alicante saltfish trade was one of the steepest within the Spanish markets.

The port of Malaga was another southern Spanish saltfish market. Its saltfish imports were not as large as those of Valencia province, but the two areas were similar in certain ways. Malaga had a small American saltfish trade which had ceased by 1820 and an even smaller Nova Scotian and Cape Breton trade which also ceased.[36] Imports of Newfoundland saltfish declined in the early 1820s because of the high tariffs, but recovered

TABLE 4.F

Valencia's Import Tariffs
on Saltfish: 1815-1828
(Sterling per cwt)

Year	Amount	Year	Amount
1815	11s. 10d.	1822	9s. 3d.
1816	9s. 4d.	1823	9s. 7d.
1817	9s. 10d.	1824	31s. 5d.
1818	12s. 10d.	1825	17s.
1819	12s. 8d.	1826	16s. 10d.
1820	12s. 2d.	1827	16s. 9d.
1821	14s. 11d.	1828	10s. 8d.

somewhat towards the end of the decade as tariffs decreased a little (see Table 4.G,[37] below). According to Mark, the British consul in Malaga, a small amount of Norwegian klippfisk had been brought there but could not be sold.[38] He said, in connection with Norwegian competition, that "Newfoundland [fish] being much drier is better adapted for conveyance on mules to the interior, and it keeps a much longer time."[39] He pointed out that the high import tariff had kept down consumption and, although

TABLE 4.G

Malaga's Saltfish Imports:
1815-1828
(cwts, prices, and tariffs)

Year	cwts	Average Import price	Average Tariff Paid
1815	15,875	22s. 5d.	?
1816	11,174	18s. 5d.	?
1817	9,830	20s. 2d.	?
1818	9,910	20s. 2d.	?
1819	25,833	21s. 2d.	13s. 5d.
1820	13,853	18s. 10d.	11s. 2d.
1821	16,572	16s. 5d.	14s. 5d.
1822	13,629	16s. 7d.	7s. 2d.
1823	6,910	19s. 2d.	8s.
1824	5,974	12s. 5d.	26s. 5d.
1825	7,597	14s. 7d.	12s. 5d.
1826	10,930	16s. 5d.	18s.
1827	9,312	15s. 7d.	18s.
1828	19,946	14s. 7d.	13s. 2d.

a necessary food item for all inhabitants, the people had been forced to find substitutes. As one can see from Table 4.G, the price of fish also declined during this period, from an average of 20s. 6d. per cwt in 1815-1819, down to 14s. 9d. in 1824-1828. At the same time, the tariff, though fluctuating, was very high; it was 215 percent of the price in 1824, and 85 percent, 110 percent, 116 percent, and 91 percent during the following four years. While Newfoundland shippers did not have to worry about competitors, high duties kept down the consumption of their produce.[40] In January 1830 the tariff was raised to 63r 6m per 100 pounds if imported in British ships and 12r less if imported in Spanish ships.[41] As Mark concluded, 63r 6m equalled about 12s. 9d. on 100 pounds of fish which cost 8s. 6d. in Newfoundland and was quite unreasonable.[42] He stated that in former times when the tariff was 15r to 18r, consumption was six to eight times as much. He said that the consumption of Newfoundland saltfish had declined from 30,000 cwts annually to 10,000, and then to 7,000 more recently. And although Newfoundland did not suffer from foreign competition, it did have competition from government-subsidized local fisheries. Mark refuted the suggestion that the quality of Newfoundland fish had deteriorated, but said that it varied from year to year. The imports remained stable at this low point for the rest of this period (1814-1833) and in 1833 it was reported that five ships from Newfoundland had entered port during that year with cargoes of saltfish.[43] With a total burthen of 420 tons, these ships could have carried up to about 8,000 cwts. There is no reason to doubt that Malaga's importance as a customer for Newfoundland saltfish declined because the extremely high tariff made the product too expensive for the consumers.

Finally, the province of Andulasia was another major market for Newfoundland saltfish. Cadiz was the centre of this trade and, indeed, had been the most important commercial port in Spain. Its British consul was also responsible for Seville and San Lucar, but Cadiz lost most of its importance to Seville, especially after the introduction of steam tug boats made the latter more accessible. The development of Cadiz as a market closely paralleled the developments that occurred in the other ports (see Table 4.H,[44] below). Here one can see that Cadiz declined from a major market to a minor one, especially, like the other markets, after 1823. San Lucar had imported several hundred hundredweight of Newfoundland saltfish annually from 1815, and this small market also disappeared. Seville declined, but not so drastically (see Table 4.I,[45] below). Seville's fish, with the exception of an occasional cargo, was imported through Cadiz during these years. Matthews, British consul in Cadiz, wrote in 1817 that the sale of saltfish was declining because of high import tariffs (and also because

TABLE 4.H

Cadiz's Imports of
Newfoundland Saltfish: 1815-1828
(cwts)

Year	Cwts	Year	Cwts
1815	40,580	1822	14,360
1816	37,600	1823	12,100
1817	28,100	1824	4,000
1818	37,260	1825	5,410
1819	18,770	1826	5,840
1820	27,120	1827	2,820
1821	4,110	1828	7,910

TABLE 4.I

Seville's Imports of
Newfoundland Saltfish: 1815-1828
(cwts)

Year	Cwts	Year	Cwts
1815	25,000	1822	16,000 – 18,000
1816	23,000	1823	16,000 – 18,000
1817	23,000	1824	11,000
1818	23,000	1825	?
1819	20,000	1826	11,000
1820	24,000	1827	12,000
1821	16,000	1828	12,000

of the increased sale of indulgences, for ten pence each, giving permission to eat meat on Fridays).[46] Cadiz tried to improve its commercial position by acquiring free-port status and was finally successful in February 1829.[47] The privilege, however, was short-lived, due primarily to complaints from other Spanish ports, and on 18 September 1832 it was cancelled by Royal Decree.[48] There is no detailed information available on the Cadiz import duty, but very likely it was similar to that charged on saltfish admitted through Cadiz for Seville (see Table 4.J,[49] below). Here the familiar pattern is repeated: high import tariffs with a major increase in 1824, followed by reduced but still expensive charges. Lying on the extreme end of a narrow spit of land which extends about seven miles out to sea, Cadiz lacked room for expansion. Although it continued to import saltfish for some time, it was never again to be an important market and the small vacuum left was filled by Seville.

TABLE 4.J

**Seville's Import Tariffs
on Saltfish: 1815-1828**
(Sterling per cwt)

Year	s. & d.	Year	s. & d.
1815	9s. 5d.	1822	7s. 6d. &7s. 10d. under non-Spanish flag
1816	9s. 5d.	1823	7s. 6d. &7s. 10d. under non-Spanish flag
1817	9s. 5d.	1824	12s. 5d. plus about 2d. per pound to O'Shea
1818	9s. 5d.	1825	16s. 5d. – O'Shea's monopoly ceased 18 Aug.
1819	9s. 5d.	1826	16s. 5d.
1820	9s. 5d.	1827	16s. 5d.
1821	13s.	1828	16s. 5d. until 18 Jan. 1828 – reduced to 12s

To recapitulate, it can be seen that the total importation of Newfoundland saltfish into Spain began to decline immediately after the war (see Table 4.K,[50] below). Furthermore, during the 1820s the

TABLE 4.K

**Spain's Imports of Newfoundland Saltfish:
1811-1828**
(cwts)

Year	Newfoundland Saltfish to Spain, Portugal & Italy	Spain	% of Column 1
1811	611,960	242,122	40
1812	545,451	329,108	60
1813	727,739	401,822	55
1814	768,010	-	-
1815	952,116	315,293	33
1816	770,693½	278,830	36
1817	681,559	239,709	35
1818	560,632	221,444	39
1819	606,689	211,911	35
1820	626,644	208,510	33
1821	699,349	149,171	21
1822	726,400	232,195	32
1823	631,089	174,008	28
1824	723,438	135,540	19
1825	512,389	105,849	21
1826	687,200	125,630	18
1827	533,092	98,162	18
1828	586,155	111,474	19

proportion of Newfoundland's exports to southern Europe which was sold in the Spanish markets declined substantially.

The factor that was most important in determining the development of Newfoundland's saltfish industry after the Napoleonic War was the deepening crisis in the Spanish markets. Spain's high tariffs were not the result of an unusual and unnatural degree of nationalism, but were the result of the government's desperate need for revenue combined with an effort to rebuild local fisheries and to correct to some degree the very unfavourable trade balance on current account.

The import tariff was increased sharply in 1814 and remained fairly steady until another increase was ordered in 1821. Then, during the brief 'liberal' administration, it was nearly halved, only to be increased again in 1824. In that year, a monopoly was established, under a Mr. O'Shea, to purchase and distribute all imports of saltfish. This monopoly received 28m (about 2d.) per pound and, in return, was required to pay the Spanish treasury $825,000 annually in twelve monthly installments.[51] Imports of saltfish declined even further, although some was smuggled in through the Basque provinces and from the vicinity of Gibraltar.[52] The monopoly quickly ran out of money; they paid their first installment in hard cash, but the second was paid in bills because of a capital shortage.[53] The tariff was impossibly high during 1824 and until 18 August 1825, when the monopoly was abolished.[54] In Seville it had risen to over 30s. per cwt;[55] in Catalonia to over 27s.; in Malaga to at least 26s.; and in Valencia to over 31s.[56] When one considers that the exporters were charged about 3s. 8d. per cwt on fish that was often valued at 40s. free-on-board during the period from 1808 to 1814 and, for example, 26s. 5d. tariff on fish valued at 12s 5d. (cost, freight and insurance paid) in Malaga in 1824 (see Table 4.G, above), one can better appreciate the increase in this financial burden: the equivalent of nine percent ad valorem duty in the war period had risen to 215 percent in 1824, and the latter was calculated on prices which included cost, freight and insurance. The monopoly failed for the charges were too high and imports declined or importers avoided payment by importing through Bilbao. Bosanquet reported in 1825 that total legal imports of saltfish had slumped to 80,000 cwts in 1824.[57] Nobody benefitted from this arrangement: neither the Spanish treasury, O'Shea's company, the suppliers, nor the consumers. That the Spanish government would be forced to lower this tariff was evident to Bosanquet by February 1825 and he suspected that they would have done so before if it had not been for England's declaration with respect to the former Spanish colonies. The protectionist movement had peaked.

Finally, on 18 August 1825 the monopoly ceased and a lower import tariff came into effect — lower than the combined 1824 charges but higher than anything prior to 1824. In January 1828 they were lowered a little but in January 1830 they were increased again and a differential was established to encourage Spanish shipping. Meade, the British consul in Madrid, reported in February 1830 that the new "National Duty per Spanish quintal" would be forty-eight reales if carried in foreign vessels, thirty-six reales if carried in Spanish vessels from the fisheries, and forty reales if carried in Spanish vessels from an American or European port.[58]

In the meantime, Bilbao was not affected by any of this. Except when an attempt was made to collect national duties during 1820-1823, it remained a free port. Nevertheless, it was also an impoverished port, and cheaper Norwegian klippfisk undersold Newfoundland's product. Norway's exports of klippfisk increased dramatically during this period, although it too was affected by Spain's high import tariffs in 1821 and 1824-1825.

The state of the Newfoundland cod fishery in the years immediately following the cessation of war has already been described. The unemployment, poverty, bankruptcies and the violent reaction to their conditions by the fishermen and servants forced the British House of Commons in 1817 to appoint a select committee to study the situation. Various recommendations were presented to this committee by interested parties, but there was a general consensus that the unemployed surplus population would have to be removed; Great Britain would have to subsidize the cod fishery to the amount of 2s. per cwt of saltfish exported; and the foreign tariffs on this product would have to be reduced.[59] High import tariffs in Spain plagued the Newfoundland cod fishery during this period, and it was the recommendation concerning this problem which was seized upon by the fishing interests; only this recommendation was acted upon by the British government.

The petitions and protests that were submitted by the Newfoundland saltfish exporters reflected their concern over these high Spanish tariffs. The Board of Trade had received a number of communications concerning this problem by 1820.[60] Liverpool merchants trading in Newfoundland complained to the Foreign Office in 1822 that the high import tariff was driving the retail price so high as to "...discourage the consumption of the Produce of the Fishery in Spain which heretofore afforded a Market for a considerable portion of the fish caught in Newfoundland."[61] In 1824 when the importation of saltfish into Spain became the monopoly of O'Shea, the Newfoundland shippers reacted immediately as merchants from Poole,[62] Bristol,[63] Greenock,[64] and Dartmouth[65] registered their dissatisfaction; and the Swedish chargé d'affaires in Madrid threatened retaliation by Sweden against Spanish products because of the difficulties placed in the way of imports of Norwegian klippfisk.[66] Similarly, in 1826 the St. John's Chamber of Commerce petitioned the Foreign Office about the extremely high level of the Spanish saltfish import tariff, and wrote: "The lately increased Duty on Dried Codfish in Spain has so considerably reduced the consumption of our staple commodity in that country as to have already occasioned a great decline in its value in this island."[67] In 1818 Benjamin Lester, on behalf of his fellow Poole-Newfoundland merchants, appealed to the Foreign Office for a reduction in the Spanish import tariff.[68] Again, in 1830, the St. John's Chamber of Commerce, concerned about Norwegian competition as well as the Spanish tariff, petitioned the Board of Trade:

> Your Memorialists beg leave to state that previous to the increase of the Duties on Cod Fish in Spain, the annual consumption of British Caught Fish in that Country was upwards of Three hundred thousand Quintals, but during the last year about Sixty thousand Quintals only were landed there, and One hundred and fifty thousand Quintals of Norwegian Caught Fish were imported into the different Ports of Spain during that year.
>
> Considering that the Norwegians take scarcely any of the Produce of Spain in exchange for their Fish, and that Great Britain and her Colonies take Spanish Wines, Wool and other articles to an amount far exceeding the Value of the British Caught Fish consumed in Spain Your Memorialists humbly presume that British Caught Fish ought to be admitted at a less rate of Duty than Fish imported into that Country by other Foreigners.
>
> Your Memorialists therefore humbly pray that His Majesty's Government will use its best influence to prevail upon the Spanish Government to admit into the Ports of Spain British Caught Fish at a less rate of Duty than Fish imported by other Foreigners, or to procure a reduction of the present enormous Duty upon Fish in Spain generally.[69]

The Chamber petitioned the Colonial Office again in May 1834 and reiterated its earlier statement about the decline in the Spanish markets.[70] It sent a similar petition in November of the same year.[71] Newfoundland was passing through the final stages of evolution from *fishing station* to *colony* during these years, and this explains why both British and local fish exporters (the latter through the St. John's Chamber of Commerce) submitted separate communications on the subject of Spanish import tariffs. Nevertheless, it was one subject about which both bodies completely agreed and both found themselves forced to rely entirely upon the British government for a resolution of this problem.

Naturally, the British government's reaction to the dilemma which the saltfish exporters described was influenced by the importance they attached to this industry and by the amount of leverage they had at their disposal in this situation. In 1817 they appointed a select committee to examine the state of the Newfoundland cod fishery; they supported Governor Cochrane's distribution of poor relief during the difficult 1820s; and they continued to keep troops and ships in and around Newfoundland to preserve the peace and protect the fishing fleet. In addition, they responded as best they could, under the circumstances, to the marketing crisis in Spain. In 1820 the Board of Trade appealed to the British Foreign Office to try again to achieve a reduction in the "ruinous" tariff on Spanish saltfish imports.[72] The Foreign Office had already made a number of unsuccessful attempts in this direction[73] and were no more successful on this occasion. In 1824, when informed about the Spanish saltfish import monopoly and the resulting peak in the tariff, the Foreign Office instructed the British embassy in Madrid to warn the Spanish Foreign Office that Great Britain was ready to retaliate in a fashion designed to disrupt Spain's commerce and trade if the tariff was not lowered.[74] The monopoly was later abolished and the tariff decreased, but, as has been shown, there were a number of other reasons for this. Furthermore, this decrease was not large and did little to help Newfoundland's trade. Again, in 1831 the Board of Trade, on behalf of the Newfoundland saltfish exporters, urged the Foreign Office to act,[75] but what the Foreign Office did in response is unclear. A similar request was made in 1835 without achieving anything.[76] All demands were ignored by the Spanish government.

It is difficult to assess the efforts of the Foreign Office to achieve a reduction in the Spanish import tariff on saltfish. On the surface they seem to have been limited, which is not consistent with the Foreign Office's efforts in 1816 when strong protests were directed at the Spanish government and an investigation into the legality of the latter's actions was ordered and carried out. Furthermore, the detailed accounts of the importation and sale of saltfish which were submitted by most British consuls in Spain indicate considerable interest in this subject on the part of the British government, as does the British government's request in 1828 to its consuls in the Spanish markets for a complete report on the saltfish trade up to 1828.[77] The explanation probably lies in the fact that the British government realized very early that Spain was not going to negotiate its import tariff schedule with Great Britain. Consequently, while Great Britain could and did provide other forms of assistance to Newfoundland, it was unable to achieve a reduction in the Spanish tariff and, by and large, it accepted this unpleasant situation quite early — possibly as early as 1816 when the Spanish finance minister accused the British of only looking after their own interests and setting unreasonable import duties on Spanish products.

In all, the period from the end of the Peninsular War in 1814 to the beginning of the Carlist War in 1833 was a difficult one for Newfoundland's Spanish saltfish trade. During the latter part of the Peninsular War Newfoundland had sold up to 400,000 quintals of saltfish to Spain annually at very high prices; in 1834 exports to the same market had declined to no more than 100,000 quintals annually,[78] and prices were ruinously low. The extremely high Spanish tariff had been the main reason for this collapse, and the British government was unable to help. In Newfoundland, the result was a falling standard of living, near-starvation in certain places, and political and socio-economic confrontation. The colony did adjust, however, to the new economic realities.

1834-1876

Although information is very scarce, it appears that by the 1840s the Spanish market had begun to improve. The improvement may not have been extensive; indeed, in comparison with the growth in the importation of Norwegian klippfisk into Spain, the increase in the sales of Newfoundland's product was probably slow. Nevertheless, it was extremely important to the colony because southern Spain bought some of the best and highest-priced fish produced. Furthermore, during certain years, Spain was once again Newfoundland's best customer (see Table 4.L,[79] below). In the 1870s, however, the Spanish market began to decline again. For this reason, the writer has decided to limit this section of the discussion on Spain to the 1834-1876 period; from the beginning of the First Carlist War to the end of the Second Carlist War. This was a period in Spanish history when more moderate trade and economic policies were implemented. For the Newfoundland-Spanish saltfish trade, it was the most prosperous period since the Napoleonic War.

Nevertheless, Spain's economic crisis continued and duties on saltfish remained high. In 1840 the Spanish treasury tried to borrow £10,000,000 in London using the resources of Cuba, the Philippines, and the Almaden mines (worth an annual income of £1,000,000) as security.[81] By that year, Spain's foreign debt amounted to about £42,000,000 including two years' arrears of interest at five percent.[80] The English stock exchange would not accept the offer.

On 1 November 1841 a new Spanish import tariff came into operation marking what is generally considered the beginning of a more liberal trade period.[82] With regard to the saltfish trade, however, this was not the case. The new tariff established the value of saltfish at eighty reales de vellon per quintal.[83] Spanish ships direct from the fisheries paid 37.5 percent ad valorem duty and non-Spanish ships, fifty percent; Spanish ships from foreign ports paid 56.25 percent and non-Spanish ships 68.75 percent.[84] Mark, the British consul in Malaga, explained the implications of this

TABLE 4.L

Spain's Imports of Newfoundland Saltfish:
1848-1876

(cwts)

Year	Spain's Imports	Total Exports from Newfoundland	% of Total to Spain
1848	291,000	920,366	32
1849	230,611	1,175,167	20
1850	237,644	1,089,182	22
1851	173,910	1,017,674	17
1852	220,208	973,731	23
1857	266,775	1,392,322	19
1858	120,127	1,038,089	12
1859	239,552	1,105,793	22
1860	259,406	1,379,804	19
1861	262,092	1,214,326	22
1862	274,737	1,241,830	22
1863	309,740	1,012,321	31
1864	242,768	1,013,037	24
1865	173,714	1,019,081	17
1866	182,940	930,447	20
1867	171,543	1,066,215	16
1868	150,128	1,169,948	13
1869	170,628	1,204,086	14
1870	211,222	1,213,737	17
1871	218,864	1,328,726	16
1872	185,551	1,221,156	15
1873	247,710	1,316,785	19
1874	259,064	1,595,827	16
1875	139,031	1,133,196	12
1876	161,983	1,068,471	15

new treaty more clearly and more extensively than any of his colleagues. He said that at the par value of 48d. per hard dollar, saltfish would pay the following respective charges in these four categories on 100 pounds of saltfish: 37.5 percent — 7s. 6d.; fifty percent — 10s.; 56.25 percent — 11s. 4d.; 68.75 percent — 13s. 10d. But, he continued, if one used the actual exchange rate of 50d. per hard dollar, the duties would be 7s. 9d., 10s. 5d., 11s. 8d., and 15s. 5d., respectively. To make the picture even gloomier, Mark went on to add that the saltfish price established in the tariff schedule of eighty reales de vellon, or four hard dollars, per quintal of 100 pounds was actually double the real value of the fish. Therefore, according to his estimation, the real duty was double his calculations. Then the minimum duty on 100 pounds of saltfish taken from a Newfoundland port would be 11s. 4d. if carried in a Spanish ship and 13s. 10d. if carried in a British-Newfoundland ship. If Mark was correct, and the value of saltfish was often lower than that fixed by the schedule, then these duties represented much higher ad valorem charges than those listed officially.

This import tariff schedule remained in operation until 1849 when it was raised from an "official average" rate of 9s. 9d. per cwt to an average rate of 12s. 10d., with a differential in favour of Spanish ships of 3s. 8d. per cwt.[85] The new rate came into effect on 5 January 1850, despite protestations from Newfoundland through the Colonial Office and the Foreign Office.[86] According to the Board of Trade, the old "official" tariff came to about 9s. per cwt on fish brought from foreign ports in Spanish ships and 11s. on similar fish brought in non-Spanish ships.[87] The new tariff was to raise these amounts to just over 11s. and just under 15s., respectively.[88] What was particularly irritating to the Newfoundland exporters was the knowledge that the new tariff schedule introduced reductions on practically all other imports. After it had gone into effect the British consul in Alicante wrote:

> It was expected that the chief article of British importation, viz, Codfish would be comprehended in the 5th paragraph of the 1st Basis which declares 'that the Foreign articles which are required for consumption and which the national industry does not produce, shall pay up to 15 per Cent, and solely in very exceptional cases this maximum can be raised to 20 per Cent.' Instead, however, codfish in Foreign Bottoms pay 50⅞ rials per Castilian Quintal or 56⅔ per Cwt. plus 5½ for consumption duty. Average price of Newfoundland fish at this port on board has been in 1849 — 54⅞ per Cwt. Duty of over 100 per Cent. In Spanish ships less 15⅓ rials so that British shipping is suffering.[89]

Thus, despite the relevant article in the new schedule, saltfish, worth slightly less than 11s. per cwt (c.i.f.), was charged more than that sum if carried in British ships and about 3s. less if carried in Spanish ships. Unlike the iron and coal trade, which were exempt from most duties and thus not affected by the Spanish differential charges, the Newfoundland saltfish carrying trade came under almost complete domination by the Spaniards by the late 1850s. As early as 1851 the local Chamber of Commerce in St. John's wrote: "...whilst during the past season 69 Spanish vessels of 8,496 tons have taken cargoes to Spain not a single British vessel has cleared for that Country from this Port."[90] In 1858 all Newfoundland saltfish to Alicante (and indeed to Spain in general) was carried by Spanish ships;[91] out of 62,000 cwts imported into Valencia port in 1858, only 8,960 were carried in British ships.[92] While it does not appear that the fish exporters changed their agents in the Spanish ports, the evidence indicates that by mid-century they were having to charter Spanish vessels instead of British ones to carry their cargoes. This change to Spanish shipping was probably one of the most important subsidiary developments of the middle decades of the century.

It can be seen that imports of Newfoundland saltfish declined during the early 1850s; there was certainly a twenty-seven percent drop in 1851 from 1850 figures and only a partial recovery in 1852 (see Table 4.L, above), but no further statistical evidence is available until 1856. The Spanish-Newfoundland fish trade was particularly strong during the 1859-1864 period. In the second half of the 1860s another decline occurred; during the five-year period ending in 1869 imports averaged 169,791 cwts annually — down about 100,000 cwts from the previous five years. This may have been caused partly by a financial crisis in Spain and partly by the outbreak of cholera in Alicante in 1866. In 1868 a constitutional crisis occurred which resulted in a more liberal government that not only removed the tariff differential in favour of Spanish shipping, but also lowered the import duties on saltfish to thirty-five percent ad valorem. In the early 1870s the trade expanded but there was a setback in 1875 possibly due to a decline in the Newfoundland catch. After the ending of the Carlist War in 1876 the commercial situation changed, bringing with it modifications to the saltfish trade.

An overview of the 1834-1876 period can explain only so much. Like the examination of the earlier period, it is necessary to subdivide the whole country into its individual regions and ports for closer examination.

Bilbao's commercial problems were increased after the outbreak of the Civil War in 1833.[93] Many Basques supported Don Carlos in his attempt to wrest the throne from his niece (who became Isobel II when she reached adulthood), and the Basque provinces provided him with the base he needed within Spain to carry out his campaign. Imports of saltfish during the following years were mostly from Norway, but sometimes imports came from Newfoundland as well (see Table 4.M,[94] below). This table is incomplete because it does not include other non-national ships bringing cargoes of saltfish, nor does it include ships from other ports whose voyages may have originated in Newfoundland or Norway. Nevertheless, the above table does give a good indication of the superior strength of the Norwegian saltfish trade compared to that of Newfoundland. Vollan states, using the Swedish consular records, that in 1839 Bilbao imported 64,999 kvintaler of klippfisk, made up as follows: 38,726 from Norway, 17,680 from Newfoundland, 6,118 from Scotland, and 2,475 from Iceland.[95] (This suggests that Table 4.M seriously underestimates Bilbao's imports; however, the table is still valid for comparison purposes).

TABLE 4.M

Bilbao's Saltfish Imports
from Newfoundland and Norway: 1834-1840
(cargoes and value)

Year	Newfoundland			Norway		
	Ships	Tons	Cargo Value £	Ships	Tons	Cargo Value £
1834	9	979	13,000	14	1,360	18,800
1835	1	137	1,800	17	1,384	15,000
1836	0			13	1,154	17,500
1837	0			26	2,307	31,000
1838	0			16	1,320	21,000
1839	0			13	1,206	18,000
1840	7	829	11,200	28	2,601	33,000

Vollan goes on to say that of the twenty-two cargoes from Norway, fifteen were carried in Norwegian ships, six in Spanish, and one in a ship from Rostock. The seven cargoes from Newfoundland and the three from Shetland were all carried in Spanish ships, while the three partial cargoes all came in Danish ships.[96] It seems that the Newfoundland-Spanish saltfish had recovered briefly in 1839 for in 1841 Bilbao bought only 1,350 kvintaler from Newfoundland but 25,000 and 10,000 from Norway and Iceland respectively.[97] However, Newfoundland had not been forced completely out of this market (as will be demonstrated later).

The defeat of Don Carlos resulted in the Spanish government becoming a little more moderate in economic and commercial matters, but at the same time, it became more centralized and the Basque provinces were forced to accept national customs houses.[98] National duties on saltfish imports into Spain were reduced if imported in Spanish vessels.[99] Spanish shipping to Norway increased and Norwegian sales of klippfisk to Bilbao also increased. By the 1840s Newfoundland's saltfish trade to Bilbao appears to have practically ceased, although statistical information concerning it is scarce.

The nearby ports of San Sebastian and Santander also shifted their saltfish trade to Norway (see Table 4.N,[100] below, for Santander's saltfish imports) and for the same reasons as Bilbao. Apparently, earlier in the period, Santander had benefitted from Bilbao's problems during the Carlist Wars and had used that opportunity to expand its trade into the interior.[101] Young, the British consul, had predicted that once Bilbao completed its railroad into the interior, this lost trade would be recaptured,[102] and he was correct. Nevertheless, as Table 4.N shows, Santander retained a fairly substantial saltfish trade during this period. When one remembers that Young, in Bilbao, had the Santander reports compiled under his supervision, it can be assumed that since no purchases of Newfoundland saltfish were reported, none were unloaded in that port. The consul reported the sale of Newfoundland saltfish worth £13,202 and Norwegian klippfisk worth £20,382 in San Sebastian during 1861.[103] Other reports stated that San Sebastian imported saltfish valued at £26,590 and £29,680 in 1864 and 1865, respectively,[104] and £19,500 worth from "France and Norway" in 1866.[105] One can safely assume that the saltfish trade in these ports was almost exclusively controlled by the Norwegians during this period.

TABLE 4.N

Santander's Saltfish Imports: 1858-1870
(value)

Year	Information
1858	£ 44,974 – Norway
	12,678 – Scotland
1859	60,860 (51,576 cwts) – Norway
	6,650 (5,000 cwts) – Britain
1861	90,000 – Norway
1865	104,431 – Total
1866	83,700 – Norway and Britain
1867	62,546 – Norway
1869	111,000 – Norway and Britain
1870	61,000 – Norway and Britain

Meanwhile, the other major northern port, Corunna, seems to have faded away almost completely as a saltfish market. In 1845 it was reported that all trade in the whole consular district of Corunna was very depressed because of the high tariffs.[106] In 1849 the port purchased saltfish worth £9,162 from Newfoundland and saltfish worth £10,508 from Norway.[107] Vollan reports that Corunna imported 3,255 kvintaler of saltfish from Europe in 1863 and none from elsewhere.[108] This city played an almost insignificant role in the saltfish trade during this period.

Norway had captured the northern Spanish markets by the late 1850s. Young wrote in his report for 1859:

> The principal article of import into Bilbao is codfish, large quantities of which are consumed in the interior, but chiefly in the

Old Castile and Aragon.... This important trade was formerly in the hands of the Newfoundland houses; British vessels exclusively conveying the cargoes to Bilbao; but our shipping and colonial interests have long since been excluded from it by the differential duties levied on importations in foreign bottoms....

The business is now nearly monopolized by the Norwegian trade, the house of the Norwegian Consul being principally engaged in it. The fish, with the exception of small quantities from Scotland, Iceland and Faroe, comes now from Norway, and is mostly imported in Spanish ships.[109]

Norway's capture of the eastern Spanish market centred in Barcelona was even swifter and more thorough than its takeover of the Bilbao market.

After the collapse of the Newfoundland saltfish trade in Barcelona in the late 1820s, there was a brief period during the early 1830s when a few cargoes from the colony were sold there.[110] By 1838 these intermittent sales had ceased.[111] John Penleaze, the British consul in Barcelona in 1842, clearly and succinctly described the changes that had occurred in British trade within that consulate area when he wrote:

> ...the trade of Barcelona with England has entirely changed its character within the last few years...up to 1832 the trade was averaging about 24 to 26 vessels per annum chiefly from cotton, fish, hides but not a single vessel laden with coals and machinery. Since that year the introduction of these articles took place, the fish trade gradually disappearing, the cotton trade was lost — and at last the fish trade also.[112]

Penleaze went on to point out that by 1841 fifty-one ships with cargoes of coal and machinery from Britain entered Barcelona and left in ballast. In the meantime, the Norwegian klippfisk industry had acquired a monopoly in the port's saltfish trade.

Barcelona's consumption of klippfisk increased steadily during this period, and a very large proportion of it was carried in Spanish ships. Systematic statistical information is lacking for the period after 1861, but indications are that the purchases of Norwegian klippfisk continued, and probably even increased; it is known that in 1872 Barcelona imported 5,500,000 kilograms (about 108,262 cwts) of klippfisk from northern Europe in fifty-three ships;[113] no doubt the vast majority of this came from Norway.

Barcelona was not a market for Newfoundland saltfish during this period, with the exception of a few cargoes in the 1830s, although it was an expanding market for the Norwegian product — buying an average of 35,981 cwts annually during the three-year period 1831-1833, and an annual average of 93,878 cwts in 1857-1859.

Valencia province remained Newfoundland's most reliable and

important Spanish market during this period, although there were temporary setbacks and the colony's shipping was adversely affected by the differential duties.

Although statistical information is incomplete, it is evident that both Alicante and Valencia bought substantial quantities of Newfoundland saltfish during the 1830s (see Table 4.O,[114] below). Unfortunaely, neither the amount of saltfish nor the price per hundredweight is known except in the case of 1840 when 83,944 cwts were imported, worth £39,132.[115] This means that the price of saltfish in that year (including cost, freight and insurance) was 8s. 7d. per cwt — a very low price and an indication

TABLE 4.O

**Valencia Province's Imports
of Newfoundland Saltfish
in British Ships: 1834-1840**
(cargoes and value)

Year	Alicante		Valencia		Total	
	Ships	Value	Ships	Value	Ships	Value
1834	9	£ 13,462	9	£ 14,910	18	£ 28,372
1835	19	29,771	15	23,495	34	53,266
1836	13	19,161	14	17,183	27	36,344
1837	10	14,927	15	19,660	25	34,587
1838	11	17,006	17	26,385	28	43,391
1839	14	31,244	18	25,895	32	57,139
1840	10	17,286	12	21,846	22	39,132

of just how low prices were during the 1830s. This also indicates that more fish was purchased by this province than the total value would suggest. Again, scattered information indicates that this market improved during the 1840s with some improvement in price (see Table 4.P,[116] below). Also, the limited use of Spanish shipping indicated in this table supports Vollan's contention that the Spanish merchant fleet preferred to go to Norway rather than Newfoundland, if given a choice. Norwegian ships entered the ports of Valencia, sometimes with timber, but usually in ballast for salt and fruit. However, during the 1840s Newfoundland saltfish was practically the only export to this province from the British Empire.[117] Barrie, the British consul in Alicante, reported that the total import tariff on saltfish was the equivalent of seventy-six percent of its real value.[118] He also stated that the average price on board ship in Alicante for saltfish (including cost, freight and insurance) was 12s. per cwt in 1848[119] — a low price but certainly an improvement over 1840. Although the province of Valencia was a big market for Newfoundland saltfish during the 1830s and 1840s, the price was very low and no doubt contributed to the economic and political problems within the colony.

TABLE 4.P

**Valencia Province's Imports
of Newfoundland Saltfish: 1840-1849**

(cwts and value)

	In British Ships		In Spanish Ships	
Year	Cwts	Value	Cwts	Value
1840	83,944	£ 39,132		£ 8,330
1841	52,379	33,300	16,500	10,500
1842	103,999	62,355	'a small amount'	
1843				
1844	110,676	60,968	3,900	7,100
1845				
1846	105,046	58,293	5,900	3,250
1847		57,773	0	0
1848		98,022		
1849		66,482		

Only £18,350 worth of saltfish was imported into Valencia province from Newfoundland in British ships in 1850, compared with £66,482 worth in the previous year (see Table 4.P, above, and Table 4.Q, below). In 1851 it was down to £15,891, but "Double this amount has been imported in Spanish Vessels, and above one half in French Vessels, the former having been able to undersell the British in consequence of the high differential duty."[120] Thus imports were down and British shipping was badly hit. In fact, Barrie reported that the Spanish government became alarmed and reduced the duty by five reales in Spanish vessels and by eight in the British ones.[121] By this time, the price had fallen again, and the average price paid for fish on board English and French ships in Alicante in 1851 was only forty-two reales, a little over 8s. per Valencian quintal (approximately 113.1 pounds avoirdupois).[122] In 1853, with imports of Newfoundland saltfish down even further, Barrie wrote:

> ...the importation of Codfish from Newfoundland has been reduced to a mere trifle. Previous to the increase of the duty in 1850 to 42 rials 40 cents per Quintal or Ten Shillings per Cwt. the yearly importation into this Consulate [the province of Valencia] amounted on an average of £70,000. This exhorbitant duty, which at the average

Market prices of last year is equivalent to about 98 per Cent, has reduced in three years the value of the importation in British vessels to £9,072, and although under the protection of a Differential Duty of 25 per Cent a great part of this traffic is monopolised by Spanish vessels it may safely be asserted that the whole of the importation does not come up to one half of what it formerly was notwithstanding that the consumption of French cured Fish has increased in consequence of the Bounty granted by the French Government on all that is sold in a foreign country.[123]

French competition did not last very long in this market on this occasion, and Barrie reported that in 1855 and 1856 no other fish had been imported besides the Newfoundland product.[124] However, at the same time, a steamer service was established between Marseilles and Cadiz, consisting of nine steamers (eight Spanish and one French) which called at Barcelona, Valencia, Alicante, Carthagena, Almeira, and Malaga for cargo and passengers.[125] Although it was of little immediate interest to the fish trade, this service later helped to facilitate the exportation of French cured saltfish. During the 1850s, however, French competition, high duties and high shipping costs could not prevent Newfoundland from remaining the sole supplier of this significant Spanish market.

TABLE 4.Q

Valencia Province's Imports
of Newfoundland Saltfish: 1850-1859
(cwts and value)

Year	In British Ships	£	Total Cwts
1850	18,350	-	-
1851	15,891	-	-
1852	9,072	-	-
1853	9,027	-	-
1854	12,393	-	-
1855	-	45,947	70,688*
1856	-	42,235	60,331*
1857	-	60,462	100,770
1858	-	-	90,980
1859	-	-	130,561

*May include Alicante imports only

In the meantime, Alicante had embarked upon a railroad building program designed to connect that port with Madrid.[126] The resulting demand for railroad materials brought about an increase in the importation of rails and machinery from Britain[127] and optimistic forecasts for the long-term prosperity of the port.[128] The railroad to Madrid opened in March 1858 and the commercial life of the port improved and its population increased.[129] This may have been one of the factors that halped raise the demand for Newfoundland saltfish in the province in 1859 (see Table 4.Q,[130] above). In fact, the construction of the railroad lines created such a demand for iron products and coal that by 1865 Alicante was leading all the Spanish ports in imports.[131] The temporary nature of this position was aptly illustrated in the following year, 1866, when Alicante slipped to ninth place in this league.[132] Although the railroad brought long-term benefits and contributed to the overall economic development of the country, its influence was uneven and often unexpected.

In the 1850s Alicante's position as a British trading partner suddenly changed. Instead of being a market for only Newfoundland saltfish it became an importer of British industrial products and coal as well. However, in 1864 imports of British railroad materials began to decline as Alicante started to buy more from France and Belgium.[133] While there is no doubt that Alicante was a large market for Newfoundland saltfish by the end of the 1850s, it is not possible to say to what degree the demand for fish was hindered by the easier access to the livestock of the interior, nor to what degree it was helped by the opening up of new interior markets.

Although statistical evidence is not available to explain fully the developments in this market during the 1860s, indications are that the market was strong during the first half of this decade. During the period from 1860 to 1864 inclusive, Spain purchased an average of 269,749 quintals of Newfoundland saltfish annually and was the colony's most important market. From what is known about the trade, it is very likely that most of this fish was sold in Alicante and Valencia. In the second half of the 1860s imports declined but in the early 1870s the trade expanded. Shipments of Newfoundland saltfish in British ships imported into Alicante increased from 10,330 quarters [quintals?] in four vessels in 1867 to 81,535 quarters [quintals?] in twenty-two vessels in 1872.[134] In 1874 these figures had risen to twenty-five vessels and 87,400 cwts and in 1874 to thirty-seven vessels and 129,566 cwts — all entering the port of Alicante.[135] However, the trade suffered a setback in 1875.

In general, from 1834 to 1876 the province of Valencia proved to be a good customer for Newfoundland saltfish. Even during the 1830s this market remained fairly strong and, except for setbacks in the early 1850s and latter 1860s, it remained consistently dependable. Furthermore, it was a Spanish market in which Newfoundland saltfish had practically no competition. Nevertheless, high tariffs kept fish prices very low and the profits, at least until the end of the 1850s, must have been very limited, although the sales to Alicante and Valencia remained a vital part of the Newfoundland trade.

In neighbouring Malaga, the saltfish market remained depressed throughout the 1830s, unlike Valencia. During the period from 1834 to 1839 inclusive, a total of five British ships entered Malaga with cargoes or partial cargoes of saltfish direct from Newfoundland. In addition, three British ships arrived from Nova Scotia and Gaspé, and two from Gibraltar[136] — the latter most probably originating in Newfoundland. One can assume that, similar to the position in Alicante and Valencia, very little, if any, saltfish was being carried from Newfoundland (or indeed anywhere else) to Malaga in Spanish ships during this decade. The British consul in the province of Valencia made no reference to any and his records were much more informative than those of his colleague, Mark, in Malaga.

Malaga experienced a slight increase in the importation of Newfoundland saltfish in British vessels during the 1840s. Between 1842 and 1849 inclusive (no information is available on 1840 and 1841), twenty British vessels arrived with cargoes valued at £26,768. Besides these, another eight arrived from Gibraltar, Halifax, Poole, Cadiz and Lisbon; with the exception of the two from Halifax, all of these probably came indirectly from Newfoundland.[137] However, this would mean a total of only twenty-six ships during this eight-year period. Once again, one wonders whether a significant quantity of Newfoundland saltfish was transported in Spanish ships, and once again, by comparing the situation in Valencia province to that in Malaga, it can be concluded that this was very unlikely during this decade.

In the 1850s there were new developments. From 1850 to 1856 inclusive (no information is available for the later 1850s), only six British ships arrived with cargoes of saltfish directly from Newfoundland.[138] However, it has already been pointed out that an increase in the use of Spanish shipping in the Newfoundland saltfish trade occurred after the Spanish tariffs were restructured in 1849. Therefore, it is safe to assume that this trend was present in the Malaga market as well, and that Malaga's total imports of Newfoundland saltfish were considerably higher than the amount carried in British vessels. Another fact that supports this contention is the knowledge that by the early 1860s the Malaga market for saltfish was a significant one (see Table 4.R,[139] below). Even this information does not entirely clear up the problem, however, since it is not absolutely clear whether fish came from other countries (and if so, how much). On the basis of what is known about this part of the southern Spanish market, it would seem that nearly all came from Newfoundland. Furthermore, according to Vollan, Malaga imported 80,491 cwts of saltfish from North

TABLE 4.R

Malaga's Saltfish Imports: 1862-1876
(cwts)

Year	Cwts	Year	Cwts
1862	40,281	1870	53,286
1863	72,721	1871	68,689
1864	61,090	1872	68,948
1865	59,177	1873	70,364
1866	57,791	1874	66,523
1867	65,531	1875	71,921
1868	70,082	1876	83,751
1869	79,711		

America in 1863 and 2,259 cwts from Europe in the same year.[140] Since only occasional cargoes were brought from Gaspé and Nova Scotia, it seems certain that the North American shipments came from Newfoundland. Thus Malaga's imports increased substantially between the 1830s and the 1870s.

In the south, Cadiz and Seville remained constant but relatively unimportant customers. The former imported an average of over 16,500 cwts each year in the 1830s,[141] and both imported a total of 23,000 cwts in 1863. This market contracted and by 1871 only a token 864 cwts were imported (chiefly from France).[142] However, by the mid-1870s Cadiz was importing several thousand cwts annually from Great Britain and a little from Norway.

Throughout this period, the Newfoundland saltfish markets in Spain had their problems. Import tariffs were fairly high and Norwegian competition was strong. Newfoundland lost completely the markets of northern and eastern Spain, including Corunna, Bilbao and Barcelona; the latter two were large, developing industrial centres, and their loss was serious. The colony, however, retained the important southern markets, but the commercial importance of this region was declining, the prime example being the decline of Cadiz. One of the few complete pictures of the Spanish saltfish trade during this period is given in the report on 1863 (see Table 4.S,[143] below), in which the importance of northern and eastern Spain as saltfish markets is made obvious. At the same time, Newfoundland's domination of southern Spain is also obvious. Although Newfoundland's share of the Spanish market during this period was quite significant, it was also quite vulnerable as Spain continued to industrialize.

TABLE 4.S

Spain's Saltfish Imports
by Individual Market
and Place of Origin: 1863
(cwts)

Destination	From Europe	From America
North		
- San Sebastian	11,174	5,606
- Bilbao	169,343	7,121
- Santander	61,191	0
- La Corunna	3,191	0
- Vigo	6,762	0
East		
- Barcelona	83,460	0
- Tarragona	48,337	0
- Palma	2,276	0
South		
- Cadiz	72	12,078
- Malaga	2,259	80,491
- Carthagena	1,471	971
- Alicante	0	78,541
- Valencia	2,695	66,183
- Seville	0	10,907
- Other Places	4,324	0
Totals	396,621	261,898

The news of the increase in the Spanish tariff in 1850 created the usual concern in Newfoundland. In 1849 Governor LeMarchant forwarded a petition to the Colonial Office from the St. John's Chamber of Commerce registering a strong protest against the proposed increase.[144] Again in May 1850, after the new tariff had gone into effect, LeMarchant transmitted an address from the Colonial House of Assembly asking the British government to try to get a reduction in the new tariff.[145] The following year another petition was forwarded from the St. John's Chamber of Commerce[146] and there the matter seems to have rested for awhile, although judging by the reaction of the Colonial and Foreign offices (which are discussed below), several unrecorded petitions were submitted by Newfoundland business interests during the remainder of this decade. With the Spanish markets buying a considerable quantity of the colony's saltfish, there were few grounds for complaint. Nevertheless, in 1861, in the midst of a depression (through no fault of the Spanish markets), the St. John's

Chamber of Commerce wrote in their annual report: "...the Chamber again drew the attention of the Colonial Minister both to the excessive rate of duty still levied on codfish imported into Spain and Portugal, and to the wide differential duty still maintained in the former country, which operates almost as a prohibition in British Vessels...."[147] However, this issue was allowed to lie dormant during the remainder of this period as Newfoundland wrestled with more urgent problems.

Meanwhile the British government did not remain idle. In 1849 the Colonial Office notified the Foreign Office of the proposed higher tariff and asked that some steps be taken to alleviate the problem.[148] The Foreign Office replied:

> Lord Palmerston...will not fail to take advantage of any opportunity that may offer itself to induce Spain and Portugal to lower their Duties upon British Fish. But frequent endeavours have been made hitherto without effect, to accomplish this purpose, and His Lordship cannot say that we anticipate much better success from future negotiations.[149]

Similarly, in 1857 the Colonial Office notified Governor Bannerman that repeated attempts had been made to achieve a reduction in the Spanish tariff on saltfish imports but without success.[150] At the same time, however, the Foreign Office had instructed its minister in Madrid to press the matter on the Spanish government.[151] In reply to the Colonial Office, the Foreign Office reported in August of the same year that Spain would reduce the duties on saltfish imports if Great Britain reduced the duties on Spanish wine imports,[152] but nothing further seems to have come of this. Finally, in 1860 the Foreign Office promised the Colonial Office that efforts would be made to have the Spanish import tariff reduced;[153] their efforts apparently had no immediate success. Nevertheless, in 1868 Spain, in a further experiment in free trade, reduced the tariff to about 8s. per cwt and this was to serve until the end of the period.

There is no doubt that there was not much motivation in Newfoundland nor in Great Britain to campaign for lower or less discriminatory saltfish duties in Spain during this period. Except during the disruptive civil war years in the 1830s and 1851, the Spanish markets do not seem to have been adversely affected throughout those middle decades.

1877-1914

The mid-1870s was a turning point in Spain's development as a Newfoundland market. Although Spain remained the major world market for saltfish and its overall purchase of that product increased, Newfoundland's sales to this market declined during the following decades.

The free-trade tariff of 1868 did not produce the economic results that had been expected and its supporters in the government became increasingly unpopular. In 1875 the British embassy in Madrid reported that Spain's commercial position had deteriorated and that there was strong pressure on the government to revise the progressive or free trade tariff of 1868, and to return to a strong policy of protection.[154] This posed a threat to saltfish imports, and one that the suppliers thought unfair, because the saltfish trade had grown by only twelve percent between 1849 and 1873 while imports of coal, iron and iron goods had increased by 400 percent and total imports by 200 percent.[155] Although the consumption of saltfish had remained widespread and its tariff provided a significant portion of the national revenue,[156] its relative importance had declined in a more industrialized Spain. In 1849 the four most important Spanish imports, in order of the amount of duties paid on them, were saltfish (bacalao), sugar, woven goods and cocoa, while in 1872 the four were cotton, silk, iron and coal.[157] Not only had Spain's economy changed significantly during this period so that revenue from saltfish was less important, but the nation also faced large military expenditures by the mid-1870s; the outbreak of the Cuban War in 1870, followed by the Second Carlist War in Spain itself in 1872, brought the country to the brink of collapse.[158] In response, a new and more protectionist tariff was introduced in 1877.

The import tariff of 1868 was quite liberal by previous standards. It established three categories: extraordinary, thirty to thirty-five percent ad valorem; fiscal, fifteen percent ad valorem; and balance, a small duty to keep track of raw materials.[159] However, since these duties were ad valorem, it was possible to keep tariffs higher than expected by raising the valuation of the goods, and it appears that this happened during the actual administration of the tariff.[160] Furthermore, although saltfish exporters believed, or at least hoped, that their product would be charged under the 'fiscal' column since it did not compete directly with a similar Spanish product, such was not the case. Saltfish was charged under the 'extraordinary' column at the full thirty-five percent because, according to the British embassy, it was so widely consumed.[161] Therefore, the 1868 tariff was not as liberal in its treatment of saltfish as would appear at first glance.

The new tariff of 1877 established the tariff on saltfish imports at 17.50 pesetas per 100 kilograms, or about 8s. per cwt.[162] The British embassy calculated that this represented a duty of fifty percent of the original cost of the top-quality fish and seventy percent of the poorer grade.[163]

In spite of commercial and fiscal difficulties and in spite of the higher tariff of 1877, Spain's importance as a market hardly changed during this transitional period (see Table 4.T,[164] below). The quantity of saltfish imports was impressive — larger than ever before in Spanish history, although the colony was finding it increasingly difficult to sell its product there.

TABLE 4.T

Spain's Total Saltfish Imports:
1875-1885
(cwts and value)

Year	Cwts	£	Year	Cwts	£
1875	686,776	697,764	1881	848,408	747,798
1876	620,356	630,282	1882	815,685	706,740
1877	650,736	661,162	1883	836,272	1,189,513
1878	696,713	688,825	1884	955,897	1,204,276
1880	870,135	849,015	1885	945,358	1,191,000

Although, high duties were a problem, Spanish imports had not been curtailed; indeed, they began to increase. The major problem, in Newfoundland's case, was the almost immediate granting of preferential tariff treatment to the colony's competitors. Joel, British consul in Cadiz, wrote in his report:

> Our North American Colonies have suffered heavily in consequence of the commercial treaties which Spain has entered into with other nations since 1877, up to which date a very large trade was done with this country by our colonies in salt fish. Sweden and Norway now virtually monopolise this market as the duty on their fish, which is 18 pesetas 50c. per 100 kilos (15s. 5d. sterling) excludes our colonial product from the market, the duty on which is 23 pesetas 50c (18s. 9d) per 100 kilos. There is a double hardship in this case, as our colonies take the salt for curing their fish from Spain, while Spain excludes the cured fish from her market by a differential duty.[165]

In 1883 a 'liberal' cabinet came to office in Spain and negotiations for commercial treaties with Great Britain and the United States began;[166] the government collapsed and the talks were suspended.[167] In the meantime, Spanish imports of saltfish had increased (see Table 4.T, above). Restrictions on British trade in the Spanish markets, however, were not confined to those on saltfish; other British products were also affected. Again Joel reported in 1885:

The causes which have so disastrously affected British trade are easily explained. In 1878 Spain entered into a commercial treaty with France, and subsequently with Belgium, Austria, Switzerland, Sweden and Norway, and the German Empire, by the terms of which the products and manufactures of those countries are admitted into Spain under the favoured nation column of the Spanish tariff, while British products and manufactures are chargeable with customs duty under the first column of the tariff, the differences in many cases being so great as virtually to exclude British manufactures from the market.[168]

Bidwell, the British consul in Malaga, had come to the same conclusion and wrote also in 1885:

A considerabnle decrease in British trade has doubtless taken place since the establishment of differential treatment of English goods in Spain. Ever since 1877 English goods have been treated differentially, whilst England has remained the only European nation excluded from the reductions from time to time made in the Spanish tariff.[169]

From 1877 to the early months of 1886, the importation into Spain of British goods in general, and saltfish in particular, was discriminated against by Spain's tariff system and commercial treaties. By 1886 the situation changed for the better. A convention between Spain and Great Britain was signed on 18 April, giving each country's product most-favoured nation treatment under their tariff regulations.[170]

Meanwhile, a new set of circumstances had already arisen and the new convention of 1886 did not produce the expansion in the importation of Newfoundland saltfish that many had hoped and expected would occur. Unfortunately for the colony, the new convention coincided with a rapid and major expansion in the French saltfish industry, which was heavily subsidized with large government bounties. Joel wrote:

The Canadian [Newfoundland] salt-fish trade with Spain has for years been heavily handicapped; and when the commercial convention between Great Britain and this country came into operation in August last by the terms of which Canadian [Newfoundland] fish was admitted into Spain at the same duty as that of the most favoured nation, it was confidently anticipated that a fair portion of this trade would accrue to our North American colonies [Newfoundland]. Experience proves that this anticipation has, in a great measure, been fallacious. This part of Spain [Cadiz] still continues to be supplied almost wholly by French fish, as the Government bounty enables the French colonies to undersell ours, and thus no sooner was the obstacle of the differential duty formerly levied on Canadian [Newfoundland] fish removed, than the still more formidable obstacle of the bounty-fed French fish comes between our colonies and this market. While French fish is sold at from 10s to 12s. the 50 kilos., Labrador fish is quoted at 15s. and Newfoundland shore fish at from 19s to 20s. So long as the difference in price continues there is but little prospect of an improvement in the Canadian [Newfoundland] trade with this market.[171]

Therefore, the problem in the Spanish markets in the 1880s changed from one of discriminatory duties to one of severe competition from government-subsidized French saltfish. Also, the expansion of the Norwegian fisheries, followed by an increase in the Icelandic and Faroese fisheries, caused Newfoundland's position in the Spanish markets to slip badly. It recovered, however, in the final years before World War I (see Table 4.U,[172] below).

TABLE 4.U

Spain's Imports of Newfoundland Saltfish:
1877-1914

(cwts)

Year	Cwts	Year	Cwts
		1896	60,424
1877	109,888	1897	20,396
1878	77,916	1898	28,632
1879	157,942	1899	24,793
1880	109,856	1900	67,380
1881	139,882	1901	84,112
1882	166,489	1902	60,115
1883	158,828	1903	92,700
1884	133,872	1904	85,583
1885	92,336	1905	111,700
1886	115,630	1906	174,970
1887	139,536	1907	203,587
1888	123,672	1908	274,998
1889	87,736	1909	280,311
1890	65,574	1910	199,662
1891	90,660	1911	174,711
1892	86,695	1912	214,934
1893	70,841	1913	248,266
1894	29,546	1914	200,562
1895	42,404		

The northern Spanish saltfish markets, Vigo to San Sebastian, remained, for the most part, outside the Newfoundland trade. As expected, Bilbao remained the major saltfish importer, while Santander, Corunna, Vigo, and smaller ports purchased varying amounts.

Norway continued to dominate the saltfish sales to Bilbao, with some competition from France in the 1880s and from Scotland in the latter part of the period. Meanwhile, the French fish that began to enter Bilbao in the early 1880s did not cause serious nor permanent competition, but it was at least partially responsible for forcing Norwegian saltfish into the southern Spanish markets, where it competed directly with the Newfoundland product (see Tables 4.W, 4.X and 4.Y, below). Newfoundland saltfish never re-entered the port of Bilbao. Smith, the British consul in Bilbao, wrote in 1895:

> Dried codfish is a stable food in this country, especially in Lent, and at all times amongst the poor. The best liked kind is that from Scotland; the supply is limited and it commands the highest prices. The fish are caught later in the year, and, therefore are fatter than Norwegian fish. Next in quality comes the Faroe fish, then those from Iceland and lastly those from Norway. Newfoundland codfish, though much eaten in the south of Spain, are not liked here. They are cured in a different way.... It appears, however, that this distaste is comparatively modern, and now that the reason for it has ceased [sic] the public might be led back to its ancient preference for Newfoundland codfish....[173]

It seems certain that the Bilbao consumers had lost whatever taste they once had for Newfoundland saltfish because in 1895 "...a small quantity of dried codfish [was] sent from Newfoundland and Labrador but...it had to be sent off to the South of Spain. It was not liked here...."[174] On the whole, Bilbao remained a very important Norwegian market while continuing to buy some fish from Scotland, France and Iceland. In the meantime, the other northern ports, Santander, Corunna, and Vigo also stopped purchasing any of the Newfoundland product.

In conclusion, several things are apparent regarding the northern Spanish markets during the period from 1876 to 1914. They were dominated by Norway, but that country was vulnerable to competition from the cheaper, subsidized French fish and from what appears to have been better quality Icelandic, Faroese and Scottish fish. Therefore, it seems that at times Norwegian fish was forced out of its traditional markets in this area and into the southern markets — Newfoundland's preserve. Also, Newfoundland's saltfish sales were hampered by the discriminatory import tariff which its fish was forced to pay prior to 1886.

Barcelona's development during this period differed significantly from that of Bilbao; its importation of Norwegian klippfisk was eventually replaced by the importation of Iceland's product (see Table 4.V,[175] below). Norway moved from having a virtual monopoly in this market to holding a position of relative insignificance while Icelandic fish took over.

TABLE 4.V

Barcelona's Imports of Klippfisk
from Norway, Iceland, and
the Faroe Islands: 1896-1913
(cwts)

Year	Norway	Iceland & The Faroe Islands
1896	107,681	42,413
1897	109,406	51,740
1898	107,529	50,319
1899	114,595	53,268
1900	78,262	72,220
1901	67,018	76,865
1902	80,509	82,994
1903	54,136	115,703
1904	38,762	112,434
1905	28,492	105,234
1906	37,325	97,709
1909	8,400	144,920
1910	5,080	113,680
1911	4,640	173,920
1912	15,540	170,000
1913	18,200	138,760

In the south of Spain, Newfoundland had long held a favoured position, probably because of the unique nature, if not the quality, of its product. Here too, however, the situation on the whole deteriorated. There was more competition from Norway and France and the absolute demand for saltfish diminished.

Alicante had always been one of the most secure markets in Spain for Newfoundland saltfish. This remained the case during the period from 1876 to 1914 also, but the city seems to have stagnated by the beginning of this period. In 1878 it lost its separate British consulate and was placed under the consulate in Barcelona.[176] In 1882 the British consul in Barcelona reported that the chief trade commodity of Alicante was "dried codfish."[177] At a time when the trade in saltfish had become a much less significant part of Spanish commerce, that classification is indicative of Alicante's stagnation.

In general, Alicante's importance as a saltfish market declined steadily in the years leading up to the end of the century but then recovered fairly briskly just before the First World War (see Table 4.W,[178] below). Newfoundland's sales were hampered by the sale of subsidized French saltfish in the mid-1880s, the late 1890s and the early 1900s. In 1889 the

TABLE 4.W

Alicante's Saltfish Imports
by Place of Origin: 1882-1913
(cwts)

Year	Newfoundland	Norway	France	Total
1882	83,000	22,600		
1884	110,000	24,000		
1885	'Decrease reported'			
1886	86,000	20,000	6,000	112,000
1887				120,000
1888	62,000	10,600	10,000	82,600
1889	52,000	18,000	8,000	78,000
1890	61,000	27,000	10,000	98,000
1891	66,000	21,000	2,000	89,000
1892	80,800	15,400	1,840	98,040
1893	42,000	18,800	1,200	62,000
1894	27,200	22,000	800	50,000
1895	65,000	9,400	1,900	76,300
1896	47,400	2,000	2,600	52,000
1897	27,000	8,000	8,000	43,000
1898	25,200	7,800	19,000	52,000
1899	28,800	5,000	29,000	62,800
1900	26,000	2,000	32,000	60,000
1901	27,000	4,000	25,000	56,000
1902	36,000	2,000	14,000	52,000
1903	36,000	0	12,000	48,000
1904	30,400	2,400	800	33,600
1905	28,600	'Plus a little from France'		
1906	58,000			
1907	54,900	1,100	0	56,000
1908	66,200	3,800	0	68,000
1910	66,200	3,800	0	84,300
1911				80,000
1913				144,000

British consul wrote that "French Newfoundland fish...aided by the heavy bounty of 8 fr. per 50 kilos. does great injury to the consumption of British staples."[179] Concern about the French was expressed again during the 1896-1903 period when competition from French saltfish became evident once more.[180] In his report for 1899, the British consul in Barcelona reported of Alicante that "The 3,140 tons of dried codfish landed here comprise 1,450 tons French 'Lavé', 1,440 tons British cure from Newfoundland, and 250 tons Norwegian cure, again demonstrating the increasing competition of French against British codfish."[181] Not only did

139

the importation of French saltfish affect the Newfoundland trade directly in Alicante itself, but its transportation into the interior of Spain by other routes affected Alicante's position as a distributing centre. In 1886 the British consul wrote that "French salt fish competes so successfully against British staples that many important *inland* markets have become quite closed to British produce."[182] Alicante's position was heavily dependent on its commerce. The building of railroads enhanced this position at first, but in the long run made the port more vulnerable to competition; the transport of saltfish from France to central Spain by rail was one example. The protectionist policies and high tariffs did not seriously affect the Bilbao economy and they were essential to Barcelona's light industry. In Alicante, they were detrimental to its position as a centre of distribution in general, and as a market for Newfoundland saltfish in particular.

As already pointed out, Newfoundland saltfish was especially susceptible to competition during the period from 1877 to 1886 when Great Britain had no commercial agreement with Spain. Agreements concluded between Spain and Norway (Sweden) and France resulted in saltfish imports from the latter countries being charged 2s. duty per fifty kilograms less than that paid by the Newfoundland product.[183] Then Norway's large catches during the late 1880s and early 1890s forced its saltfish into direct competition with Newfoundland saltfish. Similarly, French expansion in the mid-1880s and again around the turn of the century created further problems. As the British consul in Barcelona, Roberts, reported in 1902, Alicante had begun to experience an "...increase of late years of 'Lavé', or French-cured fish."[184] He continued:

> The Alicante market formerly used to take a large quantity of Labrador codfish (the cheaper British Newfoundland staple); in fact, states the British Vice-Consul there, the greater part of the consumption was of that quality, the importation of which, till the year 1894, used frequently to be double or triple the quantity of British shore-cured fish, which costs more; but latterly, it appears, this market is almost completely lost to British shippers as far as Labrador codfish is concerned, the importation of British fish being now reduced almost exclusively to shore cure, and Mr. Vice-Consul Cummings is of opinion that the consumption of Labrador fish is most seriously affected by the heavy and growing increase in the importation of French "Lavé", which, assisted by the bounty paid by the French Government, can compete successfully.[185]

Therefore, just as Newfoundland was about to benefit from the most-favoured-nation status after 1886, Norway was reaching its summit as a producer and French competition was expanding; probably even more important, Alicante was about to decline as a saltfish market. Between discriminatory import tariffs and strong competition on the one hand,

and a decreasing demand for saltfish on the other, Newfoundland's sales to Alicante declined seriously and were not to recover until the years immediately before the First World War.

In Valencia, the neighbouring port, the situation was somewhat different: it was a less important market, and it was, almost exclusively, a market for the Labrador-cured Newfoundland saltfish (see Table 4.X,[186] below). Like Alicante, it also experienced competition. In 1886 the British consul wrote that "Codfish from Labrador and Newfoundland is encountering considerable competition from French fisheries cured [sic] in Bordeaux, Fecamp, etc., having a bounty of 13 fr. per 100 kilos."[187] This port, too, lost some of its interior markets. In 1887 the consul wrote: "Labrador and Newfoundland fish has fallen off this year, having to contend against the competition of French cure (Bordeaux and Fecamp) in the towns of Aragon, which have hitherto supplied themselves almost

TABLE 4.X

**Valencia's Saltfish Imports
by Place of Origin: 1883-1912**
(cwts)

Year	Labrador	Newfoundland Shore	France	Norway	Total
1883-1884	41,150	2,276			
1884-1885	38,975				
1885-1886	35,090				
1886-1887	24,824		1,665	11,885	
1887-1888					30,837
1888-1889	25,057	0	7,826		
1889-1890	54,254	'Shore fish is not acceptable in this market.'			
1890-1891	39,637	0	1,120	14,000	
1891-1892	36,782	0	0	9,650	
1893					47,130
1894					35,726
1895					41,780
1898					27,500
1899					29,400
1900	20,300	Includes the United Kingdom			
1905					36,260
1906	46,840	Includes the United Kingdom			
1908	42,060	Includes the United Kingdom			
1909	46,100	Includes the United Kingdom			
1910	18,700	Includes the United Kingdom			
1911	17,320				
1912	31,840	'Plus 12,680 from the U.K. & other British Colonies.'			

entirely from Valencia, the bounty granted by the French Government to shipowners, masters of ships, pilots, and fishermen amounting to about 15 to 18 fr. per 100 kilos."[188] Similarly, as Table 4.X indicates, Norwegian fish made substantial inroads during at least the late 1880s and early 1890s. Valencia was not a significant market for Newfoundland and Labrador saltfish during much of this period, but it was a fairly steady market and, furthermore, very little of it was captured by the French fish exporters. In 1890 the British consul wrote that the French saltfish, with its poor keeping quality, could not compete with the Newfoundland Labrador-cured fish.[189] However, Valencia was, at best, a stagnating minor market for Newfoundland saltfish.

Malaga retained more of its original importance although its imports were also affected by the protectionist policies of the government. Bidwell, the British consul in 1882, claimed that it was second to Barcelona in its importance as a seaport.[190] With the exception of a few specific years such as 1895 and 1902-1904 when it bought very little Newfoundland saltfish, Malaga remained, generally, a steady and fairly substantial purchaser of the colony's product (see Table 4.Y,[191] below).

However, Malaga also became a market for the Labrador-cured saltfish, which does not appear to have been as susceptible to Norwegian competition as the Newfoundland shore-cured product was. The British consul wrote in 1894: "There has been an increase in the consumption of Labrador fish compared with previous seasons, but no demand whatever, for British shore[-cured fish] which has been entirely substituted by Norway fish."[192] In 1897 the consul discussed the saltfish trade issue thoroughly, but confined his remarks to the Labrador-cured product which would indicate that the Newfoundland shore-cured saltfish was not being imported in significant quantities. He wrote:

> Importation of Newfoundland codfish during 1896 amounted to 49,000 cwts. last season [1896], owing to abundant fishery and consequent oversupplies, prices ruled low, and several cargoes of Labrador fish were sold at about 9s. per cwt. to pay cost, freight, and insurance, but the heavy customs duty levied in this country (say 9s. per cwt.), and high rates of exchange, kept up prices for inland consumption. Prices this season [1897] opened in October as high as 19s. on account of short catch on Labrador coast, but no demand being found at such a rate sales have been since effected at 16s. 6d. and 14s.[193]

Although Malaga too was one of the less important major markets for Newfoundland saltfish, it was fairly reliable, considering the difficulties the colony's product experienced in Spain in general. Malaga's reliability, in this case, was no doubt helped by the fact that it was "one of the best

TABLE 4.Y

Malaga's Saltfish Imports
by Place of Origin: 1882-1912
(cwts)

Year	Newfoundland & Labrador	Norway	United Kingdom	France	Total
1882					69,058
1884					87,371
1885					57,160
1886	66,464				
1887	'Decrease.'				
1888					29,400
1889					56,520
1890	48,783	20,866			69,649
1891	59,378	9,560			68,928
1892	54,794	10,247			65,041
1893	48,000	12,000			
1894					39,949
1895	14,453	7,142	15,713		37,308
1896	49,000				
1897	34,500	14,386			45,086
1898	59,600				
1899	61,050	13,553		1,101	
1900	69,400				
1901	51,400				
1902	26,420	42,200	22,040	1,040	120,460
1903	18,580	31,780	20,620	560	93,540
1904	12,500	23,460	21,020	1,000	80,620
1905	'Drought, very little information.'				56,620
1906	40,000				64,940
1907	60,000	'Rest from Norway & Scotland.'			68,380
1908	58,000	11,100			69,000
1909					78,260
1910	49,760	4,560		13,520	67,840
1911					45,860
1912					61,760

distributing centres in Spain for dried cod fish."[194] Newfoundland's exports of shore-dried fish to Malaga were displaced by Norway's klippfisk, but the Labrador-cured fish had no competitor here and experienced a fair demand. Next to Alicante, Malaga was the colony's best Spanish market.

When Cadiz declined as a saltfish market, it was to some extent replaced by Seville (see Table 4.Z,[195] below). Information is very incomplete and it is impossible to determine from this table whether

Seville's saltfish imports came from Newfoundland or Britain or both. However, the Newfoundland-Spanish saltfish trade was growing during these latter years, so it is likely that they came from the former. In any case, it was not, on the whole, a significant market.

TABLE 4.Z

Seville's Saltfish Imports: 1883-1913
(cwts)

Year	British Sources	Other European Countries	Other Countries	Total	
1883	1,520	4,173	11,880	17,573	
1884	2,681	7,579	18,189	28,449	
1886				36,140	'all kinds of fish'
1887				27,520	'all kinds of fish'
1891				35,660	'all kinds of fish'
1892				35,960	'all kinds of fish'
1907	14,000			28,920	
1908	8,300			20,900	
1909	14,700			21,800	
1910	15,840			20,440	
1911	31,860			38,020	
1912	47,700			49,680	
1913	41,420			46,260	

The true state of the Newfoundland-Spanish saltfish trade is not well known because of the lack of statistical information about certain parts of this period. Nevertheless, it is obvious that this trade faced two major problems that helped to retard it after 1876. In the early part of this period, Spanish discriminatory duties were a problem, but only temporarily. The problem that followed was much more damaging: that of French competition. The two problems were very different and the colony's reactions to them were tailored to maximize its chances of eliminating or at least curtailing both. Naturally, the British government had an important, although not always successful, role to play in this regard.

Although the new Spanish tariff of 1877 hardly affected trade, France, in 1878, and Norway, in 1882, were both given preferential tariff treatment on their exports of saltfish to the Spanish markets that amounted to about 2s. 6d per cwt and the St. John's Chamber of Commerce became quite upset and duly notified the Colonial Office about their feelings.[196] The following January, 1883, the British Foreign Office, at the request of the

Colonial Office, instructed the British ambassador in Madrid to seek changes in this discriminatory tariff.[197] The ambassador, Morier, pointed out that the discriminatory difference amounted to 2s. per cwt in favour of France and Norway over Newfoundland and asked for further instructions.[198] Although the Foreign Office felt that Morier was wasting time they sent him additional data and instructions.[199] The situation became quite serious for Newfoundland, as already indicated. The British Foreign Office continued to pursue the matter and in 1886 a convention was concluded between Great Britain and Spain which established, among other things, the same import tariff on Newfoundland saltfish as that already enjoyed by France and Norway.[200]

The major problem between Great Britain and Spain with regard to the Newfoundland saltfish trade was thus resolved, but other lesser ones continued to create difficulties. In January 1892 a new import tariff schedule was introduced which increased the duty on saltfish from 18.70 pesetas per 100 kilograms to 36 pesetas (approximately 9s. 4d. to 18s. per cwt).[201] It was to come into effect on all saltfish imports on 30 June of that same year.[202] The Newfoundland merchants protested and the Foreign Office supported their protests.[203] The Colonial Office even went so far as to get permission from the Foreign Office for A.W. Harvey, the government leader in the Newfoundland Legislative Council, to travel to Spain to represent Newfoundland in the negotiations.[204] As the Chamber of Commerce wrote in its annual report for the year ending 30 September 1892, "...the Chamber at once sought the friendly office of the government, who not only thought the regular channel put the Chamber in touch with the Secretary of State for the Colonies, but despatched one of its members [A.W. Harvey] to Madrid...."[205] The Foreign Office pursued the issue[206] and it was resolved in July 1892 when Spain announced the reduction in the import tariff on saltfish from thirty-six to twenty-four pesetas per 100 kilograms.[207] The Colonial Office Minute reads:

> I don't know how much of this is due to Mr. Harvey's efforts [to reduce Spanish West Indian as well as Spanish tariffs]. Telegraph it to Newfoundland and send a copy to Sir C. Tupper Canada who has been asking about it [the Spanish West Indies trade].[208]

Therefore, in 1892 the import tariff on all saltfish into Spain was set at twenty-four pesetas per 100 kilograms, certainly a significant compromise on the part of Spain and a considerable victory for the saltfish suppliers and the British Foreign Office. The exchange rate was fluctuating at this time and the Foreign Office could not forecast what this would mean in sterling, but it pointed out that the peseta had declined to a rate of twenty-nine pesetas per pound (£) sterling in the summer of 1892.[209] However, the Newfoundland exporters were apprehensive that further tariff revisions would be introduced by the Spaniards and had to be reassured by the Foreign Office that their interests would be protected.[210] Nevertheless, with the exception of the issue involving Spanish raisins and Greek currants, which is fully discussed below (Chapter 7), Spain's import tariffs on saltfish ceased to be a major issue after the early 1890s. In other words, Newfoundland's requests to the Colonial Office and Foreign Office had been favourably resolved by the latter.

In the case of French competition, such was not so. The French saltfish industry expanded in the early 1880s, supported by an extensive government bounty program, and the Newfoundland exporters looked on helplessly while French saltfish began to enter the markets in large quantities.

Newfoundland's saltfish exports to Spain declined after 1876 but recovered in the twentieth century. At first, the decline was caused by the Spanish discriminatory tariffs which favoured the French and Norwegian products. Then, just as that problem was resolved in 1886, the rapid expansion of the French subsidized saltfish industry posed new problems for both Norwegian and Newfoundland saltfish in the Spanish markets. Not only did French saltfish compete directly with that of Newfoundland in certain cases, but it also forced some Norwegian saltfish out of the eastern and northern Spanish ports and into Newfoundland's traditional markets in southern Spain. This was followed by an expansion in Norwegian production during the early 1890s. To make matters worse, in the early years of the twentieth century, Icelandic saltfish entered Barcelona in large enough quantities to displace the Norwegian product, which increased the pressure on other markets (especially Portugal — see Chapter 5). Furthermore, English, Scottish and/or Shetland saltfish was also consumed in certain Spanish markets. Coupled with these developments was the fact that Newfoundland's Spanish markets were in the south of the country, an area that had remained behind the eastern and northern regions in industrialization and urbanization. Therefore, its commerce did not benefit to the same extent from the government's trade and revenue policies. Consequently, Newfoundland's share of the Spanish market, as well as its actual saltfish exports to Spain, declined, especially after 1876. In the twentieth century, however, Norway and France both experienced catch failures and other problems and Newfoundland was able to recapture some of its lost markets.

Summary

Between 1814 and 1914 the Newfoundland-Spanish saltfish trade was influenced in important ways by a number of factors. The decline in the trade after 1814 was catastrophic for the colony's economy. The trade revived during the middle decades of the century but experienced another decline in the 1880s and 1890s, followed by a revival in the twentieth century. At the same time, however, Norway and later France, sold saltfish in Spain — with Norway making enormous gains there.

A major barrier to Newfoundland saltfish exports to southern and western Spain after 1814 was the system of prohibitively high import tariffs which was established immediately after the French were driven out of the country. The other factor was the ability of Norway to produce a cheaper product. These two chief factors which determined the development of the Newfoundland-Spanish saltfish trade. At the same time, however, Norwegian klippfisk was not immune to competition. The expansion of the French-subsidized industry in the 1880s and 1890s hurt the Norwegian trade as well as that of Newfoundland, and Icelandic saltfish completely displaced the Norwegian product in Barcelona in the early twentieth century. In general, during the century, high import tariffs (sometimes discriminatory), combined with competition from Norway and later France and Iceland, created a situation in the Spanish markets whereby it was always difficult and often impossible to sell Newfoundland saltfish.

CHAPTER 5

Portuguese Markets

Background

The development of the Portuguese saltfish markets during the nineteenth century differed greatly from the development of the Spanish markets. For example, between 1815 and 1835 Newfoundland sold about 300,000 cwts of saltfish annually in Portugal, nearly all of which was purchased in Lisbon and Oporto. In spite of losing its preferential tariff treatment in these markets, the colony continued to dominate them until the last quarter of the century. Growing competition from Norway and, later, from Portugal's own fishing fleet posed problems but Newfoundland's predominance was not threatened until the years immediately before World War I. Generally developments in the Portuguese markets for most of this period were more favourable to Newfoundland saltfish than were developments in Spain. In studying the Portuguese markets the questions encountered are more positive: Why was Newfoundland able to dominate the Portuguese saltfish markets for so long? What benefits accrued to Newfoundland from this domination? What were its inherent weaknesses? And where did these weaknesses finally lead? In order to make this chapter more manageable the writer has divided it into two sections: 1814-1860 and 1860-1914.

1814-1860

Portugal was a traditional market for Newfoundland saltfish and in 1810, at Great Britain's insistence, it entered into a trade agreement which, among other things, allowed for the entry of British-Newfoundland saltfish into Portugal at a preferential tariff rate of fifteen percent ad valorem compared to the general rate of thirty percent.[1] During the following three years the importation of Newfoundland saltfish was considerable, (see Table 5.A,[2] below) averaging over 300,000 cwts per year.

Local port duties, however, increased the actual tariff rate and the Portuguese authorities had a considerable amount of latitude in the application of the tariff. For example, to cover the duty, the local authorities in Oporto in 1810 took 277 cwts out of each 1000 cwts of Newfoundland

TABLE 5.A

**Portugal's Imports of
Newfoundland Saltfish: 1811-1813**
(cwts)

Year	Lisbon	Oporto	Figueira	Vianna	Total
1811	165,238	154,241	8,442	41,917	369,838
1812	106,125	86,581	3,110	20,527	216,343
1813					325,917

saltfish imported; in addition, a small levy was placed on the remaining 723 cwts. Then, by order of the authorities, the 723 cwts were stored while the 277 cwts were distributed to the major retailers for sale; until the 277 cwts were sold, the 723 cwts were kept in storage. Consequently, glutted markets occurred, resulting in much lower prices for the fish in storage which came up for sale later. While the earlier sales brought about 8.400 milreis (8400 reis) per cwt, the later sales brought 5.600 to 5.700.[3] No doubt the confusion caused by the war was partly responsible for the local discrepancies in the application of the treaty regulations at the local level, for in 1812 the British consul, Jeffery, wrote "...I have great difficulty in hazarding an opinion, as to the measures, most advisable to recommend in the present unsettled state of the Country, and the extreme irregularity with which every branch of the Commercial Department is carried on here."[4] According to Jeffery, British saltfish in 1811 was actually paying a total of twenty-six percent ad valorem duties, made up as follows:

Dezima and Siza	19%
Donativo	4%
an additional	3%

whereas in 1804 the duty had not been much higher, at least in Oporto where it was 27.7 percent, made up as follows:[5]

Dezima	9.0%
Siza	8.7%
Donativo	4.9%
Consulado	3.9%
Fragatas	2.9%
Redizima	1.0%

According to the Committee of the Privy Council for Trade, the collection of duties in kind continued to be the practice for some time, and although the committee could admit no justification for the Portuguese action, they found they could not do anything about it.[6] Nevertheless, since the official tariff on the importation of British goods was fifteen percent, or one-half the general tariff, and in the absence of any evidence to the contrary, it is reasonable to assume that the general tariff of thirty percent was also increased at the local level by port duties and customs' manipulations. Therefore, the importation of British-Newfoundland saltfish enjoyed a substantial advantage. However, since Newfoundland had no competition in the Portuguese saltfish trade immediately after 1810, the preferential nature of the tariff was immaterial; what was important from the point of view of Newfoundland was the fact that the tariff was low. It was during the post-war years that the preferential aspect of the tariff became just as important as (and maybe even more important than) its actual rate.

The data for the years 1814, 1815, and 1816 cannot be found but one can assume that Portugal's importance to the Newfoundland saltfish trade continued undiminished; certainly after 1816 the trade remained healthy (see Table 5.B,[7] below), although, once again, the data are incomplete.

TABLE 5.B

**Portugal's Imports of
Newfoundland Saltfish: 1817-1824**
(cwts)

Year	Lisbon	Oporto	Total	Total Exports to Spain, Portugal & Italy	% of Column 4 Imported by Portugal
1817	155,474	173,473½	328,947½	681,599	48
1818	164,356	117,605	281,961	560,632	50
1819		117,154			
1820	150,070				
1821		184,493			
1822	140,257				
1823	87,179				
1824	99,567				

Throughout the 1820s and 1830s, during the considerable decline in the Spanish-Newfoundland saltfish trade, Portugal remained a steady market, although naturally fish prices declined. Sideri points out that after 1810 "the Portuguese market was flooded by larger quantities of British goods than it could absorb. Prices then began to decrease rapidly."[8] This did not happen to the importation of saltfish immediately after 1810 because of the great demand in the Spanish markets and the limited supplies available, but the decline in the Spanish saltfish trade and the re-entry of the Norwegians and French into the fishery caused prices to drop.

Systematic statistics on the importation of Newfoundland saltfish into Portugal during the 1820s and 1830s are scarce but other evidence indicates that it was substantial. Between 1822 and 1840 Oporto received a large number of cargoes of Newfoundland saltfish (see Table 5.C,[9] below), as

TABLE 5.C

British Vessels that Entered Oporto
with Newfoundland Saltfish: 1822-1840

Year	Number	Total Tonnage
1822	68	8,605
1823	69	8,397
1826	80	10,630
1830	59	7,650
1831	40	4,916
*1833	23	2,780
1834	65	7,932
1835	62	8,437
1836	56	7,292
1837	45	4,797
1839	34	4,726
1840	45	5,720

*Civil war; Pedro seizes Oporto

did Lisbon (see Table 5.D,[10] below), and by examining these figures it is possible to estimate the approximate amount of fish imported. In 1830, for example, ships totalling 16,549 tons entered Oporto and Lisbon. Under the old measure, these ships could have carried in excess of 300,000 cwts. The fact that some of these ships carried only partial cargoes is probably offset by the fact that some British ships entered each year with saltfish indirectly from Newfoundland and, therefore, are not included in these figures. Furthermore, the British consul in Lisbon reported in 1837 that "[Codfish] is one of great importance to our Commerce as upwards of 400,000 quintals of it estimated to Value £300,000 are annually imported in British Vessels to Portugal."[11] Also in 1837 the Greenock merchants trading in Newfoundland stated in a petition that the Portuguese markets were consuming "nearly *One half of the produce of the Newfoundland fishery.*"[12] In addition, Tinelli, the American consul in Oporto, reported

TABLE 5.D

**British Vessels that Entered Lisbon
with Newfoundland Saltfish: 1827-1840**

Year	Number	Total Tonnage
1827	93	10,333
1829	73	8,377
1830	78	8,899
1833	54	6,548
1834	73	8,581
1836	66	7,935
1837	79	9,439
1838	35	3,894
1839	71	7,236
1840	45	5,014

in 1841 that "Two hundred English vessels are constantly employed in bringing Cod-fish from Newfoundland to Portugal.... 5,941,615 quintals [have been imported] from 1816 to 1836...."[13] If he was speaking of a twenty-year period, then the average number of quintals (cwts) imported from Newfoundland was 297,081; if it was a twenty-one-year period, the average was 282,934. Both figures are close enough to the other sources to enable us to conclude that up to 1836 about 290,000 cwts of Newfoundland saltfish were imported annually by Portugal. To put these figures in context, Portugal imported between forty-seven and fifty percent of all Newfoundland saltfish sent to southern Europe during the period from 1816 to 1833.[14]

Meanwhile, despite its stability as a market for Newfoundland saltfish, Portugal was in deep economic, fiscal, social and political trouble during these post-war years. Sideri points out that Portugal suffered three French invasions, lost its Brazilian export and re-export trade, and was governed by a regency strongly influenced by the British general W. Carr Beresford from 1809 to 1821. Taking these things into consideration, Sideri asserts that "...Portugal could hardly have paid a higher price if she had been on the losing side."[15] With the restoration in 1821, problems continued to plague the government, which was torn between liberal and conservative factions and besieged by severe economic problems.

The loss of Brazil was probably the single most significant setback experienced by Portugal during this period. As early as 1813 the British ambassador in Lisbon wrote: "I cannot be surprised that the visible effects of the direct commerce between Brasil [*sic*] and Great Britain in the decay of the Portuguese manufactures which were more considerable than is generally imagined should have given rise to a violent outcry among the manufacturing and mercantile classes throughout this kingdom."[16] Sideri writes that "The closure of the Metropolitan ports and the opening of Brazilian harbours to all nations disrupted the Portuguese commercial system and wiped out half a century's efforts to improve her economic situation."[17] He goes on to explain that the economic loss of Brazil after 1808 eliminated the most crucial element in Portugal's industrialization program. He says that Portugal's exports in 1806 were valued at 58,000,000 cruzados, of which sixty-five percent were re-exports from Brazil, while in 1819 the total exports had declined to 28,100,000 cruzados, of which, forty percent were re-exports from Brazil.[18] Therefore, Brazilian goods re-exported from Portugal in 1806 were worth 37,700,000 cruzados, while those re-exported in 1819 were worth 11,240,000. As a protected market for its manufactured goods and as a source of gold and imports for local consumption and re-export, Brazil had played a very important role in the Portuguese economy; the loss of this colony was a crucial element in Portugal's post-1808 development. The culmination was its recognition of Brazil's independence in 1825.

The tension generated by the economic problems contributed to the growth of political and constitutional differences which led to civil disturbances and, later, civil war during 1826-1834.[19] Political conflicts and brief civil wars were to continue to disturb the country until 1851 and according to one major historian "...1851 saw the final adjustment of Portugal to the new conditions which had arisen with the loss of Brazil and breakdown of the old regime."[20]

Commercial and economic depression, political disturbances, an unfavourable balance of trade on current account, and the declining value of the Portuguese currency[21] all had implications for the Newfoundland saltfish industry. Portugal needed to become more self-sufficient in food in order to save foreign exchange and at the same time it felt it needed to improve its maritime strength. However, duties collected on the importation of saltfish were a significant part of the government's revenue. In 1835, with the civil war over, the new government turned its attention to a revision of the tariff agreement signed with Great Britain in 1810.[22] First, Newfoundland's preferential position was abolished and the official import tariff on saltfish was established at a flat rate of 3s. 6d. per Portuguese quintal (approximately 129.5 pounds avoirdupois).[23] This was not a great increase since the fifteen percent ad valorem duty was worth about 2s. 10d. at this time.[24] However, this was just the beginning, for a new tariff schedule was drawn up and took effect in April 1837.[25] The new official tariff amounted to about 7s. per cwt.[26] The British consul wrote that the poorer classes would be affected most since they were the chief consumers and exaggerating, added that this new increase nearly amounted to a "prohibition."[27] In conjunction with this action, the Portuguese government encouraged the establishment of the Portuguese National Fishing Company in 1836, which sent nine vessels to the Grand Banks during its first year.[28] In 1836 only 68,000 codfish were taken[29] (about 1,225 cwts, if one calculates that the fish when dried averaged two pounds,[30] but since the Portuguese catch was not well dried the total weight was, no doubt, somewhat more). By 1841 the fleet had increased to thirteen vessels; it employed five to six hundred sailors and fishermen at sea, sixty to one hundred persons on shore drying the fish, and had increased its catch about five times since 1836.[31] Yet the total catch was still not significant. In 1842, according to Walden, the Portuguese Fishing Company supplied 7,000 cwts of saltfish to Lisbon — the only market.[32] Not only was the quantity small, but the quality was poor, as the Swedish consul general, among others, pointed out: "...this company cannot be very injurious to the foreign fish trade especially when one adds to that [small production] the fact that the Portuguese fish is only sought after when the foreign product is not available."[33] Nevertheless, the Company had strong support. Walden wrote in 1841:

> It was founded in 1836, has never paid a dividend, shares have fallen to one-fifth their original value. Vessels, nets, etc are deteriorating. But it has strong supporters who would like to embarrass the Government, some of the main shareholders are Septembrists.[34]

By the mid-1830s Newfoundland was facing a different situation in Portugal as that country attempted to grapple with its fiscal, commercial and maritime problems.

The Newfoundland saltfish exporters were unanimous in their condemnations of the higher duties and in their opinions regarding the hardships they would bring to the industry. As early as 1834 the St. John's Chamber of Commerce sent a petition to Governor Cochrane in Newfoundland to be forwarded to the Colonial Office complaining about the planned increase in the tariff on the colony's saltfish.[35] Cochrane sent the petition to the Colonial Office and gave it his full support. Later in 1834 Governor Prescott, newly-arrived in Newfoundland, received a similar petition from the same body and sent it to the Colonial Office.[36] In 1836, another petition was forwarded to the Colonial Office and specifically drew attention to the fact that both Norway and France would be ready to enter the Portuguese markets as soon as Newfoundland lost its preferential treatment there, and that, competition aside, the higher duty would curtail the trade anyway.[37] The next year yet another petition expressing great concern about the imminent rise in the Portuguese tariff was sent to the Colonial Office via Governor Prescott.[38] This petition emphasized the fact that the new tariff would be specific and not ad valorem, thus making damaged or inferior fish comparatively very expensive. Similarly, late in 1837 the Chamber of Commerce sent a petition directly to the secretary of state for war and the colonies, Glenelg, pointing out that the chamber was "exceedingly alarmed at the effect which such a measure is calculated to produce on the Trade and Fisheries of this Island."[39] Finally, in 1841 the chamber once again asked the Colonial Office directly to work for a reduction in duties on saltfish in Portugal (and Spain).[40] Their efforts were in vain.

Although Newfoundland failed in its attempts to prevent the ending of preferential duties and the general increase in duties, as well as in its attempts to have the tariff lowered, it does appear that, under the circumstances, the British government did all they could to support the colony's interests. In 1835 the British Board of Trade recommended strongly that the Foreign Office instruct its minister in Lisbon to work to prevent the change in the tariff on saltfish and at the same time requested that the Foreign Office check the legality of the local duties at Oporto.[41] On 5 October 1837 Glenelg sent the chamber's petition, which had been forwarded by Prescott on 28 August, to Lord Palmerston enquiring as to whether it was legal for Portugal to change the saltfish tariff, given the existing commercial treaty.[42] The Committee of the Privy Council for Trade examined the consuls' reports, consulted Newfoundland merchants and came to the conclusion that the increase in the saltfish import tariff would be very harmful. They therefore asked Palmerston to instruct Walden to repeat the remonstrances which had been made to the Portuguese government.[43] The committee also forwarded to the Foreign Office a copy of a petition received from Greenock merchants trading in Newfoundland with the observation that consumption of fish in Portugal might be reduced to one-third of its former amount.[44] Similarly, Glenelg directed James Stephen, the undersecretary of state for the colonies, to forward a copy of the petition from the Chamber of Commerce, St. John's, to the Foreign Office pointing out that a revision in the proposed increase in the Portuguese tariff on Newfoundland saltfish would be most desirable and convenient to the inhabitants of the colony.[45] The Foreign Office attempted to carry out the wishes of the Newfoundland exporters and a report, signed by W.T. Strangeways, was sent to James Stephen, 1 March 1838:

I have laid before Viscount Palmerston your letter of the 17th Instant, inclosing the Copy of a Memorial addressed to Lord Glenelg by the Chamber of Commerce, of St. John's, Newfoundland, upon the subject of the serious consequences likely to result to the trade of that Island from the heavy duty imposed by the Portuguese Government upon Cod-fish imported into Portugal

Lord Palmerston directs me to acquaint you, in reply, that Her Majesty's Government do not possess the right to demand a repeal of the duty complained of; but Her Majesty's Minister at Lisbon has addressed frequent representations to the Portuguese Minister upon the impolicy and injustice of such a measure, and I inclose, for Lord Glenelg's information, the Copy of the last despatch upon the subject which has been received from Lord Howard de Walden, in which His Lordship reports the inutility of addressing any further remonstrances to the Portuguese Government upon that subject at present; but points out the probability of a speedy dissolution of the Portuguese National Fishing Company, the interest of which company form at present the only pretext for continuing the increased duty on Salt Fish imported from Newfoundland.[46]

Strangeways enclosed a despatch from Walden which stated that continuous application had been made to the Portuguese government to get them to reduce the duties charged on imports of Newfoundland saltfish, but to no avail. Walden wrote:

Codfish constitutes in the North of Portugal [the Oporto area] one of the main necessaries of life for the lower population, and from that part of this kingdom it is also imported [sic] by Traders into Spain. The Duty in question has been imposed principally as a protection to a National Fishing Company instituted, I believe, mainly under the Auspices of Admiral Sartorius. Although the Vessels bought by this Company and the Seamen employed are principally British, the affairs of this Society are at the lowest ebb. In consequences of the disadvantages under which they labour of not being able to dry their fish at Newfoundland, the waste of the raw commodity is immense, while owing to the Climate of the Western Islands, where they do attempt to cure the fish, this process is incomplete, and the article as brought into the Portuguese Market is in a very crude state and 100 per cent below the comparative value of British fish, not being of a quality to keep any length of time and unfit for transport into Spain. It is now fully expected that this Association must be dissolved during this season, when the specious pretext for this increased duty on Foreign Fish, that of protection of National Fisheries, will fall to the ground, and when I trust I shall be able to effect some suitable revision of the Law, by which this increase of duty has been imposed by the present Cortes.[47]

Smith, the British consul in Lisbon, also joined Walden in thinking that the interests of the National Fishing Company provided the key factor in the whole question of the Portuguese saltfish tariff. He wrote in 1838 that while the temporary decline in imports of Newfoundland saltfish was inevitable, "...the affairs of the National Fishing Company are generally considered to be involved in such embarrassments that its duration for any lengthened period is very questionable; and its dissolution would in all probability remove the existing restrictions and tend to revive that important branch of the British Trade with Portugal."[48] Nor did the Portuguese government take kindly to hints from Walden that Great Britain might retaliate if the duties were increased on Newfoundland saltfish. He reported that a member of the Cortes wrote "...that if England retaliated, Portugal could retaliate also, as every nation was mistress to alter its Tariffs of Duties as she pleased; the more so as England herself, while the Treaty of 1810 still existed had altered the duties on wines...."[49] Although their efforts had been in vain, the British government had tried all the avenues open to them, to help Newfoundland retain, and later regain, her preferential tariff privileges.

By the end of the 1830s Portugal was in the process of regaining more control over its economy and commerce, while Great Britain's interest in the saltfish trade was waning. As one Portuguese historian has noted,

> The 1837 customs tariff firmly protected existing national industry, while fostering the rise of new activities. For Portugal this marked the beginning of an epoch.[50]

Nevertheless, the Portuguese markets had been irreplaceable for Newfoundland during the post-war years and had been largely responsible for keeping the colony solvent. The low preferential tariff and the absence of any major local marketing problems assisted the Newfoundland saltfish industry through what was probably its most crucial period. Although it was to retain an important place in the Newfoundland markets, Portugal's role would never again be as crucial to the colony's survival as it had been during this period.

The two decades that followed the increase in the Portuguese tariff on saltfish imports in 1837 and the formation of a national fishing company in 1836 witnessed a consolidation in the changes that had recently occurred in the relationship between Newfoundland and Portugal. The negotiations which took place between Newfoundland and Great Britain on one side and Portugal on the other focused on the saltfish tariff and the National Fishing Company.

After the rise in import duties in 1837, Newfoundland exports of saltfish to Portugal declined somewhat. In 1842 it was reported by Walden that Lisbon consumed 40,000 cwts of saltfish annually, of which about 7,000 were produced by the Portuguese fishing company.[51] In 1845 the

British consul in Lisbon reported that there had been a considerable decrease in imports of Newfoundland saltfish (but a large increase in imports of British coal).[52] However, in 1848 the Portuguese Foreign Office pointed out to the resident British minister that the consumption of Newfoundland saltfish had not varied very much since the import tariff was doubled in 1837.[53] Moreover, the British consul reported that imports of fish into Portugal during 1842-1844 had been worth as follows:[54]

	Milreis	Sterling
1842	826,212,300	£ 185,898
1843	951,937,254	214,186
1844	795,672,780	179,026

The consul did not indicate the kind of fish imported, nor the port of origin, nor the nationality of the vessels, but there is no doubt that most of this was saltfish from Newfoundland.

It was about this time — mid-century — that another question developed, one very closely allied to the probliem of the saltfish import tariff. This was the question of drying rights on the Newfoundland coast for the Portuguese Grand Bank fishing fleet (the National Fishing Company) similar to those granted to French and American fishermen. The Portuguese Fishing Company had not been very successful in its ventures on the Grand Banks of Newfoundland and one reason was the lack of drying areas near the fishing grounds. It had tried drying the fish in the Azores and in Portugal itself, but had found this to be unsatisfactory because of transportation costs and the warm Portuguese climate. In 1848 the Portuguese Foreign Office wrote in reply to a British request for lower duties on imports of Newfoundland saltfish:

> The Fish supplied by the Company is inferior to the England [sic]...[and] this inferiority proceeds from the British Government having denied us a small piece of ground in Newfoundland for drying, and which it appears to me, we requested with more right than France and other Nations to whom that faculty was concerned.
> You will see that this occasions the low price of the Company's shares, whose vessels resorting to the common fishing ground with those of other nations, are exposed to twice the risk, in being obliged to bring their fish to Portugal to be dried, and consequently to bring much smaller cargoes than they otherwise would do.[55]

The Portuguese government had come to the conclusion that their National Fishing Company was failing because of a lack of drying facilities near the fishing grounds.

The negotiations over a drying area in Newfoundland had hardly got underway when the Portuguese, being ill-informed about French rights on the Newfoundland coast, decided to play their 'French' card; they approached the French for permission to dry their catch on the French Shore in Newfoundland.[56] The British Foreign Office, which was determined by now to hinder the Portuguese fishery as much as possible for Newfoundland's sake, soon disabused the Portuguese of this new notion. Howard, the secretary of legation in Lisbon, was notified "...to inform the Portuguese Minister for Foreign Affairs that the French Government may of course grant to the Portuguese what privileges it chooses in the Island of St. Pierre and Miquelon, which were restored to France at the Peace of 1814; but that it is by Treaty that French Fishermen are allowed to dry their Fish on a certain part of the British Coast of Newfoundland, and to resort to that part of the Coast for such purpose during the fishing season only; and that H.M.'s Govt is under no similar engagement to Portugal, and cannot therefore permit the Portuguese to use the British Coast of Newfoundland for such Purposes as are above mentioned."[57] By November 1850 it appeared that the Portuguese Fishing Company would have to declare bankruptcy unless it could use Newfoundland territory on which to dry its catch. Sir Hamilton Seymour summarized the situation as follows:

> I beg to enclose to your Lordship, together with a translated extract, a report just published by the Fish Company of Lisbon, from which it appears that there is little prospect of its being possible, except with adventitious assistance, that an undertaking should be carried on, the returns from which barely cover the outgoing.
>
> Your Lordship will indeed observe that...it is estimated that the accounts of the Company must be closed unless the Portuguese are admitted to dry their fish upon some of the French stations at Newfoundland, or at some of those parts of the Coast which remain unoccupied.
>
> The despatch addressed by your Lordship to Mr. Howard on the 26th of August last makes it clear that the French cannot be permitted to extend to other Foreigners the facilities to which they are admitted in possessions of Her Majesty, but is it possible that that which would not be allowed to take place in an open manner may be attempted by indirect means, it will be necessary that the overtures made by the Fish Company to the French Mission should not be overlooked.
>
> As at the same time a report has reached me of its being hoped that increase of duties upon Cured Fish might be obtained from the Cortes. I have thought it my duty to remind Count Tojal that the Duties actually levied are sufficiently onerous to have given rise to representations on the part of her Majesty's Government.
>
> Count Tojal in lieu of returning any direct answer to my

observations entered into some explanations of the grounds which had led him to hope that the Portuguese might be admitted to the same privileges with regard to the preparing of fish as are enjoyed in English Dependencies by the French and Americans — these expectations appearing to have been formed upon a somewhat liberal reading of the 4th Article of the Treaty of 3rd July, 1842.

His Excellency stated that the encouragement which was desired for the Portuguese fishermen was not sought with a view of fostering a trade which should injure that of England, but solely with that of forming a nursery for seamen from which the deficiencies caused by constant desertions from the Portuguese Navy to that belonging to Brazil, and particularly to Vessels in slaving operations, might be supplied.

The plea may be specious — but as I cannot doubt that Portuguese fish, if properly dried, would, when admitted, as is the case, duty free, supplant the England goods in the Markets of this Country, I was careful to make such a reply as must have led to the inference of the resolution taken by Her Majesty's Government being final.[58]

By now the Portuguese government had decided to stress the importance of having a nursery for their navy with an allusion to the Brazilian slave trade that was intended to elicit some sympathy. The reply from the British Foreign Office was brutally frank and Seymour was informed regarding the

...hope expressed to you by Count Tojal that Portuguese Fishermen might be permitted to dry their Fish on the Coast of Newfoundland; I have to instruct you to state distinctly to Ct. Tojal that no such Permission will or can be given to Portuguese Fishermen. You will observe to Count Tojal, that while the Portuguese Government is refusing due Redress to many British Subjects, and is levying exhorbitant Duties on British Cured Fish, and is imposing on the Wine Trade Duties and Restrictions which are at variance with the Stipulations of Treaties, that government ought not to expect that any Facilities or Indulgences should be granted by Great Britain to the Commercial Industry of Portugal; And you will state to Count Tojal that so long as the Conduct of the Portuguese Government towards British Interests, Individual & National, shall continue to be guided by that unfriendly and even hostile Spirit by which it seems at present to be animated, such a Course of Policy must produce its natural Consequences.[59]

This was strong language and indicated exasperation in the British Foreign Office. Nevertheless, there is a suggestion here that the Foreign Office was willing to bargain and was not adverse to tying together the issues — Portuguese privileges on the Newfoundland coast against lower Portuguese import duties on Newfoundland saltfish. The Portuguese government, however, refused to be lured away from its own arguments and, through its legation in London early in 1851, it once again laid its case before Palmerston pointing out that as a loyal ally Portugal deserved more consideration. This appeal did not change anything and the terms of the commercial treaty of 1842 did not apply to this situation since the French and Americans had enjoyed their privileges before this treaty had been negotiated.

Meanwhile, the revision of the Portuguese tariff which was proceeding during 1851 raised hopes that the duties on saltfish imports might be lowered from 1800 reis (8s. 1.5d.) per quintal.[60] However, these hopes were not realized[61] and with urging from the Newfoundland exporters[62] and the Board of Trade, the Foreign Office offered to grant permission to Portuguese fishermen to dry their fish on parts of the Newfoundland coast in return for a substantial reduction in the duties on imports of Newfoundland saltfish.[63] This offer the Portuguese government peremptorily dismissed, to the chagrin of the British Foreign Office. Nevertheless, although their motives were sincere and their efforts understandable, the Newfoundland exporters, the Colonial Office, the Board of Trade and the Foreign Office exhibited a fair degree of naivety if they really thought that the Portuguese government would grant a "substantial" reduction in the tariff on imports of Newfoundland saltfish in return for the privilege of drying their fish in Newfoundland. The Portuguese government could hardly have been expected to give up an important source of revenue and allow the National Fishing Company to be eliminated by the duty-free, higher-quality, and cheaper saltfish produced by the more efficient family-unit fishery in Newfoundland.[64] After this flurry of diplomatic activity, the issue subsided and the Portuguese company collapsed and disappeared in 1857; the import tariff which had helped sustain it continued to be levied for revenue purposes.[65]

The end of the Portuguese National Fishing Company in 1857 brought to a close a twenty-year era during which the national import tariff on saltfish varied from fifty-five percent to seventy percent ad valorem, depending on quality, compared with fifteen percent ad valorem previously. This probably brought on a reduction in the importation of the Newfoundland product but statistical evidence is almost totally lacking. The secretary of the British Legation in Lisbon in 1862 reported that despite the growth of the Portuguese population the consumption of saltfish during the last thirty years "has remained nearly stationary."[66] The American consul in Oporto reported that during the financial year 1855-1856 saltfish worth $410,818.47 was imported into that city from Newfoundland while only $5,434.78 was imported from Norway.[67] With the recovery of the Spanish markets and a growing Brazilian demand for saltfish, one could safely conjecture that there was stagnation in the

Portuguese trade, if not an actual decline, because the higher cost curtailed its consumption.

Although the Portuguese cod fishery on the Grand Banks survived because a few independent ship owners entered the business, the industry ceased to occupy the attention of the nation's government. Portugal, like Spain, was becoming more industrialized and other trades and commercial activities were acquiring paramountcy. While, for the most part, Portugal was to remain a good, and sometimes excellent, market for Newfoundland saltfish, the colony found itself operating within a different framework after this period.

The elimination of preferential duties in favour of Newfoundland saltfish left the Portuguese markets open to competition, and competition was to become a permanent feature there beginning in the 1860s. The situation as it existed during the previous decades was summarized best in 1862 by Herries, the secretary of the British Legation in Lisbon, who wrote:

> Salt cod has for time immemorial constituted a large proportion of the food of the Portuguese people, and it may, indeed be considered as one of the necessaries of life in this country. During the last thirty years, however, its consumption, instead of increasing, as might have been expected with the growth of the population, has remained nearly stationary, a result to be attributed not to any change in the habits of the people, but to the progressive increase of the duty from 15 per cent ad valorem, as it stood before 1837, to the present rate, which is calculated as equivalent to about 55 per cent.[68]

Herries continued and pointed out that nearly all saltfish came from Newfoundland with just a little coming from Norway.[69] This situation was soon to change.

1860-1914

Between 1860 and 1914 the Newfoundland-Portuguese saltfish trade underwent several changes. Demand for fish grew but Newfoundland experienced more problems in maintaining its share of these markets. At the beginning of this period the trade to Portugal remained steady at just over 200,000 cwts annually (see Table 5.E,[70] below) and this increased during the early 1870s until exports peaked at over 300,000 cwts in 1874. This was followed by a fairly rapid decline. There was a recovery in the early twentieth century but a further decline occurred during the last years before the war (see Table 5.F,[71] below).

Lisbon's importance as a market for Newfoundland saltfish decreased after mid-century (see Table 5.G,[72] below). In 1868 the British consul pointed out that most of the thirty vessels with saltfish from Newfoundland

TABLE 5.E

Portugal's Imports of
Newfoundland Saltfish: 1866-1880
(cwts and value)

Year	Cwts	£	Price per Cwt
1866	240,112	282,460	£13s. 6d.
1867	206,448	228,815	£12s. 2d.
1868	207,836	221,179	£11s. 3d.
1869	206,172	243,556	£13s. 8d.
1870	208,516	234,077	£12s. 5d.
1871	256,172	289,943	£12s. 8d.
1872	261,434	331,091	£15s. 4d.
1873	277,814	287,379	£18d.
1874	307,554	247,619	16s. 1d.
1875	253,968	232,101	18s. 3d.
1876	200,484	188,900	18s. 10d.
1877	188,488	170,030	18s. 10d.
1878	161,234	130,203	16s. 2d.
1879	172,460	137,551	15s. 11d.
1880	186,324	153,446	16s. 6d.

TABLE 5.F

Oporto's Imports of
Newfoundland Saltfish: 1883-1914
(cwts)

Year	Cwts	Year	Cwts	Year	Cwts
1883	133,058	1894	96,057	1905	223,928
1884	182,953	1895	168,227	1906	256,755
1885	188,366	1896	202,168	1907	236,563
1886	180,735	1897	144,466	1908	215,721
1887	149,247	1898	129,240	1909	241,855
1888	163,908	1899	125,214	1910	
1889	181,054	1900	179,998	1911	198,892
1890	103,191	1901	202,731	1912	180,603
1891	133,262	1902	231,575	1913	179,729
1892	123,211	1903	254,426	1914	132,504
1893	106,004	1904	240,109		

that entered Lisbon in 1867 cleared for the Mediterranean with the same cargo.[73] A year later he reported that forty-six vessels had entered Lisbon

TABLE 5.G

**Lisbon's Imports of
Newfoundland Saltfish: 1868-1887**

Year	Ships Entered		Ships Discharged		Cwts Fish Landed
	No.	Tons	No.	Tons	
1868	46	-	13	-	50,000
1869	38	4,614	16	1,724	50,000
1870	46	-	15	-	45,000
1872	64	7,633	14	-	41,580
1873	48	6,027	14	1,700	41,500
1874	53	-	18	2,317	56,513
1876	35	4,441	9	-	38,657
1877	33	-	16	-	55,600
1878	27	3,216	10	-	28,090
1879	46	5,819	13	-	31,125
1880	35	4,439	13	1,661	37,720
1881	45	5,897	22	2,997	65,444
1882	49	6,013	-	-	57,931
1883	59	7,388	19	2,807	65,067
1884	-	-	17	1,875	46,547
1885	69	8,873	24	3,392	67,786
1886	'Slight depression in saltfish imports in Lisbon.'				
1887	'[British ships] discharged 20,000 quintals less...than in 1866.'				

in 1868 with Newfoundland saltfish and of these, only thirteen had discharged (about 50,000 cwts) and the remaining thirty-three had proceeded to the Mediterranean.[74] Again he reported that in 1869:

> Thirty-eight vessels, measuring in the aggregate 4,614 tons, brought salt-fish from Newfoundland. Of these 16, measuring 1,724 tons, discharged at Lisbon about 50,000 quintals of fish; the others merely called for orders.[75]

Unlike Oporto, Lisbon was conveniently located and easily entered and therefore many ships called in for orders. Thus one cannot assume that ships which entered and cleared Lisbon with saltfish had expected to sell their cargoes there, as one can in the case of Oporto, for example, where a shifting sand bar made entry quite difficult and often dangerous. Again, in 1870 the consul wrote: "15 sailing-vessels with cargoes of fish, averaging each 3,000 quintals, sold their cargoes in Lisbon, and 31 more with the like cargoes put in for orders and left again."[76] In 1873, however, the same consul, Brackenbury, did indicate a decline in the sale of Newfoundland saltfish in Lisbon when he wrote:

> Sixty-four sailing vessels, measuring together 7,633 tons, entered Lisbon in 1872 with an aggregate of 187,363 quintals of salt fish, of which number fourteen vessels discharged here 41,580 quintals; the remainder proceeding generally to the Italian ports. The consumption of Newfoundland fish, it should be observed, appears to be diminishing in the southern half of Portugal....[77]

This pattern continued and during the 1868-1885 period Lisbon purchased an average of 48,000 cwts of Newfoundland saltfish annually.[78] This amount had declined to about 20,000 cwts by 1900-1901.[79] Nevertheless, the Lisbon market improved in the early twentieth century and Newfoundland's share of this market increased as well. In 1908 about 185,000 cwts of saltfish were imported of which "more than half" came from Newfoundland.[80] Lisbon continued to grow as a market but bought more Norwegian saltfish. In 1914 when a total of over 250,000 cwts was imported the British consul declared that "most of the cod came from Norway,"[81] which meant that Lisbon had become one of Norway's chief markets.

There were two other smaller markets in Portugal: Figueira and Viana. Some saltfish was imported into the former but not enough to be of any consequence. The latter imported about 30,000 cwts annually during the late 1880s but this amount soon declined by half and later records are not available.[82]

Oporto was the most important Portuguese market for Newfoundland saltfish during 1860-1914. From what has been seen of the other markets in this country it is obvious that most of the imports enumerated in Table 5.E entered Oporto while the figures in 5.F indicate that Oporto continued to remain a strong market except during the early and late 1890s and 1914. George Hawes, who was later involved in the marketing of Newfoundland's saltfish, wrote of Oporto and Portugal as follows:

> Portugal was in the past regarded as the dumping market for Newfoundland dry fish and, as such, was of value to Newfoundland in maintaining the values on other markets by relieving the pressure of an excess of supplies. Towards the end of the season, or at other times when it became apparent that there was more fish in Newfoundland than could be disposed of to other markets which had a less flexible consumption, fish was poured into Oporto without reference to that Market's stocks or prospects. The popularity of salt codfish as a foodstuff and the poverty of the consuming public in Portugal enabled the market to be used in this way. When stocks in Portugal accumulated to a high figure, prices fell and salt codfish

became one of the cheapest articles of food, resulting in demand which never failed to absorb the excess in shipments.[83]

If this was really the case, and it seems likely that it was given the fact that surplus European fish had to be disposed of somewhere, this made Oporto unique and competition was at times effectively excluded from this port.

There were several problems that affected the sale of Newfoundland's saltfish in Portuguese markets during this half century. Competition from Norway was the most important; another, which was related, involved import tariffs, especially after 1896; and finally there was competition from the Portuguese bank fishery.

Norway had been selling some saltfish in Portugal for several decades but this trade began to increase in the 1870s. During 1883-1887 Oporto bought an average of 55,000 cwts annually and this rose to over 97,000 cwts in 1888-1892. In 1894 this amount exceeded 200,000 cwts.[84] The local British consul described the situation as follows:

> With regard to colonial goods, the most important article of consumption is salted codfish, and until a little over 20 years ago [early 1870s] Newfoundland saltfish monopolised the market, which is perhaps second to none in Europe in importance. Gradually, however, popular prejudice against an innovation in the shape of Norway fish was overcome, and its sale has by degrees increased in this market to such an extent as to very nearly approach the quantity shipped from Newfoundland. This can be accounted for chiefly owing to its lower price, also to the falling-off in the curing of the Newfoundland fish.... An advantage is also enjoyed by Norway in being able to place new fish here about two months before even winter-cured fish of Newfoundland origin can reach it. Although complaints are heard of the latter fish, as compared with that of former times, it is to be observed that, especially as regards the shore-cured fish, it always obtains the preference over and commands a higher price than the Norwegian[85]

This predominance, however, was brief. In 1895 Newfoundland experienced a serious commercial crisis and most exporters were forced to sell their fish at almost any price in order to acquire working capital. The British consul wrote:

> ...[In 1895] there was a large increase in the British fish over the rival the Norwegian one. Large quantities of the former were pressed on the market at the close of the year, possibly for financial reasons not unconnected with the financial crisis in Newfoundland, this market being, not only the largest in the world for this commodity, but also considered the best as regards safety in the matter of payments.[86]

Newfoundland retained effective control over this market until just before the war. Then Norway, again, increased its sales there and even took the larger share in 1914, selling 150,000 cwts to Newfoundland's 130,000.

The import tariff in Portugal was not considered an impediment to Newfoundland's trade during most of this period. In 1887 a new table of tariffs was drawn up by Portugal and the duty on saltfish imports was fixed at a moderate 8s. 3d. per cwt.[87] This non-preferential tariff remained in effect until 1896 when Norway was granted a slight reduction of 10d. per cwt on its fish.[88] Newfoundland complained immediately through the Colonial Office to the Foreign Office. The latter explained the oblique way this situation had arisen and what it was trying to do:

> With reterence to your letter of the 30th ultimo respecting the import duty in Portugal on dried codfish, I am directed by the Marquess of Salesbury to inform you that the differences in the duty imposed on Norwegian codfish and that on Newfoundland codfish arises in the following manner:
>
> Under Tariff B of the new Treaty between Portugal and Norway, which came into force on the 19th ultimo, the duty on Norwegian salted or dried cod is thirty nine reis per kilo, which is the same as the duty in the general tariff.
>
> But Under Tariff B of the Portuguese-Russian treaty which came into force on the 28th of April last, the duty on cod of all kinds is thirty four reis in Portugal.
>
> Under Article 8 of her treaty with Portugal, Norway is accorded most favoured nation treatment in regard to this and other articles, and she consequently obtains the benefit of this reduction. On the other hand Portugal has so far declined to come to an agreement with Great Britain with regard to most favoured nation treatment and British and British Colonial goods remain subject to the general Portuguese Tariff which, as above stated, is thirty nine instead of thirty four reis; attempts have been made to secure the benefits of these Treaties for British Trade but hitherto without success.
>
> I am to add that the matter shall again be brought to the attention of Her Majesty's Minister at Lisbon, who will be directed to try once more if most favoured nation treatment can be secured in regard to this and to other Articles.[89]

Early in 1897 the Foreign Office admitted to Newfoundland that "Her Majesty's Government have no means of compelling the Portuguese Government to grant most favoured nation treatment to British Colonies."[90] Shortly after, MacDonell, Her Majesty's minister in Lisbon, warned that imports of Newfoundland fish were bound to be adversely affected by Norway's new agreement with Portugal; in fact, he foresaw correctly what could happen when he wrote that unless "British fish is admitted into Portugal on the same footing as Norwegian...the imports from Newfoundland...will cease altogether."[91] By September 1897 the negotiations between Great Britain and Portugal had been broken off,[92] but the London Chamber of Commerce took up Newfoundland's case and tried to get something done to alleviate this particular tariff problem regardless of the rest of the commercial agreement;[93] however, their efforts were to no avail. The St. John's Chamber of Commerce presented a most compelling case[94] and the governor reported that Newfoundland would reduce its import duty on port wine by $1.00 (fifty percent) per gallon;[95] however, nothing helped.

The situation remained unresolved. Newfoundland continued to appeal to the Colonial Office and the London Chamber of Commerce, where the appeals were supported and forwarded to the Foreign Office. However, despite major efforts, the Foreign Office was unsuccessful. During the next several years a constant stream of correspondence passed from the colony to London to Lisbon and back again, without effect. A new convention between Norway and Portugal was signed in 1903 and this also contained the stipulation that the import duty on the former's klippfisk would remain at thirty-four reis per kilogram as long as the Russian-Portuguese treaty stipulations remained in effect.[96] Efforts by the Foreign Office to convince Portugal to reduce the duty on Newfoundland fish continued unabated, but to no avail.

Besides the problems of Norwegian competition and, later, a discriminatory import tariff there was also an increase in the Portuguese cod fishery towards the end of this period. After 1901 the Portuguese fleet was allowed to expand in size beyond the previously stipulated eight vessels. In 1912 there were twenty-six vessels with about twenty-five men each operating out of the Oporto area and the Lisbon fleet was reported to be selling the greater part of its catch in Oporto as well.[97]

During the half century preceding the First World War the major developments that affected the sale of Newfoundland saltfish in the Portuguese markets were the growth of the Norwegian klippfisk industry, the preferential tariff treatment which that country's product received in Portugal, and finally, the expansion of the Portuguese Grand Bank cod fishery. Nevertheless, Oporto remained one of Newfoundland's best markets.

Summary

During the period 1814 to 1914, the role of the Portuguese markets in the Newfoundland saltfish industry underwent several changes. In the beginning, they were by far the most important markets and compensated, to a large extent, for the loss of the Spanish markets. In fact, without the Portuguese markets during 1815-1835 Newfoundland's fishery might have collapsed. Nevertheless, much depended upon the preferential tariff treatment of the colony's saltfish received in Portugal. When this advantage was removed, Newfoundland's position was less secure, although it continued to dominate the market until the 1860s. In the 1870s Norwegian competition became an established fact and grew considerably during the 1880s and 1890s. A moderate tariff of approximately 8s. to 9s. remained in effect but, beginning in 1896, Norwegian klippfisk was given preferential treatment. A revitalized Portuguese fishery and an expanding Norwegian fishery dominated these markets by the final years before the First World War, despite considerable efforts on the part of the British Foreign Office to arrange tariff changes and despite the long-established eating habits of the Portuguese consumers.

CHAPTER 6

Italian Markets

Background

The study of the Italian saltfish markets during the period from 1814 to 1914 reveals a situation very different from that in Portugal and Spain. Some Italian markets — notably Naples and Leghorn — enjoyed the freedom to trade with Britain during the French Revolutionary War and during the earlier stages of the Napoleonic War. However, after 1805 Newfoundland's saltfish was excluded from the Italian ports (except those on British-occupied Sicily) — to the short-lived advantage of the Americans.

The defeat of Napoleon opened the Italian markets to British trade. Britain's role in his defeat, combined with its contribution to the elimination of the Algerian pirates, put it in a position to make advantageous trading arrangements with the various Italian states. It was only natural that Newfoundland's saltfish benefitted from these bilateral agreements.

Nevertheless, compared to markets of the nation-states of Spain and Portugal (which had local diversities of their own), the market situation in the Italian states was more complex and is not well documented. Two problems existed. There were more ports over a larger area without (until later in the century) a centralized government. Thus a few cargoes of saltfish could go to each of a wide number of markets, resulting in a considerable total sale but having comparatively little significance for each individual market. Therefore, while the Italian markets were very important to Newfoundland (though the degree of importance varied during the century), Newfoundland was often much less important to these markets. Usually when the sale of a product is of considerably less significance to the buyer than to the supplier, one must look to the latter for information on the sale. It is there that one could expect to find the market discussed. However, with rare exceptions, the British-Newfoundland documents are silent. Looking at the reason for this brings one to the second problem associated with the study of the Italian markets. Some of the cargoes that cleared from Newfoundland and entered Italian ports were recorded as having cleared for Spain or Portugal, and in some cases for Gibraltar. It has already been seen that many cargoes which entered

Lisbon cleared again for other ports. This, most certainly, must have been the rule for cargoes clearing for Spain during the years immediately following the establishment of peace. Therefore, many of the relevant clearance documents are in Spanish and Portuguese port records because the British consuls did not often record them; in fact, British ships were not required to contact the local consul if their stay in port was brief and no transactions were carried out. In addition, the Italian ports purchased significant quantities of Labrador-cured saltfish, and for much of the period from 1814 to 1914 no records exist of the cargoes that cleared from the Labrador coast for Italy and other European markets. (Records are available for the twentieth century, however.) Consequently, an examination of the Italian markets has its difficulties.

Of course, not all the Italian saltfish markets were ignored officially to the same extent. Although all were ignored at times, usually, if not always, the more important the market, the greater the amount of documentation. Thus the most important markets in this group — Naples, Leghorn, and Genoa — can be analyzed with some thoroughness. Similarly, to a lesser degree, it is possible to analyze the smaller markets of Civitavecchia and Ancona in the Papal States, which were important until affected by the unification of Italy and, later, by the building of the railways. Of the markets which were small or which took small quantities of saltfish or occasional cargoes, little can be said and, indeed, little needs to be said. They included various ports along the western coast of the Italian peninsula, the island of Sicily and the Adriatic Sea. However, one cannot and should not ignore them completely because it appears (on the basis of limited evidence) that collectively they were significant in the development of the Newfoundland saltfish industry. Nevertheless, these markets will be studied in the context of developments in the larger markets. Furthermore, it should be noted that the milestone in Italy's history — 1860 — will be used here as a periodization point in the study of the Italian saltfish markets.

Naples: 1814-1860

Naples began to import Newfoundland saltfish after the war (see Tables 6.A[1] and 6.B,[2] below). The trade fluctuated but all surviving evidence indicates that it remained important during this whole period. In 1834[3] and 1835[4] Newfoundland supplied almost all the saltfish consumed in this market and in 1837 supplied 31,610 cwts out of the 33,670 cwts sold.[5] Also, in February 1838 Hammett, the American consul in Naples, reported that "The English exclusively possess the trade of this article [saltfish] here."[6] It seems conclusive that the saltfish purchased by Naples during this period and recorded here in Tables 6.A and 6.B came from Newfoundland.

TABLE 6.A

**Naples's Imports of
Newfoundland Saltfish: 1824-1860**

(cargoes)

Year	Number of Ships	Total Tonnage	Year	Number of Ships	Total Tonnage
1824	24	3,792	1836	16	2,800
*1825	33	5,100	1837	11	1,847
1826	28	-	1838	18	2,631
1827	20	3,309	1839	30	4,300
			1840	13	2,286
1829	26	4,242			
1830	-	3,246	1846	61	8,353
1831	14	2,407	1858	36	3,975
1832	17	2,645	1859	35	4,134
1833	26	3,807	1860	47	5,723

*In 1825 these ships carried 105,000 cwts of saltfish.

TABLE 6.B

Naples's Total Saltfish Imports: 1825-1837

(cwts)

Year	Cwts	Year	Cwts
1825	89,208	1832	50,039
1826	73,661	1833	87,214
1827	48,010	1834	72,709
1828	35,199	1835	54,269
1829	65,651	1836	50,136
1830	53,060	1837	33,670
1831	41,371		

It is evident that Naples continued to buy large quantities of Newfoundland saltfish. Assuming that ships carried twenty cwts per ton of burthen it can be calculated that the average annual importation of Newfoundland saltfish for the five-year period ending in 1840 amounted to approximately 55,000 cwts. While it is impossible to make definite statements about the quantity of Newfoundland saltfish imported during the 1840s and 1850s, it is clear that during the three-year period ending in 1864-1865 an average of 115,975 cwts was imported annually.[7] This fact plus the few available statistics in Table 6.A and the lack of complaints concerning this market leads one to conclude that Naples imported a minimum of 50,000 cwts of Newfoundland saltfish annually during the 1840s and 1850s and, very likely, a great deal more. On the whole, it is certain that Naples was an important Newfoundland market during the period between 1814 and 1860.

The reasons why Newfoundland dominated this market are obvious. When Naples resumed the importation of saltfish after the war, the colony's product was available. It was available because (as has already been seen) the sudden decrease in Spanish imports created a large surplus and the Italian markets, especially Naples, were indispensable. In 1826 the Newfoundland saltfish merchants residing in Poole, in a petition requesting that the Board of Trade work for a reduction in the Neapolitan saltfish tariff which had been temporarily increased (see below), stated that "...the Market of Naples has been resorted to by Your Lordship's Memorialists in preference to the Markets of Spain where the Duties have been for some years so exhorbitant...."[8] Therefore, under these circumstances, any new market with a demand for saltfish and a non-prohibitory tariff was ripe to receive Newfoundland's product.

Although details concerning the tariff rate on imports are scarce, two points are clear: the tariff was not prohibitory and British goods received preferential treatment during the early part of this period. Immediately after the war, an agreement was signed between Britain and the Kingdom of the Two Sicilies giving the former a special import tariff rate at least ten percent below that charged on the goods of other nations.[9] Furthermore, although the actual import tariff on saltfish was not revealed, a report in 1822 pointed out that the tariff on saltfish imports had been reduced by 1s. 3d. the previous year.[10] In 1824 there was a general increase in the Neapolitan import tariff, but Britain again received a ten percent reduction, as did France and Spain.[11] The same year, the number of British ships that entered Naples declined to 121 from 146 in 1823 and the British consul explained that a decrease in the importation of Newfoundland saltfish had caused this decline[12] — a significant comment on the importance of this branch of commerce. Finally, in 1826 a report specifically stated that the import tariff on this article was 15s. per cantar (approximately 196 pounds avoirdupois) or about 8s. 6d. per cwt[13] — a substantial amount, but not prohibitive. However, in that year it was raised to £1 1s. 6d. per cantar — 12s. 3d. per cwt.[14] Almost immediately that rate was reduced again by 3s. 11d. per cantar, or 2s. 3d. per cwt,[15] leaving the charge at 10s. per cwt. The tariff was increased again in 1827 and the British consul, Lushington, felt that this increase accounted for the decline in the trade that year[16] (see Tables 6.A and 6.B, above). A later report stated that in 1834 the import tariff on saltfish was

8s. 10d. per cwt, or about ninety percent of the cost of the product,[17] and it seems that during 1839 the tariff was set at 7s. 8d.[18] A lack of evidence prevents further discussion of the Neapolitan import tariff rate at this time, and this lack of evidence would suggest that at least that charge did not increase. Although the import tariff was high, it was not prohibitive and on the whole the Newfoundland saltfish exporters appeared content with the situation, even though the Neapolitan market appeared to be less favourable to them than the Portuguese markets about which they waxed so indignant. The difference was that Portugal, in addition to imposing a tariff, was also trying to develop its own deep-sea fishery.

The importance of Naples to the Newfoundland saltfish trade during the period from 1814 to 1860 has been largely ignored by historians of Newfoundland history, partly for the reasons mentioned in the introduction to this chapter, but also because it was a relatively peaceful market without serious commercial crises to adversely affect Britain's trade. Civil unrest in 1820-1821 and 1848-1849 caused problems, as did stringent quarantine regulations in 1826,[19] but compared to events in Spain and even Portugal, these were minor episodes. Indeed, except for a perfunctory complaint contained in a petition from the St. John's Chamber of Commerce to the Colonial Office in 1834 concerning the Spanish and Portuguese markets,[20] there is a complete absence of complaints about the condition of this market. Neither the consuls, the Board of Trade, the Foreign Office, nor the Newfoundland community registered any complaints. It seems certain that in this substantial market, Newfoundland saltfish was free from any competition and enjoyed comparatively problem-free conditions.

Leghorn: 1814-1860

While it is unfortunate that information about the Leghorn saltfish market is even harder to find than the data on Naples, it is obvious that Leghorn became an important Newfoundland market with the revival of British-Tuscan commerce. During the period from 1814 to 1819 the annual average total burthen of ships entering Leghorn with Newfoundland saltfish was about 4,000 tons.[21] This, assuming full cargoes and standard freight ratios, would imply around 80,000 cwts of fish per year. Between 1822 and 1828 this had fallen to around 62,000 cwts and by 1840 was only 46,500 cwts on average (see Table 6.C,[22] below).

Not only was Leghorn an important market, but it acquired a preference for Newfoundland Labrador-cured saltfish, and many of the cargoes that entered the port came directly from the Labrador coast. The demand for Labrador-cured saltfish gave Leghorn added significance at

TABLE 6.C

Leghorn's Imports of
Newfoundland Saltfish: 1814-1840
(cargoes)

Year	Number of Ships	Total Tonnage	Year	Number of Ships	Total Tonnage
1814	27		1828	22	2,996
			1829	24	
1816	29		1830	18	
1817	44				
1818	16		1832	22	
1819	26		1833	31	
1822	23	3,236	1835	19	2,775
1823	20	2,961	1836	14	1,907
1824	25	3,737	1837	19	2,444
1825	25	3,429	1838	10	1,313
1826	17	2,297	1839	20	2,531
1827	23	3,029	1840	18	2,394

this time because the island's Labrador fishery was an important industry in the process of becoming established.

While the growing demand for the Labrador-cured product depended on taste preferences and cost, Newfoundland dominated this market initially for the same reasons it dominated the Neapolitan one; it had a large surplus of saltfish available when the British-Tuscan trade revived. Furthermore, Leghorn was a free port between 1814 and 1824 and again after 1834.[23] Goods could be warehoused for one percent ad valorem, plus a small additional charge.[24] Goods for local consumption paid twenty to twenty-five percent, a moderate tariff.[25] The extraordinarily low tariff allowed Newfoundland to sell whatever the market could bear, and it is unfortunate that most statistical evidence is missing for the period from 1840 to 1860. However, it is certain that neither the United States, Norway, nor France sold any fish there,[26] although, no doubt, occasional cargoes came from Gaspé and Halifax. Furthermore, no complaints were recorded by the St. John's Chamber of Commerce nor by any section of the business and political communities in the colony, concerning this market. Therefore, it is safe to assume that the market remained healthy and that the importation of 100,812 and 96,500 cwts of Newfoundland saltfish in 1860 and 1861,[27] respectively, is a reliable indication of its importance. With a low tariff and practically no competition, Leghorn was an accessible and favourable market for Newfoundland saltfish during the period from 1814 to 1860.

Genoa: 1814-1860

After 1814 exports of Newfoundland saltfish to Genoa also resumed (see Table 6.D,[28] below). Calculating from the tonnage of the ships one can estimate that 40,000 cwts were imported during 1817-1821. The trade declined in the mid-1820s and, except for 1828, this decline continued until the trade ended in 1833. There was a partial recovery in 1838, but this was temporary, and the market remained practically closed to the Newfoundland trade. The British consul's report on the condition of the trade in 1845 stated: "France now excludes us from our natural trade in Salt Cod Fish an article of great consumption here, in Piedmont etc by the great Bounty she allows upon its Export, but a little sooner or a little later this illegitimate proceedings must come to an end, in the meanwhile it ought to be remarked that a considerable part of the large augmentation of French Tonnage arises from the Importation of Salt Cod, upon this bolstered system of bounty."[29] In the following year later he wrote that "By the false system of Bounty France still retains the Trade in the Salt Codfish...."[30] Thus Genoa is the most important early

TABLE 6.D

Genoa's Imports of Newfoundland Saltfish: 1816-1837
(cargoes)

Year	Number of Ships	Total Tonnage
1816	12	-
1817	17	2,561
1818	14	2,169
1819	16	2,227
1820	14	2,161
1824	9	1,086
1825	5	523
1826	5	680
1827	6	654
1828	16	1,852
1829	6	762
1830	6	800
1831	2	311
1832	5	712
1833	3	414
1834	0	0
1835	1	105
1836	8	1,053
1837	2	344

example of a Newfoundland market that was spoiled by subsidized competition. However, in 1850 the consul reported that "The import of French Salt Fish [during 1849] has (as I anticipated) almost ceased, while our [sic] both of cod-fish and herrings has considerably increased."[31] Similarly, two years later he wrote that "We have imported Salt Fish in English Bottoms to such an extent that in more than one instance we have been obligated to send on Cargoes to Leghorn or Naples."[32] The consul reported that the importation of Newfoundland saltfish in 1853 equalled the amount imported in 1852,[33] but in 1854 it declined 9,000 cwts to 26,000 cwts.[34] Thus the quantity imported during the earlier 1850s must have been approximately 35,000 cwts annually. There was a further unspecified decline in 1855.[35] During the remainder of the decade, the Newfoundland-Genoese saltfish trade continued to fluctuate.

Although Genoa had been an important market for Newfoundland saltfish during the early years of this period and during the 1850s, it was of very little or no importance during the intermediate years. As will be seen later, it was during the second half of the century that Genoa became a significant market for Newfoundland saltfish.

The Papal States: 1814-1860

The Papal States also purchased some Newfoundland saltfish, through Civitavecchia and Ancona principally. Civitavecchia was the port that provided access to Rome and, although a few cargoes of saltfish had entered there immediately after the war, it was written in 1821 that "This port was formerly the great Emporium that supplied Rome, and the Roman States on the Mediterranean with all kinds of imported Merchandize; that Trade has fallen off, and Leghorn, Genoa and Naples now supply Rome, and this port is small coasting vessels [sic] mostly Genoese."[36] Nevertheless, Civitavecchia continued to import some Newfoundland saltfish as did Ancona, the principal Papal port on the Adriatic (see Table 6.E,[37] below). Between them, these two ports bought a fair amount of this product, maybe nearly 50,000 cwts in 1833. Freeborn, the British consul in Rome, became interested at this point because the Papal government had drawn up plans, which they later dropped, to create a saltfish import monopoly similar to that which had been set up briefly in Spain beginning in 1822. This sudden interest, both on the part of the Papal government and Freeborn, suggests the presence of a substantial market there. Problems arise when trying to analyze this market, however, because both Civitavecchia and Ancona shared it and foreign ships also entered Anzio, near Rome, and Senigallia, on the Adriatic coast. Therefore, the importance of any single port of entrance is considerably reduced and the total market attracted attention only when measures were taken that

TABLE 6.E

Civitavecchia and Ancona
Imports of Newfoundland Saltfish: 1822-1840

	ANCONA		CIVITAVECCHIA		GRAND TOTAL	
Year	Ships Number	Ships Total Tonnage	Ships Number	Ships Total Tonnage	Ships	Tonnage
1822	4	522	-	-	-	-
1823	4	402	-	-	-	-
1824	4	-	3	-	7	-
1825	6	-	4	502	10	-
1826	5	707	6	781	11	1,488
1827	-	-	-	-	-	-
1828	6	862	-	-	-	-
1829	2	-	4	545	6	-
1830	4	584	3	361	7	945
1831	2	246	6	631	8	877
1832	2	205	3	508	5	713
1833	5	777	11	1,642	16	2,419
1834	3	403	7	1,002	10	1,405
1835	0	0				
1836	1	111				
1837	3	341				
1838	-	-				
1839	6	677				
1840	2	206				

affected all of it, as in the 1830s. In 1852 a similar situation developed and Sir Henry Bulwer, the British chargé d'affaires in Florence, was asked by the Foreign Office, following a request from Newfoundland, to work towards a decrease in the Papal tariff on saltfish imports.[38] Bulwer sent a consular official, Petre, to call on Cardinal Antonelli, the Papal secretary of state. In his report, Petre relayed the cardinal's reply which was that the Papal government needed the revenue. What is more important to this historian is Petre's accompanying statement to the effect that out of over 20,000,000 pounds of "salt or prepared fish [England] furnished the greater portion of 12,954,548 pounds of salt cod baccala..."[39] or approximately 115,666 cwts. This was a substantial amount, but it is not clear where this fish originated specifically. Most probably it was comprised of some cured in England and some from Gaspé, but most from Newfoundland. However, it is clear from the report that there had been a recent and fairly large increase in the importation of 'English' fish. The report states that 1,675,584 pounds of herring and 3,525,649 pounds of pilchards from England, for a total of 18,155,781 pounds, were imported, compared with a total of 8,700,000 pounds in 1842.[40] Given the fact that Newfoundland was concerned about the impor. tariff on saltfish in the Papal States at this time, it certainly seems that this market had become important to the colony. Nevertheless, political and transportation developments were to prevent these ports from fully participating in the saltfish trade in the latter half of the century.

Summary: 1814-1860

The Italian markets became very important to the Newfoundland saltfish trade immediately after 1814, buying an annual average of about 170,000 cwts during the period from 1814 to 1828. In fact, during those years, the Italian markets purchased much of the fish that could no longer be sold in Spain. The trade to the Italian ports declined, however, and by the late 1830s Naples and Leghorn together were importing about 75,000 cwts of Newfoundland saltfish. While it is impossible to speculate about the 1840s and 1850s, the Newfoundland-Italian saltfish trade had grown considerably by 1860.

Naples: 1860-1914

Naples became one of the most important markets for preserved fish in the Mediterranean after 1860 and the prospects for Newfoundland's exports of saltfish looked good. During the early 1860s imports of fish included saltfish, stockfish, Cornish pilchards, Spanish pilchards and herring (see Table 6.F,[41] below). However, saltfish (cod) was the most important single item in this group and it continued to be so for the

TABLE 6.F

**Naples's Total Imports
of Preserved Fish: 1862-1864**
(cwts)

Variety	1862-63	1863-64	1864-65
Codfish	128,928	120,850	98,146
Stockfish	25,000	19,000	20,593
Cornish Pilchards	28,414	55,300	37,375
Spanish Pilchards	10,000	34,000	16,270
Herring	8,036	9,000	6,010
Total	200,378	230,150	178,394
Number of Ships	78	89	72

remainder of the period. Furthermore, Great Britain and her colonies were the chief suppliers of fish (see Table 6.G,[42] below). Again, the

TABLE 6.G

**Naples's Total Fish Imports
by Place of Origin: 1871-1874**
(value)

Producer	1871	1873	1874
	£	£	£
Great Britain	225,576	119,361	177,968
France	4,893	5,545	9,656
Austria	126	298	-
Holland	76	-	-
Sweden & Norway	16,068	6,673	18,626
Others	432	1,865	18,058
Total	247,173	133,742	226,648

evidence is scarce, but it appears that most of the fish imports referred to as British actually came from Newfoundland (see Table 6.H,[43] below). However, the substantial quantities imported in the early 1860s declined and during 1875-1881 the total imports from the colony averaged about

TABLE 6.H

**Naples's Saltfish Imports
by Place of Origin: 1875-1881**
(cwts)

Year	Gaspé	NEWFOUNDLAND Shore-cured	Labrador-cured	Total
1875	10,405	18,924	19,080	38,004
1876	22,200	11,710	33,167	44,877
1878	12,672	16,550	29,154	45,704
1879	27,252	22,634	42,525	65,159
1880	31,650	16,616	62,000	78,616
1881	19,100	22,700	45,700	68,400

57,000 cwts annually. The trade declined even further during the 1880s (see Table 6.I,[44] below) and in 1894-1895 Naples imported just over 13,000 cwts of Newfoundland saltfish, nearly all Labrador cured.

There is no doubt that increased competition from Norway and France was the major reason for the drop in Naples's imports of saltfish

TABLE 6.I

Naples's Saltfish Imports
by Place of Origin: 1886-1895
(cwts)

		NEWFOUNDLAND					
Year	Gaspé	Shore	Labrador	Total	Norway	France	Grand Total
1886	14,960	21,400	34,200	55,600	26,700	12,400	109,660
1887	5,050	9,700	14,000	23,700	49,950	34,100	112,800
1888	2,900	15,300	19,800	35,100	51,500	27,200	116,700
1888-89	6,828	12,769	18,825	31,594	36,926	27,698	103,046
1889-90	11,937	4,262	11,488	15,750	29,162	29,556	86,405
1890-91	13,222	7,494	20,440	27,934	31,050	25,547	97,573
1891-92	14,100	21,000	27,000	48,000	24,000	17,000	103,100
1892-93	12,627	12,300	19,500	31,800	40,900	23,000	108,327
1893-94	13,383	600	14,558	15,158	32,766	21,642	82,949
1894-95	10,521	500	12,878	13,378	39,500	21,500	84,899

from Newfoundland. In 1887 the British consul wrote: "...owing to the abundant fishery in Norway, and to the stimulus given to French shippers by the heavy bounty paid them by the French Government, although the total quantities imported in 1886 and 1887 are about the same, the imports of British cod-fish during the past year [1887] only amounts to about 40% of the quantity imported in 1886, whereas the imports of Norwegian and French cod-fish have more than doubled."[45] Newfoundland's trade with Naples continued to be frustrated by the Norwegians and French. In 1895 the British consul reported:

> The principal importers regret that Norwegian fish is not only holding its ground, but gaining stronghold in this part of Italy. It was hoped at one time that, English fish would have had the preference, but during this season such has not been the case; the price paid for the Norwegian having been as much as £1 per English quintal, with a brisk demand, whereas Newfoundland, obtainable at 17s., has lagged....
> The Labrador cure (soft cure), has even suffered more from French competition. The French commenced at about £1 and gradually dropped to 18s., whereas for the Labrador cure 15s. only for the first arrivals could be obtained. It has now dropped to the ruinous price of 10s. 6d., and is difficult to sell. The heavy bounty of 5s. per quintal [sic] given by the French government will, in course of time, entirely prevent the sale of English soft-cured fish, to the ruin of the colonies in Newfoundland.[46]

The following year, the consul again bewailed the fact that there was "A large increase in the imports of French fish and very small sales of Labrador."[47] However, the Norwegian fishery had turned a corner because of catch failure, and the consul was pleased to report that there had been a decline in the importation of klippfisk and that "the deficiency has been made up by large arrivals of Newfoundland codfish."[48] This decline in Norwegian production in the latter 1890s gave the Newfoundland shore-cured saltfish industry a new lease on life in the Neapolitan market, although the French threat to the Labrador-cured product remained.

There is no doubt that the decline in Norwegian production after 1895 was to Newfoundland's advantage and the Neapolitan market improved for Newfoundland shore-cured saltfish. This was not so in the case of the Labrador-cured fish which was still subject to competition from the French product. In 1902 the British consul reported "A larger quantity of shore fish was imported..." while "A very insignificant quantity of Labrador fish was received...."[49] He added: "...The French are strong competitors in the soft cured fish, and will always gain ground, especially against the Labrador cure, for the reasons, firstly of the bounty they receive, secondly, because their fish being dried at Cette, Bordeaux and Marseilles it is imported weekly from the last port according to the necessities of the market, the soft cured fish being mainly consumed in the city of Naples and its immediate neighbourhood, and thirdly, because the Newfoundland merchants send their fish to Naples improperly culled [graded], and many parcels have arrived here in a very unsatisfactory condition."

The Neapolitan-Newfoundland saltfish trade, however, recovered from this decline and survived. By the final years of this period there had been a substantial increase in this trade and in both 1912 and 1913 over 100,000 cwts of Newfoundland saltfish were sold in Naples.[50]

It has been shown that Newfoundland had control over the substantial Neapolitan saltfish market in the 1860s, but began to experience competition from Norway in the 1870s and from France in the 1880s — competition so severe that it had nearly destroyed the colony's export trade to Naples by the end of the century. However, setbacks in both the French and Norwegian cod fisheries allowed the fish trade of Newfoundland to re-expand into this market at the beginning of the twentieth century.

Leghorn: 1860-1914

Like Naples, Leghorn continued to be an important market for saltfish. In 1871 the United States consul, John Howard, wrote:

> Codfish enters very largely into the Commerce of this place, and immense quantities are annually imported and from here is sent all over Northern and Central Italy. This season between thirty and forty Cargoes have been contracted....[51]

It was an important market for Newfoundland shore-cured saltfish during the early years of the century, but by the 1860s Newfoundland's Labrador-cured product was beginning to dominate. In 1871, for example, British vessels entered the port with 39,517 cwts of the Labrador-cured fish and 13,029 cwts of the Newfoundland shore-cured article.[52] By 1883 imports of the Labrador-cured product had become very substantial.[53]

Although Leghorn had lost its free port status in 1868,[54] it remained a distribution centre for various imports, including saltfish. In 1883, for example, twenty-four British ships with a total burthen of 3,132 tons entered Leghorn and unloaded 65,000 cwts of Labrador-cured saltfish, of which only 25,300 cwts were consumed in the immediate area.[55] In addition, 27,300 cwts[56] of Newfoundland shore-cured saltfish were imported to make a total of at least 92,300 cwts from Newfoundland. The British consul pointed out that the 65,000 cwts of Labrador-cured saltfish was the largest amount imported there "for years past."[57] Very little French fish was imported — only small parcels which were imported in August of each year "when the English cure has not yet come in."[58] The consul went on to explain that the French product, despite its bounties, "...cannot compete with the English, which not only sells at very much lower prices, but is more suited to the taste of the country."[59] Like the situation in Naples, imports of French saltfish into Leghorn were still insignificant in 1883. Similarly, he reported that the Norweigan klippfisk "will only be taken when the English is wanting."[60] Vollan points out that Leghorn bought some Norwegian klippfisk in 1877 when Newfoundland's production was low, but that the market returned again to the colony's product as soon as possible.[61] Thus by the early 1880s Leghorn, like Naples, was a substantial market for only Newfoundland's saltfish — especially the Labrador-cured article.

Like Naples, Leghorn also experienced French competition in the 1880s (see Table 6.J,[62] below), and in his report for 1885 Inglis, the British consul, wrote that "...in fact in many parts of Tuscany French cured codfish is now consumed, although much dearer than English, and unless these defects [poor quality] are remedied, importers here are of opinion that the French will soon monopolise the trade."[63] The following year Inglis reported that an "enormous quantity of French fish, of very good quality..."[64] had taken the place of much of the English cure. In his report on the state of trade in 1889, the British consul wrote: "...it is plain that a severer competition than ever threatens for British dealers in a market that ten years ago we had no difficulty in holding as our own."[65] In the same year, the consul reported that imports of French saltfish had risen to 85,000 cwts, a phenomenal level. Very serious competition from French saltfish had become evident in Leghorn.

TABLE 6.J

Leghorn's Saltfish Imports
by Place of Origin: 1883-1903
(cwts)

Year	Newfoundland Labrador	Shore	Total Newfoundland	French	Norway	Total
1883	66,962	27,300	94,262			
1884	45,225	14,740	59,965			
1885	64,500	13,500	78,000	25,000		
1886	45,770	9,810	55,580			
1889	58,180	14,252	72,432	85,080		
1892	51,820	16,070	67,890	46,091	4,532	118,513
1893	52,000	13,500	65,500	41,251	7,862	114,613
1894	39,896	12,231	52,127	48,404	14,869	115,400
1895	60,000	19,000	79,000	51,985	3,882	134,867
1896	34,880	19,360	54,240	88,659	0	140,899
1897	30,298	26,100	56,398	100,481	1,970	158,849
1898	45,000	13,000	58,000	81,776	4,926	144,702
1899	15,000	15,600	30,600	71,405	1,970	103,975
1900	31,604	13,972	45,576	79,889	985	126,450
1901	24,985	18,452	43,437	87,001	1,478	131,916
1902	44,118	17,494	61,612	90,525	985	153,122
1903	40,800	7,000	47,800	?	?	?

Major French competition continued to affect the colony's sales in Leghorn (see Table 6.J, above), while Norway's direct influence on this market was comparatively insignificant. One of the reasons for this was the fact that Leghorn was such an important market for Newfoundland's Labrador-cured fish. After 1889 French sales declined for a few years, but in 1896 France captured over half of this market, a proportion which was maintained until at least the early years of the twentieth century. Information becomes scarce and vague in the early years of the twentieth century, but it seems likely that Newfoundland recaptured a larger share of this market, at least temporarily (see Table 6.K,[66] below). Table 6.K probably reflects some real growth in the importation of Newfoundland saltfish for a brief period early in the century. Further, in his 1909 report, Carmichael noted that "Labrador and Shore fish continues to suffer from the competition of the bounty-fed French article and the popularity of Norwegian stock fish, the proportion of import from British sources being 63 per cent in 1907, 42 per cent in 1908 and 38 per cent in 1909."[67] Although Carmichael does not state that the fish 'from British sources' was Labrador and shore-cured saltfish, he certainly implies that a considerable proportion was. In any case, one can deduce that a fairly substantial increase occurred in the sale of Newfoundland saltfish in Leghorn in the early part of the century, to be followed by a rapid and major decline.

TABLE 6.K

**Leghorn's Imports of
Dried and Smoked Fish: 1903-1913**
(cwts)

| Year | Total | From British Sources | |
		Cwts	Percent of Total
1903	223,524	109,941	49
1904	179,735	115,874	64
1905	241,975	123,513	51
1906	172,580	113,400	66
1907	201,240	128,360	64
1908	382,832	164,482	43
1909	348,995	135,342	39
1910	351,915	73,660	21
1911	228,580	75,617	33
1912	148,720	68,236	46
1913	102,186	49,659	49

Thus Leghorn was an extremely important market for Newfoundland saltfish, especially the Labrador-cured variety, until the mid-1880s. At that point, France became a major competitor and had captured over half of this large market by 1896. After a brief recovery, the Newfoundland export trade to Leghorn again declined.

The developments in the Leghorn saltfish market were similar in many ways to those already mentioned in the examination of the Neapolitan market. There was a low import tariff and there were no complaints from the colony about the market itself, which is the major reason for the documentary silence on the subject. On the other hand, there were also differences between these two markets. Unlike Naples, Leghorn did not purchase any significant quantities of Norwegian klippfisk. Finally, Leghorn was a much more important market for Newfoundland Labrador-cured saltfish, and experienced stronger competition from the similar French product.

Genoa: 1860-1914

Genoa's development as a market for Newfoundland saltfish during the period from 1860 to 1914 was similar in certain ways to that of the other two major Italian markets. Nevertheless, it had always had closer connections with France. Although it became a market for Newfoundland saltfish after 1814, it soon began to purchase the French product and, as has been shown, it did not revert to purchasing the colony's product until the 1850s. From these limited beginnings in the 1850s, Genoa was to become, for a time, one of the colony's most important markets, especially for the Labrador-cured product (see Table 6.L,[68] below).

TABLE 6.L

**Genoa's Saltfish Imports
by Place of Origin: 1866-1890**
(cwts)

Year	Newfoundland	France
1866-67	44,000	
1867-68	73,000	
1868-69	82,897	
1869-70	92,287	
1870-71	62,440	
1871-72	88,753	
1872-73	98,749	
1873	62,907	
1874	101,681	27,000
1875	87,232	
1876	104,121	30,128
1877	89,308	22,244
1878	133,055	29,100
1879	147,388	31,500
1880	159,352	37,270
1881-82	133,681	25,000
1882-83	105,842	26,700
1883-84	122,865	30,000
1884-85	109,658	22,274*
1885-86	129,134	18,775*
1886-87	72,300	38,212*
1887-88	61,640	32,144
1888-89	70,887	5,656*
1889-90	86,490	13,407
1890-91	42,630	10,313*

*These figures are given in bales.

There were several reasons why Newfoundland recaptured the Genoese saltfish market. In spite of the French government subsidy, it seems that the colony's fish was cheaper, at least initially. In 1864 the British consul reported that Labrador-cured saltfish was sold at from 19s. to £1.0.6 per cwt (c.i.f.) while the French product fetched £1.1.6 to £1.3.6 per cwt (c.i.f.).[69] Also the French catch had declined in 1868 by over fifty percent.[70] In that year the acting British consul wrote: "In 1868 French vessels were very unfortunate in the fishery, and this caused an unusually large quantity of fish of English cure to be imported at Genoa."[71] And finally, it would seem that, as a British consul wrote, "the taste for fish of English cure is somewhat spreading."[72] It was this impetus in the 1850s and 1860s that established Newfoundland saltfish in the Genoese market. Unlike its performance in the Neapolitan and Leghorn markets, the colony's product re-entered the market in Genoa after a period of successful competition with French saltfish.

Genoa's growth as a market for Newfoundland Labrador-cured saltfish was rapid. In his report for 1867 the British consul wrote: "The import of fish of English cure has increased enormously within the last two years, and Genoa is now the most important market in the Mediterranean for this article."[73] There was a break in the growth of this market in 1870 due to a catch failure on the Labrador coast,[74] another in 1875 for the same reason,[75] and a couple of other slower seasons. On the whole, however, sales of Newfoundland saltfish — most of which was Labrador-cured — increased during the 1860s and 1870s to the exceptionally high level of almost 160,000 cwts annually in 1880-1881. The reasons why Genoa became such an important market during this time have already been noted. There was obviously a substantial demand for the lower-priced Labrador-cured saltfish, and Newfoundland was the only available supplier. Genoa certainly had consumers and a strong distribution system. In 1871 it was reported that "Genoa [was] the richest and most commercial of Italian cities...."[76] By 1880 Newfoundland's prospects in the Genoese market looked exceptionally bright.

After it hit its peak in 1880-1881, the sale of Newfoundland saltfish in Genoa declined, slowly and erratically at first, but then rapidly after the 1885-1886 season. In 1890-1891 only 42,630 cwts were imported, compared with nearly 160,000 cwts in 1880-1881. Several years later, in 1894, there were imported from all North America 9,080 cwts of "dried, salted, and pickled fish" which consisted solely of Labrador-cured saltfish.[77] During that same year imports of all preserved fish were made up as follows:[78]

	Cwts	
Great Britain	98,360	herring, pilchards
Spain	113,880	sardines, tunny (tuna)
Norway	75,220	klippfisk, stockfish, smoked herring
Iceland	10,520	klippfisk
Portugal	5,140	tunny
France	2,620	lavé (quality of large codfish)
North America	9,080	Labrador-cured saltfish
Total	314,820	preserved fish

The following year, there were very few changes, with the exception of an increase in the importation of Icelandic klippfisk to 30,220 cwts and Labrador-cured saltfish to 21,940 cwts.[79] The recovery in the sales of the latter continued in 1896, when 60,040 cwts were bought.[80] However, this appears to have been the extent of Newfoundland's recovery for a few years because it was reported that this market purchased only 3,920 cwts of preserved fish from North America in 1898, compared with 83,084 cwts from Norway.[81] Although detailed evidence is not available, it is known that Genoa imported 54,000 cwts of the Labrador-cured product in 1901[82] and it was reported in 1902 that 30,000 to 40,000 cwts annually was the usual extent of this trade,[83] Some recovery, therefore, was made. Information on the rest of this period is even scarcer. Keene, who had been the British consul since 1897, neglected to mention imports of North American and/or Newfoundland fish in his official reports for the years immediately following 1901, although he presented detailed accounts of the importation of preserved fish from Spain, Great Britain, Norway and "Others" annually. In addition, he reported the total imports of "dried cod and stockfish" in 1908 and 1909[84] without being specific. Only later did Keene again mention Newfoundland or, indeed, North America, when he reported that two sailing ships of 323 tons burthen "entered from Newfoundland with cargoes" in 1911;[85] three sailing ships of 407 tons burthen entered "from Labrador with Cargoes" in 1912;[86] and in 1914 the vice consul reported that four sailing ships of 541 tons burthen "from Labrador with Cargoes" arrived during 1913.[87] Although it is not explicit, the tone of these and other reports suggests that the sale of Newfoundland saltfish in Genoa had practically ceased during the years just before the First World War.

Newfoundland's inability to maintain her position in the Genoese saltfish market is not inexplicable. The expansion of the subsidized French fishery in the mid-1880s was the first major shock. As early as 1885 the British consul wrote with unusual prescience:

In the fish trade our English cured fish only fetches about half the price of French cured fish, and in fact I know of no article in which we are progressing as a set off against the vast number in which we are losing ground, or have been beaten out of the field.

The import of codfish of English cure in 1885 amounted to 129,134 cwts. against 109,658 cwts. in 1884 — the import of French cured fish having been of 18,775 bales in 1885 against 22,274 bales in 1884 — but a great deal of French cured fish has been imported by land this year, the quantity of which it is difficult to ascertain. It is a fact much to be regretted that year by year French cured fish are supplanting ours in the market, and meet with ready sale at high prices, whilst ours remains unsaleable at almost any price. If our trade is not to be entirely driven out of the market, it behooves our producers to listen to the warnings which they receive year after year, and to strive to adapt the goods they send here to consumers' tastes. They may rest assured that, with such keen competitors as the French, it will not do to be careless, and to continue to send to this market fish that, both in point of cure and assortment, will not bear comparison with French cured fish, more especially as the taste for fish is on the decline rather than on the increase, and the use of it in Lent is, for various reasons, by no means so prevalent in this district as it was some years ago.[88]

In 1886 the importers of Labrador-cured saltfish complained bitterly about French competition.[89] The same year, the British consul reported that the French product was "admirably cured, sorted and packed" while that of Newfoundland showed signs of neglect.[90] Furthermore, similar saltfish began to arrive from Norway and Iceland. In 1887 the consul reported that "The Norwegians are curing their fish like Labrador instead of continuing their old process."[91] In 1894 Payton, the newly-appointed British consul, wrote: "I am informed that British trade in cod-fish appears to be losing ground from year to year owing to the fact that Iceland (through Denmark) and Norway are better cured [sic], and, therfore, command higher prices than those which arrive from Labrador, the demand and price for the latter showing, so far, a steady decrease."[92] Two years later the same consul reported that fish from Iceland was preferred over the Labrador product for its cheapness and quality.[93] He concluded, "The province of Piedmont which used to take the chief portion of English fish [imported through Genoa] now consumes exclusively Iceland and French cures, and Labrador cures find no market in that large district."[94] Similarly, in 1899 it was reported that the quality of the Labrador-cured product was not very good while that from Iceland, Norway and France was better, and the latter's was also cheaper.[95] It is impossible to estimate the quantities of saltfish exported to Genoa by each of Newfoundland's competitors during this extended period because of the absence of records, but they must have been considerable. It is known that in 1908 and 1909 the total imports of dried and salted cod amounted to 302,160 cwts and 267,240 cwts, respectively.[96] Similarly, total imports of all preserved fish reached over 500,000 cwts by 1904[97] and Norway's share of this market reached an annual average of 116,313 cwts during the three-year period ending in 1904.[98] Finally, it was reported that 104 Norwegian ships with a total of 103,384 tons burthen entered Genoa with cargoes in 1912.[99] Considering the fact that codfish was Norway's chief export to Genoa, the quantity carried in these ships must have been large. Vollan writes: "Genoa gradually became the centre of the Norwegian klippfisk trade in Italy."[100] Competition — especially from the French and Norwegian products, but also from that of Iceland — in combination with deterioration in the quality of Newfoundland fish, led to the decline in the sales of Newfoundland saltfish in this market.

Genoa had been won by the Newfoundland saltfish exporters in the 1850s and 1860s and had grown to become one of the colony's most important markets. As was the case with Naples and Leghorn, Newfoundland's trade, however, experienced French competition after the mid 1880s and Norwegian competition later. Icelandic klippfisk entered this market as well. The Newfoundland trade in Genoa was adversely affected by a lack of quality control as it was in the other markets. However, its fate in this market as in the others was largely outside the colony's jurisdiction. However, because of its size, the collapse of the Genoese market was more significant to the Newfoundland economy than that of either Naples or Leghorn. The acquisition and loss of this market was one of the most significant developments in the history of the Newfoundland saltfish trade.

Other Italian Markets: 1860-1914

Bari, which is located in southern Italy on the Adriatic coast, became a fairly important saltfish market in the latter part of the nineteenth century. It seems to have developed as a market with the increase in saltfish imports into Italy from Norway because its trade in this product was virtually ignored by British consuls, and it was 1900 before the British consul reported that Bari bought its annual 40,000 or 50,000 cwts of saltfish and dried fish "chiefly from Sweden and Norway."[101] However, Bari had begun to purchase most of its saltfish imports from Newfoundland and Canada by 1909 and 1910.[102] At that time the British consul reported that "The most interesting features are a decline in the codfish imports from the United Kingdom and Norway in favour of Newfoundland fish".[103] Nevertheless, total imports from British North America amounted to a moderate 37,000 cwts.[104] The only other available document shows Bari's total imports of "Dried and salted fish" and does not provide any breakdown by type or port of origin. In 1910 and 1911, two of the latest and most important years for this trade, Bari imported 75,300 cwts and 77,240 cwts, respectively.[105] Although growing, Bari imported fish from a number of suppliers and could not be considered a large Newfoundland market, but it is a good example of the more important minor ones.

Whereas Bari was small but growing, Civitavecchia and Ancona were small and declining during the second half of the century. The latter, in fact, declined soon after the Italian unification, but Civitavecchia continued to retain some importance for several decades. The British vice consul reported from Rome that Civitavecchia had usually imported 1,000 tons (20,000 cwts) annually, but that only 142 tons were imported in 1900.[106] He went on to explain: "...Codfish used to be imported direct from Newfoundland in British sailing vessels...but since the railway company has established a special reduced tariff for the transport of large consignments of codfish via Genoa, cargoes are discharged at that port from whence they are distributed by rail to different parts of Italy."[107] A couple of years later, the same vice-consul explained the decline of Civitavecchia more fully:

> Before Rome became the capital of United Italy the port of Civitavecchia was one of the most flourishing in the Mediterranean, and its importance and the prosperous condition of its trade were due not only to the fact that it was the natural port of Rome, but also because practically it had no competitors, inasmuch as Genoa and Leghorn then belonged to different States and the entire trade of Rome was concentrated at Civitavecchia. Since 1870 a considerable portion of this trade has been diverted to other ports of the Kingdom farther away from Rome, but affording better facilities for trade, and hence Civitavecchia from being an exclusive port, and therefore necessarily an important one had dwindled down to a port of secondary importance.[108]

However, Civitavecchia continued to be a minor market, taking 4,000 to 8,000 cwts of Newfoundland saltfish annually for the remainder of this period, while the port of Ancona purchased much less.

Other small markets for Newfoundland saltfish existed throughout the Mediterranean. For example, in Sicily, both Messina and Palermo bought small quantities (Messina was also to become a major market for Norwegian klippfisk and stockfish by the end of the century). While collectively these and other small markets were important, during the period from 1860 to 1914, as in the earlier period, the success of the sales of Newfoundland saltfish in the Mediterranean region was dependent upon the major markets.

Summary: 1860-1914

During the period from 1860 to 1914, Newfoundland's experience in the Italian saltfish markets reached new levels of achievement and failure. The colony's product dominated the markets in Naples and Leghorn from the beginning of this period and recaptured the market in Genoa. By 1880 these three markets together provided the most important European outlet for Newfoundland saltfish, especially the Labrador-cured variety. While it is difficult to compare different years because fish could be forced from one market into another at certain periods, sometimes it is worth the risk to do so. Also, this risk can be reduced considerably by using averages. For example, during the three-year period 1879-1881 Leghorn imported an average of 71,000 cwts of Newfoundland saltfish annually, during the two years 1883-1884 Naples imported an average of 77,000 cwts annually, and during the six-year period 1887-1893 Genoa imported an average of 134,000 cwts annually. Given that there is some uncertainty involved, it is still not unreasonable to conclude that during the late 1870s and early 1880s, these three markets together bought a total of over 250,000 cwts of Newfoundland saltfish annually. When one takes into consideration the probable importation at Civitavecchia, Ancona and Bari, plus the occasional cargoes elsewhere in Italy, one can state with reasonable certainty that the total importation of Newfoundland saltfish into the country exceeded 300,000 cwts annually during these years. During this short period Italy was the most important European market for the colony's product. One of the reasons for its popularity in the Italian markets was Italy's low import tariff on saltfish. In 1862 West, secretary of the British Legation in Turin, reported that Italy's tariff was "perhaps one of the most liberal in Europe."[109] In 1886 it was reported by the United States consul general in Italy that the tariff on 100 kilograms of saltfish was six francs (about 3s. per cwt),[110] a very moderate amount. Even as late as 1903 the tariff on saltfish imports into Italy was only 2s. 0.5d. per cwt compared with 9s. 9d. charged in Spain and 8s. 11d. charged in Portugal.[111] However, the rate of the import tariff was not the only factor involved.

In the late 1880s and the early 1890s French and Norwegian competition in these markets became severe as both producing countries experienced good fishing seasons and Newfoundland's economy was beset by problems both in the markets and at home. In 1893 and 1894 Naples imported an annual average of 14,000 cwts and Leghorn an average of 59,000 cwts of the colony's saltfish. In 1894 and 1895 Genoa imported an average of 16,000 cwts. These figures suggest that these three markets together bought about 90,000 cwts annually during the early 1890s. Even allowing for another 10,000 cwts imported by other Italian ports, there would have been a total importation of only 100,000 cwts during this period.

A report from the British consul general in Florence in 1897 stated that the total importation of Newfoundland saltfish into Italy had declined to 47,000 cwts annually.[112] While this figure is too low for 1897 it may be closer to the truth for the very early 1890s, about which few statistics exist.

Finally, one comes to the end of the period. Here one is forced to speculate even more since the evidence shows that Naples imported an average of 125,000 cwts of saltfish annually from "Canada" in 1912 and 1913, Leghorn imported an average of 59,000 cwts annually from "British Sources" during the same period, and seven sailing ships with a total burthen of 948 tons entered Genoa "from Labrador with Cargoes" with a total of about 18,000 cwts — an average of 9,000 cwts annually. This amounts to a total of 190,000 cwts annually. Taking into account the fact that Naples probably imported some Gaspé saltfish, and allowing for the importation of Newfoundland's product into other Italian ports, one can estimate the total importation from the colony at about 200,000 cwts annually. Fortunately, one is not totally dependent upon this speculation because an analysis of the saltfish markets by Newfoundland's governor in 1914 concluded that Italy purchased 207,611 cwts of the colony's product in the year ending 30 June 1913 and he observed that this market was "stationary."[113] Briefly, then, it can be said that Newfoundland sold a considerable quantity of saltfish in Italy during the period from 1860 to the early 1880s. Sales then declined during the latter 1880s and early 1890s, but this decline was followed by a recovery in which much, but not all, of the lost ground was regained.

Nevertheless, developments in the Italian markets varied from one place to another. Leghorn seems to have been the most stable of these markets during this time, despite the competition. On the other hand, the colony's market in Naples was seriously affected by Norwegian and French competition, but then recovered and became a very important market, probably because it generally bought shore-cured fish and was safer from French competition and because at the same time Norway's fishery was having problems. Genoa had been the most important market for Newfoundland saltfish, but the colony lost this market completely, except for a brief resurgence around the turn of the century. Although Norway sold some klippfisk there, the chief competition came from the French product. The Newfoundland governor stated in 1914 that the colony's main competitor in "the North of Italy" was France.[114] In the absence of any significant import tariffs, it seems that competition from France and Norway and, to some extent, Iceland, combined with the deterioration in the cure of the Newfoundland product were the major factors that determined the varying degrees of success and failure that accompanied the sale of Newfoundland saltfish in these markets.

Newfoundland felt powerless when faced with competition in the Italian markets in the 1880s because the problem originated with the competitors and it was not a market problem per se. Consequently, the colony reacted differently than it did when confronted with *market* problems in Spain and Portugal. The first reaction was its decision to injure the French deep-sea fishery by preventing the sale of bait to this fleet. After some delay and considerable pressure the British Government approved the legislation, known as the Bait Act, in 1888. Then there was an unsuccessful attempt to improve the local product. Finally and unfortunately the exporters attempted to outmaneuver each other by sending fish to market as early and as swiftly as possible. It is possible that French expansion was curtailed by the Bait Act but, on the whole Newfoundland did not succeed in its efforts to counter the problems in the Italian markets.

Summary

From 1814 to 1914 the Italian markets played a vital role in the Newfoundland saltfish industry. Immediately after 1814 they absorbed much of the colony's saltfish destined for Spain, certainly saving many Newfoundland exporters from bankruptcy and reducing considerably the impact that the collapse of the Spanish markets had on the island's economy. In the late 1830s there was a decline in sales to these markets. This appears to have resulted from a general decline in demand but, in the case of Genoa, French competition was also a factor. The markets had recovered by the late 1850s, with the Labrador-cured product becoming very important, especially in Genoa and Leghorn. By the early 1880s Italy had become the colony's most important market, but the expansion of the French and Norwegian fisheries soon brought about a decline in Newfoundland's trade with the Italian ports. Around the turn of the century, competition lessened and Newfoundland's position in the Italian markets improved significantly.

The importance of the Italian markets to the Newfoundland saltfish industry during the period from 1814 to 1914 is obvious now. Despite setbacks during the 1830s and 1880s-1890s, these nation-states and later the unified nation provided significant outlets for the colony's saltfish, especially the Labrador-cured variety. Nevertheless, because of problems of documentation which were discussed in this chapter, the importance of these markets has not been fully appreciated by historians. Prowse, who discussed the significance of the Bait Act, did not mention the Italian markets,[115] beyond quoting a speech in the Newfoundland House of Assembly which stated that the Newfoundland saltfish exporters were meeting French competition in "Spain, Italy, and other European countries."[116] Similarly, the present writer, in a paper presented to the annual meeting of the Canadian Historical Association in June 1973, pointed out that the Italian markets were of only minor importance to the Newfoundland saltfish trade — an opinion formed from an examination of the colony's export statistics.[117] It is hoped that this chapter has succeeded in acknowledging the important place that these markets occupy in the history of Newfoundland from 1814 to 1914.

CHAPTER 7

Greek Markets

Partly in reaction to the market problems of the latter nineteenth century Newfoundland attempted to sell some of its Labrador fish to Greece. In his report of 1856, the British consul in Patras stated that it was probable that this article would "come into large consumption in Greece."[1] Information is scarce, but Patras imported £4,749 worth of salted fish from Britain and £4,264 worth from Italy in 1871.[2] No doubt these shipments included some saltfish as well as herring, pilchards and salmon and, in any case, could have amounted to only a thousand hundredweight. In 1875 the British consul reported that only 1,400 cwts of Newfoundland saltfish had been imported during that year and "considerable quantities had to be brought in country boats from Zante, where five cargoes were imported direct from Newfoundland."[3] If the consul considered five cargoes to be "considerable quantities," it is obvious that his idea of size differed greatly from his colleagues' ideas in the larger European markets. Consequently, since he wrote about relative size and rate of growth, one gets the distinct impression that this was a new and growing market for the colony's product. The following year he reported that "The consumption of Labrador codfish is gradually increasing and three cargoes arrived direct by English vessels [during 1876], altogether 9,200 [cwts], which netted £9,500."[4] Again, the tone of this report suggests that this was a new enterprise. In 1878 "Two cargoes of cod-fish were imported direct from Newfoundland, besides smaller lots from indirect ports..."[5] and in 1880 "large importations" were reported, with some cargoes being discharged at Patras and others at Zante.[6] In short, the period from the 1850s to the 1880s marked the infancy of this trade.

Information on the 1880s is scarce and, in fact, the consular reports are less informative during this decade than during the 1870s. Nevertheless, it is known that Patras and Zante together purchased fifteen cargoes of saltfish in 1883 and Wood wrote that "large quantities" had been imported into the former.[7] There are no further references to the amount of saltfish imported but several references to prices and tariffs for this product. While the price varied, the import tariff was raised (from an undisclosed figure) to 4s. 9.5d. per cwt in 1885.[8] This was well below the rate charged in Spain and Portugal but higher than that in Italy. Furthermore, its being increased may indicate that the Greek government was beginning to recognize the saltfish import tariff as a source of revenue, which would suggest that the importation of this product was becoming significant.

Although the degree of their significance during the 1880s cannot be quantified, the Greek markets — sometimes individually, sometimes collectively — were becoming quite important by at least the beginning of the 1890s (see Table 7.A,[9] below). Patras was the major market and supplied the Morea, while Zante and Corfu, at least for a while, supplied the Ionian Islands, and Syra supplied the Cyclades. It was reported by Wood, the British consul, in 1894 that "dried Labrador fish is a very favourite article of diet among the lower classes in this country."[10] The following year Wood cited the importation of 34,250 cwts of saltfish into Patras as unprecedented.[11] He continued: "The consumption of codfish in the Morea is yearly on the increase, and, luckily for British colonial

TABLE 7.A

Greece's Imports of Newfoundland Saltfish: 1891-1914

(cwts)

Year	Patras	Corfu	Zante	Syra	Total
1891	22,327	-	-	-	-
1892	19,247	-	-	-	-
1893	24,489	-	-	-	-
1894	17,515	9,913	-	-	-
1895	34,250	-	16,448	-	-
1896	37,000	13,089	14,448	-	-
1897	29,500	3,680	16,600	11,000	-
1898	40,000	-	-	-	80,000
1899	36,000	-	-	-	72,000
1900	27,000	-	-	-	56,000
1901	-	-	-	-	56,000
1902	32,440	-	-	-	-
1903	38,848	-	-	-	-
1904	41,713	-	-	-	-
1905	55,757	-	-	-	-
1906	(52,000-57,000)	-	-	-	-
1907	(55,000-60,000)	-	-	-	-
1908	55,760	-	-	-	-
1909	57,000	-	-	-	-
1910	44,000	-	-	-	-
1911	48,000	-	-	-	-
1912	42,000	-	-	-	-
1913	40,400	-	-	-	-
1914	69,500	-	-	-	-

trade, the demand runs entirely on Labrador codfish."[12] In 1898 imports of Labrador-cured saltfish reached their peak, as Patras imported 80,000 cwts; it is quite possible that some fish was imported at other Greek ports as well. A decline followed and then another increase so that by 1909 about 77,000 cwts of saltfish were imported from Newfoundland.[13] Decline recurred the next year, but having settled at this low point in 1910, the market held firm for the remainder of the period. However, problems prevented the Greek saltfish markets from living up to the expectations that they had aroused in Newfoundland during the expansionary period leading up to 1898; at that time it looked as if Greece would replace Italy in the colony's trade. Newfoundland's later disappointment over the failure of these expectations to materialize resulted in a round of diplomatic negotiations between Great Britain, Greece and other nations, which was unusual in even Newfoundland's history and illustrates some of the complexities of the saltfish trade.

Newfoundland's major saltfish market in Greece was the province of Morea, which was served by the harbour of Patras. It was an area suffering from economic depression by 1900. This region had traditionally produced olive oil, currants, sultanas and grain for export, and had practised mixed farming and livestock raising. In the early 1880s[14] many French vineyards were destroyed by phylloxera, and this created an almost unlimited demand in France for wine-making products. Large tracts of land along the western coast of Morea and the shores of the Gulf of Corinth, which had previously provided pasture for "innumerable" flocks of sheep and goats and herds of cattle, were transformed into currant and grape vineyards by the shepherds and herdsmen. In other cases, proprietors of excellent olive groves destroyed their trees in order to extend their currant and grape vineyards. The production of currants soon increased from about 75,000 tons in 1877 to 130,000 tons in 1884 and 160,000 tons in 1891. For a period, there was considerable prosperity, with France buying whatever wine-making products that came on the market, at excellent prices. In the meantime, the French vineyards recovered and tariffs on imports of wine-making products were gradually introduced and increased during the 1890s until they became prohibitive. The Greek products were then forced onto other markets, which became so glutted that the products became almost worthless. To try to correct this, the Greek government passed the *Retention Law* in 1895, which required exporters to deposit a percentage of their product in government warehouses for local sale in the wine-making industry. By 1902 the government had raised this retention to twenty percent, which still left an oversupply for export: in 1902 the total production of currants amounted to 160,000 tons. By the turn of the century, Greece desperately needed to find new markets for its currants and sultanas and/or expand its old ones.

Anxious to take advantage of the trade problems in Greece, the colony enquired in 1902 whether Greece would remove its import duties from Newfoundland saltfish if Newfoundland removed its import duties from Greek sultanas and currants.[15] If that was not possible, Newfoundland asked, could reciprocal reductions be made in the respective tariffs?[16] Governor Boyle, in his official capacity, followed up the initial request with two telegrams to the Colonial Office in February 1903 seeking information on the progress of the talks with Greece and emphasizing that he needed this information before the local House of Assembly opened. No reply arrived. The following June Prime Minister Bond requested a report on the talks and the governor again pressed the Colonial Office for an answer.[17] The Colonial Office sent the request to the Foreign Office.[18] Upon receipt of his instructions, Charles des Graz, the British minister in Athens, asked the minister for foreign affairs in the Greek government what reductions they would be willing to make in the tariff on imports of Newfoundland saltfish if the colony removed their import tariff on Greek currants and sultanas.[19] The Greek government in turn asked how much of a reduction in the import tariff on Newfoundland saltfish would be required for the abolition of the colony's import tariff on Greek products.[20] The British Foreign Office notified the Colonial Office of this reply[21] and negotiations started.

The next stage in these negotiations was somewhat confusing because there was a misunderstanding with regard to the amount of the actual Greek saltfish import tariff involved. In reply to the Greek government's request, just discussed, the Newfoundland government, in the following February, notified the Colonial Office that a reduction in the tariff on Greek imports of Newfoundland saltfish to 3s. 6d. per quintal — "one half the present duty" — would be required before the colony could abolish her import tariffs on Greek currants and raisins.[22] This instruction was forwarded to the Foreign Office, who sent it to the British minister in Athens. The confusion arose from the fact that the import tariff on saltfish entering Greece was already in the vicinity of 3s. 9d., having been reduced in 1895 from 6s.[23] However, the British legation in Athens assumed that the Newfoundland government had made a mistake and ignored the sum of 3s. 6d. mentioned in the correspondence. They simply asked the Greek government for a reduction of fifty percent in the tariff.[24] The misunderstanding may have stemmed from the fact that the Newfoundland government was referring to the metric quintal, but more than likely it is an example of the slow, and not always accurate, flow of information from the markets through the saltfish exporters to the colony's government officials. In any case, a reduction of fifty percent became Newfoundland's goal.

No sooner had the fifty percent reduction issue been sorted out when other complications arose. In February 1904 the colony was notified by the Colonial Office that, under existing treaties, both Persia and Turkey would also have to receive most-favoured-nation treatment if Greek sultanas and currants were allowed into Newfoundland duty-free.[25] If not, new arrangements would have to be drawn up by the Foreign Office with these nations, eliminating the clause which gave Newfoundland most-favoured-nation treatment in Persia and Turkey. Then the Foreign Office discovered that this was not strictly true, because as they explained:

> The Commercial Treaty between Great Britain and Turkey of 1861 has expired; and strictly speaking Turkey is not as of right entitled to most-favoured-nation treatment in the United Kingdom, though such treatment is still enjoyed by British subjects and commerce in Turkey in virtue of the capitulations. It appears however to Lord Lansdowne that it would hardly be equitable, though not contrary to treaty for Newfoundland to refuse most-favoured-nation treatment to Turkey; and it would be advisable that no ground of complaint should be offered to the Ottoman Government, by giving any preference to Greek over Turkish sultanas.[26]

However, Newfoundland's statement to the effect that it did not engage in any trade with Persia nor Turkey and did not wish to retain most-favoured-nation treatment in these countries[27] seems to have solved this problem.

With the solution of these problems, negotiations proceeded. In September 1904 Athens offered to reduce the tariff from 11 drachma 36⅓ lepta down to five drachma per one hundred okes (i.e., from approximately 3s. 8d. to 1s. 7.5d. per cwt) on all imports of salted and/or dried codfish.[28] The agreement was signed in November[29] but did not go into effect immediately. First, the Greek parliament was slow to ratify it; this necessitated additional correspondence from the colony to the British Foreign Office and from there to Athens and back again. In addition, the local valuation of saltfish on the market in Greece was raised at the beginning of 1905 from one drachma to one drachma fifty lepta per oke.[30] This allowed the local authorities to increase the amount of their local duties on the saltfish because these extra duties, called octroi duties, were always levied as a percentage of the valuation which was fixed by royal decree.[31] This increased the cost to the consumer and reduced the effectiveness of the tariff decrease. This unexpected action was also the subject of a considerable amount of correspondence. Finally, the agreement was ratified and went into effect in July 1905,[32] and in the following

November the Greek government published a royal decree, effective 1 January 1906, which reduced the valuation of saltfish, for octroi purposes, from one drachma fifty lepta to the old figure of one drachma per oke.[33] The negotiations had been successfully concluded.

Between 1905 and 1910 the importation of Labrador-cured saltfish into Greece rose. The increase, however, is not adequately reflected in Table 7.A because the figures for ports other than Patras are incomplete. In his report for 1909, Wood noted that the annual consumption of the Labrador-cured saltfish amounted to an average of 70,000 cwts[34] and, as the table shows, 77,000 cwts were imported during the year in question. However, beginning in 1910 the importation of this product declined somewhat for various reasons, including the poor quality of some fish[35] and a larger supply of local meat and vegetables because of exceptionally mild weather.[36] Nevertheless, the long-term prospects for these markets seemed very encouraging during the final years of this period.

At first, it seemed to the British Foreign Office that all had turned out well in the negotiations with Greece, but complications arose which were to occupy that office until the outbreak of the war. Once again, these complications were rather unimportant in the total context of Newfoundland's fishery and economy, but they provide another illustration of the complexity of the saltfish industry and trade and, equally important, an excellent example of the trouble to which the Foreign Office was prepared to go on behalf of the colony.

Trouble arose when Spain discovered that Greek sultanas and currants were being admitted into Newfoundland duty free. Great Britain and Spain had signed a commercial agreement in 1887, with a most-favoured-nation clause that included Newfoundland saltfish in 1894. Furthermore, neither Spain nor Great Britain admitted that special concessions could be granted to third parties in return for a consideration (as was admitted by the United States of America).[37] Therefore, it was the opinion of the Foreign Office that Spain would have to be granted the same concessions as Greece, at least in the case of sultanas, since it could be argued that currants were unique to Greece.[38] The item that caused the trouble was the Spanish raisin or *pasa*. De Bunsen reported that he had pointed out to the Spanish foreign minister that pasas were different from Greek sultanas and currants.[39] This was not satisfactory to the Spanish government and they demanded more information from the British Foreign Office on the alleged differences between their product and that of Greece.[40] The Colonial Office forwarded this information on to the colony and asked if the Newfoundland government wished to have the director of the Royal Botanic Gardens at Kew analyze and describe the fruits.[41] In reply to the Colonial Office, Michael Cashin, the Newfoundland minister of finance, stated that the Spanish pasa was a seedless raisin very similar to the sultana but with a much thicker skin, while the currant was a dried grape peculiar to the Corinth.[42] In the meantime, the Foreign Office had taken independent action and had received an opinion from the Board of Agriculture and Fisheries. The board ruled that berries containing seeds were raisins and berries without seeds which were yellow, oblong, and small were sultanas, while those without seeds but black or dark, round and very small were currants. They came to the conclusion that pasas could be classified as raisins or as sultanas, depending on whether they contained seeds.[43] Since Spain produced both pasas with seeds and without seeds, the Foreign Office notified the Colonial Office to advise the Newfoundland government to examine each consignment of pasas to determine in which category to place it and to allow the importation of the seedless pasas duty free.[44] Following another request from the Colonial Office, Governor Williams reported in November 1911 that the Newfoundland customs department had examined the Spanish pasas and had found them entirely different from Greek sultanas and currants.[45] Newfoundland did not allow any of the pasas to enter duty free, as can be seen from the customs records in the Sessional Papers of the Newfoundland House of Assembly. Since there are no records of further deliberations on this subject, it is probable that the Spanish Foreign Office did not consider the limited Newfoundland market of sufficient consequence to pursue the matter further.[46] On the other hand, the British government may have decided to ignore any further correspondence on this tedious topic. In any case, the outbreak of the war made the issue irrelevant.

The issue involving the French vineyards, the Greek currants and sultanas, and the Spanish pasas illustrates several things. First of all, one must appreciate the complexities of the international saltfish trade when one sees the extent to which disease in the French vineyards in the 1880s affected the sale of Newfoundland Labrador-cured saltfish after 1900. There were many difficulties involved in trying to change trade or tariff policies, and negotiations were long and drawn out. In addition, one is impressed by the British Foreign Office's successful effort to negotiate a change in the Greek tariff on saltfish, considering the limited benefits and the more important negotiations it was already pursuing on behalf of Newfoundland and other colonies. Finally, this is one of the most outstanding examples of a bilateral arrangement between Newfoundland and a saltfish market. (The fact that Newfoundland had very little leverage in negotiations with her fish markets has already been noted.) As an example of the various factors that affected the sale of Newfoundland's saltfish and the activity necessary to deal with them, the Greek-Newfoundland agreement is particularly important.

Meanwhile, the French were becoming competitors in the Greek markets as well. In the first half of the century France had supplied 10,000 to 20,000 cwts of saltfish annually to the Greek markets.[47] This amount declined and had become inconsequential by the 1880s. The trade recovered, however, by the late 1890s and in 1896 Wood reported from Patras: "The importation of French codfish in large quantities is a new feature in the codfish trade of this Consular district, and is causing great uneasiness to the importers of Labrador and Newfoundland fish, which used formerly to have the monopoly."[48] Imports from France rose to over 37,000 cwts in 1897, declined by over fifty percent during the following decade, and recovered to about 45,000 cwts annually during the years before the war.[49]

The reasons for the increase in sales of Newfoundland saltfish in Greece, especially in the Morea area, have been intimated but not clearly stated. The increase in currant exportation beginning in the 1880s brought prosperity to the region and thus enabled the peasants to make more purchases. In addition, the reduction in the grain and livestock yield increased the need for imported food. Also, as pointed out above, the depletion of the Greek fishery was probably another factor. At first, the tariff rate on saltfish imports may have posed something of a problem for suppliers of that product. In 1885 it was fixed at 4s. 9.5d. per cwt,[50] not high compared to the rates in Spain and Portugal, but given the longer voyage and compared to Italy, it was high. In 1893 the tariff was increased to about 6s. (approximately fifty percent of the value of the product).[51] However, it was reduced to about 3s. 9d. per cwt in 1895.[52] As has been shown, this figure was reduced by fifty percent in 1905 and for the remainder of this period the tariff rate remained unchanged, encouraging the importation of saltfish. Finally, the rate of exchange of the drachma changed radically. In 1879 the rate was twenty-eight drachma twelve lepta per pound sterling[53] but by 1895 this had declined to forty-five drachma per pound sterling.[54] It began to strengthen in 1896 due, at least partly, to the "sudden growth of remittances from Greek emigrants in America"[55] and reached twenty-five drachma, or par, in 1910.[56] This increased strength in the drachma benefitted Greek importers and consumers, for wages remained steady,[57] although the price of basic foods declined only fifteen percent during the seven-year period ending in 1909 while the c.i.f. price of all foreign imports declined by about thirty percent during the same period.[58] Finally, one must take into consideration the problems that Newfoundland saltfish was experiencing, for various reasons, in the other markets during the early 1890s, especially those in Italy. All of these factors encouraged the exportation of the colony's product to Greece.

Summary

The Greek markets were unusual in that they were new or modern markets for the three-hundred-year-old Newfoundland fishery. During the 1890s they became almost as important to Newfoundland as the Italian markets, and for a while it looked as if they would go on to become the major markets for Labrador-cured saltfish and replace the Italian markets in this trade. This did not happen, most probably because Patras and the other Greek markets did not command the level of consumption that the larger ports of Italy did. Nevertheless, Greece remained a significant buyer of Newfoundland's Labrador-cured saltfish; during the year ending 30 June 1913 it purchased, in all, 60,527 cwts from the colony and Governor Davidson reported that this market was "steady."[59]

The study of the Greek markets involves not only an examination of the quantity and quality of the saltfish imported and the factors governing this importation, it is also a micro-study of the international saltfish trade during this period. The study of these markets provides an opportunity to acquire a more complete appreciation of the factors involved in the arrangement of bilateral trade agreements. Furthermore, it demonstrates the British Foreign Office's professional approach to Newfoundland's problems. Therefore, while the Greek markets, per se, were at best of only limited importance to Newfoundland, and for much of the period of no importance, the study of these markets is of considerable interest to the Newfoundland historian.

CHAPTER 8

Brazilian Markets

Background

One of the most striking developments in the marketing of Newfoundland saltfish took place after 1808 when the product found new outlets in Brazil. The Brazilian markets had always been supplied with manufactured goods and various other commodities by the Portuguese mother country in return for dye woods, precious metals, sugar, and other local products, following the classical European colonial practice of the period. In 1807, however, Napoleon decided to coerce Portugal into enforcing his continental blockade of British goods, and when General Junot led his army into Lisbon, the British navy evacuated King John VI and his government from the city. The king established his court in Rio de Janeiro in 1808. As a result, the mercantilist policies governing Brazilian trade and commerce were no longer appropriate, since the colony was now the seat of government and the mother country was occupied by enemy forces (although the latter condition did not continue to be the case for long). Therefore the king lifted the restrictions on Brazilian industry and opened the colony's ports to foreign trade. Naturally, this was a great boost to British trade and a severe blow to that of Portugal. Even before the end of 1808 there were about 100 British merchants residing in Rio de Janeiro alone.[1] Burns has written that after 1808 "Great Britain rapidly and completely replaced the mother country in commerce...."[2] This situation was officially recognized in 1810 when a commercial treaty was signed between the Portuguese government in Rio de Janeiro and Great Britain, setting the maximum tariff on imports of British goods at fifteen percent ad valorem. Portuguese goods were required to pay a minimum of sixteen percent. It was reported by the Swedish minister in the Brazilian capital that the treaty made Brazil a colony of Great Britain.[3] The treaty was renewed after Brazil acquired its independence and remained in effect until 1844. In that year, the rate on British goods was raised to the general level of thirty percent and Brazil would not agree to any new commercial treaties.[4] The import tariffs underwent certain modifications during the remainder of the period until 1914, but Great Britain remained the dominant trading partner until the last quarter of the nineteenth century when the United States became the major customer for Brazil's exports of coffee and rubber. It was within this context that Newfoundland's saltfish was sold in certain Brazilian ports.

The history of Brazil during the period from 1814 to 1914 is part of the history of the New World with, naturally, its own unique developments. Brazil produced colonial products; it suffered from internal local independence movements; frontier expansion and settlement were encouraged; and the country had border disputes with its neighbours. On the other hand, it acquired its independence quickly and with a minimum of force; it had a constitutional monarchical government until 1889; slavery was legal until 1888; and, unlike its Spanish-speaking neighbours, it was able to remain united. Finally, it was the only new Latin American nation to provide major markets for Newfoundland's saltfish.

The study of the Brazilian saltfish markets, like that of the other major markets, has its own individual peculiarities. The study of these markets is the only one that allows the historian to use freely Newfoundland's export statistics. While a cargo of saltfish that cleared from Newfoundland for a specific European country could eventually be sold in another country, such was not the case with Brazil. Ships that cleared from Newfoundland for Brazilian ports did not have the option of proceeding to another country and, consequently, the cargoes were always sold in Brazil. Therefore, the statistical evidence concerning the amount of saltfish exported from Newfoundland to Brazil is highly reliable although, unfortunately, it was not systematically recorded between 1833 and 1857. Nevertheless, there is a sufficient amount of this evidence to facilitate the study of these markets.

1814-1850

The opening of the Brazilian ports to foreign trade in 1808 had very little immediate effect on the Newfoundland saltfish industry. In 1810, the first year in which statistics on these markets were recorded, the Newfoundland governor reported that 6,710 cwts of saltfish had been exported to Brazil.[5] According to the records, 2,600 cwts were sent there in 1812 and 2,049 cwts in 1814.[6] There were no further reports of Newfoundland saltfish exports to Brazil until 1819. It is not difficult to understand how booming fish markets in Europe, which also fitted into an established trading pattern, would make the Brazilian ports appear rather unattractive to Newfoundland exporters.

Understandably, the difficulties created by the virtual collapse of the Spanish markets had their implications for the Brazilian-Newfoundland trade because the colony suddenly needed new markets. During the period from 1819 to 1833 a fairly substantial trade developed between Newfoundland and the Brazilian markets (see Table 8.A,[7] below), especially after Portugal recognized the independence of its former colony in 1825. The preferential treaty that had been signed in Rio de Janeiro in 1810 was then renewed and British goods continued to receive advantageous treatment under the same import tariff of fifteen percent ad valorem. From these modest beginnings, a very important trade was to develop.

TABLE 8.A

**Newfoundland's Saltfish Exports
to Brazil: 1819-1833**
(cwts)

Year	Cwts	Year	Cwts	Year	Cwts
1819	13,067	1824	39,703	1829	84,713
1820	7,723	1825	64,025	1830	54,650
1821	14,817	1826	49,665	1831	40,387
1822	13,681	1827	34,088	1832	32,078
1823	16,201	1828	63,569	1833	47,407

The sale of Newfoundland saltfish to Brazil was confined to two markets, Pernambuco and Bahia — both on the northeast coast, and both well established, prosperous provinces. Newfoundland was not their only supplier during these early years, as each market purchased some fish from Halifax and a little from elsewhere (see Table 8.B[8] and 8.C,[9] below), but by mid-century both markets had become almost entirely dependent on the Newfoundland product. (As well, some fish from Gaspé was exported to Rio de Janeiro.)

These Brazilian markets quickly became consumers of codfish. In 1829, for example, a total of fifty-one cargoes of saltfish entered these markets (see Table 8.D,[10] below): twenty-nine from Newfoundland and twenty-two from elsewhere. In that year, 84,713 cwts of saltfish were exported from Newfoundland directly to Brazil. Therefore, one can calculate that another 60,000 cwts were carried in ships from elsewhere; thus total consumption was over 140,000 cwts in the area. The figures for 1829 are unusually high, both the total number of cargoes and the amount exported from Newfoundland; also, imports declined during the early 1830s. Yet in 1833, a year for which there is fairly complete information and one which was quite successful for this trade during the

TABLE 8.B

Pernambuco's Saltfish Imports: 1825-1843

Year	Ships	From Newfoundland Tonnage	Value of Cargo	Ships from Elsewhere
			£	
1825	20	3,697	-	10
1826	14	2,486	-	4
1827	12	1,933	-	4
1828	20	3,617	-	13
1829	20	3,550	-	7
1830	15	2,445	-	3
1931	14	2,361	-	3
1833	14	2,325	-	5
1835	8	1,352	11,974	5
1836	20	3,319	38,192	7
1837	20	3,551	42,126	13
1838	18	3,094	36,369	6
1839	15	2,881	33,993	6
1843	18	3,495	39,931	3

TABLE 8.C

Bahia's Saltfish Imports: 1825-1850

Year	From Newfoundland Ships	Tonnage	Ships from Elsewhere
1825	6	1,021	5
1826	10	1,878	6
1828	13	2,130	4
1829	9	1,473	15
1831	7	1,187	8
1832	7	1,294	7
1833	9	1,525	12
1834	8	1,366	8
1836	13	2,414	9
1839	14	2,538	4
1847	15	2,945	4
1848	10	1,929	4
1849	10	1,998	1
1850	18	3,465	2

period, a total of forty ships entered this port — twenty-three from Newfoundland carrying 47,000 cwts and seventeen from elsewhere carrying a possible 35,000 cwts for a total estimated importation of over 80,000 cwts, a substantial amount. However, by 1850 (see Table 8.C) Newfoundland's share of the Bahia market had probably increased (and later developments indicate that the same thing was most probably true for Pernambuco). In the meantime, the importation of saltfish into Pernambuco and Bahia remained fairly high throughout the 1840s (see Tables 8.E,[11] 8.F[12] and 8.G,[13] below). With some exceptions, by the 1850s Newfoundland was the sole supplier of these markets.

TABLE 8.D

**British North American Saltfish Shipments
to Pernambuco and Bahia: 1825-1839**

Year	From Newfoundland	From Elsewhere	Total
1825	26	15	41
1826	24	10	34
1828	33	17	50
1829	29	22	51
1831	21	11	32
1833	23	17	40
1836	33	16	49
1839	29	10	39

TABLE 8.E

Bahia's Saltfish Imports: 1842-1850
(value)

Year	From British Sources	Grand Total
	£	£
1842	29,409.12. 9	33,223.16. 9
1843	20,660. 2.10	21,190.19. 6
1844	21,599.11. 9	23,688. 7.10
1845	29,740.17. 2	30,494. 8. 6
1846	28,887.15. 0	33,022. 0. 0
1847	36,801. 7. 6	37,238. 5.11
1848	34,663. 9. 2	35,124. 7. 8
1849	25,515.12.11	32,233.16. 4
1850	16,905.19. 4	32,493.11. 2

TABLE 8.F

**Pernambuco's Saltfish Imports
from British Sources: 1841-1846**
(cwts)

Year	Cwts
1841	62,961
1842	52,546
1843	49,634
1844	59,513
1845	67,739
1846	59,675

TABLE 8.G

**Pernambuco's Saltfish Imports
from British Sources: 1844-1859**
(value — each year ending 30 June)

Year	Value
	£
1844	73,812.13. 1
1845	64,150.17. 1
1846	69,212. 5. 6
1847	77,267.18.11
1848	74,529. 5.10
1851	97,131. 7. 0
1859	253,117. 0. 0

The reasons for the growth of saltfish markets in Pernambuco and Bahia during the first half of the century have been intimated already. As pointed out, Lisbon lost its monopoly over Brazilian imports, and imports of British goods were given preferential tariff treatment set at fifteen percent ad valorem until 1844, when the commercial treaty between Great Britain and Brazil expired and all imports were to pay the general but not immoderate tariff of thirty percent. Plentiful supplies of saltfish were available from British North America, especially Newfoundland, after 1814, and these supplies received the preferential treatment applied to all British goods. By the time this special treatment had been eliminated in 1844, the United States saltfish exporters (who had been considered the most dangerous potential competitors) were leaving the trade. The British consul in Bahia wrote in 1834 that some fish came from the United States but the quality was "very inferior and not liked."[14] A few years later, one of his successors wrote that the codfish all came from Halifax and St. John's.[15] In addition, the American consuls in Pernambuco reported that all the saltfish imports came from the British colonies during this period.[16] Furthermore, the Norwegian industry had not reached the point where this trade was viable. Finally, these two Brazilian markets demanded a very dry, small fish (ten to eighteen inches long) and with Newfoundland's large production, this specific requirement could be met.[17] These markets were not interested in the larger (and sometimes moister) saltfish demanded by the European markets and this gave Newfoundland exporters more flexibility. It was fortunate for this British colony that Brazil needed, and Newfoundland could supply, saltfish of a special quality.

These Brazilian markets purchased this special quality fish at good prices but demanded a distinctive type of packaging. The fish was packed in wooden barrels or "drums" and "half-drums" which were lined at the top and bottom with tree rinds.[18] Apparently, the drums and half-drums were used to facilitate local distribution, which was generally performed by pack mules. Thus the product and its packaging differed significantly from the loose bulk shipments to Europe.

This small dried fish seems to have received its greatest competition (ignoring other fish imports for the moment) from the dried or *jerked* beef that was produced in the interior and south of Brazil and imported from Argentina and Uruguay. In 1831, for example, the British consul in Bahia reported that "the reduced importations of the season of 1830 are attributable to the glut of jerked beef from Rio Grande do Sul and Buenos Ayres."[19] However, saltfish had the advantage of the Lenten regulations of Roman Catholic Brazil, as Parkinson reported in 1834: "Codfish is of extended sale during the months of January to April or about Lent, the Consumption being during these three Months about 5000 Drums per month, during the remainder of the year 1500 drums per month is a sufficient supply."[20] Nevertheless, in 1830 the consul reported from Pernambuco that "The reduction in this branch of Commerce [the saltfish trade] arises from the free Importation of Jerked Beef from the Southern Brazilian Ports, which were comparatively closed during the war between the governments of Brazil and Buenos Ayres."[21] In 1843 Pernambuco imported jerked beef valued at a total of £38,000, while the total value of saltfish imports was £37,000.[22] In 1844 Bahia's imports of jerked beef were worth £10,000, while the imports of saltfish were valued at £24,000.[23] The degree of competition varied from year to year but a demand for some variation in their diet by even the poorest consumers, plus the Lenten regulations, probably guaranteed that both producers found a ready sale in these markets.

Therefore, by the 1850s Newfoundland saltfish had become an important article of importation in two South American markets, Pernambuco and Bahia, and through these two provinces was being consumed throughout northeast Brazil. Moreover, Brazil's economy was still a colonial one, with a strong emphasis on the exportation of cotton and sugar (and, later, coffee and rubber) and this orientation compelled the Brazilian government to encourage the production of their staple exports at the cost of self-sufficiency in food (among other things).

It was probably this emphasis on the exportation of their basic staples which encouraged the Brazilian authorities to help keep food and production costs as low as possible by establishing low import tariffs. The import tariff on saltfish was increased to thirty percent ad valorem in 1844, which meant a charge of between 5s. 5d. and 5s. 11d. per cwt in 1846[24] and an average of 5s. 10d. in 1848.[25] Only once did the St. John's exporters complain about the Brazilian tariff or, indeed, about any problems in these markets, and on that occasion the Chamber of Commerce sent a petition to the governor (to be forwarded to the Colonial Office) criticizing the high import tariff in Spain, Portugal and Brazil.[26] This does not appear to have been a very serious indictment of the Brazilian markets. Furthermore, an even better trading climate was soon to develop.

As indicated earlier, Brazil began to experience major changes in the 1850s — changes which involved an expansion in its economy, a war and a revolution. Combined with these events there was competition from jerked beef producers and, later, competition from other saltfish producers. All these factors affected the importation of Newfoundland saltfish, but Pernambuco and Bahia continued to play a prominent role in the colony's trade.

1850-1914

Beginning in the 1850s there was a rapid expansion in the importation of Newfoundland saltfish into Brazil. Although systematic statistical evidence is missing for the period immediately prior to 1857, it is apparent that there had been a swift and significant increase in this trade. It was reported by the British consul in Bahia that the imports of Newfoundland saltfish into that province had increased from nearly 77,000 cwts in 1855 to over 153,000 cwts in 1858.[27] Similarly, the British consul in Pernambuco reported in 1863 that saltfish imports from British North America had increased steadily from 117,000 cwts in 1853-1854 to over 283,000 cwts in 1858-1859.[28] However, from a peak of over 394,000 cwts (almost forty percent of Newfoundland's total sales) in 1858 Brazil bought a steadily declining quantity of Newfoundland's saltfish until only 98,000 cwts were imported in 1868 (see Table 8.H,[29] below). The trade recovered again, reaching a peak of nearly 327,000 cwts in 1874. This was followed by another smaller decline but in 1881 exports again peaked at over 471,000. The trade continued to fluctuate and the amount declined to just over 218,000 cwts in 1890. This was followed by another recovery to over 450,000 cwts at the beginning of the century but exports had dropped again by 1905 to about 237,000 cwts. After this exports rose almost steadily to over 462,000 cwts in 1914. The magnitude of the Newfoundland-Brazilian saltfish trade can be better appreciated when it is seen that Brazil, which bought five to six percent of Newfoundland's saltfish in the 1830s, was purchasing over thirty percent by 1911-1914.

TABLE 8.H

**Newfoundland's Saltfish Exports
to Brazil: 1857-1914**
(cwts)

Year	Cwts	Year	Cwts	Year	Cwts
		1876	228,470	1896	338,193
1857	368,205	1877	292,129	1897	321,910
1858	394,092	1878	268,455	1898	402,724
1859	358,568	1879	362,429	1899	464,531
1860	268,937	1880	395,044	1900	458,240
1861	232,219	1881	471,244	1901	458,249
1862	203,400	1882	312,078	1902	367,398
1863	163,528	1883	295,094	1903	297,301
1864	154,528	1884	375,089	1904	315,112
1865	178,462	1885	259,818	1905	236,553
1866	149,749	1886	294,267	1906	301,487
1867	171,456	1887	315,150	1907	334,416
1868	98,426	1888	276,058	1908	341,203
1869	201,212	1889	262,501	1909	382,180
1870	249,425	1890	218,833	1910	395,143
1871	255,708	1891	250,663	1911	368,794
1872	246,292	1892	255,347	1912	423,980
1873	266,577	1893	352,160	1913	417,155
1874	326,969	1894	356,929	1914	462,233
1875	275,482	1895	342,692		

Although the general developments mentioned above governed the importation of Newfoundland's saltfish into Brazil, the colony's product remained restricted to its two traditional markets, Pernambuco and Bahia, especially the former. From the scattered pieces of information available, it is known that Bahia imported saltfish worth over £34,000 in 1872[30] and over £44,000 in 1874.[31] During these same two years, Pernambuco imported over 191,000 and 121,000 cwts, respectively.[32] Although further information is not readily available regarding Bahia's imports, a number of sources indicate that Pernambuco had become the principal Brazilian market for Newfoundland's product. In fact, in 1888 it was practically the only market because reports from there claim that fish from Newfoundland valued at £252,000 was imported while Newfoundland records show that total exports to Brazil amounted to fish worth approximately $1,324,000.[33] Pernambuco remained the principal market during the period up to 1914 (see Table 8.I,[34] below). With few exceptions this province bought over 200,000 cwts of Newfoundland saltfish annually and in one year, 1900, bought over 363,000 cwts, making it the best single market the colony had ever had since 1814.[35] The British vice consul wrote from Pernambuco in 1908:

TABLE 8.I

**Pernambuco's Imports of
Newfoundland Saltfish: 1891-1914**

Year	Cwts	Year	Cwts
1891	211,042	1906	193,542
1892	169,049	1907	187,363
1893	255,003	1908	206,920
1894	246,177	1909	200,000
1895	221,008	1910	200,000
1896	195,395	1911	200,000
1897	221,318	1912	
1898	285,944	1913	178,569
1899	282,318	1914	215,362
1900	363,714		
1901	302,503		
1902	196,371		
1903	-		
1904	207,555		
1905	200,086		

Dried codfish is very extensively used here; it is still almost exclusively imported from Newfoundland and is practically a monopoly in the hands of two firms. The imports for 1907 were 10,160 tons and for 1908, 10,346 tons. Special methods of packing are required for this market. Codfish for Pernambuco market is packed in drums and half drums. A drum equals 128 lbs. Fish should neither be very large or very small. A good average is, say 16 to 17 inches down to 9 to 10 inches. Fish must be bright yellow colour and thoroughly dried. Sweated fish is only a drug on the market. Pickled fish is liable to sweat after arriving in a warm climate. Great care should be taken in cleaning the fish so as to leave no blood clots, which, if left, cause rapid decay and consequent smell.[36]

Another British consul also felt obliged to comment upon this large trade. In 1909 he wrote:

> It seems strange that so far no really organized attempt has been made to take cultural advantage of the rich soil of this wonderful country: cereals and food supplies are imported which would well and profitably be grown in the country, and provided that the labour supply was sufficient, grown on a large scale....
> The coast waters are very rich in excellent fish and with proper curing stores it should be possible successfully to compete with the importation of codfish. Codfish is imported each year to the extent of some 10,000 tons from St. John's, Newfoundland; ...The fish is packed tightly in drums and half-drums of 128 and 64 lbs. weight respectively, and arrive in sailing ships, an average cargo being equal to 4,000 large drums. As half-drums are preferred by the local dealers, as more saleable, they form a considerable part of each cargo....[37]

Despite fluctuations, the province of Pernambuco was unequalled in its importance to Newfoundland's saltfish trade.

Although the Pernambuco port of Recife was the entrepôt for saltfish imports into the surrounding provinces, it is clear that Maceió, the major port of the neighbouring province of Alagoas, also imported some fish directly, especially during this period. Earlier references to the trade through Maceió are missing or do not include saltfish, but it was reported in 1885 that this city had imported a quantity of this product valued at £12,385.[38] The problem, however, is that there is no way of telling, at present, whether this fish was imported by coasting vessels from Pernambuco or directly from overseas. This writer is inclined to believe that the former was the case. Furthermore, because the consular district of Pernambuco included Maceió, it is not clear to what extent statistics concerning the latter were combined as part of the general report. Nevertheless, it is conclusive that by 1895 Maceió was carrying on a direct trade with overseas suppliers. In that year the vice consul wrote: "Formerly a large trade in imports was done with the states of Pernambuco and Bahia, but of late years...shopkeepers (who do all their own importing) have been getting their goods direct from abroad."[39] During the next few years, there were reports of British sailing ships that entered Maceió with cargoes but no further information was given, although these ships probably carried Newfoundland saltfish. Eight of these ships entered in 1896[40] and twelve in 1897.[41] These short reports dealing with Maceió provided no other details and during the next few years, even this type of information was not given. However, in the final years of this period, when Newfoundland's exports of saltfish to Brazil were reaching their peak, the number of British sailing ships that entered Maceió with cargoes of Newfoundland saltfish were recorded and during the four-year period ending in 1914, an average of thirteen ships totalling an average of 2,668 tons entered this port annually.[42] Maceió's imports of Newfoundland saltfish had become fairly important by this time.

As already indicated, Bahia's importance as a Newfoundland saltfish market was considerably less than that of Pernambuco during the 1870s. However, the later shipping records indicate that a considerable increase in this trade took place in the mid-1890s and continued, with fluctuations, into the twentieth century (see Table 8.J,[43] below). In 1900 the British consul reported on the Newfoundland saltfish trade with Bahia:

> The sea [along the Bahian coast] abounds in fish, many of which are excellent, resembling red mullet and mackerel in flavour, and there is game within easy distance of the town (snipe, pigeons, quail, etc). The fish market is most irregularly supplied with any other than salt codfish, of which there is ever an abundance.[44]

Later, in 1910, the British consul reported that "the number of small sailing vessels engaged in the dried codfish trade between Newfoundland and Bahia shows no diminution."[45] Both statistical and literary evidence

TABLE 8.J

Bahia's Imports of Newfoundland Saltfish in British Sailing Ships: 1890-1914

Year	Number of Cargoes	Total Tonnage	Year	Number of Cargoes	Total Tonnage
1890	13	2,553	1903	19	3,628
1891	16	3,182	1904	17	3,469
1892	13	2,608	1905	18	3,087
1893	19	3,928	1906	23	4,076
1894	21	4,342	1907	21	5,635
1895	23	4,728	1908	21	3,858
1896	18	3,472	1909	29	5,237
1897	25	4,720	1910	-	-
1898	37	6,705	1911	24	4,236
1899	-	-	1912	25	4,596
1900	29	5,094	1913	30	5,140
1901	27	4,721	1914	31	5,706
1902	25	5,526			

indicate that Bahia had become an important saltfish market by the end of this period and it seems that the growth in the Newfoundland-Brazilian saltfish trade occurred partly because of the expansion of Bahia's imports. By 1914 Bahia was importing yearly in excess of 100,000 cwts of Newfoundland's saltfish.

The sale of Newfoundland saltfish in Brazil was very closely related to the general economic developments of the importing nation. The degree of such dependence was probably greater in Brazil than in any other saltfish market (with the possible exception of the Caribbean).

The nature of Brazil's economy by mid-century has already been indicated. It had an export-oriented economy, largely dependent on cotton and sugar and heavily influenced commercially and economically by Great Britain. The country was inclined towards free trade so that the workers could be clothed and fed at minimum cost, and thus the cost of its export products could be kept down. The merchants who controlled the import and export trade had interests similar to those of the landholders. Therefore, although there was the modest increase in the import tariff in 1844, the free-trade philosophy remained as strong as ever. In 1853 Brazil reduced its import tariffs, citing extensively Adam Smith's *Wealth of Nations* and the views of twenty-eight contemporary English writers, including the most prominent free-trade thinkers.[46] The commission charged with revising the tariff law concluded that protective tariffs were "a denial...of justice, a denial of liberty, and a denial of the right of property."[47] Newfoundland saltfish imports were charged the low rate, about 2s. 4d. per cwt.[48] In 1858 this was reduced to between 10d. and 12d. per cwt,[49] in order "...to help large landowners to feed and cloth their slaves," according to one report.[50] It was certainly no coincidence that imports of Newfoundland saltfish increased during these years. Also, cotton and sugar exports from Brazil's northeast coast increased rapidly, almost entirely due to the growth in the British market.[51] Therefore, a demand for British goods, markets for Brazil's major exports, lack of competition, a free-trade climate, and very low tariffs, all combined to turn Brazil into a major market for Newfoundland saltfish during the 1850s.

After 1858 the Newfoundland-Brazilian trade began to falter for various reasons. Burns claims that the world financial crisis of 1857 severely affected Brazil.[52] In the meantime, the government faced financial problems because of the declining revenue from the lower import tariffs.[53] This was accompanied by drought and an agricultural failure. The British consul reported from Bahia that "never in the memory of man has this fine province of Bahia encountered a more disastrous financial, commercial, and agricultural crisis than the one we have just witnessed."[54] He pointed out that Bahia's trade had risen substantially in the earlier part of the decade, but had fallen off in 1859-1860.[55] In addition, a financial crisis in 1864 placed a severe strain upon the economy.[56] Also the Paraguayan War was very costly and the exchange rate of the empire's currency declined from about 25d. per milreis to a low of 15d.[57] This impeded the import trade. The government contracted large debts as a result of the war[58] and to help repay the loans, they raised the import tariff; the new tariff came into effect on 1 July 1869.[59] (The available records do not contain specific details of the new tariff, but its application to saltfish imports did not elicit any response from Newfoundland exporters. Therefore, this writer believes that the extra charge must have been moderate.)

Meanwhile, the relative importance of Brazil's northeast declined steadily as its sugar and cotton faced serious world-wide competition. In the south, the area around Rio de Janeiro prospered from the increased production of coffee and new railroads were built in the south to open up Sao Paulo to coffee production. Pernambuco and Bahia, however, stagnated and general alienation of the older landholding classes occurred.

Beginning in the 1880s a number of developments added to the instability of the country. The slaves were freed in 1888 and the emperor was overthrown in 1889. Although the latter incident was essentially a bloodless revolution and the royal family went into exile, civil disorders followed. It is sufficient to note that not until 1904 was peace finally restored when the last of the pro-monarchy forces were defeated and the republican government could make a real effort "To bury the dead, to bind up the wounds of the suffering, and to reconstruct the civil and political life of Brazil...."[60] Economic problems accompanied these political troubles and Pernambuco was hit by a depression in the mid-1880s. It was reported that in 1895 and 1896 this province suffered "agricultural and industrial disaster" after five years of relative prosperity.[61] But agricultural and industrial distress could work both ways. While the latter reduced the purchasing power of the consumers the former forced them to buy imported food. However, in 1900 drought in the neighbouring province of Ceará increased the demand for Newfoundland saltfish and thus raised the quantity imported to over 363,000 cwts, an amount thirty percent higher than that of the previous year.[62] Similarly, in 1901 Pernambuco imported over 300,000 cwts of the colony's saltfish and the acting British consul wrote: "Food stuffs have decreased as compared with 1900, still the value of the imports — codfish from Newfoundland, jerked beef from the Argentine Republic, and flour from the United States and Trieste — form the heaviest item in the year's figures."[63] Nevertheless, it was reported in 1902 that the imports of Newfoundland saltfish had declined by over thirty-five percent because of the continuing depression and the decline in the purchasing power of the people.[64] Likewise in Bahia, in 1899, a terrible drought caused the deaths of hundreds of people and greatly damaged the tobacco crop. "Immense numbers of cattle" were slaughtered or died from the results of the drought and the value of the total trade declined.[65] The scarcity of local cattle could help explain the greater number of shipments of Newfoundland saltfish imported during the 1900-1902 period. Then the exchange rate dropped steadily from an average of 27d. per milreis to a low of only 6d. in March 1898.[66] This "reduced the purchasing power of the native consumers."[67] In 1902 it was reported that "The consumption of both Canadian and Norwegian codfish tends to diminish in favour of cheaper foods owing to the diminished purchasing power of the people."[68] Nevertheless, this decline in purchasing power was partially offset by the benefits it brought the Brazilian exporters. For most of the country's problems the secretary of the British legation in Rio de Janeiro blamed the expense of railroad building, the inflation of the paper currency, the unfavourable balance of trade due to the remittances of sterling to Europe, speculation, the fall in the price of coffee, and poor financial and monetary policies.[69] Meanwhile the import tariff on saltfish had been established at 3s. 3d. per cwt in 1881[70] and was raised to 6s. 2d. in 1887.[71] This remained unchanged, in theory, for the remainder of this period, but, in its application, it became slightly more onerous during the late 1890s because the government requested that part of this tariff be paid in gold at artificially high exchange rates.[72] It was within this political and economic framework that the importation of saltfish proceeded during the 1890s. The situation would soon change, however, as political peace and economic growth and stability would become the hallmarks of the early twentieth century.

Beginning in the late 1850s competition from jerked beef became a major factor in the Newfoundland-Brazilian trade. In 1863 the British consul reported that the importation of jerked beef into Bahia had increased significantly from over 78,000 cwts in 1854 to over 294,000 cwts in 1863.[73] Similarly, in 1860, the American consul in Pernambuco reported that the price paid for saltfish was declining because of the importation of large stocks of jerked beef.[74] Newman, Hunt and Company, which exported saltfish regularly to Brazil, complained in 1870 about the competition from jerked beef imported from the Rio de la Plata.[75] During the following thirty-seven years that the company remained in the saltfish trade there were additional reports of competition from jerked beef and it was the only other competing product mentioned. Because of the lack of comparable records for other firms, these are the only business records that deal specifically with individual exporters' experiences with competition from jerked beef. There are scattered statistics available, but they indicate only the presence of jerked beef imports; they do not add anything to the discussion of its importance as a direct competitor of saltfish. One small set of figures shows that Bahia imported saltfish and jerked beef worth over £34,000 and £101,000, respectively, in 1872, and in 1874 imported over £44,000 worth of saltfish and £93,000 worth of jerked beef.[76] Similarly, there is a little statistical information available on Pernambuco's imports in 1876 and 1877-1878:[77]

| | Saltfish | | Jerked Beef | |
	Cwts	Price Per	Cwts	Price Per
1876	79,781	17/3	264,953	3/6
1877-78	274,762	11/-	108,494	£1.0.9

The prices recorded here present some problems which cannot be fully resolved, given the lack of additional evidence. If they are accurate, they indicate that a relatively small quantity of saltfish was imported in 1876 and that this fish fetched a relatively high price. This suggests that consumers purchased some saltfish despite the fact that it was much more expensive than jerked beef. Such purchases may have been made for religious reasons, but since it is not known how much jerked beef was available when the fish arrived, one cannot be sure. The low prices fetched by the jerked beef might have been due to dumping on the market or caused by a glut brought about by simultaneous shipments. In any case, certainly by the late 1870s jerked beef was a serious competitor in the saltfish markets of Brazil.

There is no doubt that jerked beef, which was a by-product of the leather industry, was apt to be dumped at sacrifice prices. A retired British sea captain wrote about his attempt to find work in the slaughterhouses of Montevideo:

> In these slaughter houses they in the killing season killed some thousands a day of cattle, both horses & horned cattle, for the sake of their hides, tallow & bones, and they were then [1863] really just learning to dry the beef, but before this the meat & bones were spread on a plain. The vultures and the sun would soon put the meat out of sight. The bones would then with the hides and tallow be shipped away on board some ship. I believe now [1883] nothing goes to waste; The beef is all cured now in some way or other.[78]

If jerked beef had to be sold at a loss in 1876, this would help explain the severe reduction in exports from the Rio de la Plata the following year and the consequent rise in price (which appears rather large). However, it is not known what other local factors were active. Of course, the figures for Newfoundland are much easier to explain. Given what is known about the lack of organized marketing by Newfoundland exporters, it is reasonable to assume that a comparatively high price for saltfish in 1876 would encourage exporters to send more fish the following year and thus create a glut and lower prices. All in all, the evidence from the 1830s already quoted, combined with that contained in the Newman, Hunt and Company papers, certainly indicates that jerked beef was sold in competition with Newfoundland saltfish.

The importance of jerked beef in Pernambuco grew as the century progressed and exceeded by a considerable amount the importation of Newfoundland saltfish (see Table 8.K,[79] below). The British consul reported in 1902 that the reason for the decline in the importation of Newfoundland saltfish was "...the low prices which prevailed for jerked beef."[80] However, importations of jerked beef had declined by 1907-1908 while saltfish imports were relatively unchanged. Nevertheless, the amount of jerked beef consumed remained substantial. In 1909 a report stated that:

> Jerked beef is imported into this city and district, chiefly from the Argentine and South Brazil, to the value of some £250,000 annually. Numerous districts are to be found within easy reach where cattle could be raised to supply fresh beef, but the liking for jerked beef seems to have fixed itself so strongly in the population that it would take some endeavour to alter it.[81]

Meanwhile, Pernambuco was producing jerked beef locally and this might have had an impact on imports of this product.

TABLE 8.K

Pernambuco's Imports of
Jerked Beef and Saltfish: 1899-1908
(value)

Year	Jerked Beef	Newfoundland Saltfish
	£	£
1899	798,074	284,082
1900	898,165	365,987
1901	657,100	330,865
1902	592,280	193,303
1907	253,967	294,605
1908	265,511	268,038

In Bahia the situation was similar. Despite the scattered information it is obvious that, at least by the latter years of this period, imports of jerked beef were substantial (see Table 8.L,[82] below).

TABLE 8.L

**Bahia's Imports of
Jerked Beef and Saltfish: 1908-1911**

Year	Cwts	Jerked Beef Value	Price Per Cwt	Cwts	Saltfish Value	Price Per Cwt
		£	£		£	£
1908	100,960	173,321	1.14. 4	115,640	186,702	1.12. 3
1909	96,560	163,713	1.13.11	120,360	163,714	1. 7. 2
1910	112,560	194,166	1.14. 6	135,000	222,750	1.13. 0
1911	123,820	216,685	1.15. 0	135,600	236,300	1.14.10

The importation of jerked beef into Brazil from the southern part of the continent remained a major factor (see Table 8.M,[83] below), although saltfish was certainly showing every indication that it was increasing in popularity while jerked beef imports were declining. However, jerked beef imports may have been replaced to some extent by Brazil's local product.

TABLE 8.M

**Brazil's Imports of
Saltfish and Jerked Beef: 1902-1912**
(cwts)

Year	Saltfish	Jerked Beef
1902	554,843	955,354
1903	491,654	938,819
1904	399,567	1,013,110
1905	474,902	1,023,130
1906	510,472	659,469
1907	518,189	682,520
1908	610,669	649,173
1909	658,898	691,102
1910	666,161	663,583
1911	674,035	524,626
1912	725,925	453,976

The explanations for the growth in the Newfoundland-Brazilian saltfish trade during this period are not too difficult to find. In the first place, as has been seen, the import tariff was generally low. Furthermore, there was an increase in immigration and over seventy-five percent of the immigrants came from Italy, Portugal and Spain, where saltfish had always been a staple food.[84] Between 1893 and 1913 over 1,500,000 people arrived from these three countries.[85] Schurz reports that "The Portuguese brought with them to Brazil an obsession for cod fish or bacalhau,"[86] while he quotes a nineteenth century account which states that "..whilst the river flowing before their door [on the Sao Francisco River] produces the best of fish, the townspeople eat the hard, dry bacalhau or codfish...from Newfoundland."[87] Similarly, in 1875 the British consul in Bahia submitted the translation of part of a report by the inspector of customs houses in Bahia, which contained the following commentary: "The coasts of Brazil are in general well supplied with fish, and if a perfected system of fishery and salting were established, fish, which as a rule is good, of various qualities, and abundant, might constitute a great branch of export; but on the contrary the country imports yearly for its consumption enormous quantities of dried codfish."[88] In 1881 the British consul in Pernambuco reported in a similar vein:

> The chief food of the inhabitants is farinha flour obtained from the root of the mandioca, saltfish imported from Newfoundland, and jerked beef from the River Plate and the south of the Empire....
> Salt or Dried Cod-fish comes from Newfoundland, and forms a very important article of food. The pack animals which come into the town with produce carry this and jerked beef back for the food of the natives.[89]

Finally, of course, one must remember that the northeast coast of Brazil became more important during the early years of this period. In 1864 the American consul in Pernambuco reported that the four most populous provinces in Brazil were Minas Gerais, Rio de Janeiro, Bahia, and Pernambuco, each containing over 1,000,000 inhabitants and together accounting for over one-half the total population of the twenty provinces of the empire.[90] Furthermore the traditional export orientation of the Brazilian economy remained evident to the end. Even as late as 1907 the American consul was dismayed by the absence of a market for American goods among the poorer classes in Pernambuco. He wrote: "The poorer classes along the coast, it is true, consume enormous quantities of dried cod from St. John's and jerked beef from the South but aside from these two items the limited well-to-do class makes up the whole market."[91] As Graham points out, the modernization of Brazil was still some way off even in 1914.[92] Finally, of course, Newfoundland had established trade connections with northeastern Brazil and this aided it in maintaining dominance over this market. Also, it is likely that the Newfoundland saltfish was better suited to the hot climate of Pernambuco and Bahia. This product consisted of small fish (usually less than fourteen inches long) which was extremely well dried. Governor Davidson wrote from Newfoundland in 1914:

> Newfoundland supplies the northern ports of Brazil, especially Bahia and Pernambuco, whereas the Gaspé fish is in demand in the southern ports of Brazil and in the Argentine. There is a sharp line of demarcation, said to be due to a difference in the methods of curing, the Newfoundland fish keeping best in the extreme heat.[93]

Therefore, entrepreneurial habits, consumer habits, Lenten regulations, low to moderate tariffs, free-trade and export-oriented governments, the general economic situation, and the quality of the Newfoundland product all encouraged Brazil to purchase the colony's fish.

While Newfoundland experienced no problems with saltfish competitors and no import tariff problems in Pernambuco and Bahia it did not participate very successfully in the growing saltfish market in Rio de Janeiro where two competitors became established. This region, which was close to the extensive supplies of jerked beef from Rio Grande do Sul, Uruguay, and Argentina, did not acquire the same early dependence on saltfish imports that characterized the northeast. However, the market expanded during the later years of the century, probably encouraged by the increased immigration, and in the 1890s Rio de Janeiro purchased about 140,000 cwts of saltfish annually.[94] Only a small portion came from Newfoundland while Canada and Norway supplied the bulk. Canada and Norway imported coffee from Brazil and it is very likely that this encouraged Brazil's importation of Canadian and Norwegian saltfish. Return cargoes of coffee also must have helped reduce shipping costs and it was reported that Norway was underselling Newfoundland in this market.[95] In any case this market expanded and the British consul general reported in 1906 that Brazil imported a total of 515,680 cwts of saltfish as follows:[96]

Newfoundland	307,040
Norway	97,500
Canada	85,840
United Kingdom	14,100
United States	8,180
France	3,020

With Newfoundland's product going to the northern markets most of the remaining 200,000 cwts was sold in Rio de Janeiro. In 1911 and 1912 it was calculated by the acting British consul general that Brazil imported forty-nine percent of its saltfish from Newfoundland, twenty-five percent from Norway, and twenty percent from Canada.[97] Since Newfoundland exported an average of 380,000 cwts to Brazil annually during these two years (and this was about half of the total amount imported by that nation), and since nearly all of the Newfoundland product went to Pernambuco and Bahia, one must conclude that a similar amount was purchased by Rio de Janeiro during these years, which made the capital one of the largest saltfish markets in the world. This is substantiated by the fact that Norwegian sources state that in 1912 and 1913 Brazil bought 17.63 percent and 19.25 percent of Norway's total exports of klippfisk, which would mean about 200,000 cwts annually,[98] with the remainder from Canada. Rio de Janeiro purchased probably less than 100,000 cwts of saltfish in 1892, increased its importation for a few years, and then experienced a decline to just over 100,000 cwts in 1899.[99] This was followed by a rapid increase, and the high level of trade held steady at about 200,000 cwts annually until the final years of this period, when the capital imported between 300,000 cwts and 400,000 cwts, or approximately half the republic's importation of saltfish.

During the period from 1850 to 1914 Newfoundland sold a tremendous amount of saltfish to Pernambuco and Bahia, especially to the former which, at times, became the colony's principal market. Although they were unable to take advantage of the growing market in Rio de Janeiro and had to deal with economic problems in Brazil and competition from jerked beef, Newfoundland's exporters on the whole were pleased with the train of events during this period. Their satisfaction was reflected in the absence of any complaints directed towards the market or the British Foreign Office.

Summary

The Newfoundland-Brazilian saltfish trade was a phenomena of the nineteenth century. Anglo-Newfoundland merchants pioneered this trade beginning in 1808 and as the fishery became increasingly *Newfoundland* oriented local merchants shipped some of their product to Brazil as well. This trade increased dramatically about mid-century and with the exception of the 1860s, the late 1880s, and early 1890s it remained very substantial. By 1914 over 400,000 cwts of Newfoundland's saltfish, more than one-third of the colony's total production, was sold in two Brazilian markets. Despite competition from jerked beef and some other local problems the Newfoundland-Brazilian saltfish trade was certainly the most progressively positive experience the colony enjoyed in the entire international saltfish trade during the period from 1814 to 1914.

CHAPTER 9

Caribbean Markets

Background

The Caribbean was the location of another major group of saltfish markets. Like Brazil, it was part of the New World but, unlike that country, it was composed of a large number of markets of varying size which generally purchased the cheapest varieties of saltfish. The principal markets in this region were the British West Indies, the Spanish West Indies and the French West Indies. There were some Dutch and Danish possessions as well (part of the former became British Guiana), and Haiti. The French West Indies were major markets for French saltfish; they were protected to some extent by import tariffs prior to the mid-1880s and very much so after this decade. Their role, in the context of this study, was minor. The Spanish West Indies,[1] although tightly governed by Madrid, were dependent on saltfish from all sources, but particularly from the United States of America and British North America. The significance of these West Indian islands varied throughout the century. The British West Indies (including British Guiana)[2] provided the markets which are of most interest to this study, for it was in these markets that Newfoundland sold substantial quantities of saltfish. The other colonial possessions (and Haiti) need no comment. The Caribbean was a conglomeration of saltfish markets united by similar climates, fairly similar economies, and a common demand for a well-preserved protein-rich food. Saltfish, including some from Newfoundland, played an important part in supplying this demand.

By the early years of the nineteenth century, the British West Indies included the old English colonies of Barbados, Jamaica and the Leeward Islands; the *ceded islands* (lost by France during the Seven Years' War) — Grenada, Dominica and St. Vincent; and the territories acquired during the French Revolutionary and Napoleonic Wars — St. Lucia, Trinidad, Berbice and Demerara (the latter two were united to form British Guiana). Jamaica, Barbados, Trinidad and British Guiana became the major saltfish markets within this group.

Since the beginning of European settlement, the British West Indies had been primarily dependent on the New England colonies for their supplies of saltfish. It was reported that during the three-year period ending in 1773, these islands imported saltfish as follows:[3]

From	Hogsheads
The Thirteen Colonies	51,344
Newfoundland	2,307
The Rest of British North America	449

After the American Revolutionary War, the new republic's place as saltfish supplier was challenged by the Newfoundland saltfish industry.[4] Indeed, the two-way trade that developed between Newfoundland and the British West Indies, as saltfish was sold and sugar, molasses and rum purchased, encouraged the growth of settlement in Newfoundland and thereby aided the island's transition from fishing station to colony. Nevertheless, the United States continued to supply a major part of the saltfish consumed in the British West Indies. For example, in 1805 Newfoundland exported 70,000 cwts to these markets while the remainder of British North America (chiefly Nova Scotia) supplied 115,000 cwts. At the same time the United States provided 175,000 cwts.[5] Within a few years the Americans were excluded from these markets and Newfoundland and Nova Scotia became the suppliers.

The Newfoundland-British West Indian saltfish trade was influenced by several factors. The British West Indies was the source of the sugar, molasses and rum consumed in Newfoundland, and it purchased the inferior qualities of saltfish. Furthermore, they were not expanding markets like those in Brazil. The British West Indian sugar cane suffered severe competition from other cane sugar during the first half of the century and its problems were exacerbated by the production of European beet sugar later in the century. Finally, Nova Scotia became the major supplier of these markets and, in fact, the British West Indies bought the largest share of that colony's production. Meanwhile, the foreign West Indies remained, for the most part, on the periphery of the Newfoundland trade.

British West Indies: 1814-1850

During the Napoleonic War, Newfoundland's saltfish exports to the British West Indies became quite large (see Table 9.A,[6] below). No doubt this was partly a response to the colony's rapidly growing population and the consequent increase in the demand for West Indian products. This is not to suggest that the trade to the British West Indies was determined by Newfoundland's needs alone. There were push and pull factors operating on both sides. Exports rose to over 150,000 cwts annually in 1810 and 1811, but declined sharply the following year, no doubt because of increasing demand in Europe, where the prices were very high. After

TABLE 9.A

**Newfoundland's Saltfish Exports to the
British West Indies: 1803-1833**
(cwts)

Year	Cwts	Year	Cwts
1803	64,248	1818	116,716
1804	41,590	1819	126,995
1805	81,488	1820	139,484
1806	100,936	1821	127,105
1807	103,418	1822	88,181
1808	115,677	1823	118,414
1809	133,359	1824	126,625
1810	151,869	1825	137,561
1811	152,184	1826	105,411
1812	91,864	1827	146,033
1813	119,354	1828	123,611
1814	97,249	1829	158,493
1815	159,233	1830	129,525
1816	176,603	1831	110,801
1817	150,827	1832	127,687
		1833	136,830

the war, the British West Indian trade recovered and in 1816, with serious market problems in Europe, Newfoundland sent over 176,000 cwts of saltfish south to these markets. Thereafter, this commerce stabilized at a lower level, and during the seventeen-year period from 1817 to 1833, the exportation of Newfoundland saltfish to the British West Indies averaged over 127,000 cwts annually. A comparison can be drawn between Newfoundland and Nova Scotia during part of this period: during the five-year period ending in 1833, the latter colony exported an annual average of just over 142,000 cwts to these markets, compared with over 132,000 cwts from Newfoundland during the same period. However, a portion of the Nova Scotian trade actually involved the re-exportation of Newfoundland saltfish, as will be discussed later. Newfoundland's saltfish exports to the British West Indies appear to have remained static during the 1830s and 1840s. Unfortunately, it is impossible to be precise about the actual quantity exported to the British West Indies during this period. Nevertheless, calculations based upon Colonial Office statistics indicate that between 145,000 cwts and 163,000 cwts of Newfoundland saltfish were exported to the British West Indies during the five-year period from 1836 to 1841 and between 153,000 and 172,000 cwts annually during the five-year period ending in 1855.[7] In any case, it can be seen that there was a general stagnation in the trade during this period, although some additional Newfoundland saltfish may have entered these markets via Nova Scotia and the United States.

Jamaica, Barbados, Trinidad, British Guiana and the lesser islands all bought Newfoundland saltfish during the first half of the nineteenth century. Between 1837 and 1850 Jamaica imported an average of 100,000 cwts annually but its peak years were 1842 and 1843 when 130,000 and 150,000 cwts were imported respectively.[8] Barbados imported about 34,000 cwts in 1841, 79,000 cwts in 1850, and 59,000 cwts in 1852.[9] During 1825-1839 Trinidad imported an average of £23,000 worth of saltfish annually. This declined a little to £21,000 annually during 1840-1850.[10] At 10s. per cwt this would mean 40,000 to 45,000 cwts. Meanwhile, British Guiana imported an average of 90,000 cwts annually.[11] All the saltfish imports mentioned were British North American in origin and amounted to between 250,000 and 300,000 cwts per year at least; they were shared between Newfoundland and Nova Scotia and accounted for almost all the fish going to the Caribbean from British North America.

Although there were many similarities each market had individual characteristics. Jamaica's imports of saltfish were accompanied by substantial imports of British herring: for example, in 1827 this market bought 53,816 cwts of saltfish from "the British Colonies" and 61,375 barrels of herring from Great Britain;[12] herring was a popular food in the other colonies as well. Barbados very early became an entrepôt for the Windward Islands and much of its saltfish importation was re-exported: almost one-half of the total of 60,000 to 70,000 cwts was imported annually. While British Guiana, Jamaica, and, to a lesser extent, Trinidad had agricultural land to spare and local provisions were an important part of their diets and economies, Barbados, as the smallest of the four, had no excess land and depended almost totally on imported food. There were other complexities in this trade as well. As already mentioned, Newfoundland exported some fish to these markets via Halifax. During the five-year period ending in 1833, an average of 56,862 cwts of Newfoundland saltfish was exported to Nova Scotia.[13] However, while both Nova Scotia and Newfoundland exported fish to these markets via the United States later in the century, it was not common to do so during the earlier period. Despite the complexities in this trade and the imprecise documentation available, it can be concluded that during the first half of the century, the trade was an important part of the Newfoundland economy and essential to the prosperity of the cod fishery.

Although the major purchasers of saltfish in the British West Indies were Jamaica, Trinidad, Barbados and British Guiana the product was consumed throughout the British West Indies. One of the reasons for its widespread importation was the comparatively moderate import tariff imposed on this article. The rate varied a little (see Table 9.B,[14] below), but it is known it was a favourable rate in 1851 and it changed very little throughout the century. (Table 9.B also gives one a better appreciation of the number of markets which were included in the British West Indies.) Among the important markets, the more self-sufficient Jamaica had the highest tariffs and the largest population while Barbados — small, densely populated, and having no land to spare from sugar cane production — charged the lowest rate. Furthermore, saltfish retailed more cheaply than other types of protein-rich foods.[15] Also, British North America enjoyed preferential import tariffs in the British West Indies during most of this period. The ending of these preferential arrangements during the free trade years of the 1840s and American reciprocity in the 1850s created new market conditions but did not affect the trade to any great extent.

TABLE 9.B

British West Indian
Saltfish Import Tariffs: 1851

Colony	Tariff	Import
Jamaica	2s. per cwt	dried fish
Trinidad	ls. per 100 pounds	dried fish
Barbados	4d. per cwt	dried fish
British Guiana	50 cents per cwt	dried fish
St. Vincent	1s. per cwt	dried or salted fish
Grenada	1s. per cwt	dried or salted fish
Tobago	1s. per cwt	dried or salted fish
St. Lucia	1s. per cwt	dry salt cod
Antigua	1s. per cwt	dried fish
Montserrat	1s. per 100 pounds	dried salted fish
St. Christopher	1s. ½d. per 100 pounds	pickled and dry fish
Nevis	1s. per cwt	dried fish
Virgin Islands	2s. per cwt	dried salted fish
Dominica	1s. 6d. per cwt	dried salted fish
Bahamas	5s. per cwt	dried or salted fish
Turks Island	5s. per cwt	dried or salted fish

British West Indies: 1850-1914

In the mid-1850s Newfoundland was engaged in a substantial trade in saltfish to the British West Indies, both directly and through Halifax (see Table 9.C,[16] below). However, it's saltfish was only part of the total trade of these markets. In the 1850s the total importation into the British

West Indies amounted to about 285,000 cwts annually[17] valued at about 11s. per cwt, according to market import records. Information regarding the later years is scarce but the total trade experienced some real growth, then stagnation and some decline towards the end of the period. The Newfoundland-British West Indian saltfish trade declined in the 1860s and 1870s, increased again in the late 1880s, and declined towards the end of the period.

TABLE 9.C

Newfoundland's Saltfish Exports to the British West Indies & Nova Scotia: 1856-1914

(cwts, five year averages)

Year	British West Indies	Nova Scotia	Total
1856-1860	112,063	54,391	166,454
1861-1865	92,092	24,498	116,590
1866-1870	91,278	14,763	106,041
1871-1875	87,960	29,032	116,992
1876-1880	69,267	17,063	86,330
1881-1885	84,103	23,259	107,272
1886-1890	96,373	24,723	121,096
1891-1895	86,643	87,222	173,865
1896-1900	97,927	63,345	161,272
1901-1905	83,048	64,383	147,431
1906-1910	82,638	120,733	203,371
1911-1914	77,510	97,782	175.292

Barbados's total importation remained stable at about 90,000 cwts annually until the 1890s, when it began to decline. By the end of the period the total had dropped to about 50,000 cwts.[18] Imports into this market were not distinguished by place of origin until the final years of this period. During 1905-1909 Barbados bought on average about 17,000 cwts from Nova Scotia and 9,000 cwts from Newfoundland. In 1910-1913 the figures were 21,000 from Nova Scotia and 22,000 from Newfoundland. Barbados was probably Newfoundland's best British West Indian customer for most of this period although statistical evidence is very scarce. One report, written in 1885, stated that Nova Scotian saltfish was disliked in that island and could not be sold.[19] Another report in 1887 stated that "Newfoundland supplies nearly all the codfish consumed; the 'hard cured' being preferred to the quality shipped from Nova Scotia."[20] However, Barbados's importation of the product declined.

If Barbados was buying most of its fish from Newfoundland, then from the statistics available the other British West Indies were purchasing comparatively little from this source. However, they continued to consume significant quantities of the product. Jamaica imported annually an average of about 98,000 cwts in the 1850s. There were considerable fluctuations in the trade during the remainder of the period and in 1910-1914 imports averaged about £140,000 in value annually. However, there seems no doubt that this market was dominated by Nova Scotia. The Canadian commercial agent in Kingston wrote in 1892:

> Fish stuffs — No remarks necessary on this class of goods. The shippers are fully aware of the requirements of this market. Halifax, N.S., having had the monopoly for years. Within the last two, however, Newfoundland has been endeavouring to secure a share, and will do so if shippers in Canada are not careful to send good quality stuffs and at reasonable cost, as now supplied by Newfoundland.[21]

It was further reported that in 1913 and 1914 saltfish imports from Newfoundland were worth about £6,000 and £10,000, respectively, which indicates that Newfoundland had not captured much of this market.[22] Trinidad's trade in saltfish was also substantial. In the 1850s it imported on average £26,000 worth annually and this rose to over £56,000 by the late 1870s. During the remainder of the period the value of the trade hovered around £60,000-£70,000 per year.[23] British Guiana, for which more figures are available, purchased about 65,000 cwts in 1859 and an annual average of 75,000 cwts in the 1860s. There was a rise to 84,000 in the 1870s, followed by fluctuations, and a decline to less than 45,000 cwts during 1905-1914.[24] In 1880 it bought over 58,000 cwts from Canada, and over 6,000 cwts from Newfoundland.[25] Again, in 1881 it was reported that Newfoundland supplied under 9,000 cwts while Canada supplied over 53,000 cwts.[26] Incidentally, Barbados exported to this market about 4,000 and 12,000 cwts of saltfish during 1880 and 1881 respectively; these shipments were, no doubt, originally from Newfoundland. Nevertheless, it seems that these three British Caribbean markets bought only minor amounts of Newfoundland saltfish for most of this period. However, since it is apparent that the colony's trade to Barbados declined during the final years of this period it must be concluded that Newfoundland's product was more widely sold throughout the British Caribbean during the early twentieth century.

Beginning in mid-century the overall market situation in the British West Indies changed and conditions became somewhat more difficult for the British North American saltfish suppliers. On the one hand, the latter lost their preferential position in these markets. Consequently, some fish from the United States was imported. Jamaica began importing American fish in the 1880s and during the 1890s this trade rose to be worth over

£30,000 annually. However, these imports declined considerably during the final years before the war.[27] Barbados was purchasing 10,000-15,000 cwts annually from this producer by the late 1880s and over 20,000 cwts annually in 1905-1909 but then this trade collapsed.[28] The pattern in Trinidad and British Guiana was similar. The United States thus became a minor but fairly constant factor in this trade. In addition to this problem the British North American saltfish exporters were confronted with the fact that the British market in the Caribbean was declining in importance in relation to the whole region. For example, in 1828 the British West Indies produced nearly one-half the world's sugar while in 1850 its share had dropped to about one-ninth (see Table 9.D,[29] below). During the same time total production had declined while competitors, including the Spanish West Indies, had increased production. The problems in the British West Indian economies during the last half of the century[30] in combination with some foreign competition created problems for the Newfoundland exporters.

TABLE 9.D

World Production of Sugar: 1828 and 1850

(cwts)

Source	1828	1850
British West Indies	4,210,000	2,590,000
Other British Producers	516,000	2,200,000
Cuba & Puerto Rico	1,300,000	5,920,000
Brazil	560,000	2,200,000
Louisiana	400,000	2,480,000
Other Foreign Producers	1,700,000	5,260,000
European Beet Sugar	140,000	3,800,000
Total	8,826,000	24,450,000

However, the British West Indies were always dependent on saltfish imports for cheap, easily-preserved, protein. Furthermore, the British West Indies included, in addition to the principal markets mentioned above, a considerable number of markets with export-oriented economies. Also, these markets continued to charge a moderate import tariff on saltfish. In 1890 the four principal markets charged as follows:[31]

Jamaica	3s. per 100 lbs.
Barbados	2.5d. per cwt
British Guiana	2s. 1d. per cwt
Trinidad	No Tariff

Although the tariffs were rising and Barbados soon began to charge 1s. 6d. per cwt while Jamaica added another 6d. to its rate[32] import tariffs were never considered, by the Newfoundland exporters, to be a hindrance to this trade. Nevertheless, towards the end of this period the general British West Indian saltfish trade stagnated and by the very end of the period it was in actual decline. In the 1870s, for example, Nova Scotia sold on average over 270,000 cwts annually in these markets. Although there was a gradual decline by 1911-1914 this trade still averaged over 180,000 cwts per annum.

These markets had their limitations, in the context of the Newfoundland saltfish trade, in that they purchased the cheapest product and thereby forced this colony to compete with the more cheaply-produced Nova Scotian deep-sea product. Furthermore, these markets had major economic problems. Still, they provided an important outlet for Newfoundland's "West India" fish, served as a place to dump surplus fish, and, at the same time, satisfied the colony's demand for sugar, molasses, and rum.

The Foreign West Indies: 1814-1914

The Foreign West Indian saltfish markets were of considerable importance during this century. The Spanish colonies and, to a lesser extent, the French colonies, dominated this trade while there was lesser activity in the Dutch and Danish possessions and Haiti. Although these markets were almost exclusively supplied by the United States and Nova Scotia by mid-century Newfoundland had acquired a fair-size market in the Spanish West Indies. In the latter 1850s the colony exported on average over 68,000 cwts annually to three markets.[33] However, there was a decline in the trade and in the late 1870s this amount had been reduced to less than 14,000 cwts annually. By the end of the century the trade was insignificant although some Newfoundland fish may have reached there through Nova Scotia.

Summary

For the most part, the West Indian markets played an important role in the development of the Newfoundland saltfish industry throughout this period. These markets, however, were almost entirely confined to the British West Indies. The British West Indies had their attractions for the colony's saltfish. They purchased the cheapest and poorest quality thus providing a useful outlet for that type of product. No doubt, in the early decades this was due to the desire of the planters to economize on the food they supplied the slaves. However, the abolition of slavery does not appear to have changed the trade, probably because of the general economic decline which the British West Indies began to experience. Newfoundland imported its sugar, molasses and rum from there which was a further encouragement for this trade. Moreover, the British West Indies served as a place to dump surplus fish, especially fish that was inferior according to European market standards. However, the nature of this trade and the stiff competition from Nova Scotia prevented the British West Indies from becoming a viable market for the good-quality shore-cured and Labrador-cured saltfish which was the colony's economic mainstay.

CHAPTER 10

Conclusion

Access to foreign markets had always been a deciding factor in the development of the Newfoundland cod fishery. When the fishery came under the control of the West Country merchants in the sixteenth century, markets were at first found in France, and soon these were replaced by permanent and substantial markets in Spain, Portugal and Italy. It became a well-defined trade: saltfish from Newfoundland to southern Europe; salt, wine, fruit and other products, plus specie to England; then fishing equipment and supplies, and dry provisions from the West Country and wet provisions from southern Ireland to Newfoundland. After the American Revolutionary War, a two-way trade in sugar products and saltfish was established directly between Newfoundland and the British Caribbean. In the nineteenth century, as has been shown, Brazil became a market of considerable importance and Greece also became a regular, though rather minor, customer.

Newfoundland's fishing industry in the nineteenth century faced the same basic market problem that had been faced by the sixteenth century West Country fishermen — the absence of a significant home market such as the French had always enjoyed or the Americans acquired in the nineteenth century. Furthermore, unlike their nineteenth century contemporaries, the Norwegians, whose more diverse economy cushioned some of the setbacks in the saltfish industry, Newfoundlanders were completely exposed to the forces of the market place and the very existence of their economy depended on developments in southern Europe, the Caribbean and, later, Brazil. During the period of almost continuous peace in the North Atlantic between 1814 and 1914, there were some changes in the processes of production, but the fundamental factor which had prompted the sixteenth century English to destroy the Spanish and Portuguese cod fisheries remained — the need for reliable foreign markets.

During the latter years of the Napoleonic War, when the Anglo-American War removed the remaining competitor in the saltfish markets, Newfoundland's position was enviable, with Spain purchasing, at record-high prices, fifty-five to sixty percent of the colony's European-quality product. The conditions, however, which allowed this situation to develop — low import tariffs and no competition — changed once the wars were over. The Spanish government immediately raised its national import tariff from 3s. 8d. per cwt to about 10s. 7d. per cwt. Local port duties were also increased to varying levels so that by 1817 a cwt of saltfish imported into Barcelona paid 36s., while one imported into Alicante paid 15s. 7d. Charges at the other ports were set between these two extremes. (Bilbao was a special case.) In addition, the Spanish economy had been weakened by the Peninsular War and the colonial wars and by the impending loss of its colonial resources. Spain was determined to limit imports and, at the same time, to collect as much revenue as possible from those necessities that were imported. This general discouragement, combined with Norway's re-entry into the saltfish trade, dampened Newfoundland's sales to Spain. With the aid of an expanding seal fishery and the expansion of the saltfish trade into other markets, the Newfoundland economy adjusted, and after the moderation of the import tariff following the First Carlist War, the colony's trade to Spain revived; instead of remaining the least important of the southern European markets, Spain became, briefly, the most important. In the latter 1870s Norwegian and French saltfish imports were given preferential tariff treatment by the Spanish government. This was, no doubt, partly responsible for the decline in Newfoundland's exports to Spain during this period. In 1886 preferential tariff treatment was extended to the colony's saltfish also, but by then the French saltfish industry, aided by government subsidies and improved technology, had become a major competitor. French competition in the 1880s and 1890s was joined by Icelandic competition in the early twentieth century. This development, combined with the well-established competition from the Norwegian fishery, which continued to dominate the northern Spanish markets, placed limitations on Newfoundland's share of Spain's saltfish imports until the reduction in competition from France during the first decade of the twentieth century. During this brief period, Spain once again replaced Portugal and Italy as the colony's chief European market.

After 1814 Portugal replaced Spain as Newfoundland's most important saltfish market and purchased nearly one-half of the colony's total exports to southern Europe until at least 1836. This was partly owing to the fact that Newfoundland's product enjoyed considerable preferential tariff treatment until the mid-1830s when all foreign saltfish imports were placed on the same level and a Portuguese deep-sea cod fishery was revived and given official encouragement. For a while, it seemed to the Newfoundland exporters that Portugal was about to replace gradually foreign imports of saltfish with the Portuguese product. This did not happen, however.

There is a major gap in the evidence during the middle decades of the century, but the absence of major complaints from Newfoundland is indirect, albeit inconclusive, evidence that the Portuguese markets remained important to the colony, although they probably surrendered first place to the Spanish markets at times. In the 1870s Portugal began to buy fairly large quantities of Norwegian klippfisk and this continued to be the case during the remainder of this period. A commercial agreement between Norway (Sweden) and Portugal in 1896 gave Norwegian klippfisk a price advantage in the Portuguese markets. The Norwegian fishery and Portugal's own fleet captured an ever-growing slice of the Portuguese markets during the latter years of this period. Oporto, however, remained the colony's single most important European market for shore-cured fish during the early years of the twentieth century, and Portugal continued to compete for first place with Spain and Italy as the colony's most important European market.

The Italian ports became important markets for Newfoundland saltfish after the defeat of France and, during these early years, it is very likely that much of the colony's product originally intended for Spanish ports was diverted into the Mediterranean, especially to Naples, Leghorn and Genoa. As has been seen, an average of about 172,000 cwts was imported yearly by the Italian ports during the period from 1816 to 1828, but these markets apparently became less important during the 1830s and the Genoese market appears to have been captured entirely by the French. It is impossible to ascertain the developments during the 1840s and 1850s, but by the 1860s Naples and Leghorn were importing annually over 100,000 cwts of saltfish each, while smaller amounts were being imported into Genoa and the Papal States. A decade later Italy's total importation of Newfoundland saltfish amounted to over 300,000 cwts annually, mostly of the Labrador-cured variety, and this country was, briefly, the colony's most important consumer of saltfish. However, the increase in exports of the French government-subsidized saltfish after the mid-1880s severely affected these markets and their imports from Newfoundland declined significantly. These markets regained much of their former importance to the colony's trade in the early years of the twentieth century, partly, no doubt, because of catch failures in the French fishery.

The Greek markets were of only minor importance in the international saltfish trade and were relatively late in acquiring any significance for the Newfoundland industry. When the area around the Gulf of Corinth switched from subsistence agriculture to the production of currants and grapes, a demand for saltfish was created and this was met by Newfoundland saltfish which was unable to find a market in Italy and Spain. Greece was the only market — and many felt it had considerable potential — where Newfoundland, with the support of the British Foreign Office, managed to negotiate a bilateral trade agreement offering a reduction in the import tariff on currants and sultanas in return for a reduction in the Greek import tariff on saltfish. However, the anticipated expansion of the Greek markets failed to materialize.

The Brazilian markets for Newfoundland saltfish became established in 1808 when British goods were granted the right of direct importation and preferential import tariff rates. The two markets which developed a preference for the colony's small, well-dried saltfish were the northeastern provinces of Pernambuco and Bahia and the neighbouring, smaller provinces that were supplied by them. These markets had a modest beginning in the saltfish trade, but in the 1850s northeastern Brazil began to expand its economy rapidly and Newfoundland saltfish became a major source of protein, with competition only from jerked beef. While the Canadians and Norwegians captured the Rio de Janeiro market, which acquired prominence later, and also exported fish to Argentina, Newfoundland continued to dominate Pernambuco and Bahia and the surrounding area. With the exception of a couple of depressed periods which occurred during the Paraguayan War and during the late 1880s and early 1890s, these markets remained extremely important, one could say vitally important, to the Newfoundland trade. While various reasons have been put forth for this development, it is obvious that the colony's gradual acquisition of these markets after 1808 allowed it time to perfect the product most suitable for this region and to establish firmly its reputation. Therefore, when demand accelerated during the economically prosperous 1850s, Newfoundland's product was already familiar and its trade connections organized so that the colony was in a perfect position to take advantage of the increased demand.[1] In any case, the Brazilian markets provided the one almost unbroken success story in the history of the Newfoundland saltfish trade during this period; by 1914 Brazil was the largest single consumer of Newfoundland saltfish.

The Caribbean was the area where Newfoundland had always sold its most inferior saltfish in exchange for sugar, molasses and rum. This continued to be the case during this period, with most of the colony's product going to the British West Indies and Britian Guiana, sometimes via Halifax and New York. These were not very profitable markets because their economies were troubled, fish prices were low, and competition from Nova Scotia was extensive. Therefore, the trade tended to depend on the colony's consumption of Caribbean produce, which was quite high. Although the colony was not adverse to dumping surplus European-quality saltfish in the Caribbean markets when necessary, these markets remained reasonably constant, given the factors already mentioned, and during most of this period Newfoundland seems to have enjoyed its closest West Indian trade links with Barbados.

The developments in each of Newfoundland's saltfish markets during the period from 1814 to 1914 have been analyzed on an individual basis. While the gaps in the evidence, both literary and quantitative, make it impossible to do a century-long comparative study of these markets, there is enough information available to present a complete illustration of this subject during the early years and the latter years of the period. For most of the middle years, one can make only tentative comparisons, but even these are useful.

During the period from 1814 to 1833, for which almost complete statistics are available, it can be seen that Europe's share of Newfoundland produce declined, especially in the 1830s (see Tables 10.A[2] and 10.B,[3] below). Also, sales to the British West Indies had increased by 1833 and

TABLE 10.A

**Newfoundland's Saltfish Exports
to Individual Markets: 1814-1833**

(cwts)

Year	Spain Portugal & Italy	British Europe	British West Indies	British America	United States	Brazil	Total
1814	768,010	55,791	97,249	24,712	0	2,049	947,811
1815	952,116	46,116	159,233	24,608	588	0	1,182,661
1816	770,693½	59,341½	176,603	37,443	2,545	0	1,046,626
1817	681,559	79,746	150,827	20,656	2,848	0	935,636
1818	560,632	57,258	116,716	0	0	0	751,818
1819	606,689	57,737	126,995	3,762	0	13,067	808,250
1820	626,644	81,014	139,484	19,741	0	7,723	874,606
1821	699,349	95,935	127,105	26,686	0	14,817	963,892
1822	726,400	73,931½	88,181	22,090	0	13,681	924,283½
1823	631,089	65,140	118,414	27,324	636	16,201	858,813
1824	723,438	65,592	126,625	28,221	104	39,703	963,683
1825	512,389	146,106	137,561	32,285	0	64,025	892,366
1826	687,200	93,739	105,410½	57,945	54	49,665	994,013½
1827	533,092	118,738	146,033	44,831	0	34,088	876,782
1828	586,155	112,696	123,611	48,201	0	63,569	934,232
1829	474,236	156,378	158,493	54,998	0	84,713	928,818
1830	560,620	125,449	129,525	35,875	0	54,650	906,119
1831	425,427	89,051	110,801	61,215	0	40,387	726,881
1832	426,673	62,359	127,687	58,585	0	32,078	707,382
1833	515,880	89,765	136,830	73,637	3,668	47,407	867,187

TABLE 10.B

Newfoundland's Saltfish Exports to Europe, the British West Indies and Brazil: 1814-1833

(cwts and percentages of total)

Year	Total	Europe		West Indies		Brazil	
		Amount	% of Total	Amount	% of Total	Amount	% of Total
1814	947,811	823,801	87	121,961	13	2,049	N/A
1815	1,182,661	998,232	84	216,591	21	N/A	N/A
1816	1,046,626	830,035	79	184,429	16	N/A	N/A
1817	935,636	761,305	81	174,331	19	N/A	N/A
1818	751,818	617,890	82	116,716	16	N/A	N/A
1819	808,250	664,426	82	130,757	16	13,067	2
1820	874,606	707,658	81	159,225	18	7,723	2
1821	963,892	795,284	83	153,791	16	14,817	1
1822	924,283½	800,331½	87	110,271	12	13,681	1
1823	858,813	696,229	81	146,374	17	16,201	2
1824	963,683	789,030	82	154,950	16	39,707	4
1825	892,363	658,495	74	169,846	19	64,025	7
1826	994,013½	780,939	79	163,409½	16	49,665	5
1827	876,782	651,830	74	190,864	22	34,088	4
1828	934,232	698,851	75	171,812	18	63,569	7
1829	928,818	630,614	68	213,491	23	84,713	9
1830	906,119	686,069	76	165,400	18	54,650	6
1831	726,881	514,478	71	172,016	24	40,387	6
1832	707,382	489,032	69	186,272	26	32,078	5
1833	867,187	605,645	70	214,135	25	47,407	5

Brazil was beginning to acquire some significance. Furthermore, as has been shown, Spain's share of the European markets was in decline, Portugal's held steady, and Italy, once the Napoleonic War was over, resumed its trade with Newfoundland. Since Newfoundland usually dumped in the British West Indies the saltfish that could not be sold in Europe, the higher proportion of exports that went to the Caribbean in 1831-1833 probably indicates that the market situation in Spain was even more unfavourable during these years than it had been during the 1820s, although no statistics are available for the Spanish markets during the 1830s. Among the push and pull factors in operation during these years, Spain and Italy occupied important positions. The high import tariffs imposed on saltfish by Spain and the successful inroads that were made in the northern and eastern Spanish markets by Norwegian klippfisk reduced the importation of the Newfoundland product. Meanwhile, the re-opening of the Italian markets to British trade created markets that had been closed during the wars to which the colony's saltfish could be sent. On the whole, several developments seem to have characterized this period: the decline of the Spanish markets; the recovery of the Italian markets; the stability of the Portuguese markets; the opening of new Brazilian markets; and the steady demand of the British West Indies, where surplus European-quality saltfish could be dumped if necessary.

As has been pointed out, the developments in the saltfish trade after 1833 are not systematically documented in either the statistical or literary sources. Nevertheless, it has been possible to deduce the general trends and to explain them, at least in part. Sales of Newfoundland saltfish to Spain increased generally during mid-century and declined again beginning in the 1870s. As far as the evidence indicates it seems that sales to Portugal remained steady, while sales to the Italian ports declined in the 1830s but had recovered by the 1860s and were quite substantial by the 1870s. Given the conditions in the British West Indies in particular, and the Caribbean in general, and given the statistical information available, it seems that this area continued to play the same role in the trade which had been established much earlier: it remained the market for inferior saltfish and the dumping ground for the surplus European-quality product. The markets in northeastern Brazil were the ones to show most change during this period, and during the 1850s these markets were briefly the most important to the trade although, unfortunately, there is insufficient information to freely quantify this trend. In general it would seem that the more moderate duties in Spain and the increasing demand in Brazil acted as the pull factors during the 1840s and 1850s, while the stagnation in the Newfoundland-Portugese trade, the decline in the quality of Newfoundland saltfish sold to the Italian markets, and the growth in the production of saltfish in Newfoundland in the 1850s were the push factors.

During the final decades of the nineteenth century major changes occurred in the international saltfish trade. Although exports of Newfoundland saltfish to Spain declined after 1876 when Norwegian and French saltfish were given preferential tariff treatment in that country the real crunch came in the 1880s. The expansion in total world exports of saltfish during this period, especially in French exports to Spain and Italy (see Table 10.C,[4] below), caused decreased demand and lower prices for Newfoundland fish — and probably for all saltfish. The bulge in the total amount of fish going to Spain and Italy, in the 1880s in particular, created problems in the Newfoundland trade.

TABLE 10.C

Saltfish Exports by Newfoundland, Norway, and France: 1876-1890

(cwts)

Year	Newfoundland	Norway	France	French Exports to Spain	French Exports to Italy
1876	1,068,471	650,319	68,287	3,102	37,042
1877	1,034,101	902,903	59,813	0	26,791
1878	1,035,013	806,274	75,535	3,276	34,115
1879	1,387,770	879,560	93,881	7,805	43,490
1880	1,383,531	1,042,506	122,922	15,700	41,569
1881	1,535,573	825,125	118,126	23,617	37,175
1882	1,391,102	789,726	97,407	31,419	32,092
1883	1,532,023	678,169	180,010	95,860	37,142
1884	1,397,637	741,412	226,901	131,601	47,571
1885	1,284,710	735,630	275,120	164,023	62,906
1886	1,344,180	875,762	355,700	199,155	84,292
1887	1,080,024	830,817	362,539	180,113	126,780
1888	1,175,720	842,817	314,674	150,524	91,212
1889	1,076,507	934,578	295,187	144,833	70,901
1890	1,040,916	1,093,976	261,623	123,579	71,521

At the same time, in order to make the purchase of their products more convenient, both the French and Norwegians made adjustments in shipping, packaging, and payment. They began to export their fish in small parcels or bales on a regular basis. Norwegian steamers of 300 or 400 tons called at "almost every port along the coast of the Mediterranean and Adriatic; and deliver[ed] 50 or 100 bales at each according to requirements; [and]...also at places where neither safe anchorage nor shelter are to be found."[5] In addition, this fish was packed in fifty kilogram bundles "...thus saving great expense in weighing."[6] Similarly, the French exported their fish in bales of sixty kilograms and "with three boats weekly from Marseilles [to markets], the French merchant is content to send two or three bales at a time — in other words, he is in a position to supply the smallest order."[7] Meanwhile, Newfoundland's exporters insisted on selling whole cargoes. Also, both Norwegian and French shippers gave buyers three months' credit and accepted local currency unlike Newfoundland shippers who demanded immediate payment in sterling drafts drawn on London banks.[8] Thus French and Norwegian shippers offered more convenient shipping and credit arrangements, which enhanced their popularity and thus increased their business.

Problems in the European and Brazilian markets continued and the only positive development was the opening of new markets in Greece which, however, did not live up to expectations. As already indicated, Newfoundland experienced a severe depression during the early 1890s and even the government was barely able to avoid defaulting on its loans. However, during the late 1890s Norwegian production declined, the Brazilian markets expanded, and Newfoundland began to recover from this depression by the turn of the century.

It is possible to get a clearer picture of the market developments during the last sixteen years of this period. From 1899 to 1914, there is a complete record of Newfoundland's exports of shore-cured and Labrador-cured saltfish by destination. While the records are not completely accurate because of Gibraltar's inclusion as a market, it is possible to determine the amount of the colony's saltfish production consumed in southern Europe as well as in Brazil and the Caribbean (see Tables 10.D,[9] 10.E[10] and 10.F,[11] below). The proportion of the colony's total saltfish production which was sold in southern Europe had declined significantly from the beginning of the century, while the proportion sold to Brazil had grown. Excluding 1831-1833, there was not much difference throughout

TABLE 10.D

**Newfoundland's Saltfish Exports
to Europe: 1899-1914**
(cwts)

Year	Portugal	Italy	Spain	Greece	Gibraltar	United Kingdom	Total
1899	211,991	38,726	24,793	N/A	220,951	81,057	577,518
1900	226,366	24,114	67,380	N/A	272,555	104,893	695,308
1901	276,647	6,500	84,112	N/A	181,625	95,559	644,443
1902	333,130	24,711	60,115	N/A	198,853	123,738	740,547
1903	388,225	52,892	92,700	800	240,351	107,079	882,047
1904	377,924	107,647	85,583	12,040	207,429	41,841	832,464
1905	322,287	111,447	111,700	3,632	215,507	40,737	805,310
1906	304,203	273,453	174,970	66,724	51,409	46,601	917,360
1907	307,960	265,782	203,587	34,908	0	51,382	863,619
1908	292,651	252,173	274,998	50,053	0	51,308	921,183
1909	256,080	380,762	280,311	65,202	0	58,548	1,040,903
1910	321,296	253,542	199,662	89,708	0	25,755	889,963
1911	258,523	132,153	174,711	42,715	0	10,968	619,070
1912	206,206	212,061	214,934	69,280	0	12,866	715,347
1913	203,899	207,617	248,266	60,527	0	21,167	741,476
1914	153,023	170,634	200,562	69,602	0	12,275	606,096

TABLE 10.E

Newfoundland's Saltfish Exports
to the West Indies: 1899-1914
(cwts)

Year	Canada	United States	British West Indies	French West Indies	Total
1899	46,039	24,926	103,489	9,800	184,254
1900	44,286	31,413	68,166	2,518	146,383
1901	21,921	37,594	67,425	1,941	128,881
1902	43,624	32,261	93,267	9,625	178,777
1903	87,480	34,115	112,861	12,734	247,190
1904	107,430	13,642	75,926	12,000	208,998
1905	61,459	9,072	65,763	12,063	148,357
1906	148,701	19,208	68,226	20,500	256,635
1907	110,407	19,962	70,479	15,417	216,265
1908	130,276	14,038	75,319	15,855	235,488
1909	128,344	24,732	105,282	40,798	299,156
1910	85,938	8,565	93,885	18,508	206,896
1911	77,159	16,234	78,719	13,434	185,546
1912	109,169	34,425	90,876	8,251	242,721
1913	125,088	29,315	73,323	14,356	242,082
1914	79,713	17,556	67,123	10,155	174,547

the century in the proportion sold in the Caribbean. In Europe, Portugal, Spain and Italy alternated for first place in the consumption of Newfoundland saltfish, with Spain becoming the most important of the three by 1914. At the same time, Portugal was importing large quantities of Norwegian klippfisk and in 1914 that country slipped behind both Italy and Spain in its importance to Newfoundland. In the meantime, the colony's most important markets were located in Brazil.

As indicated earlier, the exportation of Newfoundland's saltfish, when examined statistically, presents a picture of fluctuations around a rising trend during the period from 1814 to 1914. However, when one examines the per capita exportation, one sees a picture of fluctuations around a declining trend. At the same time, the fluctuations that did occur did not follow the same cyclical patterns. Thus the history of the Newfoundland-Spanish trade, with its early decline followed by growth, decline and, finally, growth, differed from that of the Newfoundland-Portuguese trade with its long history of stability followed by decline. Both of these trades, of course, differed from the Newfoundland-Italian trade where there was a picture of growth, decline, growth, decline and, finally, growth. Only

TABLE 10.F

Newfoundland's Saltfish Exports to Europe, the British West Indies, and Brazil: 1899-1914

(cwts and percentages of total)

Year	Total	Europe		West Indies		Brazil	
		Amount	% of Total	Amount	% of Total	Amount	% of Total
1899	1,226,303	577,518	47	184,254	15	464,531	38
1900	1,299,931	695,308	53	146,383	11	458,240	35
1901	1,233,101	644,443	52	128,881	10	458,249	37
1902	1,288,921	740,547	57	178,777	12	367,398	29
1903	1,429,246	882,047	62	247,190	17	297,301	21
1904	1,360,219	832,464	61	208,998	15	315,112	23
1905	1,196,774	805,310	67	148,357	12	236,553	20
1906	1,480,734	917,360	62	256,635	17	301,487	20
1907	1,422,129	863,619	61	216,265	15	334,416	24
1908	1,509,020	921,183	61	235,488	16	341,203	23
1909	1,732,172	1,040,903	60	299,156	17	382,180	22
1910	1,502,020	889,963	59	206,896	14	395,143	26
1911	1,182,480	619,070	52	185,546	16	368,794	31
1912	1,387,930	715,347	52	242,721	17	423,980	31
1913	1,408,501	741,476	53	242,082	17	417,155	30
1914	1,247,234	606,096	49	174,547	14	462,233	37

in the Newfoundland-Brazilian trade does one find the classic case of fluctuations around a rising trend to which economists such as Rau refer.[12]

The Newfoundland economy began to display weaknesses in the 1880s and 1890s which were eventually to lead to the colony's political bankruptcy in 1934, when self-government was surrendered in return for the assumption of the public debt by Great Britain. Despite a period of prosperity from 1900 to 1907, when the markets were favourable, there were, beginning in the 1880s, obvious signs that the Newfoundland saltfish trade was in trouble. As has been pointed out, the seal industry declined and the fleet of sailing ships which had prosecuted that fishery was replaced by a much smaller fleet of steamers based in St. John's. In 1894 a number of well-established firms went bankrupt, and the remainder were forced to curtail their businesses. At the same time, the St. John's firms — those which survived — consolidated their control over the trade by supplying small outport firms and traders. Ian McDonald, who studied the history of the Fishermen's Protective Union, writes of the period leading up to the formation of this union:

In the last quarter of the century...this [established] marketing pattern began to undergo radical alterations because of changes in the organization of the fishery, technological innovation, the bankruptcy of many old firms, and the gradual introduction of steam shipping. The general consequences were a decline in the standard of Newfoundland's salt fish and the creation of an inherently unstable system of exporting which perpetuated lower quality standards and artificially depressed the value of salt fish exports. The inability of Newfoundlanders to modify these trends does much to account for the Island's eventual bankruptcy in 1933.[13]

McDonald was concerned primarily with the conditions in Newfoundland that led to the growth of a fishermen's union and, consequently, not with the market developments during this pre-war period.[14] Nevertheless, while he emphasizes the decline in the cure, the growing practice of purchasing talqual, the competition between the St. John's steamers and the gluts it caused, and the general internal problems in the trade, he writes that "...the practices of Newfoundland fish marketing...now bordered on the chaotic."[15] Furthermore, he points out that the merchants "...made the bulk of their profits on the supplies they sold to the fishermen [and] there was a natural inclination among many of them to treat fish essentially as a form of currency, as merely a means of repayment, rather than as an export article of food which had to meet certain minimum standards and return a profit itself."[16] McDonald identifies other problems as well: he mentions foreign competition, exchange rate and currency problems, local speculators, the system of credit from the banks to the exporters to the small fish buyers to the fishermen,[17] and then makes the point about the lack of information about the markets which illustrates the need for the detailed research in this study.

Some contemporary writers have felt that the blame for the local problems of the Newfoundland saltfish industry must be shared by merchants and government alike. The Royal Commission appointed in 1933 to examine the colony's conditions wrote of the merchants:

Intent only on outdoing their local rivals in a scramble for immediate profits, they have failed to realise that time does not stand still. While the industry in Newfoundland, with its haphazard and hand-to-mouth methods and an entire lack of organisation, has stagnated, if indeed it has not declined, the industries of Norway and Iceland, Newfoundland's chief competitors in the saltfish markets, have been modernised, on a national and scientific basis....[18]

The positive role which the Fishermen's Protective Union hoped the Newfoundland government would play was indicated by the union's *Bonavista Platform*, which was announced at its annual general meeting in December 1912. S.J.R. Noel has summarized its recommendations on the fishery as follows:

(1) the introduction of a standardized cull of fish, to be administered in conjunction with a system of government inspection, under the control of a permanent commission...;

(2) the appointment of trade agents abroad;

(3) the publication of weekly reports on the price of fishery produce in foreign markets;

(4) the erection and maintenance of state-owned cold storage bait depots;

(5) the utilization of the government's cash reserve to assist the modernization of the fishery by the introduction of gasoline engines;

(6) the closing down of the whale factories, which were held to pollute inshore waters;

(7) the introduction of legislation to make fishing debts outstanding for more than two years uncollectable by process of law;

(8) the reorganization of the Fisheries Department to accommodate these innovations.[19]

While some of these recommendations were responses to local problems, the first three dealt specifically with market issues. Even by 1933 neither business, nor government, nor labour had come to grips with either the marketing or productions problems.

It is at this point that another question arises — why Newfoundland was able to do as well as it did in the production and marketing of its saltfish. The answer to this question can be found by looking at the nature of the Newfoundland economy and the variety of its saltfish.

As pointed out earlier, the colony's economy was most dependent on the production and sale of saltfish (although the seal fishery bore some of the economy's burden in the earlier decades of the nineteenth century, and the mines and pulp and paper industries were doing likewise by 1914). Nevertheless, with few exceptions (and ignoring seals, mining, and pulp and paper for the moment), saltfish production was only one part of a dual economy — exchange and subsistence.[20] Saltfish could be exchanged for goods which were unobtainable locally, while the fishermen and their families, under ideal conditions, provided themselves with many necessities from the land and sea. Various products of the sea were consumed fresh and/or preserved. Cod, caplin, salmon and herring were important sources of food, as was seal meat and, on occasion, meat from other marine mammals. Cattle, goats, sheep, fowl, and pigs were raised for food (and the sheep for wool, also), and usually foraged for themselves on the unoccupied, uncultivated crown lands on the outskirts of the villages during the spring, summer and autumn months. Horses were kept for hauling wood from the interior, for ploughing the vegetable plots in the spring, and for local transportation. Potatoes were grown extensively and cabbage, turnips, carrots, and parsnips were also cultivated to varying degrees. Wild berries and fruits were gathered for jams and wines, and caribou, hare, and an assortment of island birds and sea birds were hunted. The skins of seals and land animals were converted into leather for harnesses and boots. In addition, wood was available inland and the fishermen could cut, on crown land, timber for their boats, houses, sheds, wharves, stages, and other buildings as well as for oars, chests, furniture, carts, sleds, and fences. In addition, the houses were heated by firewood. (Only flour, ship's biscuit, cotton goods, twine, and salt for preserving the fish were necessities which had to be purchased. However, tea and molasses were also considered necessities.) Nevertheless, all of these local products were available only under ideal circumstances. Usually the resources of the small coastal villages were stretched to the limit. In some cases, people lived on rocky islands or on headlands which were near good fishing grounds but which had no other resources; fishermen often lived in such places in summer residences for the fishing season only; this was especially so on the coast of Labrador. In addition, Newfoundland fishermen migrated to jobs on the mainland of North America, especially to the Boston area, in order to find temporary employment during slow seasons. This feature of the Newfoundland economy has not been examined but there is no doubt that money remitted to the colony by these workers was considerable. In the year ending 30 June 1896, for example, twenty-seven complaints were registered with the Newfoundland Postal Department concerning the non-receipt in Newfoundland of unregistered letters containing money which were mailed from the United States.[21] The sums of money varied from $2 to $20 and in only three cases were money orders used. When one considers that most senders, no doubt, registered their letters and a further number of migratory workers saved their money and brought it home with them the amount of earnings accruing to Newfoundland could be considerable.[22] Thus in varying degrees, most fishermen were not totally dependent on the sale of saltfish for their livelihood.

In addition, as already intimated, much of Newfoundland's strength lay in the varied nature of its saltfish production. In the first place, Newfoundland produced a number of qualities of saltfish, partly, of course, because of the individualistic nature of the curing of its product. Varying quantities of salt were used and the fish was dried to various levels of moisture content. Combined with the different sizes of fish and the varying degrees of care and attention given to curing, the result was the exportation of a variety of grades which were in demand in the individual markets. The Amulree Commission recognized the strengths and weaknesses of Newfoundland's saltfish trade when it wrote in 1933:

> Had Norway and Iceland been producers of light-salted fish, of the same type as Newfoundland's shore fish, the industry in Newfoundland would many years ago have been compelled, in the interest of self-preservation, to organise itself on a competitive basis. But Norway and Iceland produce only heavy-salted fish, of the "Labrador style," and, while these have gradually ousted Labrador fish from the first place in the European markets taking heavy-salted fish, they have not so far interfered with the markets for Newfoundland's shore fish. Seeing that the Labrador fishery has been accustomed to produce annually about 320,000 quintals and supports a considerable proportion of the population, it could hardly have been supposed that the loss of first place in the markets would have been accepted by the Newfoundland exporters with indifference. Yet, instead of being alarmed at this development and exerting themselves to recover the lost ground, the exporters have been content to explain with pride that no country in the world can compete with Newfoundland's shore-fish, which is therefore in an impregnable position. The loss of the principal markets for Labrador fish, which has involved the selling of the fish to the poorer markets at low prices, is dismissed as a temporary phase of no great consequence so long as the markets for shore-fish are retained.[23]

Given the nature of the Newfoundland economy and the different kinds of saltfish it produced, the saltfish industry could not be eliminated by depression as long as there was any demand in the markets.[24] At the same time, given the common property nature of the resource, the laissez-faire system of production and marketing which prevailed, and the growth of foreign competition, it was impossible for Newfoundland to experience a long-term period of prosperity and growth — in fact, decline in the economy and the standard of living is evident throughout the century, but especially after 1880. Furthermore, as pointed out, the industry's history during that century is best described as fluctuations around a downward trend.

Thus the market played a significant role in the development of the colony's industry and, consequently, in the history of the colony itself. Newfoundland experienced a serious depression, partly because of the decline of the Spanish importation of the colony's saltfish after 1814, and probably only survived because of the opening of the Italian markets, the stability of the Portuguese markets, and the growth of a new industry — the seal fishery. The economy fluctuated during the century and nearly collapsed during the 1880s and 1890s. Setbacks in the French and Norwegian fisheries in the years immediately prior to the First World War brought some prosperity to the colony, but the intrinsic weaknesses in the trade remained very obvious.

The weaknesses in the Newfoundland economy had noticeable effects on the colony during the latter decades of the nineteenth century and these have already been indicated. Businesses declared bankruptcy, fishermen emigrated, and the government borrowed. Between 1831 and 1833 the public debt increased to a comparatively moderate $1.5 million; by 1914 it had reached $30 million.[25] Borrowing to cover operating and capital expenditures and neglecting to establish a sinking fund set the stage for the collapse of the economy and political bankruptcy in 1934. Leaving aside the fact that Newfoundland neglected to develop other industries one is forced to see the colony's problems in terms of the faltering saltfish trade.

The problems of Newfoundland's saltfish industry resulted from the nature of the fishery, with its relatively short season, and from the nature of the economy itself, with its exchange and subsistence components. At the same time, as has been strongly suggested, there were external factors which also influenced the colony's saltfish trade, and these related to marketing. Newfoundland's product faced competition from those of Norway, France, Iceland, the United States, and Canada (Nova Scotia and Quebec) to varying degrees. Furthermore, its fish also faced competition from other foods, especially jerked beef in Brazil. There is no doubt that other local foods also competed with saltfish, but evidence is almost non-existent regarding competition of this kind. However, it must be noted that saltfish was the cheapest source of a plentiful supply of protein-rich food which would not spoil in hot climates. In addition, since saltfish was sold predominantly in large coastal urban centres, which were often more efficiently and cheaply supplied by sea than by land, there would not appear to be any reason for its being replaced by subsistence agriculture or local products. Only in Jamaica, Trinidad and British Guiana does it appear likely that some poorer rural inhabitants abandoned the use of saltfish for home-grown products. Because of the small size of Barbados, subsistence agriculture was much less common. Another aspect of competition is taste preference and, again, the evidence is inconclusive. While it was maintained in the colony that Newfoundland's good-quality shore-cured saltfish was superior to most others, there are also reports which testify to the superiority of the competitors' products on occasion. Given that saltfish was purchased by the poorer classes as a necessity, it is most likely that price was more important than taste, provided the product was reasonably acceptable in terms of quality. Customers undoubtedly balked at trying a different cure for the first time, but evidence indicates that local preferences could be changed in a relatively short time. The advances of Norway, France, and Iceland in the saltfish markets attest to this. It would seem that the ability to produce an acceptable product in terms of quality and price was a major determinant in saltfish sales.

As this study has tried to show, there were problems in the saltfish markets involving the lack of quality control and price. Also, it is obvious that, despite delays in communications, the government and the merchants were made aware of these problems. Their responses to these problems and to all the signals emanating from the markets varied very little throughout the century even after the improvements in communications already discussed in Chapter 2.

Quality control was one major problem that became particularly evident in the 1880s. While each market had its preference, competition from foreign producers, combined with competition among the local Newfoundland merchants, created a situation in which each exporter attempted to deliver the first cargo to market. A solution to this problem was not attempted in Newfoundland until after the First World War and it was not solved until the 1930s, when the appointed commission of government imposed standards and controls. Only when competition was reduced by failures in the fisheries of the foreign producers or by the failure of the Newfoundland fishery was there a respite from this problem.

Closely related to the problem of quality control was price. Because saltfish had to be sold at a cheap price, there was very little profit margin in dealing with this product. Thus it often paid to send poorly-cured fish to market if this meant that the cargo was the first to arrive in a port which was experiencing a shortage of saltfish. Even more important, at times, the slim profit margin meant that a slight difference in the cost of production could be significant. Norway's more diversified economy, longer fishing season, and cheaper transportation costs could allow that country to sell its products at a lower price in the markets. Similarly, the French, with their generous government subsidies, had an important advantage over their competitors. Finally, any import tariff preferences granted by a consuming country to an exporting country could be significant in determining which produce was imported. Providing a reasonable quality at a competitive price was an overriding necessity for a successful trade.

When the Newfoundland exporters were presented with market problems relating, in the final analysis, to competitive prices, they felt they had very few available options. It has already been shown that the merchants responded by trying to get cargoes of saltfish to market before their competitors. In addition, as has been seen throughout this study, they appealed to the British Foreign Office for assistance in acquiring and/or maintaining preferential, or at least equal, import tariff treatment by the importing countries. Their efforts were, for the most part, condoned and usually supported by the Newfoundland government.

It has been shown that the policy of early shipments was not a wise solution but, in the long term, was very detrimental; on the other hand, appeals to Great Britain resulted in some positive action. In fact, one of the significant findings of this study has been the discovery of the extent to which the British Foreign Office was often prepared to act in order to try to satisfy the colony's demands for imperial action. The only work that has thoroughly examined the role of the British Foreign Office in Newfoundland affairs has been Thompson's study of the French Shore problem.[26] The imperial government was equally involved in other, less well-known issues: the American Shore problem and Portugal's attempts to acquire access to part of the Newfoundland coast are the most important examples.[27] While the Foreign Office was concerned with the more conspicuous matters mentioned above, it also kept steady pressure on all the colony's saltfish markets whenever support was requested. This was most obvious in the Spanish markets in the early part of the nineteenth century and in the late 1870s, at which time Norwegian and French saltfish received preferential treatment in this market: within a few years, Britain had procured similar treatment for Newfoundland's product. Later, when Norwegian klippfisk received preferential tariff treatment in the Portuguese markets in 1896, the Foreign Office tried, although without success, to have this preferential treatment extended to its colony. And finally, the most famous, although not the most significant example, was the British handling of the colony's conflict with Spain over whether Spanish pasas should receive the same preferential tariff treatment as Greek currants and sultanas. There were, of course, many other foreign issues which affected the Newfoundland saltfish trade over which Britain had no control, including the French system of government bounties and Norwegian and Icelandic competition. However, where action could be taken, the British government seemed willing to take it. Only in the area of direct financial support for the colony's fisheries could Britain have done more, but given the fact that the fisheries were no longer British, and given the fact that Britain (unlike its continental neighbours) firmly believed in free trade, it is not surprising that the imperial government offered no subsidies to the Newfoundland saltfish industry (anymore than it offered financial support to the extremely troubled British West Indian sugar industry). But considering the fact that Newfoundland was of little importance to Britain either as a colony, a source of trade, or a recruitment ground for sailors, it is remarkable to observe the seriousness with which the Foreign Office approached the colony's problems and the amount of success it had. While the Colonial Office often gave the impression of being somewhat jaded by Newfoundland's complaints, the Foreign Office dealt with them all with a degree of enthusiasm that leaves one with the impression that Britain's support of Newfoundland on the international scene during this period has not been sufficiently appreciated hitherto.[28]

The role played by the British Foreign Office on behalf of Newfoundland in the saltfish markets does require an explanation. There were at least two reasons for this activity. The first reason was probably an historical one. The Foreign Office had always been aware of the importance of the Newfoundland (West of England) saltfish trade to Britain because of the foreign exchange it earned and because it was a recruitment ground for British sailors. The Foreign Office probably continued to treat the Newfoundland saltfish trade during the nineteenth century as a British trade although, in fact, it had ceased to be a British trade during the Napoleonic War. Thus in 1842 the British ambassador in Lisbon reported, without qualifications, that the two main points of difficulty between Britain and Portugal concerned woollens and saltfish.[29] Similar matter-of-fact statements from British embassy officials and consular officers were common throughout most of the period. In fact, Newfoundland saltfish gradually lost its importance in the eyes of most of these officials, not because it was non-British, but because British exports of coal and manufactured goods became more important. To the end of this period, however, the Foreign Office in London continued to support the Newfoundland saltfish trade.[30] The second reason for this support is related to the first, and that is the fact that Newfoundland saltfish was sold outside Great Britain and in markets where the mother country had extensive trade interests. Thus Newfoundland's exports could be accommodated in a way that Canada's timber and the British West Indies' sugar products (to name just two other colonial examples) could not. It is also for this second reason that the British free-trade movement was welcomed in Newfoundland, because of the possibility that the saltfish markets would reciprocate and lower their import tariffs on British (and Newfoundland) goods. Given the origins of the Newfoundland saltfish industry and the nature of the saltfish trade, one can understand why the British Foreign Office actively supported it during 1814-1914.

Nevertheless, nothing illustrates Newfoundland's vulnerability as much as the correspondence between the colony and the mother country about marketing problems. Newfoundland's saltfish trade was probably as dependent upon Britain's commercial links and policies as Britain's Chilean nitrate trade, for example. Therefore, while it can be argued that the mercantile profits from Newfoundland's saltfish trade could have been more equitably shared between fishermen and merchants and government income could have been more judiciously spent, the fact remains that Newfoundland was forced to sell its product under conditions set by the markets. Newfoundland, on its own, had very little leverage in these markets and was practically powerless to make changes. This powerlessness is almost identical to that of modern Third World single-product exporters such as Zambia with its copper and Bolivia with its tin (and Zambia, at least, enjoys climatic and agricultural advantages). It was the infrastructure and the support provided by the British connection which helped Newfoundland's saltfish trade to compete as effectively as it did during the nineteenth century.

While one must face the fact that Newfoundland depended heavily on Great Britain for improvements in the colony's saltfish trade — and the mother country could provide only limited help — one must ask what action Newfoundland should have taken to maintain and improve its trade situation. The signals that came from the markets indicated that production of a reasonable-quality, cheap product might be the answer. Certainly, the merchants seemed willing to allow the price to fall, as they demonstrated by their talqual shipments, but the quality declined also. Furthermore, the colony was sometimes the victim of stubborn entrepreneurial habits. For example, the markets which the colony controlled in southern Spain experienced stagnation during the period, while Norway's markets in northern and eastern Spain expanded as Bilbao and Barcelona became leading industrial centres. It could be argued that Newfoundland could have competed most effectively by concentrating more fully on the deep-sea or bank fishery. An editorial in the St. John's *Trade Review* in 1901 stated:

> The Norwegians are going out of sailing vessels in their fishery entirely, and they think that if Newfoundland do not follow suit, European fishermen will come over and carry off our fish from under our nose. The same feeling is gaining ground in England and Scotland, and the fishery fleet is becoming more and more a steam fleet everyday.[31]

Or like the French after 1900, Newfoundland could have invested in a fleet of steam trawlers to be used on the Grand Banks. The capital was available, but it was invested in a fleet of wooden and iron-clad sealing steamers to engage in an industry which was obviously dying, but from which quick returns could be obtained. The colony, for a while, had the largest and best fleet of sealing ships and ice breakers in the world — a luxury it could not afford. Internationally, these ships were most famous for their use in arctic and antarctic expeditions — one was sent to bring back Scott's body from the South Pole ice cap — but their usefulness to Newfoundland was limited. Had Newfoundland invested in a fleet of steam trawlers during these years, its proximity to the fishing grounds would have given it an advantage over two of its competitors, France and Portugal. Larger quantities of cheaper Newfoundland deep-sea saltfish would certainly have had an impact on the markets. The most expensive inshore fisheries of Gaspé, Newfoundland, Iceland, and Norway, with their limited fishing seasons, would have been adversely affected, provided the colony's steam trawlers operated throughout much of the year. Perhaps such competition would have meant a lower standard of living for everyone as fish prices fell; or perhaps the situation would not have changed very much, except that a few more Portuguese would have emigrated to Brazil and a few more Norwegians, Icelanders and Newfoundlanders would have emigrated to the United States. As David Alexander pointed out, the exploitation of a common property resource cannot stabilize at a point where all involved in it can expect a reasonable standard of living unless the surplus population moves elsewhere or into other activities. The very nature of a common property resource precludes this, unless some outside force intervenes.

At the same time the saltfish trade was only part, although a major part, of a larger trade in cured fish. Stockfish from Norway and Iceland, herring from northern Europe and North America, and pilchards, sardines, and tunny fish from many countries combined to make up a substantial international trade. In addition, by the latter years of the century the exportation of canned sea products, including salmon and lobster, added to the world supply of fish. Saltfish sometimes competed in some of these trades but, for the most part, it was confined to its own traditional consumers. These consumers bought the product because it was a cheap and easily preserved source of protein and because Roman Catholicism required that its adherents refrain from eating meat at certain times.

Also, the trade in saltfish must be seen in the context of the international trade in food. An examination of the trade in grain and meat, for example, establishes the fact that there was a marked price decrease during the 1870s and 1880s. Woodruff attributes this decrease to a number of factors including the increase in world production and the decline in freight rates.[32] All producers and exporters of food were affected but especially those economies dependent upon the export of a single product as in the case of Newfoundland.

Newfoundland's saltfish trade was affected by many factors. It was subject to international developments to an extent unmatched by any other British colonial trade. In addition, it was extensively affected by the changes occurring in British trade and navigation and in Britain's changing international role and commitments. It was also influenced by the British North American free-enterprise ethos of the nineteenth century. Finally, there were general technological developments and local colonial developments which must also be taken into account. Newfoundland failed to make necessary local adjustments and on the international level Britain did not contribute much to the improvement of the saltfish trade. The latter point leads one to question the commitment of the mother country to British North America. It would have been different had the market countries, especially Spain and Portugal, followed Britain's early lead and lowered the import tariff on the colony's saltfish. Newfoundland would have benefitted enormously. However, since the saltfish markets did not adopt reciprocal free-trade policies one must question whether the laissez-faire philosophy associated with free trade was suited to the development of Newfoundland. Instead of spending funds on Foreign Office salaries to provide, as John Bright put it, outdoor relief for the privileged classes, maybe Britain should have spent money on direct subsidies to the colony's fisheries (as France and Portugal did for their national fisheries). Indeed even the efforts of the Foreign Office to assist Newfoundland's trade can be questioned. For example, in the 1890s when the Portuguese moved from Mozambique into British-occupied Shona territory (in what is now Zimbabwe) the Foreign Office moved swiftly and forced them to withdraw. Britain's concern for Newfoundland, or even Canada, was not on the same level as its concern for its new African possessions. However, while it can be questioned whether the overall development of the British Empire was favourable to Newfoundland (and it seems that the answer is no) it is certain that given Britain's declining interests in its North American and Caribbean possessions and given its commitment to free trade and laissez-faire it provided considerable assistance to Newfoundland's saltfish trade.

In 1914 Newfoundland could look back on one hundred years of peace, living standards comparable to that of the rest of British North America, and industrialization attempts. Nevertheless its economy remained primarily dependent upon the saltfish trade which, in turn, was dependent upon the resources, connections, and support of Great Britain's international commmercial arrangements and activities. Within twenty years Newfoundland would be forced to call a halt to its journey along the road to political independence and would ask the imperial government to reverse this political process in a futile effort to save its trade. Although the Great War and the Great Depression contributed to the Colony's economic collapse, developments during the nineteenth century demonstrated that Newfoundland's political independence was incompatible with the commercial reality of the international saltfish trade.

Appendix

TABLE INTRODUCTION.1[1]

Newfoundland's Saltfish Exports (cwts) and Population: 1803-1914

Year	Cwts	Population		Cwts Per Capita
		Winter	Summer	
1803	582,849	19,034	25,445	22.9
1804	559,442	20,380	24,922	22.5
1805	625,519	21,975	26,505	23.6
1806	772,809			
1807	674,810	25,234	32,542	20.7
1808	576,132	24,625	29,115	19.8
1809	810,219	25,157	30,359	26.7
1810	884,474	-	-	-
1811	923,540	25,985	33,605	27.5
1812	711,056	30,772	38,398	18.5
1813	912,183	32,749	41,775	21.8
1814	947,811	35,952	45,718	20.7
1815	1,182,661	40,568	55,284	21.4
1816	1,046,626	41,898	52,672	19.9
1817	935,636	43,409	50,211	18.6
1818	751,818	40,854	47,676	15.8
1819	808,250	40,937	48,920	16.5
1820	874,606	42,535	51,427	17.0
1821	963,892	47,083	55,292	17.4
1822	924,284	47,530	54,982	16.8
1823	858,813	49,503	56,547	15.2
1824	963,683	-	-	-
1825	892,366	55,504	62,839	14.2
1826	994,014	-	63,644	15.6
1827	876,782	53,238	16.5	
1828	934,232	59,101	15.8	
1829	928,818	59,035	-	
1830	906,119	60,088	15.0	
1831	726,881	-	-	
1832	707,382	-	-	
1833	867,187	-	-	

Year	Cwts	Population Winter	Summer	Cwts Per Capita
1834	674,988	-	-	
1835	712,588	-	-	
1836	860,354	74,993	11.5	
1837	-	-	-	
1838	724,575	-	-	
1839	865,377	-	-	
1840	915,795	-	-	
1841	1,009,725	-	-	
1842	1,007,980	-	-	
1843	936,202	-	-	
1844	852,162	-	-	
1845	1,000,233	96,296	10.4	
1846	879,015	-	-	
1847	837,973	-	-	
1848	920,366	-	-	
1849	1,175,167	-	-	
1850	1,089,182	-	-	
1851	1,017,674	-	-	
1852	973,731	-	-	
1853	922,718	-	-	
1854	774,118	-	-	
1855	1,107,388	-	-	
1856	1,268,334	-	-	
1857	1,392,322	124,228	11.2	
1858	1,038,089	-	-	
1859	1,105,793	-	-	
1860	1,379,804	-	-	
1861	1,214,326	-	-	
1862	1,241,830	-	-	
1863	1,012,321	-	-	
1864	1,013,037	-	-	
1865	1,019,081	-	-	
1866	930,447	-	-	
1867	1,066,215	-	-	
1868	1,169,948	-	-	
1869	1,204,086	146,536	8.2	
1870	1,213,737	-	-	
1871	1,328,726	-	-	
1872	1,221,156	-	-	
1873	1,316,785	-	-	
1874	1,595,827	161,374	9.9	
1875	1,133,196	-	-	
1876	1,068,471	-	-	
1877	1,034,101	-	-	
1878	1,035,013	-	-	

Year	Cwts	Population		Cwts Per Capita
		Winter	Summer	
1879	1,387,770	-	-	
1880	1,383,531	-	-	
1881	1,535,573	-	-	
1882	1,391,102	-	-	
1883	1,532,023	-	-	
1884	1,397,637	197,335	7.0	
1885	1,284,710	-	-	
1886	1,344,180	-	-	
1887	1,080,024	-	-	
1888	1,175,720	-	-	
1889	1,076,507	-	-	
1890	1,040,916	-	-	
1891	1,244,834	202,040	6.2	
1892	-	-	-	
1893	1,160,335	-	-	
1894	1,107,696	-	-	
1895	1,312,608	-	-	
1896	1,436,083	-	-	
1897	1,135,817	-	-	
1898	1,145,540	-	-	
1899	1,226,336	-	-	
1900	1,300,622	-	-	
1901	1,233,107	220,249	5.6	
1902	1,288,921	-	-	
1903	1,429,246	-	-	
1904	1,360,219	-	-	
1905	1,196,774	-	-	
1906	1,480,734	-	-	
1907	1,422,129	-	-	
1908	1,509,020	-	-	
1909	1,732,172	-	-	
1910	1,502,020	-	-	
1911	1,182,480	242,619	4.9	
1912	1,387,930	-	-	
1913	1,408,501	-	-	
1914	1,247,234	-	-	

TABLE 2.1

Part A[2]

Export Prices of Newfoundland Saltfish (f.o.b.):
1801/1914

Year	Price (Shillings & Pence) Minimum Maximum
1801	14s. 6d. to 22s. 6d.
1802	-
1803	12s. to 15s.
1804	10s. 6d. to 16s. 6d.
1805	10s. to 14s. 6d.
1806	-
1807	8s. 6d. to 13s. 6d.
1808	9s. to 14s. 6d.
1809	9s. 6d. to 13s. 6d.
1910	8s. to 14s. 6d.
1811	11s. 6d. to 22s.
1812	11s. to 22s. 6d.
1813	24s. to 32s.
1814	14s. 6d. to 24s. 6d.
1815	14s. to 21s.
1816	9s. to 15s.
1817	8s. to 14s.
1818	10s. to 17s.
1819	9s. to 17s.
1920	9s. to 14s.
1821	8s. to 14s.
1822	6s. to 10s. 6d.
1823	6s. to 13s.
1824	7s. to 13s.
1825	7s. to 12s.
1826	8s. to 12s.
1827	8s. to 12s. 6d.
1828	7s. to 12s. 6d.
1829	7s. 6d. to 13s.
1830	8s. to 12s.
1831	8s. to 12s.
1832	8s. to 13s.
1833	7s. to 12s.

Year	Average Overall Price	Newfoundland Shore Fish	Labrador Fish
1836	12s.		
1837	-		
1838	13s. 4d.		
1839	11s. 8d.		
1840	12s. 7d.		
1841	12s.		
1842	-		
1843	11s. 4d.		
1844	11s. 4d.		
1845	11s. 11d.		
1846	11s. 6d.		
1847	11s. 8d.		
1848	10s. 10d.		
1849	10s.		
1850	9s. 9d.	10s.	
1851	9s. 8d.	10s.	
1852	9s. 6d.	10s.	
1853	12s. 2d.	12s.	
1854	13s. 5d.	13s.	
1855	12s. 3d.	12s.	
1856	12s. 5d.	12s.	
1857	14s. 5d.	14s.	
1858	14s. 9d.	15s.	
1859	16s. 2d.	16s.	
1860	12s. 3d.	19s.	
1861	11s.	13s.	
1862	12s. 8d.	15s.	
1863	15s.	19s.	
1864	15s. 8d.	19s.	
	$	$	$
1865	3.33	4.23	
1866	3.93	5.09	
1867	2.79	3.62	
1868	2.03	3.45	
1869	2.91	4.00	
1870	3.20	4.01	
1871	2.95	4.09	
1872	3.07	4.08	
1873	3.88	4.06	3.30
1874	3.88	4.13	2.97
1875	4.29	4.54	3.38
1876	4.81	5.32	4.16
1877	4.10	4.53	3.17

Year	Average Overall Price	Newfoundland Shore Fish	Labrador Fish
1878	3.90	4.44	3.28
1879	3.20	3.51	2.35
1880	3.20	3.33	2.17
1881	4.00	4.36	3.00
1882	4.30	4.84	
1883	3.80	4.06	
1884	3.80	3.94	
1885	3.10	3.20	
1886	3.00	3.15	
1887	3.80	4.11	
1888	4.20	4.38	3.40
1889	4.20	4.39	3.40
1890	3.70	4.12	2.60
1891	3.90	4.25	2.80
1892	3.45	-	-
1893	3.60	4.00	2.80
1894	3.29	3.46	2.80
1895	2.92	3.13	2.30
1896	2.99	3.16	2.30
1897	2.46	2.56	2.00
1898	2.82		
1899	3.62		
1900	4.19		
1901	4.19		
1902	4.27		
1903	3.94		
1904	4.37		
1905	5.14		
1906	5.31		
1907	5.53		3.50
1908	5.10		2.70
1909	4.20		3.70
1910	4.08		4.00
1911	5.54		4.20
1912	5.07		3.50
1913	5.66		4.70
1914	5.80		3.97

TABLE 2.1

Part B[3]

Value of Newfoundland Saltfish
in Various Markets: 1856-1900

Year	Spain	Portugal	Italy	Brazil	British West Indies
	£	£	£	£	£
1856	-	-	-	-	-
1857	14/6	14/6	12/	17/6	13/
1858	13/9	13/9	13/9	16/8	13/4
1859	15/	15/	14/6	19/	16/
1860	15/	15/	15/	17/	12/
1861	13/	13/	13/	15/	11/
1862	15/	15/	15/	15/	13/
1863	19/6	19/6	16/	20/	15/
1864	20/	20/	16/	20/	15/
	$	$	$	$	$
1865	4.50	4.50	3.50	4.50	3.50
1866	5.50	5.50	5.50	5.50	4.00
1867	4.00	4.00	3.00	4.00	2.75
1868	3.50	3.50	3.50	4.00	3.00
1869	4.00	4.00	4.00	4.50	3.50
1870	4.00	4.00	4.00	4.50	3.50
1871	4.00	4.00	4.00	4.50	3.50
1872	4.00	4.00	4.00	4.50	3.50
1873	4.20	4.40	3.60	4.40	3.20
1874	4.40	4.40	3.80	4.20	3.50
1875	4.80	4.50	4.50	4.80	4.00
1976	5.40	5.70	5.40	5.50	4.40
1877	5.00	5.00	3.20	5.00	3.20
1878	4.90	5.00	3.20	4.80	3.30
1879	3.70	3.90	2.60	3.80	3.00
1880	3.50	3.80	2.60	3.60	2.60
1881	4.50	5.00	3.60	4.50	3.20
1882	4.70	5.30	4.20	5.00	4.00
1883	4.00	4.50	3.60	4.00	3.00
1884	3.80	4.50	3.20	4.20	2.60
1885	3.20	3.40	2.60	3.50	2.40
1886	3.30	3.30	2.80	3.50	2.00
1887	4.10	4.30	3.50	4.60	3.00
1888	4.50	4.60	3.80	4.80	3.40
1889	4.20	4.50	4.20	4.80	3.40
1890	4.00	4.60	3.00	4.50	3.60
1891	4.40	4.80	3.90	4.40	3.40
1892	3.30	4.50	3.00	3.60	3.00

Year	Spain	Portugal	Italy	Brazil	British West Indies
1893	3.40	4.80	3.40	4.00	3.00
1894	3.50	4.00	3.00	3.40	3.00
1895	3.40	3.50	3.00	3.20	2.60
1896	3.40	3.50	3.00	3.20	2.60
1897	2.80	2.80	2.40	2.60	2.00
1898	2.40	3.20	2.50	3.20	2.40
1899	3.54	3.77	3.61	4.12	3.68
1900	4.32	4.46	4.67	4.51	4.24

TABLE 2.2[4]

The Shore, Labrador & Bank Catch:
1890, 1900 and 1910
(cwts)

District	Shore Catch			Labrador Catch			Bank Catch		
	1890	1900	1910	1890	1900	1910	1890	1900	1910
St. John's East	10,707	27,790	45,725	40,590	17,204	180	8,300	0	0
St. John's West	7,854	21,206	23,268	0	0	1,000	2,200	0	0
Harbour Main	1,765	2,696	3,299	27,044	15,356	5,319	2,050	0	0
Port de Grave	1,555	2,457	5,549	51,444	76,667	20,674	2,000	0	0
Harbour Grace	1,506	3,309	6,795	107,699	74,874	30,162	5,570	0	250
Carbonear	735	872	1,717	40,057	38,521	16,088	1,860	0	0
Bay de Verde	23,348	37,571	57,101	36,428	19,671	11,805	0	0	0
Trinity Bay	25,642	47,225	72,242	52,159	55,065	78,566	24,998	18,711	6,931
Bonavista Bay	39,309	69,461	55,769	82,093	78,847	68,319	1,720	0	0
Fogo	21,398	44,837	40,303	19,255	16,450	9,758	0	0	0
Twillingate	26,777	57,276	63,553	18,485	41,613	24,416	0	12	0
St. Barbe	33,941	50,369	62,086	250	1,046	2,112	0	0	0
Ferryland	33,143	62,860	52,546	56	0	0	11,949	2,200	0
Placentia & St. Mary's	72,561	128,938	150,752	0	0	2,800	20,900	0	0
Burin	28,830	68,520	63,697	0	0	0	45,318	70,155	84,439
Fortune Bay	39,018	35,031	29,700	100	2,828	2,257	3,760	20,720	57,877
Burgeo & La Poile	41,249	41,587	59,737	225	462	35	7,004	7,340	5,159
St. George's	16,617	16,763	15,584	1,000	1,703	2,173	0	0	886
Labrador	0	0	0	11,903	16,000	11,597	0	0	0
Totals	425,955	718,768	809,423	488,788	456,307	287,261	137,604	119,138	155,542

TABLE 2.3[5]

Newfoundland's Population by District:
1857-1911

District	1857	1869	1874	1884	1891	1901	1911
St. John's East	17,352	17,204	17,811	22,183	20,776	21,511	25,135
St. John's West	13,124	11,646	12,763	15,962	15,251	18,483	20,550
Harbour Main	5,386	6,542	7,174	8,935	9,189	9,492	9,471
Port de Grave	6,489	7,536	7,919	8,698	7,986	7,445	6,986
Harbour Grace	10,067	12,740	13,055	14,727	13,881	12,671	11,925
Carbonear	5,233	5,633	5,488	6,206	5,765	5,024	5,114
Bay de Verde	6,221	7,057	7,434	8,403	9,708	9,929	10,213
Trinity Bay	10,726	13,817	15,677	19,005	18,872	20,695	21,788
Bonavista Bay	8,850	11,560	13,008	16,486	17,849	20,538	22,894
Twillingate	9,717	13,067	15,135	14,058	16,780	18,843	22,705
Fogo				6,264	6,700	7,569	8,257
St. Barbe[6]				6,500	6,690	8,126	10,481
Included in St. George's							
Ferryland	5,228	5,991	6,419	6,472	5,853	5,697	5,793
Placentia &							
St. Mary's	8,334	8,794	9,857	11,789	12,801	15,206	16,099
Burin	5,529	6,731	7,678	8,502	9,059	10,402	11,616
Fortune Bay	3,493	5,233	5,788	6,917	7,671	8,762	9,989
Burgeo &							
La Poile	3,545	5,119	5,098	6,544	6,471	7,010	7,793
St. George's	3,334	5,387	8,654	5,473	6,632	9,205	11,861
Labrador	1,650	2,479	2,416	4,211	4,106	3,634	3,949
Total	124,228	146,536	161,374	197,335	202,040	220,249	242,619

TABLE 2.4[7]

Newfoundland Bank Fishery:
1889-1914

Year	Number of Vessels	Tonnage	Men	Cwts Caught
1889	230	18,890	4,401	238,821
1890	279	15,212	3,719	147,948
1891	165	9,838	2,175	103,688
1892	100	6,270	1,392	90,467
1893	71	4,409	957	54,494
1894	58	3,516	785	54,541
1895	43	2,537	565	46,984
1896	48	2,652	616	54,802

Year	Number of Vessels	Tonnage	Men	Cwts Caught
1897	66	3,684	872	58,762
1898	74	4,224	1,000	74,002
1899	90	4,722	1,163	97,399
1900	112	5,757	1,400	116,278
1901	118	6,282	1,531	113,841
1902	110	5,964	1,444	131,102
1903	100	5,529	1,386	89,321
1904	87	5,039	1,215	70,872
1905	-	-	-	-
1906	-	-	-	-
1907	83	4,286	1,261	88,086
1908	107	5,976	1,433	120,000
1909	100	5,818	1,377	131,452
1910	101	6,630	1,567	144,524
1911	122	-	-	149,924
1912	124	8,281	1,924	155,517
1913	104	7,551	1,830	152,374
1914	105	7,790	1,892	124,067

TABLE 2.5[8]

**Newfoundland's Exporters
and Saltfish Exports: 1865**

Places/Exporters	Cwts Saltfish
St. John's	
Walter Grieve & Co.	97,432
Bowring Brothers	57,929
Baine Johnston & Co.	57,123
P. & L. Tessier	58,571
Job Brothers & Co.	45,430
J. & W. Stewart	35,850
Brooking & Co.	23,329
McBride & Co.	29,277
Muir & Duder	20,099
Harvey Tucker & Co.	24,631
L. O'Brien & Co.	16,066
C.F. Ancell	15,800
Stabb, Row & Holmwood	15,186
Kenneth McLea & Sons	13,938
C.F. Bennett & Co.	8,975

Places/Exporters	Cwts Saltfish
Charles Cowan	3,400
H.C.B. Thomas	3,248
Ridley & Sons	2,430
Punton & Munn	2,402
A. Shea	0
Evans & LeMessurier	700
Edward Meehan	0
A. Goodridge & Sons	2,122
Edward White	0
P. Hutchins	1,051
M.H. Warren & Co.	3,197
Hunt & Henley	1,106
E. Stabb	290
N. Stabb & Sons	510
Wm. Hounsell & Co.	424
W.H. Mare	6
A. Pearce	0
Sundry Shippers	0
Total	540,522

Twillingate	
W. Cox & Co.	6,000
Muir & Duder	5,220
Executors of J. Slade Co.	2,115
Total	13,335

Fogo	
Wm. Cox & Co.	4,648
Muir & Duder	2,200
Total	6,648

Greenspond	
Brooking & Co.	4,500
Wm. Cox & Co.	4,248
Total	8,748

Catalina	
Ridley & Sons	10,700
Bowring Brothers	3,030
Total	13,730

Places/Exporter	Cwts Saltfish
Trinity	
Brooking & Co.	13,222
W. Grieve & Bremner	4,750
Total	17.972
Hants Harbour	
Job Brothers & Co.	2,200
Total	2,200
Carbonear	
John Rorke	7,089
Ridley & Sons	3,703
Total	10,792
Harbour Grace	
Ridley & Sons	71,546
Punton & Munn	37,256
W.J.S. Donnelly	0
Rutherford Bros.	159
M.H. Warren & Co.	1,573
Daniel Green	0
Total	110,534
Ferryland	
W. Grieve & Co.	6,100
Total	6,100
St. Mary's	
W. Grieve & Co.	2,626
Stabb, Row & Holmwood	2,000
Total	4,626
Placentia	
Kenneth McLea & Sons	2,045
Total	2,045

Places/Exporters	Cwts Saltfish
Burin	
R. Falls & Co.	13,303
Thomas Foley	0
Total	
St. Lawrence	
James Dunn	630
Total	630
Harbour Breton	
Newman & Co.	14,699
Nicholle & Co.	9,262
Baine Johnston & Co.	3,000
Punton & Munn	2,600
Joseph Gorman	82
Onslow Ludlow	0
F.W. Levers	0
Peter Smith	0
Henry Hickman	0
Solomon Trellick	0
A. Givonani	0
Total	29,643
English Harbour	
Sundry Shippers in 28 vessels	352
Total	352
Gaultois	
Newman & Co.	9,965
Total	9,965
Burgeo	
Degroucy, Renouf & Co.	179
Joseph Small	400
Nathan Crowell	290
Joseph Pippy	0
Total	869

Places/Exporters	Cwts Saltfish
La Poile & Rose Blanche	
Ridley & Sons	13,580
Nicholle & Co.	3,400
Degroucy, Renouf & Co.	12,302
F.A. Cook	0
Sundry Shippers	0
Total	29,282
Channel	
W. Pryon & Sons	1,810
John Poole	0
Joseph Parmetin	0
George Evans	0
Ridley & Sons	0
Sundry Shippers	0
Total	1,810
Labrador *(Newfoundland Houses)*	
Punton & Munn	58,104
Ridley & Sons	50,078
W.J.S. Donnelly	9,715
Daniel Green	0
Rutherford Bros.	0
J. & R. Maddock	0
John Rorke	10,102
P. & L. Tessier	5,753
McBride & Co.	3,600
W. Grieve & Co.	3,115
Baine Johnston & Co.	8,030
M.H. Warren & Co.	6,000
J. & W. Stewart	9,147
Job Brothers & Co.	11,160
Bowring Brothers	8,900
Stabb, Row & Co.	8,970
L. O'Brien & Co.	3,101
Total	195,775

Notes

INTRODUCTION

[1] Saltfish is the term used in Newfoundland to describe salted dried codfish.

[2] See David Alexander, *The Decay of Trade: An Economic History of the Newfoundland Saltfish Trade, 1935-1965* (Memorial University of Newfoundland, 1977).

[3] For competent studies of earlier and later periods in the history of Newfoundland's cod fishery, see Keith Matthews, "A History of the West of England-Newfoundland Fishery" (unpublished D.Phil. thesis, Oxford University, 1968) for the period prior to the Napoleonic War; Ian McDonald, "W.F. Coaker and the Fishermen's Protective Union in Newfoundland Politics" (unpublished Ph.D. thesis, University of London, 1971) for the First World War and post-war period; and David Alexander, *The Decay of Trade.*

[4] For the most recent survey of Newfoundland historiography, see Peter Neary, "The Writing of Newfoundland History: An Introductory Survey," in James Hiller and Peter Neary (eds.), *Newfoundland in the Nineteenth and Twentieth Centuries* (Toronto: 1980), pp. 3-15.

[5] Harold A. Innis, *The Cod Fisheries: The Study of an International Economy* (Toronto: 1940, 1954).

[6] McDonald, "Coaker."

[7] David Alexander, "A New Newfoundland: The Traditional Economy and Developments to 1934" (paper presented to the Canadian Historical Association, Kingston, 1973).

[8] Grant Head, *Eighteenth Century Newfoundland* (Toronto: 1976), p. 249.

[9] Alexander, *Decay of Trade*, p. 21.

[10] *Ibid.*, pp. 20-21.

[11] Rosemary Ommer, "From Outpost to Outport: The Jersey Merchant Triangle in the Nineteenth Century" (unpublished Ph.D. thesis, McGill University, 1979), p. 149.

[12] Fiott Papers, Letter to John Fiott from his agents in Alicante, 10 December 1771, quoted in Ommer, "Outpost to Outport," p. 122.

[13] Alexander, *Decay of Trade*, p. 21.

[14] Ommer, "Outpost to Outport," p. 117.

[15] Alexander, *Decay of Trade*, p. 21.

[16] *Ibid.*, p. 45.

[17] Department of Marine and Fisheries, Standardization Committee, 1920, *Bulletin*, 1 July 1920.

[18] *Ibid.*

[19] Newman, Hunt and Company Limited, Letter Books, Book 64, pp. 339-41, Newman, Hunt and Company, London, to Newman and Company, Newfoundland, 30 September 1864. (See Bibliography entry.)

[20] Charles Robin and Company Papers, Charles Robin to Burns and Woolsey, Quebec, 1 August 1789, quoted in Ommer, "Outpost to Outport," p. 117.

[21] Lawrence George Small, "The Interrelationship of Work and Talk in a Newfoundland Fishing Community" (unpublished Ph.D. thesis, University of Pennsylvania, 1979), p. 166.

[22] *Ibid.*, p. 14.

[23]John R. Hanson II, "Export Instability in Historical Perspective: Further Results," *Journal of Economic History*, Vol. XL, No. 1 (March 1980), 17-23. Hanson argues that the situation in the less developed countries that are dependent on the sale of one or two products in unregulated world markets, during the post-war era, is similar to the situation that was faced by some of the modern affluent countries during the nineteenth century. Without commenting on the validity of this argument, one might note that the degree of dependence on one product and the lack of an agricultural base made Newfoundland's situation in the nineteenth century much more extreme than that of Canada, Australia and the United States – examples used by Hanson.

[24]C.O.194/111, fol. 222, Chamber of Commerce to C.O., 20 April 1841.

[25]*Morning Chronicle* (St. John's), 20 November 1879.

[26]Trygve Solhaug, *De Norske Fiskeriers Historie: 1815-1880* (Bergen: 1976), p. 744. The original figures are in våger and have been converted into hundredweight by the present writer at 2.8 våger per cwt and rounded off to the nearest whole number. Throughout this book the British hundredweight (cwt) of 112 pounds, avoirdupois, is the basic unit of weight used in most calculations because until relatively recently the hundredweight (referred to locally as the quintal) was generally used throughout the industry.

[27]*Norges officielle statistikk*, Annual Reports, 1910-1914.

[28]Shannon Ryan, "Abstract of C.O.194 Statistics" (unpublished manuscript, Memorial University of Newfoundland, 1969), p. 93.

[29]See Table Introduction.1, Appendix. Tables are identified by section: for example, Introduction, Chapter 1, 2. If the first part of the table's designation is followed by another number the table is rather long and can be found in the Appendix (e.g. Introduction.1, 2.1, 2.2). If, however, it is followed a letter (e.g. 1.A,) it will be found in the text.

[30]F.O.63/1189, No. 1, Crawford to F.O., 28 April 1886.

[31]Walter Scott, *The Antiquary*, Chapter XI.

CHAPTER 1

[1]*Oxford English Dictionary.*

[2]Odd Vollan, *Den Norske Klippfiskhandels Historie* (Ålesurd: 1956), p. 524.

[3]P.P., 1884, LXXX, pp. 252-83, Inglis, British Consul, Leghorn, Report, 1883.

[4]P.P., 1890, LXXV, pp. 755-80, O'Neill, British Consul, Leghorn, Report, 1889.

[5]William J. Kirwin, "Selected French and English Synonyms in Newfoundland," *Regional Language Studies Newfoundland*, No. 9 (December 1980), 14.

[6]For a complete discussion of the origins of the English-Newfoundland saltfish industry, see Matthews, "West of England-Newfoundland Fishery."

[7]These combine the functions of a shed and a wharf. The Norwegians call them *sjøhus* (seahouses).

[8]A fishing room was that area of shoreline needed from which to carry on the fishery. This explanation has been greatly simplified.

[9]Ryan, "Abstract," pp. 12, 46, 47.

[10]Ryan, "Abstract," pp. 59, 63, 67.

[11]Collingwood Collection, copy of a letter dated 27 December 1790 and written in St. John's, Newfoundland. The writer's signature is missing but it may have been written by someone associated with Newman and Company, Newfoundland.

[12]End of statistics regarding bye boat men.

[13]Shannon Ryan, "Fishery to Colony: A Newfoundland Watershead, 1793-1815," *Acadiensis*, XII, No. 2 (Spring 1983), 34-52.

[14]C.O.194/55, fol. 101, Keats, Governor, Newfoundland, to C.O., 29 December 1814.

[15]See Shannon Ryan, *The Labrador and Seal Fisheries of Newfoundland* (Ottawa: The National Film Board, Canada's Visual History Series, 1978); Ryan, "Introduction," in Ryan and Small (eds.), *Haulin' Rope and Gaff: Songs and Poetry in the History of the Newfoundland Seal Fishery* (St. John's: Breakwater Books, 1978); and Ryan, "Fishery to Colony."

CHAPTER 2

[1]See Table Introduction.1, Appendix.

[2]Nicholas Rau, *Trade Cycles: Theory and Evidence* (London: 1974), p. 14.

[3]David Alexander, "A New Newfoundland."

[4]*JHA*, 1850-1915, Appendices, Reports of the Protection of the Fisheries, and Reports of the Department of Fisheries. Since many letters, petitions, and memorials also mention catch failures in different areas, one can easily get the mistaken idea that such failures were widespread and a major threat to the whole economy. It is essential to remember that even the most convincing memorial of this nature usually refers to only a limited area.

[5]*Ibid.*, 1869, Appendix, pp. 530-37, Abstract of the Report of Captain Parish, H.M.S. Sphinx, for the period between 5 June and 22 August 1868. There is no evidence to suggest that over-fishing was an important factor in the nineteenth century.

[6]A.W. Parsons, "An Economic Study of the Newfoundland Fisheries" (unpublished B.Sc. thesis, Mount Allison University, 1935), pp 112-13.

[7]P.P., 1890, LXXV, pp. 621-54, Turner, Report, 1889.

[8]*Ibid.*

[9]Charles L. Cutting, *Fish Saving: A History of Fish Processing from Ancient to Modern Times* (New York: 1956), pp. 175-80. The following information about curing techniques has been taken from this source.

[10]Newman, Book 64, p. 85, 31 December 1859.

[11]*Ibid.*, and Book 67, p. 113, 6 July 1880.

[12]*JHA*, 1882, Appendix, p. 616; and the Maurice Job Taylor Collection, Job Brothers and Company Special Circular and Price List, 20 July 1911.

[13]Chamber of Commerce Minute Book, 1834-1841, Vol. I, Annual Report, 5 August 1835.

[14]Newman, Book 64, pp. 80-81, 3 December 1859.

[15]*Ibid.*, pp. 101-02, 3 April 1860.

[16]*Ibid.*, pp. 307-08, 5 March 1864; and p. 320, 30 April 1864.

[17]*Ibid.*, Book 65, pp. 332-34, 7 November 1871; Book 67, pp. 7-8, 12 November 1878; *Ibid.*, p. 113, 6 July 1880; Book 69, pp. 155-57, 9 December 1890; *Ibid.*, pp. 164-65, 9 January 1891.

[18]*Ibid.*, Book 69, pp. 164-65, 6 January 1891.

[19]Chamber of Commerce Minute Book, 1866-1875, Vol. V, Annual Report, 8 August 1868.

[20]*JHA*, 1897, Appendix, p. 309, Report of the Department of Marine and Fisheries for 1896; and *Ibid.*, 1898, Appendix, p. 342, Report of the Department of Marine and Fisheries for 1897.

[21]*Ibid.*, 1910, Appendix, p. 377, Report of the Department of Marine and Fisheries for 1909.

[22]*Ibid.*, 1911, Appendix, pp. 410-11, Report of the Department of Marine and Fisheries for 1910.

[23]Baine Johnston Letter Book, 1893-1898, pp. 48-49, 2 June 1894.

[24]*JHA*, 1908, Appendix, p. 137, Report of the Department of Marine and Fisheries for 1907.

[25]Maurice Job Taylor Collection, Job Brothers and Company Special Circular and Price List, 20 July 1911.

[26]Punton and Munn, Old Letters.

[27]Newman, Book 69, pp. 214-16, 23 March 1893.

[28]*Ibid.*, Book 63, pp. 240-41, 6 November 1885.

[29] William White Collection of Trinity Bay Manuscripts, Fish and Oil Collection Book, 1852.

[30] W. Waterman and Company, Fogo, Produce Book, 1878-1883.

[31] Grieves and Bremner Fish Collection Books, 1855-1890.

[32] John Munn and Company Miscellaneous Papers, Statements of Dry Bank Fish received at Beach Premises [Harbour Grace] by the Company.

[33] The Earle Collection of One Hundred and Twenty Documents.

[34] Newman, Book 69, pp. 200-01, 7 July 1891.

[35] Baine Johnston Letter Book, 1893-1898, p. 43, 10 May 1894; and John and Charles Steer Letter Book, 1890-1898, p. 156, 16 November 1891.

[36] Nicholas Smith, *Fifty-Two Years at the Labrador Fishery* (London: 1936), p. 17.

[37] *Ibid.*, pp. 17-18.

[38] *JHA*, 1908, Appendix, p. 137, Report of the Department of Marine and Fisheries for 1907.

[39] Matthews, "West of England-Newfoundland Fishery," p. 592.

[40] See Ryan, "Abstract," pp. 86 and 112.

[41] C.O.194/45, fol. 23, Gower to C.O., Report, 10 October 1804.

[42] C.O.194/60, fol. 293, Report of the Select Committee on Newfoundland Trade, 1817.

[43] C.O.194/87, fols. 175-76, Newfoundland House of Assembly to C.O., 1 May 1834.

[44] *Ibid.*, fol. 273, Chamber of Commerce to C.O., 2 June 1834.

[45] C.O.194/139, fols. 327-28, K.B. Hamilton, Governor, Newfoundland, to C.O., 28 September 1853.

[46] C.O.194/63, fol. 128, C. Hamilton, Governor, Newfoundland, to C.O., 14 November 1820.

[47] *JHA*, 1877, Appendix, pp. 730-43.

[48] *Ibid.*, pp. 732-33.

[49] *Ibid.*

[50] William Cox and Company Letter Book, 1858-1859, Charles Edmonds, Agent at Twillingate, to John B. Highmore, Agent at Fogo, 2 July 1859.

[51] Chamber of Commerce Minute Book, 1834-1841, Vol. I, Annual Report, 5 August 1835.

[52] C.O.194/87, fols. 272-73, Chamber of Commerce to C.O., 2 June 1834.

[53] *Ibid.*, fols. 175-76, Newfoundland House of Assembly to C.O., 1 May 1834.

[54] Ryan, "Abstract," p. 112.

[55] Chamber of Commerce Minute Book, 1846-1851, Vol. II, Chamber of Commerce to the Lord Commissioners of the Admiralty, 4 December 1848.

[56] C.O.194/112, fols. 383-88, C. Wyville, Captain of the Fishery Protection Vessel H.M.S. *Cleopatra*, to Governor Harvey, Report, September 1841.

[57] Harbour Grace Police Letter Book, Vol. I, 1847, Police Office to James Crowdy, Colonial Secretary, 30 September 1847. The Police Office in Harbour Grace had jurisdiction over the area from Mosquito to Bay Roberts.

[58] *JHA*, 1890, Appendix, p. 32.

[59] *Ibid.*, 1851, Appendix, p. 146, Captain Decourcy of H.M.S. *Helena*, Report on the Fisheries of Newfoundland, 5 September 1850.

[60] Grieves and Bremner Fish Collection Books, 1855-1890.

[61] W. Waterman and Company Produce Books, Fogo, 1864-1883.

[62] Job Family Papers, Job Brothers and Company Book of Statistics.

[63] *Ibid.*

[64] Book of Coasting and Fishing Ships cleared from Harbour Grace, 1866-1918.

[65]*JHA*, 1875-1914, Appendices. Information on shipments from the Labrador coast is not always given.

[66]The latter problem will be discussed in detail in later chapters.

[67]Baine Johnston Letter Book, 1893-1898, pp. 169-70, J.C. Hepburn, Managing Director, to his partners and superiors in Scotland, 5 February 1897.

[68]*JHA*, 1908, Appendix, p. 137, Report of the Department of Marine and Fisheries for 1907.

[69]*Ibid.*

[70]*Ibid.*, 1909-1915, Appendices, Reports of the Department of Marine and Fisheries, 1908-1914.

[71]*Ibid.*, 1909, Appendix, p. 228, Report of the Department of Marine and Fisheries for 1908.

[72]*Ibid.*, 1911, Appendix, p. 405, Report of the Department of Marine and Fisheries for 1910.

[73]*Ibid.*, 1912, Appendix, pp. 456-67, Report of the Department of Marine and Fisheries for 1911.

[74]*Ibid.*, 1915, Appendix, p. 544. Report of the Department of Marine and Fisheries for 1914.

[75]*Ibid.*, 1913, Appendix, p. 570, Report of the Department of Marine and Fisheries for 1912.

[76]See Table 2.3, Appendix.

[77]The Bell Island iron ore mines, which opened in 1895, provided some work for the unemployed sealers and Labrador fishermen, particularly in the Harbour Grace area.

[78]*JHA*, 1907, Appendix, p. 279, Report of the Department of Marine and Fisheries for 1907.

[79]C.O.194/175, fols. 42-43, Musgrave, Governor, Newfoundland, Address on the Opening of the First Session of the Ninth General Assembly, 30 January 1866.

[80]*JHA*, 1877, Appendix, p. 21.

[81]*Ibid.*, 1878, Appendix, p. 14.

[82]*Ibid.*, 1915, Appendix.

[83]Newman, Book 68, pp. 115-16, 5 January 1886; Book 69, pp. 229-30, 27 October 1891; *Ibid.*, pp. 243-45, 28 January 1892; and Book 70, p. 240, 18 January 1898.

[84]See *JHA*, Appendices, for petitions requesting that bultows be banned.

[85]Captain George Whiteley, "How the Cod Trap was Invented," *Western Star* (Corner Brook), 1 July 1949, pp. 17, 22.

[86]See Note 22, Chapter 2.

[87]McDonald, "Coaker," p. 28.

[88]C.O.194/251, fol. 257, Keene, British Consul, Genoa, to F.O., 25 February 1902.

[89]C.O.194/55, fols. 954-115, Keats, Governor, Newfoundland, to C.O., Report, 10 October 1814.

[90]*Public Ledger* (St. John's), 29 April 1831.

[91]*Ibid.*, 24 May 1831.

[92]During periods of over-extension of credit, such as 1815-1820 and 1894, some of the St. John's merchants also went bankrupt.

[93]Sir Brian Dunfield (ed.), *Newfoundland Law Reports*, Vol. II (St. John's: 1916), pp. 27-47. The similar case of the Insolvent Estate of Fergus and Glen was also settled at this time.

[94]*JHA*, 1882, Appendix, pp. 615-19, Patrick Hogan to E.D. Shea, Colonial Secretary, 27 February 1882. The word *planter* was used to describe an independent fisherman who had fairly substantial premises and equipment and who hired other fishermen as servants. The planters, rather than the independent fishermen, had always controlled the major part of the resident fishery. However, the planter fishery declined during the century as it became more difficult to operate profitably in this manner.

[95]C.O.194/131, fol. 269, James Simms to LeMarchant, 23 June 1849.

[96]See Shannon Ryan, "Newfoundland's Saltfish Markets: 1814-1914" (unpublished Ph.D. Thesis, University of London, 1982), pp. 155-64 (hereafter cited as Ryan, "Ph.D. Thesis"), and Table 2.5, Appendix.

[97] William White Collection, Nimshi Crewe, "A Descriptive Monograph on the Slades."

[98] William Cox and Company Letter Book, 1858, Charles Edmonds, Agent at Twillingate, to William Cox and Company, Poole, 30 April 1858.

[99] *Ibid.*

[100] Crewe, "Slades."

[101] *Ibid.*; and *JHA*, 1870, Appendix, pp. 501-07, R.J. Pinsent, Judge of Labrador, Report, 27 November 1869.

[102] Newman, Book 64, pp. 279-80, 27 June 1863.

[103] *Ibid.*, p. 300, 28 November 1863; and pp. 337-39, 17 September 1864.

[104] *Ibid.*, pp. 121-24, 9 June 1860.

[105] William Cox and Company Letter Book, 1865-1867, Charles Edmonds, Agent at Fogo, to Thomas Cox, Poole, 12 September 1866; Edmonds to Robert Bristowe, Agent at Twillingate, 9 March 1867; Edmonds to Samuel Evans, Agent at Greenspond, 19 March 1867; and Edmonds to Bristowe, 29 March 1867.

[106] Newman, Book 65, pp. 258-63, 22 October 1870; and C.O.194/179, fols. 546-47, Stephen Hill, Governor, Newfoundland, to C.O., 2 November 1870.

[107] Newman, Book 64, pp. 279-80, 27 June 1863.

[108] *Ibid.*, Book 66, pp. 10-12, 30 July 1872.

[109] *Ibid.*, Book 65, p. 369, 4 June 1872.

[110] John and William Boyd Letter Books, 1875-1878, 16 May 1877. The Boyds were independent agents who were involved, on a small scale, in shipping.

[111] Newman, Book 67, pp. 233-36, 4 July 1882.

[112] *Ibid.*, Book 68, pp. 117-18, 28 January 1886. Degroucy owed the bank £30,000.

[113] *Ibid.*, Book 70, pp. 328-29, 6 January 1889.

[114] C.R. Fay, *Life and Labour in Newfoundland* (Toronto: 1956), p. 15.

[115] Newman, Book 67, pp. 195-96, 8 November 1881.

[116] *Ibid.*, Book 70, pp. 216-17, 8 October 1897.

[117] *Ibid.*, Book 65, pp. 264-65, 5 November 1870; and Book 70, pp. 201-02, 16 July 1897.

[118] William Cox and Company Letter Book, 1865-1867, Charles Edmonds, Agent at Fogo, to William Waterman and Company, Fogo, 19 March 1867.

[119] *Ibid.*, 1858, Charles Edmonds, Agent at Twillingate, to William Cox and Company, Poole, 8 April 1858.

[120] Dawe, Agent at Burgeo, was called back to London in 1862 and dismissed from his post; Newman, Book 64, pp. 212-14, 22 February 1862. Morry, the firm's representative in St. John's, was likewise dismissed in 1864; *Ibid.*, p. 345, 12 November 1864.

[121] Job Family Papers, Thomas R. Job to his father, 16 December 1864.

[122] *Ibid.*

[123] Newman, Book 65, p. 334, 21 November 1871.

[124] *Ibid.*, Book 67, pp. 233-36, 4 July 1882.

[125] *Ibid.*, pp. 225-28, 23 May 1882.

[126] *Ibid.*, Book 70, pp. 126-27, 1 May 1898.

[127] *Ibid.* During the entire summer of 1899, Newman and Company discussed their plans for stopping credit to all planters.

[128] Job Family Papers, 16 December 1864.

[129] *Ibid.*, Business Papers, 1810-1885.

[130] *Ibid.*

[131] *Ibid.*

[132] Newman, Book 69, p. 307, 26 January 1893; and pp. 314-16, 23 March 1893.

[133] *Times and General Commercial Gazette* (St. John's), 30 January 1895.

[134] *Ibid.*

[135] *The Crown vs. The Directors and Manager of the Commercial Bank of Newfoundland* (St. John's: 1894), n.p. See also *The Crown vs. The Directors of the Union Bank of Newfoundland* (St. John's: 1895), n.p.

[136] *Evening Telegram* (St. John's), 1 and 2 June 1897, Speech by Whiteway to the House of Assembly, 11 May 1897.

[137] Newman, Book 66, pp. 99-100, 27 January 1874; *Ibid.*, pp. 106-08, 7 April 1874; *Ibid.*, pp. 112-14, 21 April 1874; *Ibid.*, pp. 150-52, 1 December 1874; *Ibid.*, pp. 339-42, 7 March 1878; *Ibid.*, p. 376, 30 August 1878; Book 67, pp. 4-5, 15 October 1878; *Ibid.*, p. 231, 6 June 1882; *Ibid.*, pp. 248-49, 12 September 1882; Book 68, pp. 76-80, 21 July 1885; and *Ibid.*, pp. 98-100, 13 October 1885.

[138] *Ibid.*, Book 69, pp. 61-62, 26 November 1889.

[139] Frederic F. Thompson, *The French Shore Problem in Newfoundland* (Toronto: 1961), p. 75.

[140] James K. Hiller, "The Political Repercussions of the Harbour Grace Affray" (lecture delivered to the Newfoundland Historical Society, St. John's, 27 January 1971).

[141] Alexander, *Decay of Trade*, p. 21.

[142] *Ibid.*

[143] *Newfoundland and Labrador Census Returns*, 1911.

[144] *JHA*, 1850-1859, Appendices.

[145] *Ibid.*, 1853, Appendix, pp. 132-42.

[146] *Ibid.*, 1889, Appendix, p. 619.

[147] *Ibid.*, 1896, Appendix, pp. 395-406, Annual Report of the Department of Marine and Fisheries for 1895.

[148] *Ibid.*, 1916, Appendix.

CHAPTER 3

[1] Canada, *Fisheries Report, 1930-31* (Ottawa: 1931), Graph, Appendix.

[2] United States Consular Reports, Printed Extracts, Vol. September-December, 1890, Bourn, U.S. Consul General, Rome, Report, 1889.

[3] Douglas Hall, *Free Jamaica: 1836-1865* (New Haven: 1959), p. 166.

[4] Innis, *Cod Fisheries*, p. 192.

[5] Ryan, "Ph.D. Thesis," pp. 392, 440, 546. Statistics on Naples were taken from the British Consular Reports, while those on Brazil and Italy were taken from the *Canadian Sessional Papers*.

[6] Ruth F. Grant, *The Canadian Atlantic Fishery* (Toronto: 1934), p. 12.

[7] C.O.194/288, fols. 86-95, Davidson to C.O., 25 February 1914.

[8] Ryan, "Ph.D. Thesis," pp. 548-49

[9] See Burton Alexander Balcom, "Production and Marketing in Nova Scotia's Dried Fish Trade: 1850-1914" (unpublished M.A. thesis, MUN, 1981).

[10] Ryan, "Ph.D. Thesis," pp. 579-81.

[11] *Ibid.*, pp. 594-97. Statistics for the French West Indies end in 1888. There are no statistics for 1892-95. Note that these periods range from four to six years.

[12] Grant, *The Atlantic Fishery*, p. 24.

[13] P.P., 1857-58, LV, pp. 382-84, Hunt, Report, 1856.

[14] P.P., 1873, LXV, pp. 372-75, Basanta, British Vice Consul, Ponce, Report, 1872.

[15] R. McFarland, *A History of the New England Fisheries* (University of Pennsylvania: 1911), pp. 390-91.

[16] Grant, *The Atlantic Fishery*, p. 16.

[17] See also Canada, *Fisheries Reports* (Ottawa), and *The Canada Year Book* (Ottawa).

[18] McFarland, *New England Fisheries*, p. 97; and R.G.59. Despatches from United States Consuls, Alicante, 1788-1905, Vol. I, Montgomery to Secretary of State, n.d.

[19] McFarland, *New England Fisheries*, p. 165.

[20] *Ibid.*, p. 168.

[21] *Ibid.*, p. 371.

[22] *Ibid.*, pp. 164-66.

[23] *Ibid.*, pp. 290-91.

[24] *Ibid.*, p. 165.

[25] U.S. *Foreign Commerce and Navigation Reports.*

[26] Ryan, "Ph.D. Thesis," pp. 200, 260.

[27] *Ibid.*, pp. 179, 187, 200.

[28] *Ibid.*, pp. 215, 221.

[29] *Ibid.*, pp. 216, 217.

[30] *Ibid.*, p. 279.

[31] *Ibid.*, pp. 258, 287.

[32] *Ibid.*, p. 282.

[33] *Ibid.*, p. 284.

[34] *Ibid.*, p. 262.

[35] *Ibid.*, p. 290.

[36] Vollan, *Klippfiskhandels*, p. 286.

[37] P.P., 1881, XC, pp. 563-81, Grant, British Consul, Naples, Report, 1880.

[38] Ryan, "Ph.D. Thesis," p. 406.

[39] P.P., 1895, XCVIII, pp. 783-842, Payton, British Consul, Genoa, Report, 1894.

[40] *Ibid.*, 1899, C, pp. 315-50, Keene, British Consul, Genoa, Report, 1898.

[41] Ryan, "Ph.D. Thesis," p. 422.

[42] Vollan, *Klippfiskhandels*, p. 290.

[43] Ryan, "Ph.D. Thesis," pp. 338, 339, 367.

[44] Vollan, *Klippfiskhandels*, p. 483.

[45] Ryan, "Ph.D. Thesis," pp. 519-20.

[46] P.P., 1900, LXXXVI, Annual Statement of the Trade of the United Kingdom with Foreign Countries and British Possessions, 1899. At this time Norwegian statistics listed only the immediate destination of exports.

[47] P.P., 1900, XCV, pp. 171-254, Dundas, Report, 1899.

[48] P.P., 1901, LXXXIII, pp. 779-890, Dundas, Report, 1900.

[49] Fritz Hodne, *An Economic History of Norway* (Bergen: 1975), p. 24.

[50] T.K. Derry, *A History of Modern Norway* (Oxford: 1973), p. 3.

[51] F.O.72/358, n.p., Bosanquet, British Ambassador, Madrid, to F.O., 21 March 1829.

[52] P.P., 1890, LXXV, pp. 621-54, Turner, Report, 1888.

[53] Vollan, *Klippfiskhandels*, p. 167.

[54] Innis, *The Cod Fisheries*, p. 375.

[55] France, Direction Général des Douanes, *Tableau Général du Commerce et de la Navigation*, Vols. 1823-1914.

[56] Innis, *The Cod Fisheries*, p. 376.

[57] P.P., 1887, LXXXIV, pp. 637-86, Hartwell, British Consul, Naples, Report, 1886.

[58] P.P., 1902, CVIII, pp. 127-50, Neville-Rolfe, Report, 1901.

[59] Ryan, "Ph.D. Thesis," p. 406.

[60] *Ibid.*, p. 422.

[61] *Ibid.*

[62] P.P., 1910, XCIX, pp. 933-50, Carmichael, British Consul, Leghorn, Report, 1910.

[63] Ryan, "Ph.D. Thesis," p. 414.

[64] *Ibid.*, p. 444.

[65] P.P., 1887, LXXXIV, pp. 597-607, Yeats Brown, Report, 1886.

[66] *Ibid*, LXXXVI, pp. 185-202, Joel, British Consul, Cadiz, to F.O., 19 April 1887.

[67] Ryan, "Ph.D. Thesis," p. 279.

[68] *Ibid.*, p. 290.

[69] P.P., 1906, CXXIV, pp. 501-54, MacDonald, Report, 1905.

[70] Ryan, "Ph.D. Thesis," p. 402.

[71] P.P., 1906, CXXIV, pp. 825-40, Woodhouse, Report, 1905.

[72] Ryan, "Ph.D. Thesis," pp. 403-04.

[73] P.P., 1908, CXI, pp. 411-85, MacDonald, Report, 1907.

[74] Ryan, "Ph.D. Thesis," p. 405.

[75] *Ibid.*

[76] William S. Mattox, Jr., "The Fishing Industry of Iceland" (unpublished M.A. thesis, McGill University, 1960), p. 37.

[77] Halldor Hermannson, "Sir Joseph Banks and Iceland," *Islantica*, XVIII, 1928 (Reprint; New York: 1966), p. 82.

[78] Mattox, "Iceland," p. 38.

[79] *Report of the Trade Commissioners on the Mediterranean Markets* (St. John's: 1989), p. 13.

[80] Ryan, "Ph.D. Thesis, " p. 279.

[81] *Ibid.*, p. 287.

[82] Denmark, *Statisk Aarbog*, 1898-1916. There is very little information about Icelandic saltfish markets.

[83] Ryan, "Ph.D. Thesis," p. 279.

[84] Denmark, *Statisk Aarbog*, 1898-1916.

[85] Ryan, "Ph.D. Thesis," p. 279.

[86] *Ibid.*, p. 295.

[87] *Ibid.*, p. 2176.

[88] C.O.194/251, fol. 250, Cowper, British Consul, Lisbon, to F.O., 17 February 1902.

[89] *Ibid.*, fols. 250-52, Cowper to F.O., 22 February 1902.

[90] *Ibid.*

[91] C.O.194/253, fols. 343-45, F.O. to C.O., 9 February 1903.

[92] R.G.94/C8.2, American Consular Agency, Oporto, Miscellaneous Correspondence, Vol. IV, 15 April 1911 to 2 January 1915, pp. 191-92, Stuve to Department of State, 19 September 1912.

CHAPTER 4

[1] Jaime Vicens Vives, *An Economic History of Spain*, trans. by Frances M. Lopez-Morilles (Princeton: 1969), p. 694.

[2] *Ibid.*, pp. 705-12.

[3] *Ibid.*, pp. 711-12.

[4] R.G.59, Despatches from United States Consuls in Alicante, 1788-1905, Vol. I, Montgomery to Secretary of State, 14 June 1810; 4 July 1810, 14 October 1810, 6 July 1811, 22 November 1811; and 14 October 1812. On 10 December 1813 Montgomery reported that the preferential tariff was immaterial since the outbreak of war between Great Britain and the United States halted all American trade to Spain.

[5] R.G.59, Despatches from the United States Consuls in Alicante, 1788-1905, Vol. I, 5 August 1788-14 December 1834, Montgomery to Secretary of State, 14 June 1810.

[6] *Ibid.*

[7] C.O.194/93, fols. 364-65, St. John's Chamber of Commerce to C.O., 30 May 1834; F.O.72/187, fols. 40-45, Charles Vaughan, British Ambassador, Madrid, to F.O., 27 July 1816.

[8] P.P., 1817, VI, p. 469; F.O.72/187, fols. 54-59, Letter from Spanish Finance Minister to Charles Vaughan, 15 January 1816, translated in the British Embassy. Unless otherwise stated, all £.s.d. are in sterling and all cwts are British.

[9] F.O.72/163, fol. 51, Allen to F.O., 2 November 1814.

[10] F.O.72/163, fol. 160, Athy to F.O., 22 November 1814. One real de vellon contained thirty-four maravedis. Where there is repetition, the writer will use 'r' and 'm'. The Castilian quintal contained 101.4 pounds (avoirdupois). See Vollan, *Klippfiskhandels*, p. 463.

[11] F.O.72/201, fols. 23-30, Colonel Meade to F.O., 10 June 1817.

[12] F.O.72/187, fols. 40-45, Vaughan to F.O., 27 July 1816. Enclosed in this despatch is the translation of a letter received from the Spanish Finance Minister, 15 January 1816.

[13] *Ibid.*

[14] F.O.72/189, fols. 21-22, Hunter to F.O., 20 January 1816.

[15] F.O.72/201, fols. 159-60, Allen to F.O., 21 February 1820.

[16] Edgar Holt, *The Carlist Wars in Spain* (London: 1967), pp. 42-43. The fueros allowed the Basques to have their own parliament and courts of law, to raise their own militia, and to make fixed payments to Madrid in lieu of taxes.

[17] F.O.72/238, fols. 175-76, Dawson to F.O., 24 February 1820.

[18] F.O.72/358, n.p., Bosanquet to F.O., 2 March 1829. Note the attempt by the Madrid government to collect duties during 1820-1823. The report states that 72r equalled 14s. 4d., and 42r equalled 8s. 4d. Therefore, the exchange rate was almost exactly five reales de vellon per shilling.

[19] R.G.59, Despatches from United States Consuls in Bilbao, 1791-1871, Vol. I, Francisco Xavier de Ealo to John Quincy Adams, 18 November 1818.

[20] R.G.59, Despatches from United States Consuls in Bilbao, 1791-1871, Vol. I, Francisco Xavier de Ealo to John Quincy Adams, 28 September 1820.

[21] *Ibid.*, 3 July 1824 and 1 January 1825.

[22] *Ibid.* See reports dated 13 January 1826; 18 January 1827; 14 February 1828; 1 March 1829; 28 May 1830.

[23] *Ibid.*, 26 February 1831.

[24] *Ibid.*, 10 September 1832.

[25] F.O.72/201, fol. 55, Allen to F.O., 5 November 1819.

[26] One of the major advantages that saltfish had over pickled beef, pork and herring as a source of protein was the comparative ease with which it could be transported inland, often by pack animals.

[27] F.O.72/163, fol. 55, Allen to F.O., 5 November 1819.

[28]F.O.72/354, no. 67, Bosanquet to F.O., 4 June 1829. The original statistics were in Castilian quintals (101.4 pounds avoirdupois) and the writer converted these to cwts rounded off to the nearest whole number.

[29]*Ibid.*

[30]The import tariffs on saltfish will be discussed in greater detail later.

[31]F.O.72/358, n.p., Bosanquet to F.O., 21 March 1829.

[32]F.O.72/163, fol. 160, Athy to F.O., 22 November 1814.

[33]R.G.59, U.S. Consuls, Alicante, 1788-1905, Vol. I, Montgomery to Secretary of State, 14 June 1810; 4 July 1810; 14 October 1810; and other despatches during this period. Montgomery reported that Mediterranean Spain normally bought about 100,000 cwts of American saltfish annually. Since the other U.S. consular despatches record little, if any, imports of American saltfish, it appears that Alicante was the major European market for the American product.

[34]F.O.72/353, no. 36, Bosanquet to F.O., 21 March 1829. Total British fish for 1822 includes a shipment of 2,500 quintals unloaded at Denia. This must have been the result of an emergency since Denia was not permitted to receive fish imports, although it had a prosperous coastal and export trade.

[35]*Ibid.* The exchange rate varied a little during this period but remained very close to five reales de vellon per shilling. It is not quite clear whether this table refers to both Valencia and Alicante.

[36]*Ibid.* In four years, 1816-1819, Malaga imported 13,532 quintals of saltfish from the United States and 2,600 quintals from Cape Breton and Nova Scotia, compared with 52,975 quintals from Newfoundland.

[37]*Ibid.* The original contains the number of 112 pound quintals, 100 pound quintals, average import price (reales per 100 pounds), and average duty paid (reales per 100 pounds). The writer calculated the average price and duty in reales de vellon per 112 pounds. Using five reales de vellon per shilling, these prices were converted into s. & d. and rounded off to the nearest penny.

[38]*Ibid.*

[39]*Ibid.*

[40]F.O.72/370, fol. 56, Mark to F.O., 24 March 1830.

[41]*Ibid.*

[42]This is the equivalent of almost exactly five reales de vellon per shilling.

[43]F.O.72/448, no. 9, Mark to F.O., 1 June 1833.

[44]F.O.72/354, no. 48, Bosanquet to F.O., 16 April 1829. Original report submitted to Bosanquet by Brackenbury, British Consul, Cadiz.

[45]*Ibid.*

[46]B.T.6/71, fols. 7-14, Matthews to F.O., 27 January 1818. This is the only reference to the sale of indulgences.

[47]F.O.72/354, no. 49, Bosanquet to F.O., 16 April 1829.

[48]F.O.72/381, no. 77, Addington, British Ambassador, Madrid, to F.O., 22 September 1832.

[49]F.O.72/354, no. 48, Bosanquet to F.O., 16 April 1829. The writer has converted reales de vellon into sterling at the rate of five reales per shilling. In 1824 importation of saltfish was assigned to a company led by a Mr. O'Shea in return for monthly payments to the Spanish treasury.

[50]Figures for total exports were taken from Ryan, "Abstract," pp. 93-120. Figures for Spain (1811-1813) were computed using the total figures and the figures for Portugal as given in Table 5.A. The present writer has assumed that no Newfoundland saltfish went to Italy during this period (see Chapter 6). The figures for Spain (1815-1828) were computed from the tables on each market.

[51]F.O.72/289, fols. 207-09, Bosanquet to F.O., 20 October 1824.

[52]*Ibid.*

[53]*Ibid.*

[54]F.O.72/354, no. 48, Bosanquet to F.O., 16 April 1829.

[55] *Ibid.*

[56] See Tables 4.D, 4.F, 4.G and 4.J, above.

[57] F.O.72/310, fols. 360-62, Bosanquet to F.O., 16 May 1825. This would, of course, exclude Bilbao.

[58] F.O.72/371, no. 4, Meade to F.O., 11 February 1830.

[59] P.P., 1817, VI, pp. 465-514. The evidence of the Select Committee appointed to examine the state of the Newfoundland cod fishery in 1817.

[60] F.O.72/242, fols. 57-58, B.T. to F.O., 5 August 1820.

[61] F.O.72/267, fols. 248-49, Newfoundland-Liverpool merchants to F.O., [n.d.] December 1822.

[62] F.O.72/296, fols. 191-92, Newfoundland-Poole merchants to F.O., 21 March 1824.

[63] *Ibid.*, fols. 196-97, Newfoundland-Bristol merchants to F.O., 29 March 1824.

[64] *Ibid.*, fols. 184-86, Newfoundland-Greenock merchants to F.O., 30 March 1824.

[65] *Ibid.*, fols. 200-01, Newfoundland-Dartmouth merchants to F.O., 6 April 1824.

[66] F.O.72/299, fols. 195-96, Spanish Foreign Office to Swedish Chargé d'Affaires, Madrid, 16 January 1825. The original was translated in the British Embassy.

[67] C.O.194/72, fols. 227-28, St. John's Chamber of Commerce to F.O., 25 July 1826.

[68] F.O.72/351, fols. 128-30, Lester to F.O., 15 November 1828.

[69] C.O.194/81, fols. 16-17, St. John's Chamber of Commerce to B.T., 20 December 1830.

[70] C.O.194/93, fols. 364-65, St. John's Chamber of Commerce to C.O., 30 May 1834.

[71] *Ibid.*, fols. 366-67, St. John's Chamber of Commerce to C.O., 20 November 1834.

[72] F.O.72/242, fols. 57-58, B.T. to F.O., 5 August 1820.

[73] *Ibid.*

[74] F.O.72/284, fols. 63-66, F.O. to W.A. Court, 30 March 1824.

[75] C.O.194/82, fol. 175, B.T. to C.O., 23 March 1831, with a copy of the request to F.O.

[76] C.O.194/92, fol. 45, B.T. to C.O., 18 February 1835, with a copy of the request to F.O.

[77] F.O.72/338, fol. 85, F.O. to Bosanquet, 21 November 1828. The replies to this instruction provide much valuable information on saltfish imports into Spain prior to 1828.

[78] C.O.194/93, fols. 364-65, St. John's Chamber of Commerce to C.O., 30 May 1834.

[79] B.T.3/48, no. 95, B.T. to F.O., 7 March 1855; *JHA*, 1857-1876.

[80] F.O.72/564, no. 92, British Treasury to F.O., 4 February 1840.

[81] *Ibid.*

[82] Vicens Vives, *Spain*, pp. 711-12.

[83] F.O.72/606, no. 7, Mark, British Consul, Malaga, to F.O., 7 March 1842. It was assumed by Mark that one quintal was equal to 100 pounds avoirdupois; most probably, the Spanish authorities were using the Castilian quintal of 101.4 pounds avoirdupois.

[84] *Ibid.*

[85] F.O.72/763, C.O. to F.O., 11 December 1849; C.O.194/132, fols. 94-96, LeMarchant to C.O., 15 November 1849; and B.T.3/38, fols. 402-11, B.T. to F.O., 8 January 1850.

[86] Ryan, "Ph.D. Thesis," p. 210.

[87] B.T.3/38, fols. 402-11, B.T. to F.O., 8 January 1850.

[88] *Ibid.*

[89] F.O.72/769, no. 4, Barrie to F.O., 17 January 1840.

[90] C.O.194/134, fols. 6-7, Chamber of Commerce to Secretary of State for the Colonies, 6 January 1851.

[91] P.P., 1859, XXX, pp. 730-31, Barrie, Report, 1858.

[92] F.O.72/963, no. 5, Barrie to F.O., 19 February 1859; and P.P., 1859, XXX, pp. 768-71, Barrie, Report, 1858.

[93] F.O.72/414, fol. 133, Hoyles, British Consul, Bilbao, to F.O., 15 October 1833. Hoyles said that business was at a standstill.

[94] F.O.72/582, no. 6, Clark, British Consul, Bilbao, to F.O., 30 June 1841. The ships from Norway sailed under the Swedish flag and were designated as Swedish.

[95] Vollan, *Klippfiskhandels*, pp. 165-66. A kvintaler equals 100 pund; one pund equals 498.11 grammes and 109.8 pounds (avoirdupois) equals one kvintaler.

[96] *Ibid.*

[97] *Ibid.*, p. 167.

[98] F.O.72/626, no. 119, Aston, British Ambassador, Madrid, to F.O., 27 June 1843.

[99] Vollan, *Klippfiskhandels*, p. 167.

[100] Ryan, "Ph.D. Thesis," p. 216.

[101] P.P., 1862, LVIII, pp. 581-86, Young, Report, 1859.

[102] *Ibid.*

[103] F.O.72/1066, no. 10, Young to F.O., 28 January 1863.

[104] P.P., 1866, LXX, pp. 493-504, Young, Report, 1865.

[105] P.P., 1867-68, LXVIII, pp. 87-97, Young, Report, 1866.

[106] F.O.72/679, no. 7, Baker, British Consul, Corunna, to F.O., 24 March 1845.

[107] *Ibid.*, no. 13, Baker to F.O., 17 June 1850.

[108] Vollan, *Klippfiskhandels.*, p. 221.

[109] P.P., 1862, LVIII, pp. 581-86, Young, Report, 1859.

[110] F.O.72/430, no. 1, Annesley, British Consul, Barcelona, to F.O., 10 January 1834; F.O.72/449, no. 1, Montague, British Consul, Barcelona, to F.O., 10 April 1835; F.O.72/512, no. 1, Annesley to F.O., 1 January 1838; *Ibid.*, no. 4, Annesley to F.O., 23 February 1838.

[111] F.O.72/558, no. 1, Annesley to F.O., 31 January 1840; *Ibid.*, no. 2, Annesley to F.O., 31 January 1840; F.O.72/583, no. 1, Annesley to F.O., 29 January 1841.

[112] F.O.72/607, no. 6, Penleaze to F.O., 30 January 1842.

[113] P.P., 1874, LXVI, pp. 437-39, Prat, Report, 1872.

[114] Ryan, "Ph.D. Thesis," p. 223.

[115] F.O.72/583, no. 4, Waring to F.O., 4 January 1841.

[116] Ryan, "Ph.D. Thesis," p. 225.

[117] F.O.72/680, no. 4, Waring to F.O., 10 January 1845.

[118] F.O.72/758, no. 4, Barrie to F.O., 8 October 1848.

[119] *Ibid.*

[120] F.O.72/810, no. 6, Barrie to F.O., 27 January 1852.

[121] *Ibid.*

[122] *Ibid.*

[123] F.O.72/851, no. 7, Barrie to F.O., 3 February 1854.

[124] F.O.72/910, no. 7, Barrie to F.O., 25 February 1856; and F.O.72/923, no. 6, Barrie to F.O., 19 February 1857.

[125] F.O.72/851, no. 7, Barrie to F.O., 3 February 1854.

[126] F.O.72/875, no. 4, Barrie to F.O., 12 February 1856.

[127] *Ibid.*; F.O.72/901, no. 7, Barrie to F.O., 25 February 1856; and F.O.72/987, no. 5, Barrie to F.O., 10 February 1860.

[128] F.O.72/1016, no. 6, Barrie to F.O., 22 February 1861.

[129] *Ibid.*; F.O.72/1043, no. 7, Barrie to F.O., 25 February 1862; F.O.72/1085, no. 6, Barrie to F.O., 11 February 1864; and P.P., 1862, LVIII, p. 577, Barrie, Report, 1860.

[130] Ryan, "Ph.D. Thesis," p. 228.

[131] F.O.72/1188, Separate, Young, British Consul, Bilbao, to F.O., 13 March 1868.

[132] *Ibid.*

[133] P.P., 1865, LIII, p. 641, Barrie, Report, 1864.

[134] P.P., 1875, LXIV, pp. 398-423, Phipps, Secretary, British Legation, Madrid, to F.O., 25 May 1875.

[135] P.P., 1875, LXXVI, pp. 3-5, Barrie, Report, 1874.

[136] F.O.72/448, no. 10, Mark to F.O., 30 June 1835; F.O.72/466, no. 7, Mark to F.O., 15 March 1836; F.O.72/488, no. 7, Mark to F.O., 28 February 1837; F.O.72/536, no. 3, Mark to F.O., 3 February 1839; and F.O.72/558, no. 5, Mark to F.O., 27 February 1840.

[137] Ryan, "Ph.D. Thesis," p. 234.

[138] *Ibid.*

[139] P.P., 1878, LXXIII, pp. 490-501, Wilkinson, British Consul, Malaga, Report, 1877.

[140] Ryan, "Ph.D. Thesis," p. 237.

[141] *Ibid.*, p. 236.

[142] P.P., 1872, LVIII, pp. 655-93, Reade, British Consul, Cadiz, Report, 1871.

[143] Vollan, *Klippfiskhandels*, p. 221. The present writer has converted Vollan's figures from kvintaler to cwts using 109.8 pounds avoirdupois per kvintal, rounded off to the nearest whole number.

[144] C.O.194/132, fols. 94-96, LeMarchant to C.O., 15 November 1849.

[145] C.O.194/133, fols. 147-62, LeMarchant to C.O., 4 May 1850.

[146] C.O.194/134, fols. 5-9, LeMarchant to C.O., 8 January 1851.

[147] C.O.194/166, fol. 274, Report of the Chamber of Commerce, 9 August 1861.

[148] F.O.72/763, no. 61, C.O. to F.O., 11 December 1849.

[149] C.O.194/133, fols. 363-66, F.O. to C.O., 22 June 1850.

[150] C.O.194/150, fol. 513, C.O. to Bannerman, 21 July 1857.

[151] *Ibid.*

[152] C.O.194/151, fols. 441-61, F.O. to C.O., 18 August 1857.

[153] C.O.194/163, fol. 145, F.O. to C.O., 27 July 1860.

[154] P.P., 1875, LXXIV, pp. 398-423, Phipps to F.O., 25 May 1875.

[155] *Ibid.*

[156] *Ibid.*

[157] *Ibid.*

[158] P.P., 1877, LXXXI, pp. 30-58, Phipps to F.O., 25 January 1877. See also Vicens Vives, *Spain*, and C.A.M. Hennessey, *The Federal Republic in Spain* (Oxford: 1962).

[159] P.P., 1871, LXV, pp. 455-63, Young, British Consul, Bilbao, to F.O., 17 June 1870.

[160] *Ibid.*

[161] P.P., 1875, LXXIV, pp. 398-423, Phipps to F.O., 25 May 1875.

[162] P.P., 1882, LXIX, pp. 650-78, Fane, Representative of the Secretary of the British Legation, Madrid, to F.O., 30 September 1882.

[163] *Ibid.*

[164] Ryan, "Ph.D. Thesis," p. 247,

[165] P.P., 1884, LXXX, pp. 569-94, Joel, Report, 1883.

[166] P.P., 1886, LXV, pp. 81-130, Gosling, Secretary of the British Legation, Madrid, to F.O., 25 May 1886.

[167] *Ibid.*

[168] *Ibid.*, pp. 473-85, Joel, Report, 1885.

[169] *Ibid.*, pp. 487-96, Bidwell, Report, 1885.

[170] P.P., 1887, LXXXVI, pp. 61-72, Crowe, British Consul General, Havana, to F.O., 12 June 1886; and pp. 91-122, Wooldridge, British Consul, Barcelona, to F.O., 14 February 1887.

[171] *Ibid.*, pp. 185-202, Joel to F.O., 19 April 1887. See Chapter 3 for a more complete discussion of the French saltfish industry.

[172] Ryan, "Ph.D. Thesis," p. 253.

[173] P.P., 1895, C, pp. 611-56, Smith to F.O., 6 May 1895.

[174] P.P., 1896, LXXXVIII, pp. 639-71, Smith to F.O., 12 May 1896.

[175] Ryan, "Ph.D. Thesis," pp. 258, 287. Beginning in 1909 the figures in column two refer to Iceland only.

[176] P.P., 1880, LXXIV, pp. 154-59, Prat, British Consul, Barcelona, Report, 1879. This is the first consular report from Barcelona to include Alicante.

[177] P.P., 1883, LXXIV, pp. 421-29, Prat, Report, 1882. The report does not indicate the types of "dried codfish."

[178] Ryan, "Ph.D. Thesis," pp. 290-92.

[179] P.P., 1889, LXXX, pp. 555-82, Wooldridge to F.O., 5 March 1889.

[180] P.P., 1887, XCIII, pp 435-60, Wyndham, British Consul, Barcelona, Report, 1896; P.P., 1898, XCVIII, pp. 641-80, Roberts, British Consul, Barcelona, Report, 1897; P.P., 1899, CII, pp. 657-97, Roberts, Report, 1898; P.P., 1900, XCVI, pp. 236-300, Roberts, Report, 1899; and P.P., 1903, LXXVIII, pp. 1041-90, Roberts, Report, 1902.

[181] P.P., 1900, XCVI, pp. 236-300, Roberts, Report, 1899.

[182] P.P., 1886, LXV, pp. 455-71, Wooldridge to F.O., 15 March 1866.

[183] P.P., 1884-1885, LXXVIII, pp. 76-77, Cummings, British Vice Consul, Alicante, Report, 1884.

[184] C.O.194/251, fols. 254-55, Roberts to F.O., 25 February 1902.

[185] *Ibid.*

[186] Ryan, "Ph.D. Thesis," pp. 293-94.

[187] P.P., 1886, LXV, pp. 455-71, Wooldridge to F.O., 15 March 1886.

[188] P.P., 1887, LXXXVI, pp. 91-122, Wooldridge to F.O., 14 February 1887.

[189] P.P., 1892, LXXXIV, pp. 285-308, Macpherson, British Consul, Barcelona, to F.O., 16 May 1892.

[190] *Ibid.*

[191] Ryan, "Ph.D. Thesis," pp. 295-97.

[192] P.P., 1895, LXXXVIII, pp. 187-228, Finn to F.O., 5 July 1894.

[193] P.P., 1897, XCIII, pp. 519-24, Finn, Report, 1896.

[194] P.P., 1913, LXXII, pp. 567-623, Staniforth, British Consul, Malaga, Report, 1912.

[195] Ryan, "Ph.D. Thesis," pp. 298-99.

[196] C.O.194/204, fols. 96-97, Chamber of Commerce to C.O. and F.O., 9 September 1882.

[197] C.O.194/205, fols. 23-26, F.O. to C.O., 13 January 1883.

[198] *Ibid.*, fols. 195-203, F.O. to C.O., copy, 12 September 1883.

[199] *Ibid.*

[200] C.O.194/210, fols. 16-17, des Voeux, Governor, Newfoundland, "Speech on the Opening of the 2nd Session of the Fifteenth General Assembly of Newfoundland," 17 February 1887.

[201] C.O.194/221, fol. 84. O'Brien, Governor, Newfoundland, to C.O., 29 February 1892.

[202] C.O.194/202, fol. 209, F.O. to C.O., 18 January 1892.

[203] *Ibid.*, fols. 307-08, F.O. to C.O., 24 March 1892.

[204] C.O.194/221, fol. 434, Chamber of Commerce to C.O., 1 June 1892.

[205] *Ibid.*, fols. 751-52.

[206] C.O.194/222, fols. 207-08, F.O. to C.O., 24 March 1892.

[207] *Ibid.*, fols. 393-94, F.O. to C.O., 12 July 1892.

[208] *Ibid.*, C.O. Minute, 13 July 1892.

[209] *Ibid.*, fol. 405, F.O. to C.O., 15 July 1892, with enclosures.

[210] C.O.194/229, fols. 363-65, British Ambassador, Madrid, to F.O., 2 March 1894.

CHAPTER 5

[1] F.O.63/100, fol. 104, Committee of the Privy Council for Trade to F.O., 8 August 1810.

[2] Ryan, "Ph.D. Thesis," p. 302.

[3] F.O.63/99, fols. 187-91, Committee of the Privy Council for Trade to F.O., 16 August 1810; and F.O.63/100, fol. 104, Committee of the Privy Council for Trade to F.O., 8 August 1810. The 1811 exchange rate was 3.556 milreis per pound sterling; see F.O.63/106, fols. 158-64, "Exchange Rates in 1811;" and F.O.63/137, fols. 28-31, Jeffery to F.O., 25 February 1812, where the exchange rate is also given as 3.556 milreis per pound, or 67s.5d. per milrea.

[4] F.O.63/135, fols. 27-42, Jeffery to Stuart, 4 September 1812.

[5] F.O.63/137, fols. 58-77, Jeffery to F.O., 31 January 1811.

[6] F.O.63/178, fols. 145-49, Thomas Sack, Office of the Privy Council for Trade, to F.O., 12 March 1814.

[7] Ryan, "Ph.D. Thesis," pp. 358-59.

[8] S. Sideri, *Trade and Power: Informal Colonialism in Anglo-Portuguese Relations* (Rotterdam: 1970), p. 126.

[9] Ryan, "Ph.D. Thesis," pp.360-61.

[10] *Ibid.*, pp. 362-63.

[11] F.O.63/469, no. 29, Smith to F.O., 27 June 1837.

[12] F.O.63/473, fol. 284, C.O. to F.O., 10 July 1837.

[13] R.G.59, Despatches from United States Consuls in Oporto, Vol. I, no. 8, Tinelli to U.S. Secretary of State, 31 December 1841.

[14] Computed from the figures in Ryan, "Abstract." The C.O. reports which were used in the "Abstract" do not go beyond 1833. Percentages have been rounded off to the nearest whole number.

[15] Sideri, *Trade and Power*, p. 121. See also Eric N. Baklanoff, *The Economic Transformation of Spain and Portugal* (London: 1978), p. 102; and J.B. Trend, *Portugal* (London: 1957), pp. 175-76.

[16] F.O.63/156, fols. 140-41, Stuart to F.O., 18 September 1813.

[17] Sideri, *Trade and Power*, p. 121.

[18] *Ibid.*

[19] A.H. de Oliveira Marques, *History of Portugal* (2nd ed.; New York: 1976), Vol. 2, Chapter 10, "Constitutional Monarchy," pp. 1-76.

[20] *Ibid.*

[21]Sideri, *Trade and Power*, p. 131. By 1822 the Portuguese currency had lost twenty-three percent of its value: 4600 reis per pound instead of 3555.

[22]F.O.63/445, no. 110, Lord Howard de Walden, British Ambassador, Lisbon, to F.O., 25 March 1835. This is only one of a number of despatches concerning this problem.

[23]Chamber of Commerce, Newfoundland, Minute Book, 1834-41, Vol. I, Chamber of Commerce to C.O., 25 August 1837.

[24]*Ibid.*

[25]F.O.63/469, no. 8, Smith to F.O., 21 January 1837.

[26]F.O.63/474, fol. 229, Office of the Privy Council for Trade to F.O., 24 November 1837.

[27]F.O.63/469, no. 29, Smith to F.O., 27 June 1837. The real fear came from the fact that Portugal had already begun to build a deep-sea cod fishing fleet. See below.

[28]F.O.63/574, no. 132, Walden to F.O., 11 June 1842. This company was sometimes referred to as the Lisbon Fishing Company, after the port from which it sailed, and sometimes it was referred to as the National Fishing Company.

[29]*Ibid.*

[30]Solhaug, *De Norske Fiskeriers Historie*, Vol. 2, p. 597. Solhaug estimates that eighteen or nineteen klippfisk weighed one våg (approximately 39.5 pounds avoirdupois).

[31]F.O.63/547, no. 132, Walden to F.O., 11 June 1842.

[32]F.O.63/551, no. 290, Walden to F.O., 26 November 1842.

[33]Vollan, *Klippfiskhandels*, pp. 148-49.
...dette kompani ej kan vara sardeles skadlig får unlandske fiskenhandel isynnerhet da man dertil legger at den portugisiske fisken är först eftersöke da det ej finnas at tinga utlandsk.

[34]F.O.63/547, no. 32, Walden to F.O., 11 June 1842. The Septembrists were a left-wing group that enjoyed varying degrees of influence during 1836-1842.

[35]C.O.194/88, fol. 55, Cochrane to C.O., 26 July 1834.

[36]C.O.194/90, fols. 23-25, Prescott to C.O., 5 January 1835.

[37]C.O.194/93, fols. 129-32, Prescott to C.O., 29 January 1836.

[38]C.O.194/97, fols. 527-33, Prescott to C.O., 28 August 1837.

[39]C.O.194/98, fols. 233-35, Chamber of Commerce, St. John's, to C.O., 15 December 1837.

[40]C.O.194/111, fols. 98-99, Chamber of Commerce, St. John's, to C.O., 30 January 1841.

[41]C.O.194/92, fols. 45-56, B.T. to C.O., 18 February and 11 March 1835.

[42]C.O.194/97, fols. 27-33, Prescott to C.O., with enclosures and duplicates, 28 August 1837.

[43]F.O.63/471, no. 42, Committee of the Privy Council for Trade to F.O., 24 November 1837.

[44]F.O.63/474, fol. 229, Committee of the Privy Council for Trade to F.O., 24 November 1837.

[45]C.O.194/98, fols. 233-35, Chamber of Commerce, St. John's, to Glenelg, with enclosures and duplicates, 15 December 1837.

[46]C.O.194/102, fols. 43-44, F.O. to C.O., 1 March 1838, with despatch from Walden, fols. 45-47, 19 December 1837.

[47]*Ibid.*

[48]F.O.63/480, no. 10, Smith to F.O., 13 February 1838.

[49]F.O.63/462, no. 108, Walden to F.O., 25 March 1837.

[50]de Oliveira Marques, *History of Portugal*, Vol. 2, p. 5.

[51]F.O.63/551, no. 290, Walden to F.O., 26 November 1842. This seems to be a low figure for Lisbon but it is probable that a fair quantity was imported into Figueira. There is very little information on Figueira but Table 5.D, and the accompanying footnotes, seem to indicate that imports into this market were irregular, often rising when those into Lisbon fell. Neither Figueira nor Vianna received much notice in the records, with a brief exception late in the century.

[52] F.O.63/607, no. 10, Smith to F.O., 24 February 1846.

[53] F.O.63/688, no. 426, Sir Hamilton Seymour, British Minister, Lisbon, to F.O., 27 October 1848. Enclosed is the communication from the Portuguese Foreign Office.

[54] F.O.63/691, no. 15, Smith to F.O., 10 March 1848. Smith gave the value in milreis and the exchange rate of 54d. per milrea. The present writer computed the value in pounds rounded off to the nearest whole number.

[55] F.O.63/688, no. 426, Seymour to F.O., 27 October 1848. Enclosed is the communication from the Portuguese Foreign Office.

[56] F.O.63/723, no. 169, Howard to F.O., 8 June 1850.

[57] F.O.63/719, no. 87, F.O. to Howard, 27 August 1840. Howard was acting Chargé d'Affaires in Lisbon on certain occasions while serving as full-time Secretary of Legation.

[58] F.O.63/725, no. 24, Seymour to F.O., 8 November 1850.

[59] F.O.63/719, no. 7, F.O. to Seymour, 26 November 1850.

[60] F.O.63/757, no. 81, Pakenham, British Chargé d'Affaires, Lisbon, to F.O., 18 May 1852; F.O.63/754, no. 34, F.O. to Pakenham, 22 June 1852.

[61] F.O.63/762, no. 45, Smith to F.O., 28 August 1852.

[62] F.O.63/767, n.p., B.T. to F.O., 17 September 1852.

[63] F.O.63/769, no. 22, F.O. to Pakenham, 16 June 1853.

[64] F.O.63/770, no. 28, Pakenham to F.O., 10 March 1853.

[65] F.O.63/879, no. 17, Smith to F.O., 8 April 1862.

[66] P.P., 1863, LXX, pp. 662-68, Herries, Report, 1862.

[67] R.G.59, Despatches from U.S. Consuls in Oporto, Vol. 3, no. 43, Pike to Secretary of State, 24 December 1856.

[68] P.P., 1863, LXX, pp. 662-68, Herries, Report, 1862.

[69] *Ibid.*

[70] Ryan, "Ph.D. Thesis," p. 330.

[71] *Ibid.*, pp. 338, 339.

[72] Ryan, "Ph.D. Thesis," pp. 364-66.

[73] P.P., 1868-69, LIX, pp. 556-75, Brackenbury, British Consul, Lisbon, to F.O., 28 May 1868. See Table 5.G.

[74] P.P., 1870, LXIV, pp. 66-75, Brackenbury to F.O., 12 June 1869.

[75] P.P., 1871, LXV, pp. 434-41, Brackenbury to F.O., 17 May 1870.

[76] P.P., 1871, LXVI, pp. 318-33, Brackenbury to F.O., 31 May 1871.

[77] P.P., 1873, LXV, pp. 301-09, Brackenbury to F.O., 18 May 1873.

[78] *Ibid.*, p. 364.

[79] *Ibid.*, p. 333.

[80] P.P., 1910, CI, pp. 655-80, Somers-Cocks, British Consul, Lisbon, Report, 1909.

[81] P.P., 1914-16, LXXIV, pp. 651-80, Somers-Cocks, Report, 1914.

[82] Ryan, "Ph.D. Thesis," p. 333.

[83] George Hawes and C.W. Hawes, "Memorandum on the Marketing of Salt Codfish on the European Markets" (London: 1936).

[84] Ryan, "Ph.D. Thesis," pp. 338-39.

[85] P.P., 1893-94, XCV, pp. 899-918, Grant, Report, 1893.

[86] P.P., 1897, XCII, pp. 681-95, Hay-Newton, British Consul, Oporto, Report, 1895.

[87] *Board of Trade Journal*, 1887, Vol. 3, pp. 254-63.

[88] P.P., 1897, XCII, pp. 681-91, Hay-Newton, Report, 1895.

[89] C.O.194/236, fols. 104-05, F.O. to C.O., 6 October 1896.

[90] C.O.194/239, fols. 157-58, F.O. to C.O., 27 April 1897.

[91] Ibid., fols. 186-87, MacDonell to F.O., 12 May 1897.

[92] Ibid., fol. 223, F.O. to C.O., 14 September 1897.

[93] Ibid., fol. 342, London Chamber of Commerce to C.O., 2 September 1897.

[94] Ibid., fol. 436, Holmwood & Holmwood to C.O., 14 April 1897.

[95] C.O.194/240, fol. 54, Governor Murray to C.O., 28 January 1898.

[96] C.O.194/253, fols. 469-70, Gosselin to F.O., 9 May 1903.

[97] R.G.84/C8.2, American Consular Agency, Oporto, Miscellaneous Correspondence, Vol. IV, 15 April 1911 to 2 January 1915, pp. 191-92, Stuve, American Consul, to Department of State, 19 September 1912.

CHAPTER 6

[1] Ryan, "Ph.D. Thesis," pp. 432-33.

[2] Ibid., p. 373.

[3] B.T.1/309, no. 20, Gallwey, British Consul, Naples, to F.O., 21 March 1835.

[4] B.T.2/2, fols. 48-67, Gallwey to F.O., 11 March 1836.

[5] B.T.2/4, fols. 128-35, Gallwey to F.O., 10 April 1838.

[6] R.G.59, Despatches from U.S. Consuls in Naples, no. 64, Hammett to State Department, 4 February 1838.

[7] P.P., 1866, LXIX, pp. 456-63, Bonham, British Consul-General, Naples, Report, 1864.

[8] F.O.70/115, n.p., Petition from the Poole merchants to B.T., 26 June 1826.

[9] F.O.70/85, no. 74, Lushington, British Consul, Naples, to F.O., 20 September 1818.

[10] F.O.70/98, n.p., Lushington to F.O., 8 January 1822.

[11] F.O.70/106, n.p., Lushington to F.O., 7 May 1824.

[12] F.O.70/111, n.p., Lushington to F.O., 5 January 1825.

[13] F.O.70/114, no. 11, Lushington to F.O., 24 June 1826.

[14] Ibid.

[15] Ibid., no. 15, Lushington to F.O., 11 September 1826.

[16] F.O.70/120, no. 10, Lushington to F.O., 1 March 1828.

[17] P.P., 1837, XXXIX, pp. 429-46, Memorials of British Merchants on the expediency of revising the Commercial Relations between Great Britain and Spain.

[18] P.P., 1840, XXI, p. 673, J. Macgregor, Report of the Commercial Statistics of the Kingdom of the Two Sicilies.

[19] F.O.70/114, no. 22, Lushington to F.O., 29 December 1826.

[20] C.O.194/93, fols. 366-67, St. John's Chamber of Commerce to C.O., 20 November 1834.

[21] Ryan, "Ph.D. Thesis," pp. 378-79.

[22] Ibid., pp. 434-35.

[23] P.P., 1872, LVIII, pp. 531-44, Macbean, British Consul, Leghorn, Report, 1871.

[24] F.O.79/40, n.p., Falconar to F.O., 11 January 1823.

[25] Ibid.

[26] See Vollan, Klippfiskhandels, pp. 289-90; and R.G.59, Despatches from U.S. Consuls in Leghorn, 1793-1906, 11 vols.

[27] R.G.59, Despatches from U.S. Consuls in Leghorn, Vol. 5, Andrew Stevens, American Consul, to State Department, 24 February 1862.

[28] Ryan, "Ph.D. Thesis," pp. 382, 436-37.

[29] F.O.67/138, no. 5, Yeats Brown to F.O., 9 January 1846.

[30] F.O.67/145, no. 5, Yeats Brown to F.O., 11 January 1847.

[31] F.O.67/173, no. 5, Yeats Brown to F.O., n.d., January 1850.

[32] F.O.67/187, no. 7, Yeats Brown to F.O., 26 January 1852.

[33] F.O.67/202, no. 4, fols. 41-43, Yeats Brown to F.O., 30 January 1854.

[34] F.O.67/209, no. 7, fols. 47-49, Yeats Brown to F.O., 27 January 1855.

[35] F.O.67/219, no. 7, fols. 39-40, Yeats Brown to F.O., 19 January 1856.

[36] B.T.6/51, fols. 145-51, Charles Denis, British Consul, Civitavecchia, to F.O., 13 February 1821.

[37] Ryan, "Ph.D. Thesis," pp. 386, 438-39.

[38] C.O.194/137, fols. 180-84, F.O. to C.O., 19 July 1852.

[39] Ibid.

[40] Ibid.

[41] Ryan, "Ph.D. Thesis," p. 390.

[42] Ibid., p. 391.

[43] Ibid., p. 392.

[44] Ibid., p. 440.

[45] P.P., 1888, CI, pp. 617-50, Hartwell, Report, 1887.

[46] P.P., 1896, LXXXVI, pp. 445-82, Neville-Rolfe, Report, 1895.

[47] P.P., 1897, XCI, pp. 615-36, Neville-Rolfe, Report, 1896.

[48] Ibid.

[49] P.P., 1903, LXXVI, pp. 879-98, Neville-Rolfe, Report, 1902.

[50] Ryan, "Ph.D. Thesis," p. 406.

[51] R.G.59, Despatches from U.S. Consuls in Leghorn, Vol. 7, 30 May 1870 and 30 September 1880, Howard to State Department, 26 October 1871, no. 45.

[52] P.P., 1872, LVIII, pp. 531-44, MacBean, Report, 1871.

[53] P.P., 1884, LXXX, pp. 252-83, Inglis, British Consul, Leghorn, Report, 1883.

[54] P.P., 1872, LVIII, pp. 531-44, MacBean, Report, 1871.

[55] P.P., 1884, LXXX, pp. 252-83, Inglis, Report, 1883. In his report for the following year, Inglis stated that the amount of Labrador-cured saltfish imported in 1883 was 66,962 cwts. See P.P., 1884-85, LXXVII, pp. 504-35, Inglis, Report, 1884.

[56] P.P., 1884-85, LXXVII, pp. 504-35, Inglis, Report, 1884.

[57] Ibid.

[58] Ibid.

[59] Ibid.

[60] Ibid.

[61] Vollan, Klippfiskhandels, p. 289.

[62] Ryan, "Ph.D. Thesis," pp. 442-43.

[63] P.P., 1886, LXV, pp. 435-40, Inglis, Report, 1885.

[64] P.P., 1887, LXXXIV, pp. 591-94, Inglis, Report, 1886.

[65] P.P., 1890, LXXV, pp. 755-80, O'Neill, Report, 1889.

[66] *Ibid.*, p. 413.

[67] P.P., 1910, XCIX, pp. 935-50, Carmichael, Report, 1909.

[68] Ryan, "Ph.D. Thesis," pp. 444-46. From 1866 to 1872 and 1881 to 1891 the reports refer to the fish importing season, i.e. early autumn to late winter. In 1873-1880 the reports refer to the calendar year.

[69] P.P., 1866, LXIX, pp. 134-46, Brown, Report, 1864.

[70] France, *Tableau Général du Commerce*, Vols. 1823-1868.

[71] P.P., 1870, LXIV, pp. 34-50, De Thierry, Report, 1868.

[72] P.P., 1867-68, LXVIII, pp. 41-52, Brown, Report, 1866.

[73] P.P., 1868-69, LIX, pp. 435-44, Brown, Report, 1867.

[74] P.P., 1871, LXVI, pp. 29-36, Brown, Report, 1870.

[75] P.P., 1876, LXXIV, pp. 406-15, Brown, Report, 1875.

[76] P.P., 1872, LVIII, pp. 521-30, Brown, Report, 1871.

[77] P.P., 1895, XCVIII, pp. 783-842, Payton, British Consul, Genoa, Report, 1894.

[78] *Ibid.* The original figures were in tons and were converted by the present writer at twenty cwts per ton.

[79] P.P., 1896, LXXXVI, pp. 483-534, Payton, Report, 1895.

[80] P.P., 1897, XCI, pp. 695-748, Payton, Report, 1896.

[81] P.P., 1899, C, pp. 315-50, Keene, Report, 1898.

[82] P.P., 1902, CVIII, pp. 195-242, Keene, Report, 1901.

[83] C.O.194/251, fol. 257, Keene to F.O., 25 February 1902.

[84] P.P., 1909, XCVI, pp. 71-116, Keene, Report, 1908.

[85] P.P., 1912-13, XCVII, pp. 191-226, Keene, Report, 1911.

[86] P.P., 1913, LXXI, pp. 79-108, Keene, Report, 1912.

[87] P.P., 1914, XCII, pp. 409-42, Kohan, British Vice Consul, Report, 1913.

[88] P.P., 1886, LXV, pp. 423-34, Yeats Brown, Report, 1885.

[89] P.P., 1887, LXXXIV, pp. 597-607, Yeats Brown, Report, 1886.

[90] *Ibid.*

[91] P.P., 1888, CI, pp. 535-47, Yeats Brown, Report, 1887.

[92] P.P., 1895, XCVIII, pp. 583-642, Payton, Report, 1894.

[93] P.P., 1897, XCI, pp. 695-748, Payton, Report, 1896.

[94] *Ibid.*

[95] P.P., 1900, XCIV, pp. 403-15, Keene, Report, 1899.

[96] P.P., 1910, XCIX, pp. 657-733, Keene, Report, 1909.

[97] P.P., 1905, XC, pp. 323-74, Keene, Report, 1904. These are the only figures available.

[98] P.P., 1903, LXXVII, pp. 899-952, Keene, Report, 1902; P.P., 1904, XCIX, pp. 831-80, Keene, Report, 1903; and P.P., 1905, XC, pp. 323-74, Keene, Report, 1904. There are no figures for the years after 1904.

[99] P.P., 1913, LXXI, pp. 79-108, Keene, Report, 1912.

[100] Vollan, *Klippfiskhandels*, p. 290.
"Genova gikk mer og mer over til a bli hovedinnførselsbyen for norske klippfisk i Italia."

[101] P.P., 1901, LXXXIII, pp. 259-65, Berner, British Vice Consul, Report, 1900.

[102] P.P., 1910, XCIX, pp. 982-90, Berner, Report, 1909; and P.P., 1911, XCIII, pp. 529-35, Berner, Report, 1910.

[103]P.P., 1912-13, XCVII, pp. 409-17, Berner, Report, 1911.

[104]P.P., 1914, XCII, pp. 477-86, Berner, Report, 1913.

[105]P.P., 1912-13, XCVII, pp. 409-17, Berner, Report, 19ll.

[106]P.P., 1902, CVIII, pp. 76-84, MacKenzie, Report, 1900.

[107]*Ibid.*

[108]P.P., 1908, CXIII, pp. 86-95, MacKenzie, Report, 1907.

[109]P.P., 1864, LXI, pp. 715-31, West, Report, 1861-62.

[110]*United States Consular Reports*, Printed Extracts, Vol. January-March 1887, Aiden, Report, 1886.

[111]C.O.194/225, fols. 379-424, MacGregor, Governor, Newfoundland, to C.O., 31 January 1905. These were the general tariffs.

[112]C.O.194/239, fols. 165-77, F.O. to C.O., 12 May 1897. Enclosed is Chapman's report.

[113]C.O.194/288, fols. 86-95, Davidson, Governor, Newfoundland, to C.O., 25 February 1914.

[114]*Ibid.*

[115]Prowse, *A History of Newfoundland*, pp. 515-19.

[116]*Ibid.*

[117]Ryan, "Cod Trade," in Hiller and Neary (eds.), *Newfoundland.*

CHAPTER 7

[1]P.P., 1857, XVI, pp. 477-81, Wood, Report, 1856.

[2]P.P., 1872, LVIII, pp. 86-90, Ongley, British Consul, Patras, Report, 1871.

[3]P.P., 1876, LXXV, pp. 539-44, Wood, British Consul, Patras, Report, 1875.

[4]P.P., 1877, LXXXIII, pp. 559-64, Wood, Report, 1876. In this report Wood also stated that during 1876 there were "considerable importations of pickled salmon." Like Genoa, Patras became a market for Labrador pickled salmon as well as Labrador-cured saltfish.

[5]P.P., 1878-79, LXX, pp. 436-42, Wood, Report, 1878.

[6]P.P., 1881, LXXXIX, pp. 663-69, Wood, Report, 1880.

[7]P.P., 1884, LXXIX, pp. 576-82, Wood, Report, 1883.

[8]P.P., 1886, LXV, pp. 287-91, Wood, Report, 1885.

[9]Ryan, "Ph.D. Thesis," pp. 466-68.

[10]P.P., 1894, LXXXVI, pp. 473-92, Wood, Acting British Consul, Patras, Report, 1893.

[11]P.P., 1896, LXXXVI, pp. 213-19, Wood, Report, 1895.

[12]*Ibid.*

[13]P.P., 1910, XCIX, pp. 357-74, Wood, Report, 1909.

[14]P.P., 1901, LXXXIII, pp. 43-60, Wood, Report, 1900. Most of the follwoing discussion has been taken from this excellent and detailed report.

[15]C.O.194/250, fols. 740-44, C.O. Minute, 23 December 1902.

[16]C.O.194/252, fols. 50-55, Boyle, Governor, Newfoundland, to C.O., 23 and 26 February 1903.

[17]*Ibid.*, fols. 307-08, Boyle to C.O., 12 June 1903, enclosing Bond's request dated 10 June 1903.

[18]*Ibid.*, fol. 306, C.O. Minute, 7 July 1903.

[19]C.O.194/253, fols. 324-25, des Graz to Greek Minister for Foreign Affairs, 24 July 1903.

[20]*Ibid.*, fols. 577-78, Edwin Egerton, British Minister, Athens, to F.O., 15 October 1903.

[21]*Ibid.*, fol. 576, F.O. to C.O., 26 October 1903.

[22]C.O.194/254, fol. 90, Boyle to C.O., 18 February 1904.

[23] P.P., 1896, LXXXVI, pp. 207-12, Alexander, Acting British Consul, Corfu, Report, 1895.

[24] C.O.194/255, fol. 126, Elliott, British Legation, Athens, to F.O., 24 February 1904.

[25] C.O.194/254, fol. 118, Boyle to C.O., 11 March 1904, copy enclosed.

[26] C.O.194/255, fols. 175-76, F.O. to C.O., 15 March 1904.

[27] C.O.194/254, fol. 118, Boyle to C.O., 11 March 1904.

[28] Ibid., fol. 427, MacGregor, Governor, Newfoundland, to C.O., 17 October 1904; Ibid., fol. 426, C.O. Minute, 18 October 1904; Ibid., fol. 430, MacGregor to C.O., 17 October 1904.

[29] C.O.194/259, fol. 483, F.O. to C.O., 1 April 1905.

[30] Ibid., fols. 335-37, Elliott to F.O., 17 February 1905.

[31] The Board of Trade Journal of Tariffs and Trade Notes and Miscellaneous Commercial Information, Vol. 51, October-December 1905, 30 November 1905, p. 409.

[32] C.O.194/260, fol. 417, F.O. to C.O., 27 July 1905.

[33] C.O.194/261, fols. 43-44, Young, British Legation, Athens, to F.O., 8 November 1905.

[34] P.P., 1910, XCIX, pp. 357-74, Wood, Report, 1909.

[35] P.P., 1911, XCIII, pp. 175-88, Wood, Report, 1910.

[36] P.P., 1912-13, XCVII, pp. 17-32, Wood, Report, 1911.

[37] C.O.194/278, fols. 152-53, F.O. to C.O., 1 July 1909.

[38] Ibid. Like port wine, champagne and sherry, the currant also took its name from its place of origin, Corinth. In fact, the French translation of currants then in use was les raisins de Corinthe. See C.O.194/255, fols. 160-62, Elliott to F.O., 24 February 1904. Enclosed with this correspondence is a copy of Elliott's note, in French, to M. Romanos, Greek Minister of Foreign Affairs.

[39] C.O.194/282, fols. 96-97, De Bunsen, British Minister, Madrid, to F.O., 10 November 1910.

[40] C.O.194/284, fols. 18-19, F.O. to C.O., 20 January 1911.

[41] Ibid.

[42] C.O.194/283, fol. 116, C.O. to Newfoundland, 14 March 1911; and Ibid., fol. 117, Cashin to C.O., 14 March 1914.

[43] C.O.194/284, fols. 283-88, Board of Agriculture and Fisheries to F.O., 12 July 1911.

[44] Ibid., fols. 281-82, F.O. to C.O., 12 August 1911.

[45] Ibid., fol. 258, Williams to C.O., 10 November 1911.

[46] JHA, 1912, Appendix. In 1911 imports of Spanish pasas into Newfoundland were worth less than $10,000 and imports of Greek sultanas and currants were valued at about $40,000.

[47] France, Tableau.

[48] P.P., 1897, XCI, pp. 399-416, Wood, Report, 1896.

[49] France, Tableau.

[50] P.P., 1886, LXV, pp. 287-91, Wood, Report, 1885.

[51] P.P., 1894, LXXXVI, pp. 473-92, Wood, Acting British Consul, Patras, Report, 1893.

[52] P.P., 1896, LXXXVI, pp. 207-12, Alexander, Report, 1895.

[53] P.P., 1881, LXXXIX, pp. 679-87, Canale, British Vice Consul, Zante, Report, 1879.

[54] P.P., 1896, LXXXVI, pp. 213-29, Wood, Report, 1895.

[55] P.P., 1906, CXXV, pp. 567-96, H.P. Harvey, British Delegate on the International Commission, Athens, Report, 1905.

[56] P.P., 1910, XCIX, pp. 357-74, Wood, Report, 1909.

[57] P.P., 1907, XC, pp. 465-85, Wood, Report, 1906.

[58] P.P., 1910, XCIX, pp. 357-74, Wood, Report, 1909.

[59] C.O.194/288, fols. 86-95, Davidson, Governor, Newfoundland, to C.O., 15 February 1914.

CHAPTER 8

[1] E. Bradford Burns, *A History of Brazil* (New York: 1970), p. 101.

[2] *Ibid.*

[3] *Ibid.*

[4] *Ibid.*, p. 126.

[5] Ryan, "Abstract," p. 93.

[6] *Ibid.*

[7] *Ibid.*, pp. 93, 120.

[8] Ryan, "Ph.D. Thesis," pp. 534-35.

[9] *Ibid.*, pp. 536-37. Most ships from 'elsewhere' came from Halifax.

[10] *Ibid.*, p. 476.

[11] *Ibid.*, pp. 538-39. The writer cannot account for the large proportion of non-British fish imported in 1850. Either there is an error in the records or this is an aberration.

[12] F.O.13/252, no. 11, fols. 67-90, Cowper, British Consul, Pernambuco, to F.O., 20 March 1847.

[13] Ryan, "Ph.D. Thesis," p. 478.

[14] F.O.13/113, no. 2, fols. 162-69, Parkinson, British Consul, Bahia, to F.O., 31 January 1834.

[15] F.O.13/139, no. 8, fols. 42-59, Robilliard, Acting British Consul, Bahia, to F.O., 1 January 1837.

[16] R.G.59, Despatches from U.S. Consuls in Pernambuco, 1817-1906, Vol. 2, no. 22, Joseph Ray to Secretary of State, 30 September 1844; *Ibid.*, n.p., George Manonorier to Secretary of State, 7 July 1846.

[17] Newman, Hunt and Company, London, exported fish to Brazil through their company in Newfoundland, Newman and Company. The maximum length of this fish was usually set at fourteen inches and sometimes at twelve. See Newman Letter Books, Book 63, pp. 357-61, 24 March 1858; Book 64, pp. 285-86, 8 August 1863; Book 67, pp. 192-95, 8 November 1881; and Book 68, pp. 72-75, 7 July 1885.

[18] *Ibid.*, Book 66, pp. 25-27, 8 October 1872.

[19] F.O.13/88, no. 2, fols. 13-34, Parkinson to F.O., 29 January 1831.

[20] F.O.13/113, no. 2, fols. 162-69, Parkinson to F.O., 31 January 1834.

[21] F.O.13/76, no. 4, fols. 49-52, Parkinson to F.O., 10 January 1830.

[22] F.O.13/217, no. 9, fols. 37-60, Cowper to F.O., 26 January 1844.

[23] F.O.13/216, no. 20, fols. 299-311, Whately, Acting British Consul, Bahia, to F.O., 31 January 1844.

[24] F.O.13/251, no. 10, fols. 77-85, Hesketh, British Consul, Rio de Janeiro, to F.O., 20 February 1847.

[25] C.O.194/130, fols. 125-26, Chamber of Commerce, St. John's, to C.O., 11 March 1848.

[26] C.O.194/134, fols. 5-9, LeMarchant to C.O., 8 January 1851. Enclosed is the petition from the Chamber of Commerce.

[27] F.O.13/374, no. 8, fols. 246-67, Morgan to F.O., 8 April 1859.

[28] P.P., 1865, LIII, pp. 345-68, Hunt, Report, 1863.

[29] *JHA*, 1857-1915, Appendices.

[30] P.P., 1873, LXV, pp. 31-38, Morgan, Report, 1872.

[31] P.P., 1875, LXXV, pp. 536-45, Morgan, Report, 1874.

[32] P.P., 1873, LXIV, pp. 424-40, Corfield, Acting British Consul, Pernambuco, Report, 1872; and P.P., 1875, LXXVII, pp. 71-90, Corfield, Report, 1873-74.

[33] *JHA.*, 1889, Appendix; and P.P., 1890, LXXIV, pp. 113-35, Cohen, British Consul, Pernambuco, Report, 1888.

[34]Ryan, "Ph.D. Thesis," pp. 542-43.

[35]*Ibid.*, pp. 500, 542.

[36]P.P., 1909, XCII, pp. 605-22, Baile, Report, 1908.

[37]P.P., 1910, XCVI, pp. 447-72, Pearson, British Consul, Pernambuco, Report, 1909.

[38]P.P., 1886, LXVI, pp. 23-43, Cohen, British Consul, Pernambuco, Report, 1885.

[39]P.P., 1896, LXXXV, pp. 103-18, Howard, Report, 1895.

[40]P.P., 1897, LXXXIX, pp. 409-40, Howard, Report, 1896.

[41]P.P., 1898, XCIV, pp. 299-324, Williams, British Vice Consul, Maceió, Report, 1897.

[42]Ryan, "Ph.D. Thesis," p. 503.

[43]Ryan, "Ph.D. Thesis," pp. 544-45. The figures for 1906 include one British steamship of 1,971 tons burthen with a cargo of Newfoundland saltfish. There is no indication of the size of this cargo.

[44]P.P., 1902, CV, pp. 359-74, Medhurst, Report, 1900.

[45]P.P., 1911, XC, pp. 363-74, Sinclair, Report, 1910.

[46]Richard Graham, *Britain and the Onset of Modernization in Brazil: 1850-1914* (Cambridge: 1968), p. 107.

[47]Quoted by Graham, *Ibid.*

[48]P.P., 1860, LXV, pp. 490-95, Morgan, Report, 1858.

[49]*Ibid.*

[50]P.P., 1861, LXIII, pp. 460-83, Baille, Secretary of the British Legation, Rio de Janeiro, Report, 1859.

[51]Graham, *Brazil*, p. 75.

[52]Burns, *Brazil.*, p. 1452.

[53]P.P., 1862, LVIII, pp. 87-97, Baille, Report, 1860.

[54]*Ibid.*, pp. 633-49, Morgan, Report, 1860.

[55]*Ibid.*

[56]Clarence Henry Haring, *Empire in Brazil* (Cambridge, Massachusetts: 1868), p. 69.

[57]Joao P. Calogeras, *A History of Brazil* (North Carolina: 1939), p. 246.

[58]P.P., 1871, LXVI, pp. 166-70, Morgan, Report, 1870.

[59]St. John's Chamber of Commerce Minute Book, 1866-1875, Vol. 5, Annual Report, 4 August 1869.

[60]Calogeras, *Brazil*, p. 296.

[61]P.P., 1897, LXXXIX, pp. 409-40, Howard, Report, 1896.

[62]P.P., 1901, LXXXI, pp. 269-300, Howard, Report, 1901.

[63]P.P., 1902, CV, pp. 467-92, Williams, Report, 1901.

[64]P.P., 1903, LXXVI, pp. 447-60, Howard, Report, 1902.

[65]P.P., 1900, XCII, pp. 337-50, Nicolini, British Consul, Report, 1899.

[66]P.P., 1899, XCVIII, pp. 215-54, Beaumont, Secretary of the British Legation, Rio de Janeiro, Report, 1899.

[67]*Ibid.*

[68]P.P., 1903, LXXVI, pp. 471-96, Chapman, British Consul General, Rio de Janeiro, Report, 1902.

[69]P.P., 1899, XCVIII, pp. 215-54, Beaumont, Report, 1899.

[70]C.O.194/201, fols. 402-08, Maxse, Governor, Newfoundland, to C.O., 19 November 1881. Enclosed is a letter from the Chamber of Commerce.

[71] C.O.194/210, fols. 158-59, Executive Council, Newfoundland, to Blake, Governor, Newfoundland, 29 August 1887.

[72] P.P., 1900, XCII, pp. 351-408, Rhind, Report, 1899.

[73] P.P., 1865, LIII, pp. 345-68, Hunt, Report, 1863.

[74] R.G.59, Despatches from U.S. Consuls in Pernambuco, 1817-1906, Vol. 6, Stapp to the Secretary of State, 13 February 1860.

[75] Newman, Book 65, pp. 221-22, 21 May 1870.

[76] P.P., 1873, LXV, pp. 31-38, Morgan, British Consul, Report, 1872; and P.P., 1875, LXXV, pp. 536-45, Morgan, Report, 1874.

[77] P.P., 1878, LXXIII, pp. 37-58, Walker, British Consul, Report, 1875-76; P.P., 1878-79, LXX, pp. 112-35, Walker, Report, 1877-78; P.P., 1878, LXXIII, pp. 37-58, Walker, Report, 1875-76; P.P., 1876, LXXV, pp. 404-18, Corfield, Report, 1875.

[78] Aled Eames, *Ship Master: The life and letters of Capt. Robert Thomas of Llandwrog and Liverpool, 1843-1903* (Gwynedd Archives Service: 1980), pp. 44-45.

[79] Ryan, "Ph.D. Thesis," pp. 505-06.

[80] P.P., 1903, LXXVI, pp. 447-60, Howard, Report, 1902.

[81] P.P., 1910, XCVI, pp. 447-72, Pearson, British Consul, Pernambuco, Report, 1909.

[82] Ryan, "Ph.D. Thesis," p. 513.

[83] Great Britain, *Statistical Abstract for the Principal and Other Foreign Countries*, No. 37 and 39 (London). Note that Rio de Janeiro imported saltfish from Norway and Canada.

[84] Simon Kuznets, et al (eds.), *Economic Growth: Brazil, India, Japan* (Durham, N.C.: 1955), p. 256.

[85] Rollie E. Poppino, *Brazil: The Land and People* (New York: 1968), p. 193.

[86] William Lytle Schurz, *Brazil: The Infinite Country* (New York: 1961), p. 123.

[87] *Ibid.*

[88] P.P., 1875, LXXVII, pp. 50-58, Morgan, Report, 1874.

[89] P.P., 1881, XCI, pp. 94-123, Bonham, Report, 1880.

[90] R.G.59, Despatches from U.S. Consuls in Pernambuco, 1817-1907, Vol. 7, Finke to Secretary of State, 14 October 1864.

[91] R.G.84/C8.46, Pernambuco, Correspondence: Commercial Reports, 1907 and 1908, George Chamberlain, Report, 11 May 1907.

[92] Graham, *Brazil*, p. 398.

[93] C.O.194/288, fols. 86-95, Davidson to C.O., 25 February 1914.

[94] Ryan, "Ph.D. Thesis," pp. 514-15.

[95] P.P., 1895, XCVI, pp. 403-40, Ancell, Acting British Consul General, Rio de Janeiro, Report, 1894.

[96] P.P., 1907, LXXXVIII, pp. 217-66, Chapman, Rio de Janeiro, Report, 1906.

[97] P.P., 1913, LXIX, pp. 197-238, Hambloch, Rio de Janeiro, Report, 1911 and 1912.

[98] Vollan, *Klippfiskhandels*, p. 483.

[99] Ryan, "Ph.D. Thesis," pp. 514-21.

CHAPTER 9

[1] The status of Cuba and Puerto Rico changed after the Spanish-American War in 1898.

[2] Hereafter, the term "British West Indies" will be understood to include British Guiana unless otherwise stated.

[3] Lowell Joseph Ragatz, *The Fall of the Planter Class in the British Caribbean: 1763-1833* (London: 1928), pp. 88-89. According to Raymond McFarland, *A History of the New England Fisheries* (New York: 1911), p. 97, a hogshead of saltfish in British West Indian terminology in the mid-eighteenth century contained six to seven cwts.

[4] See Matthews, "West of England-Newfoundland Fishery," Chapter 10.

[5] B.T.6/91, fols. 104-07, Petition of St. John's merchants to C.O., 24 September 1805.

[6] Ryan, "Abstract," p. 93 (1803-20) and p. 120 (1821-33).

[7] *Ibid.*, pp. 93, 98, 120, 125; and Ryan, "Ph.D. Thesis," p. 556.

[8] Ryan, "Ph.D. Thesis," p. 582.

[9] *Ibid.* Information is available for these years only.

[10] *Ibid.*, p. 585.

[11] *Ibid.*, p. 591.

[12] C.O.142/40, *Jamaica Blue Book*, 1827.

[13] Ryan, "Abstract," p. 120.

[14] P.P., 1851, XXXIV, Customs Duties in the British Colonies, pp. 41-98; and C.O.142/69, *Jamaica Blue Book*, 1855. In 1854 Jamaica charged 2s. on imports of saltfish but it is not clear whether this was charged on units of 100 pounds or 112 pounds avoirdupois.

[15] Ryan, "Ph.D. Thesis," pp. 559-60.

[16] *JHA*, Appendices; and *Newfoundland Blue Books*, 1856-1914.

[17] *Ibid.*, pp. 582-93.

[18] Ryan, "Ph.D. Thesis," pp. 588-90.

[19] S.P.43 (1887), John Wylde, Commercial Agent of Canada in the West Indies, Report on Trade Relations between Canada and the West Indies.

[20] Harvey and Company Papers, Diary of a Trip to the West Indies in 1885, 21 February 1885.

[21] S.P.2E (1893).

[22] Ryan, "Ph.D. Thesis," pp. 582-84.

[23] *Ibid.*, pp. 585-87.

[24] *Ibid.*, pp. 591-93.

[25] C.O.116/249, *British Guiana Blue Book*, 1880.

[26] C.O.116/250, *British Guiana Blue Book*, 1881.

[27] Ryan, "Ph.D. Thesis," pp. 582-84.

[28] *Ibid.*, pp. 588-90.

[29] Douglas Hall, *Free Jamaica: 1836-1865* (New Haven: 1959), p. 83.

[30] Grant, *Canadian Atlantic Fishery*, p. 22.

[31] *U.S.A. Consular Reports*, Vol. January-April 1891, pp. 365-68, Pierce, American Consul, Trinidad, to Secretary of State, 22 December 1890.

[32] C.O.194/255, fols. 379-424, MacGregor to C.O., 31 January 1905.

[33] Ryan, "Ph.D. Thesis," p. 576.

CHAPTER 10

[1] It should be noted that Norway's position in Bilbao followed a similar course during the century.

[2] Ryan, "Ph.D. Thesis," pp. 629-30.

[3] *Ibid.*, pp. 631-32. Included under "West Indies" is fish exported to British North America and the United States.

[4] France, *Tableau*, Vols. 1876-1890; *JHA*, 1877-1891; and Ryan, "Ph.D. Thesis," p. 260. See also Tables 3.F and 3.I, above.

[5] F.O.414/171, fols. 30-31, Chapman, British Consul General, Florence, to F.O., 25 February 1902.

[6] Ibid., fols. 31-32, Vecqueray, British Consul, Cadiz, to F.O., 22 February 1902.

[7] Ibid., fols. 30-31, Chapman to F.O., 25 February 1902.

[8] Ibid., fols. 31-32, Vecqueray to F.O., 22 February 1902; and Ibid., fols. 32-33, Roberts, British Consul, Barcelona, to F.O., 25 February 1902.

[9] JHA., 1900-1915, Appendices. Beginning in 1899, saltfish exports from the Labrador coast to the various markets were included in the records. After 1906 the statistics concerning each market appear to be reasonably accurate. Note that beginning in 1907 Gibraltar was no longer designated as a market, despite the fact that ships continued to sail to that port for orders.

[10] Ibid. For the purposes of this table the author assumes that all saltfish exported to Canada and the United States was re-exported to the West Indies.

[11] Ryan, "Ph.D. Thesis," p. 611.

[12] See Chapter 2, Note 2.

[13] McDonald, "Coaker," p. 15.

[14] McDonald examines very thoroughly the post-war marketing developments.

[15] McDonald, "Coaker," p. 24.

[16] Ibid., pp. 26-27.

[17] Ibid., pp. 25-28.

[18] Newfoundland, Royal Commission, 1933, Report [Amulree Report], p. 108.

[19] S.J.R. Noel, Politics in Newfoundland (Toronto: 1971), pp. 98-99.

[20] Cato Wadel, Marginal Adaptations and Modernization in Newfoundland (St. John's: 1969), p. 9.

[21] JHA, 1896, Appendix, pp. 232-35.

[22] The direct financial contribution of migratory and expatriate Newfoundlanders, especially during the period from 1880 to 1914, needs to be fully examined.

[23] Amulree Report, p. 109.

[24] However, prosperity in the form of employment on the new Canadian and American armed forces bases, which were built in the colony in the 1940s, resulted in many men giving up the fishery. Confederation with Canada in 1949 added to this movement away from the saltfish industry. See Alexander, Decay of Trade.

[25] JHA, 1884, 1914, Appendices.

[26] Thompson, French Shore.

[27] For example, in Zara S. Steiner, The Foreign Office and Foreign Policy, 1898-1914 (Cambridge University Press: 1969), neither Canada, Australia, New Zealand, nor Jamaica are mentioned in the index while there are eight references to Newfoundland.

[28] Newfoundland historiography has been coloured by the colony's relationship with the Colonial Office. During the nineteenth century, Newfoundland felt it was discriminated against by the Colonial Office because attempts by the colony to acquire representative government and, later, responsible government were delayed in Britain. This frustration with the Colonial Office introduced some anti-British sentiment into the colony's historiography.

[29] F.O.63/551, n. 290, Walden to F.O., 26 November 1842.

[30] "The principal object of the appointment of British Consular Officers is the protection and promotion of the commercial interests of Her Majesty's subjects." P.P., 1886, LX, p. 89, General Instructions to Her Majesty's Consuls, quoted in D.C.M. Platt, "The Role of the British Consular Service in Overseas Trade: 1825-1914," Economic History Review, Vol. 15 (1962-63), 494-512.

[31] Trade Review (St. John's), 2 March 1901.

[32] William Woodruff, The Impact of Western Man: A Study of Europe's Role in the World Economy, 1750-1960 (London: 1966), pp. 269-70.

APPENDIX

[1] Export figures for 1803-1833 have been taken from Ryan, "Abstract;" figures for 1836-1850 have been taken from the *Newfoundland Blue Books*, Annual Statistics; figures for 1851-1914 have been taken from *JHA*, Appendices. For information missing from the above, the present writer used the table found in *JHA*, 1890, Appendix, pp. 323-24. Any fractions have been rounded off to the nearest whole number. For the period prior to 1860 figures showing the amount of saltfish exported directly from the Labrador coast have not been located. Population statistics for the 1803-1830 period have been taken from Ryan, "Abstract," while all others, except those for 1845, have been taken from the *Newfoundland Census Returns*. The statistics for 1845 have been taken from *Censuses of Canada: 1665-1871* (Ottawa: 1876), p. 160. Up to 1830 there was usually an annual census, but after the colony received representative government the census was taken only at certain intervals. Figures for 1857-1911 include Labrador, but since only several thousand people lived on that coast at the end of the century the presence or absence of these figures is not significant. The per capita figures for the period up to 1826 were calculated by using the summer population statistics.

[2] The figures for 1801-1833 have been taken from Ryan, "Abstract." The figures for 1836-1914 have been taken from the *Newfoundland Blue Books* and *JHA*, 1836-1915, and Ryan, "M.A. Thesis," pp. 269-70.

[3] Ryan, "M.A. Thesis," pp. 293-94.

[4] *Newfoundland and Labrador Census Returns*, 1891, 1901, 1911.

[5] *Newfoundland and Labrador Census Returns*. The amount of codfish caught in each of these districts during certain years is shown in Table 2.2, above.

[6] Referred to as the *French Shore* prior to 1884.

[7] *JHA*, 1890-1915, Appendices. Information for the years 1905 and 1906 is not available.

[8] Chamber of Commerce Minute Book, 1866-1875, Vol. V, pp. 46-52.

Bibliography

PRIMARY SOURCES

Manuscripts

1. The British Consular Reports and Despatches in the Foreign Office General Correspondence (Public Record Office, Kew) contain the basic information on Newfoundland's foreign saltfish markets for the earlier part of the period. The following volumes contain reports and despatches which were found particularly useful:

Great Britain. Foreign Office. General Correspondence. British Consular Reports and Despatches. Brazil. F.O.13/13, 29, 41, 52, 65, 66, 76, 87, 88, 95, 105, 113, 114, 121, 138, 139, 157, 164, 188, 203, 216, 217, 228, 251, 252, 260, 261, 268, 269, 277, 288, 297, 374, 385.

_____ . Italian States and Rome. F.O.43/16, 18, 19, 20, 21, 22, 23, 25, 26, 27, 28, 29, 30, 32, 33.

_____ . Portugal. F.O.63/99, 100, 135, 137, 156, 158, 176, 178, 253, 271, 290, 313, 325, 337, 349, 361, 407, 424, 425, 440, 445, 454, 462, 469, 470, 471, 473, 474, 480, 494, 512, 530, 531, 547, 551, 607, 688, 691, 719, 723, 725, 750, 757, 762, 767, 769, 770, 879, 1189.

_____ . Sardinia. F.O.67/78, 80, 81, 82, 90, 94, 117, 138, 145, 173, 187, 196, 202, 209, 219.

_____ . Sicily and Naples. F.O.70/85, 95, 98, 106, 111, 114, 115, 117, 120, 126, 129, 132, 135, 139, 153, 158, 164, 170, 177, 309, 322

_____ . Spain. F.O.72/163, 187, 189, 201, 238, 242, 267, 284, 289, 296, 299, 310, 338, 351, 353, 354, 358, 370, 371, 381, 414, 429, 430, 448, 449, 465, 466, 467, 487, 488, 512, 536, 557, 558, 564, 582, 583, 600, 602, 606, 607, 626, 633, 653, 679, 680, 702, 703, 729, 746, 747, 758, 763, 768, 769, 775, 777, 791, 792, 810, 828, 850, 851, 874, 875, 900, 901, 923, 946, 963, 987, 988, 1016, 1018, 1043, 1066, 1085, 1088.

_____ . Tuscany. F.O.79/25, 34, 38, 40, 43, 45, 48, 50, 52, 54, 56, 61, 68, 73, 77, 84, 88, 91, 95, 98, 102.

2. The most important manuscript source for Newfoundland's local history during this period is the original correspondence from the colonial governors to the Colonial Office.

Great Britain. Colonial Office. Newfoundland. Original Correspondence. 1760-1921. C.O.194/15-303.

3. Other manuscript sources consulted and found to be useful to a limited degree are as follows (Unless otherwise indicated these documents are located at the Public Record Office, Kew.):

Great Britain. Board of Trade. Correspondence. Bound Papers. B.T.1.

_____ . In Letters. 1833-1845. B.T.2/1-14.

_____ . Out Letters. 1852-1863. B.T.3/38-64.

_____ . Registers with Notes. B.T.4.

_____ . Minutes of Meetings. B.T.5.

_____ . Miscellanea. 1806-1835. B.T.6/51-271.

Note: Most papers received by the Board of Trade up to 1845 survived but those received after that date were heavily weeded and very few were kept except for some in B.T.6 where it is very difficult to trace them.

Great Britain. Colonial Office. Reciprocity, Fisheries, Emigration. 1854-1859. C.O.6/21-25.

─────────── . Newfoundland. Entry Books. 1786-1867. C.O.195/11-23.

─────────── . Newfoundland. Miscellanea. 1677-1903. C.O.199/1-98. [Several collections of Newfoundland newspapers, and most of the Newfoundland *Blue Books* are found here. Vol. 16 is an account of Newfoundland in 1677 and Vols. 17 and 18 deal with the eighteenth century.]

Great Britain. Foreign Office. Oslo. Correspondence and Letter Books. 1815-1854. F.O.236/1-4. [Oslo was then known as Christiania.]

─────────── . Oslo. Correspondence and Letter Books. 1832-1839. F.O.237/1.

─────────── . Shipping in Bahia. 1853-1914. F.O.271/1-33.

Individual volumes within the following series contained some useful information: these volumes were consulted on a selective basis.

Great Britain. Colonial Office. Barbados. Original Correspondence. 1806-1859. C.O.28/75-189.

─────────── . British North America. Entry Books. 1810-1873. C.O.43/49-158.

─────────── . Gibraltar. Original Correspondence. 1825-1833. C.O.91/83-127.

─────────── . British Guiana. Original Correspondence. 1841-1873. C.O.111/201-400.

─────────── . Jamaica. Original Correspondence. 1794-1843. C.O.137/117-274.

─────────── . St. Lucia. Original Correspondence. 1843. C.O.253/79.

─────────── . St. Vincent. Original Correspondence. 1844-1873. C.O.260/63-118.

─────────── . Tobago. Original Correspondence. 1843-1870. C.O.285/52-88.

─────────── . Trinidad. Original Correspondence. 1842-1873. C.O.295/139-270.

5. United States official documentation provided a useful supplement to the mainly British sources used in this work.

United States of America. Department of State. Despatches from United States Consuls in Alicante. 1788-1905. Research Group [R.G.] 59. 3 vols. [National Archives, Washington.]

─────────── . Despatches from United States Consuls in St. Salvador (Bahia). 1808-1849. R.G.59. 4 vols.

─────────── . Despatches from United States Consuls in Bahia. 1850-1906. R.G.59. 8 vols.

─────────── . Despatches from United States Consuls in Barbados. 1823-1906. R.G.59. 17 vols. [There is a microfilm copy in the British Library. Copies in the British Library are not catalogued under R.G.59 – this code applies only to the collection in the National Archives, Washington.]

─────────── . Despatches from United States Consuls in Barcelona. 1797-1906. R.G.59. 15 vols.

─────────── . Despatches from United States Consuls in Bilbao. 1791-1871. R.G.59. Vol. 1.

─────────── . Despatches from United States Consuls in Cadiz. 1791-1904. R.G.59. 20 vols.

─────────── . Despatches from United States Consuls in Genoa. 1799-1906. R.G.59. 13 vols.

─────────── . Despatches from United States Consuls in Gibraltar. 1791-1906. R.G.59. 17 vols. [Copy in British Library.]

─────────── . Despatches from United States Consuls in Halifax, Nova Scotia. 1833-1906. R.G.59. 18 vols. [Copy in British Library.]

─────────── . Despatches from United States Consuls in Kingston, Jamaica. 1796-1906. R.G.59. 39 vols. [Copy in British Library.]

─────────── . Despatches from United States Consuls in Leghorn. 1793-1906. R.G.59. 11 vols.

─────────── . Despatches from United States Consuls in Lisbon. 1791-1906. R.G.59. 11 vols.

_____ . Despatches from United States Consuls in Malaga. 1793-1906. R.G.59. 17 vols.

_____ . Despatches from United States Consuls in Naples. 1796-1906. R.G.59. 12 vols.

_____ . Despatches from United States Consuls in Oporto. 1821-1877. R.G.59. 5 vols.

_____ . Despatches from United States Consuls in Patras. 1874-1906. R.G.59. 4 vols.

_____ . Despatches from United States Consuls in Pernambuco. 1817-1906. R.G.59. 17 vols.

_____ . Despatches from United States Consuls in St. John's, Newfoundland. 1852-1906. R.G.59. 9 vols. [Copy in British Library.]

_____ . Despatches from United States Consuls in Trinidad. 1824-1906. R.G.59. 13 vols. [Copy in British Library.]

_____ . Despatches from United States Consuls in Valencia. 1816-1906. R.G.59. 4 vols.

_____ . Decimal File. General Despatches. 1910-1949. R.G.59.

_____ . Pernambuco. Record of Imports. 1854-1857. R.G.84/C36.1. 1 vol.

_____ . Pernambuco. Record of Imports and Circulars. 1863. R.G.84/C36.2. 1 vol.

_____ . American Consulate General. Genoa. Despatches to State Department. 1908-1912. R.G.84/C8.1. 5 vols. [Vols. 1-5.]

_____ . American Consulate General. Lisbon. Despatches. 1906-1912. R.G.84/C8.1. 5 vols. [Vols. 6-10.]

_____ . American Consular Agency. Oporto. Miscellaneous Correspondence. 1911-1915. R.G.84/C8.2. 1 vol.

_____ . Letters to the Consulate General, Barcelona, from Consulate, Bilbao. 1905-1913. R.G.84/C8.2. 2 vols. [Vols. 37 and 38.]

_____ . Despatches from the Consulate General, Rio de Janeiro, to the State Department. 1907-1909. R.G.84/C8.0. 3 vols. [Vols. 253-255.]

_____ . Correspondence. Commercial Reports. Pernambuco. 1907-1908. R.G.84/C8.46. 1 vol.

The despatches for the period prior to 15 August 1906 are arranged chronologically in bound volumes. The despatches for the period from 15 August 1906 to 1910 are arranged in a numerical file; those for the period from 1910 to 1949 are arranged in a decimal file. All are located at the National Archives, Washington, D.C.

6. Miscellaneous:

Baine Johnston Letter Book. 1893-1898. [Located at the Maritime History Group Archives, Memorial University of Newfoundland, hereafter referred to as MHG, MUN.]

Baine Johnston Papers. 1808/1910. [MHG, MUN]

Benjamin Smith Papers. 1833/1887. [Located at the Provincial Archives of Newfoundland, hereafter referred to as PANL]

Collingwood Collection. Newman, Hunt and Company Brochures and Letters. [PANL]

Earle Collection of One Hundred and Twenty Documents. [PANL]

Grieves and Bremner Fish Collection Books. 1855/1890. 20 vols. [MHG, MUN]

Harvey and Company Papers. Diary of a Trip to the West Indies in 1885. [PANL]

Hawes Papers. Memorandum on the Marketing of Saltfish on the European Markets [by George Hawes]. London. 1836. [MHG,MUN]

Job Family Papers. 1761/1952. [PANL]

John Munn and Company. Miscellaneous Papers. [Conception Bay Museum, Newfoundland.]

John T. Duckworth Papers. 1810-1812. [PANL]

John and William Boyd Letter Books. 1875-1878. [PANL]

Maurice Job Taylor Collection. 1824/1911. [PANL]

Newfoundland. Book of Coasting and Fishing Ships Cleared from Harbour Grace. 1866-1918. [Conception Bay Museum]

_____ . Police Letter Books. Harbour Grace. 1843-1860. 3 vols. [Conception Bay Museum]

_____ . St. John's Chamber of Commerce. Annual Reports. 1849-1884. [PANL]

_____ . St. John's Chamber of Commerce. Minute Books. 1834-1875. 5 vols. [PANL]

Newman, Hunt and Company Limited. Letter Books. 1804-1899. Vols. 39/70. [PANL]

In combination with various other West of England families, the Newmans from Dartmouth were involved in the Newfoundland saltfish trade for about 300 years. During the nineteenth century the parent company was known as Newman, Hunt and Company, while the Newfoundland operation was known as Newman and Company. Newman, Hunt and Company kept excellent records, which were preserved in England and thus escaped the fate of most St. John's records which were lost in the two major fires of the century, in 1846 and 1892. This is a rare and valuable collection and much if not all of it is available on microfilm in the PANL. The letter books contain instructions from the head office in London to the Newfoundland branches.

Punton and Munn. Old Letters. n.d. [Martin R. (Mac) Lee Estate, Placentia, Newfoundland]

Whiteley, Captain W.H. A petition to the Department of Marine and Fisheries, Ottawa. 1876. [In the possession of Dr. W.H. Whiteley, MUN.]

William Cox and Company Letter Books. 1858/1867. [PANL]

William Waterman and Company Produce Book. 1864/1883. [MHG, MUN, and PANL]

William White Collection of Trinity Bay Manuscripts. [PANL]

Printed

1. The reports from the consuls and foreign office representatives printed in the Parliamentary Papers (located in the British Library) provided the main source of information on Newfoundland's foreign markets during the latter part of the period examined. The reports cited can be found in the following volumes:

Great Britain. Parliament. *Parliamentary Papers.* 1817 (VI), 1837 (XXXIX), 1840 (XXI), 1851 (XXXIV), 1857 (XVI), 1857-58 (LV), 1859 (XXX), 1860 (LXV), 1861 (LXIII), 1862 (LVIII), 1863 (LXX), 1864 (LXI), 1865 (LIII), 1866 (LXIX, LXX), 1867 (LXVII), 1867-68 (LXVIII), 1868-69 (LIX), 1870 (LXIV), 1871 (LXV, LXVI), 1872 (LVIII), 1873 (LXIV, LXV), 1874 (LXVI), 1875 (LXIV, LXXIV, LXXV, LXXVI, LXXVII), 1876 (LXXIV, LXXV), 1877 (LXXXI, LXXXII, LXXXIII), 1878 (LXIII, LXXIII, LXXIV), 1878-79 (LXIX, LXX, LXXI, LXXII), 1880 (LXXIII, LXXIV), 1881 (LX, LXXXIX, XC, XCI), 1882 (LXIX, LXX, LXXI), 1883 (LXXI, LXXII, LXXIII, LXXIV), 1884 (LXXIX, LXXX, LXXXIV), 1884-85 (LXXVII, LXXVIII, LXXIX), 1885 (LXXV), 1886 (LXV, LXVI), 1887 (LXXXIV, LXXXV, LXXXVI, XCIII), 1888 (CI, CII, CIII), 1889 (LXXX), 1890 (LXXIV, LXXV, LXXVII), 1890-91 (LXXXVI, LXXXVII), 1892 (LXXXII, LXXXIV), 1893-94 (XCIV, XCV, XCVI), 1894 (LXXXVI, LXXXVII, LXXXVIII), 1895 (XCVI, XCVIII, C), 1896 (LXXXV, LXXXVI, LXXXVIII), 1897 (LXXXIX, XCI, XCII, XCIII), 1898 (XCIV, XCVI, XCVII, XCVIII), 1899 (XCVIII, C, CII), 1900 (XCII, XCIV, XCV, XCVI, XCIX), 1901 (LXXXI, LXXXII, LXXXIII, LXXXIV), 1902 (CV, CVI, CVII, CVIII, CIX, CX), 1903 (LXXVI, LXXVII, LXXVIII), 1904 (XCVII, XCVIII, XCIX, C, CI), 1905 (LXXXVIII, LXXXIX, XC, XCI, XCII), 1906 (XCII, CXXIII, CXXIV, CXXV, CXXVI, CXXVII, CXXVIII), 1907 (LXXXVIII, LXXXIX, XC, XCII), 1908 (CIX, CXI, CXII, CXIII, CXIV, CXV, CXVI), 1909 (XCII, XCIV, XCV, XCVI, XCVII, XCVIII), 1910 (XCVI, XCVIII, XCIX, C, CI, CII), 1911 (XC, XCI, XCIII, XCV, XCVI), 1912-13 (XCIV, XCV, XCVII, XCIX, C), 1913 (LXIX, LXX, LXXI, LXXII), 1914 (XCI, XCII, XCIV), 1914-16 (LXXI, LXXIII, LXXIV), 1916 (XXIV).

2. Other Printed Sources:

Canada. Census Office. *Censuses of Canada, 1665-1871.* Vol. IV.

_____ . Fisheries Reports. Ottawa.

_____ . Parliament. *Sessional Papers*. 1876 (S.P.2), 1877 (S.P.1), 1878 (S.P.2), 1879 (S.P.2), 1880 (S.P.1), 1881 (S.P.2), 1882 (S.P.1), 1883 (S.P.2), 1884 (S.P.1), 1885 (S.P.2), 1886 (S.P.1), 1887 (S.P.1, 43), 1888 (S.P.3), 1889 (S.P.1), 1890 (S.P.2), 1891 (S.P.4), 1892 (S.P.5), 1893 (S.P.2E, 5), 1901 (S.P.10), 1906 (S.P.10), 1911 (S.P.10b), 1915 (S.P.10b)

_____ . *Canada Year Book*. Ottawa.

Denmark. *Statisk Aarbog*. 1898-1916.

France. Direction Général des Douanes. *Tableau Général du Commerce et de la Navigation*. Vols. 1823-1914.

Great Britain. Board of Trade. *The Board of Trade Journal of Tariff and Trade Notices and Miscellaneous Commercial Information*. 1866-1915. Vols. 1-88. [Located in the British Library.]

_____ . Colonial Office. Barbados. *Blue Books*. 1824-1914. C.O.33/36-124. [All *Blue Books* listed are located at the Public Record Office.]

_____ . British Guiana. *Blue Books* (Berbice). 1826-1841. C.O.116/174-189.

_____ . British Guiana. *Blue Books* (Demerara and Essiquibo). 1828-1838. C.O.116/197-205.

_____ . British Guiana. *Blue Books*. 1859-1914. C.O.116/228-283.

_____ . Jamaica. *Blue Books*. 1827-1914. C.O.142/40-128.

_____ . Nova Scotia. *Blue Books*. 1829-1865. C.O.221/42-75.

_____ . Trinidad. *Blue Books*. 1825-1914. C.O.300/39-126.

_____ . *Statistical Abstract for the Principal and Other Foreign Countries*. Nos. 9, 20, 27, 37, 39. [Located in the British Library.]

Newfoundland. *Blue Books*. 1835-1915. [Some of the *Blue Books* are also located in the C.O.199 files; see above.]

_____ . Census Returns. 1836, 1857, 1869, 1874, 1884, 1891, 1901, 1911, 1921.

_____ . *The Crown vs. The Directors and Manager of the Commercial Bank of Newfoundland*. 1894.

_____ . *The Crown vs. The Directors of the Union Bank of Newfoundland*. 1895.

_____ . Department of Marine and Fisheries. Standardization Committee, 1920. *Bulletin*. 1 July 1920.

_____ . *Journals of the House of Assembly*. 1833-1916.

_____ . *Royal Commission, 1933, Report*. Cmd. 4880. [Amulree Report.]

_____ . *Report of Judge Bennett together with Evidence respecting Bait Protection Service*. 1890.

_____ . *Report of the Trade Commissioners on the Mediterranean Markets*. 1898.

Norway. *Norges officielle statistik*. Annual Reports. Kristiania [Oslo]. 1866-1915. [Located in the University Library, Oslo.]

United States of America. *Foreign Commerce and Navigation Reports*.

_____ . *U.S.A. Consular Reports*. Reports from the Consuls of the United States on the Commerce, Manufactures, etc., of their Consular Districts, 1880-1910. 97 vols. [Beginning in 1882 the reports are referred to as *U.S.A. Monthly Consular Reports*. Located in the British Library.]

3. Newspapers:

Evening Telegram [St. John's, Newfoundland]. 1897.

Gibraltar Chronicle. 1839-1913. [Listed in the Public Record Office as C.O.94/1-110.]

Morning Chronicle [St. John's, Newfoundland]. 1879.

Public Ledger [St. John's, Newfoundland]. 1831.

Times and General Commercial Gazette [St. John's, Newfoundland]. 1895.

Trade Review [St. John's, Newfoundland]. 1901.

Western Star [Corner Brook, Newfoundland]. 1949.

SECONDARY SOURCES

Published

1. Books:

Adams, William Forbes. *Ireland and Irish Emigration to the New World from 1815 to the Famine.* New Haven: Yale University Press, 1932.

Adamson, Alan Hubert. *Sugar Without Slaves: The Political Economy of British Guiana, 1838-1904.* London and New Haven: Yale University Press, 1972.

Aflalo, F.G. *The Sea-Fishing Industry of New England and Wales.* London: Edward Stanford, 1904.

Alexander, David. *The Decay of Trade: An Economic History of the Newfoundland Saltfish Trade, 1935-1965.* St. John's: Memorial University of Newfoundland, 1977.

Baklanoff, Eric N. *The Economic Transformation of Spain and Portugal.* New York: Holt, Rinehart and Winston, 1978.

Bellet, Adolfe. *La Grande Pêche de la Morue à Terre Neuve Depuis la Découverte du Nouveau Monde par les Basques.* Paris: Augustin Challamel, 1902.

Burns, E. Bradford. *A History of Brazil.* New York: Columbia University Press, 1970.

Calogeras, Joao Pandia. *A History of Brazil.* Translated and edited by Percy Alvin Martin. North Carolina: University of North Carolina Press, 1939.

Cell, Gillian. *English Enterprise in Newfoundland: 1577-1660.* Toronto: University of Toronto Press, 1969.

Chadwick, John. *Newfoundland: Island Into Province.* Cambridge: Cambridge University Press, 1967.

Chafe, Levi. *History of the Newfoundland Seal Fishery from the Earliest Available Records down to and Including the Voyage of 1923.* 3rd. ed. St. John's: Trade Printers and Publishers Limited, 1924.

Coull, James R. *The Fisheries of Europe: An Economic Geography.* London: G. Bell and Sons, Ltd., 1972.

Cushing, Caleb. *The Treaty of Washington.* New York: Harper and Brothers, 1973.

Cutting, Charles L. *Fish Savings: A History of Fish Processing from Ancient to Modern Times.* New York: Philosophical Library, 1956.

Derry, T.K. *A History of Modern Norway: 1814-1972.* Oxford: Clarendon Press, 1973.

Dunfield, Sir Brian, ed. *Newfoundland Law Reports.* Vol. II. St. John's: 1916.

Eames, Aled. *Ship Master: The Life and Letters of Capt. Robert Thomas of Llandwrog and Liverpool, 1843-1903.* Gwynedd Archives Service, 1980.

England, George Allan, *The Greatest Hunt in the World.* Montreal: Tundra Books, 1924, 1969.

Fay, C.R. *Life and Labour in Newfoundland.* Toronto: University of Toronto Press, 1956.

Fisher, Harold Edward Stephen. *The Portuguese Trade: A Study of Anglo-Portuguese Commerce, 1700-1770.* London: Methuen and Co., 1971.

Goodlad, C.A. *Shetland Fishing Saga.* The Shetland Times, 1970.

Graham, Richard, *Britain and the Onset of Modernization in Brazil: 1850-1914.* Cambridge: Cambridge University Press, 1968.

Grant, Ruth Fulton. *The Canadian Atlantic Fishery.* Toronto: Ryerson Press, 1934.

Gray, Malcolm. *The Fishing Industries of Scotland, 1790-1914: A Study in Regional Adaptation*. Oxford: Oxford University Press, 1978.

Gunn, Gertrude. *The Political History of Newfoundland: 1832-1864*. Toronto: University of Toronto Press, 1966.

Hall, Douglas. *Free Jamaica: 1836-1865*. New Haven: Yale University Press, 1959.

Haring, Clarence Henry. *Empire in Brazil*. Cambridge, Massachusetts: Harvard University Press, 1968.

Head, Grant. *Eighteenth Century Newfoundland*. Toronto: McClelland and Stewart, 1976.

Hennessy, C.A.M. *The Federal Republic of Spain: Pi y Margall and the Federal Republican Movement, 1868-1874*. Oxford: Clarendon Press, 1962.

Hiller, James, and Neary, Peter, eds. *Newfoundland in the Nineteenth and Twentieth Centuries*. Toronto: University of Toronto Press, 1980.

Historical Association, Lisbon Branch, Annual Reports. Vols. 1-5. 1937-41.

Hodne, Fritz. *An Economic History of Norway: 1815-1970*. Bergen: The Norwegian School of Economics and Business Administration, 1975.

Holt, Edgar. *The Carlist Wars in Spain*. London: Putnam and Co., Ltd., 1967.

Hutchinson, Harry William. *Village and Plantation Life in Northeastern Brazil*. Seattle: University of Washington Press, 1957.

Innis, Harold A. *The Cod Fisheries: The Study of an International Economy*. Toronto: University of Toronto Press, 1940, 1954.

Jackson, Gordon. *The British Whaling Trade*. London: Adam and Charles Black, 1978.

Kuznets, Simon, et al, eds. *Economic Growth: Brazil, India, Spain*. Durham, North Carolina: Duke University Press, 1955.

Larsen, Karen. *A History of Norway*. New York: Princeton University Press, 1950.

Levine, Robert M. *Pernambuco in the Brazilian Federation: 1889-1937*. Stanford, Callfornia: Stanford University Press, 1978.

March, Edgar J. *Sailing Trawlers*. Maine: International Marine Publishing Co., 1970.

Marques, A.H. de Oliveira. *History of Portugal*. 2nd ed. London and New York: Columbia University Press, 1976.

Masters, Donald C. *The Reciprocity Treaty of 1854*. London: Longmans, Green and Company, 1936.

McClintock, A.H. *The Establishment of Constitutional Government in Newfoundland: 1783-1832*. London: Longmans, Green and Co., 1941.

McFarland, Raymond. *A History of the New England Fisheries*. New York: University of Pennsylvania Press, 1911.

Morandiere, Charles de la. *L'Historie de la Pêche Françcaise de la Morue de l'Amerique Septentrionale*. Paris: G.P. Maisonneuve et Larose, 1962.

Neary, Peter. *The Political Economy of Newfoundland: 1929-1972*. Toronto: Copp-Clark, 1973.

Noel, S.J.R. *Politics in Newfoundland*. Toronto: University of Toronto Press, 1971.

Oxford English Dictionary.

Pedley, Charles. *History of Newfoundland*. London: Longman, 1963.

Poppino, Rollie E. *Brazil: The Land and People*. New York: Oxford University Press, 1968.

Prowse, D.W. *History of Newfoundland*. London: Macmillan and Co., 1895.

Ragaty, Lowell Joseph. *The Fall of the Planter Class in the British Caribbean: 1763-1833*. London: The Century Co., 1928.

Rau, Nicholas. *Trade Cycles: Theory and Evidence*. London: Macmillan, 1974.

Rogers, J.D. *A Historical Geography of Newfoundland*. Oxford: Oxford University Press, 1931.

307

Ryan, Shannon. *The Seal and Labrador Cod Fisheries of Newfoundland*. Canada's Visual History Series. Vol. 26. Ottawa: National Film Board of Canada, 1978.

————————— . *Newfoundland-Spanish Saltfish Trade: 1814-1914*. St. John's: Harry Cuff Publications, 1983.

Ryan, Shannon, and Small, Larry, eds. *Haulin' Rope and Gaff: Songs and Poetry in the History of the Newfoundland Seal Fishery*. St. John's: Breakwater Books, 1978.

Schurz, William Lytle. *Brazil: The Infinite Country*. New York: E.P. Dutton & Co., 1961.

Scott, Walter. *The Antiquary*.

Sheridan, Richard Best. *Sugar and Slavery: An Economic History of the British West Indies, 1623-1775*. Baltimore: The Johns Hopkins University Press, 1974.

Sideri, S. *Trade and Power*. Rotterdam: Rotterdam University Press, 1970.

Smith, Nicholas. *Fifty-two Years at the Labrador Fishery*. London: A.H. Stockwell Ltd., 1936.

Solhaug, Trygve. *De Norske Fiskeriers Historie: 1815-1880.*. Bergen: Universitetsforlaget, 1976.

Steiner, Zara S. *The Foreign Office and Foreign Policy, 1898-1914*. Cambridge: Cambridge University Press, 1969.

Story, G.M., Kirwin, W.J., and Widdowson, J.D.A., eds. *Dictionary of Newfoundland English*. Toronto: University of Toronto Press: 1982.

þorsteinsson, Björn. *Tíu borstastríd: 1415-1976*. Sögufélagid: 1976.

Talbot, Thomas. *Newfoundland: A letter addressed to a friend in Ireland in relation to the condition and circumstances of the Island of Newfoundland, with an especial view to emigration*. London: Sampson, Low, Marston, Searle and Rivington, 1882.

Thompson, F.F. *The French Shore Problem in Newfoundland*. Toronto: University of Toronto Press, 1961.

Tocque, P. *Newfoundland: As It Was and As It Is in 1877*. London: Law, Marsden, Seals and Rivington, 1878.

Trend, J.B. *Portugal*. London: Ernest Benn Ltd., 1857.

Vicens Vives, Jaime. *An Economic History of Spain*. New Jersey: Princeton University Press, 1969.

Villiers, Alan. *The Deep Sea Fishermen*. London: Hodder and Stoughton, 1970.

Vollan, Odd. *Den Norske Klippfiskhandels Historie*. Ålesund: Øens Førlag-Forde, 1956.

Wadel, Cato. *Marginal Adaptations and Modernization in Newfoundland*. St. John's: Institute of Social and Economic Research, Memorial University of Newfoundland, 1969.

Woodruff, William. *The Impact of Western Man: A Study of Europe's Role in the World Economy, 1750-1960*. London: Macmillan, 1966.

Worcester, Donald E. *Brazil: From Colony to World Power*. New York: Charles Scribner's Sons, 1973.

2. Articles:

Conrad, Robert. "Neither Slave nor Free: The Emancipation of Brazil, 1818-1868." *Hispanic American Historical Review*, LIII (February 1973), 50-70.

Eisenberg, Peter L. "Abolishing Slavery: The Process on Pernambuco's Sugar Plantations." *Hispanic American Historical Review*, LII (November 1972), 580-97.

Flory, Rae, and Smith, David Grant. "Bahian Merchants and Planters in the Seventeenth and Early Eighteenth Centuries." *Hispanic American Historical Review*, LVIII (November 1978), 571-94.

Hanson, John R. "Export Instability in Historical Perspective: Further Results." *Journal of Economic History*, XL (March 1980), 17-23.

Hermannson, Halldor. "Sir Joseph Banks and Iceland." *Islantica*, XVIII (1928). Reprint. New York: Kraus Reprint Corporation, 1966.

Keene, Charles A. "American Shipping and Trade, 1798-1820: The Evidence from Leghorn." *Journal of Economic History*, XXXVIII (September 1978), 681-700.

Kennedy, John Norman. "Bahian Elites: 1750-1822." *Hispanic American Historical Review*, LIII (August 1973), 415-39.

Kirwin, William J. "Selected French and English Synonyms in Newfoundland." *Regional Language Studies Newfoundland*, No. 9 (December 1980).

Leff, Nathaniel H. "Economic Retardation in Nineteenth-Century Brazil." *Economic History Review*, XXV (August 1972), 489-507.

Lydon, James G. "Fish and Flour for Gold: Southern Europe and the Colonial American Balance of Payments." *Business History Review*, XXXIX (Summer 1965), 171-83.

Morton, F.W.O. "The Royal Timber in Late Colonial Bahia." *Hispanic American Historical Review*, LVIII (February 1978), 41-61.

Platt, D.C.M. "The Role of the British Consular Service in Overseas Trade: 1825-1914." *Economic History Review, XV (1962-63), 494-512.*

Ridings, Eugene W. "Class Sector Unity in an Export Economy: The Case of Nineteenth-Century Brazil." *Hispanic American Historical Review*, LVIII (August 1978), 432-50.

Ryan, Shannon. "Fishery to Colony: A Newfoundland Watershed, 1793-1815." *Acadiensis*, XII, No. 2 (Spring 1983), 34-52.

Unpublished

Adamson, Alan Herbert. "Sugar and the Economy of British Guiana, 1838-1904." Ph.D. thesis, University of London, 1964. [Revised and published in 1972. See above.]

Alexander, David. "A New Newfoundland: The Traditional Economy and Development to 1934." Paper presented to the Canadian Historical Association, Kingston, 1973. [Revised and published later in Hiller and Neary (eds.), *Newfoundland*. See above.]

Antler, Steven David. "Colonial Exploitation and Economic Stagnation in Nineteenth Century Newfoundland." Unpublished Ph.D. thesis, University of Wisconsin, 1975.

Balcom, Burton Alexander. "Production and Marketing in Nova Scotia's Dried Fish Trade: 1850-1914." M.A. thesis, Memorial University of Newfoundland, 1981.

Davis, David. "The Bond-Blaine Negotiations: 1890-1891." Unpublished M.A. thesis, Memorial University of Newfoundland, 1970.

Fairly, Susan Elizabeth. "The Anglo-Russian Grain Trade: 1815-1861." Unpublished Ph.D. thesis, University of London, 1959.

Field, Agnes Mary. "The Development of Government in Newfoundland, 1638-1713." Unpublished M.A. thesis, University of London, 1924.

Fisher, Harold Edward Stephen. "Anglo-Portuguese Trade: 1700-1750." Ph.D. thesis, University of London, 1961. [Revised and published 1971. See above.]

Hiller, James. "The Political History of Newfoundland: 1874-1901." Unpublished Ph.D. thesis, University of Cambridge, 1972.

_____ . "The Political Repercussions of the Harbour Grace Affray." Lecture delivered to the Newfoundland Historical Society, St. John's, 27 January 1971.

Jones, John Stoddard. "English Foreign Trade in the First Half of the Nineteenth Century, Together with some Observations on the War Period of 1793-1814." Unpublished M.Sc. thesis, University of London, 1928.

_____ . "Historical Study of the Anglo-South American Trade with Special Reference to the Period 1807-1825." Unpublished typescript, 1934. [Located in the London School of Economics Library.]

Matthews, Keith. "A History of the West of England-Newfoundland Fishery." Unpublished D.Phil. thesis, Oxford University, 1968.

Mattox, William S. "The Fishing Industry of Iceland." Unpublished M.A. thesis, McGill University [Quebec], 1960.

McDonald, Ian. "W.F. Coaker and the Fishermen's Protective Union in Newfoundland Politics." Unpublished Ph.D. thesis, University of London, 1971.

Neary, Peter. "The French Shore Problem in Newfoundland." Unpublished M.A. thesis, Memorial University of Newfoundland, 1961.

Ommer, Rosemary. "From Outpost to Outport: The Jersey Merchant Triangle in the Nineteenth Century." Unpublished Ph.D. thesis, McGill University [Quebec], 1979.

Parsons, A.W. "An Economic Study of the Newfoundland Fisheries." Unpublished B.Sc. thesis, Mount Allison University [Nova Scotia], 1935.

Paterson, Janet. "The History of Newfoundland, 1713-1763." Unpublished M.A. thesis, University of London, 1931.

Rothney, Gordon. "British Policy in the North American Cod Fisheries, with special reference to Foreign Competition, 1775-1819." Unpublished Ph.D. thesis, University of London, 1939.

——————— . "The History of Newfoundland and Labrador, 1754-1783." Unpublished M.A. thesis, University of London, 1934.

Rothstein, Natalie K.A. "The Silk Industry in London, 1702-1766." Unpublished M.A. thesis, University of London, 1961.

Ryan, Shannon. "Abstract of C.O.194 Statistics." Unpublished typescript, Memorial University of Newfoundland, 1969.

——————— . "The Newfoundland Cod Fishery in the Nineteenth Century." Unpublished M.A. thesis, Memorial University of Newfoundland, 1972.

——————— ."Newfoundland's Saltfish Markets: 1814-1914." Ph.D. thesis, University of London, 1982.

Saw, Sick Hwa. "The Rice Industry of Burma, 1852-1940." Unpublished Ph.D. thesis, University of London, 1963.

Sheridan, Richard Best. "The Sugar Trade of the British West Indies from 1660 to 1756, with special reference to the Island of Antigua." Ph.D. thesis, University of London, 1951. [Revised and published 1974. See above.]

Small, Lawrence George. "The Interrelationship of Work and Talk in a Newfoundland Fishing Community." Unpublished Ph.D. thesis, University of Pennsylvania, 1979.

Thompson, Frederic F. "A Background of the Newfoundland Clauses of the Anglo-French Agreement of 1904." Unpublished Ph.D. thesis, University of London, 1953.

Index

Note: Page references followed by the letter t refer to the table on that page; those followed by the letter m refer to the map.

319

An illustration from Herman Moll's map of 1710. The sketch was accompanied by a description of the complete operation. Briefly stated, the description included: A — clothing; B — fish hook; C — fishing; D,E,F — splitting and salting; G,H — washing the salted fish; I,K.L — extracting oil from the cod livers; M — fish drying on the flakes.

Bay de Verde, Conception Bay. This is representative of an inshore (or shore) fishing community. Note the fish flakes in the foreground and on the other side of the harbour. These fish flakes, which are almost completely covered with fish, are known as broad-flakes or standing-flakes (see DNE) because the men, women, and children walked on them to spread the fish. (Captain George C. Whiteley, Jr. Collection)

Petty Harbour, one of the oldest Newfoundland communities noted for its inshore fishery. (Martin R. (Mac) Lee Collection)

Fish drying on broad-flakes at the P & L Tessier premises, St. John's. (PANL Collection)

Labrador fishing station at Venison Tickle. Note the low hand-flakes with room for the workers to walk between them. (Holloway photo, PANL Collection)

Women and children spreading fish on broad-flakes. Flakes were often covered with fir and spruce boughs. (Newfoundland Book Publishers (1967) Ltd. Collection)

Spreading fish in Portugal Cove, c.1900. By the middle of the 1800s children and older people did much of the shore work (i.e. curing the fish) while the able-bodied men fished and the women carried out the necessary household tasks. (Gordon King Collection)

Flakes were often built on steep inclines as this example from Bay Bulls illustrates. (Captain George C. Whiteley, Jr. Collection)

The premises of W.H. Whiteley and Sons, Bonne Esperance, Labrador. (Captain George C. Whiteley, Jr. Collection)

Broad flakes covered with fish at Strong's premises in Little Bay Islands, Notre Dame Bay. (Holloway photo, PANL Collection)

Drying fish on broad-flakes in Torbay. The fish was usually made up overnight into small piles called "faggots." (Gordon King Collection)

The premises of A.H. Murray, St. Anthony. This was a twentieth century operation built in the tradition of the early nineteenth century ourport fishing establishments. (Mrs. Gertrude Crosbie Collection)

In places, flakes covered walkways and roadways as in Quidi Vidi in the nineteenth century. (From Prowse, **History of Newfoundland** *(London: 1895), p. 366.)*

Burin, c.1900. In the background the broad-flake has been covered with fish, while in the foreground more fish is being spread on the beach. (Gordon King Collection)

On the Labrador coast where wood was scarce, fish was spread on the rocky surface. This rocky surface was referred to as "bawn" (see **DNE**). *(Hal Andrews, 1975.)*

Fish spread on the bawn on the Labrador coast. (Martin R. (Mac) Lee Collection)

Workers spreading fish on a beach at Grand Bank. In certain locations fish was dried in this way. Note the piles of fish in the background. (PANL Collection)

Another view of fish spread on the beach, possibly in Grand Bank as well. Note the pile in the foreground. (Provincial Reference and Resource Library Collection)

Some fishermen, on occasion, spread fish on the wharf and on the roof of the stage, or indeed on practically any dry clean surface. (Provincial Reference and Resource Library Collection)

Labrador schooners under sail. (Martin R. (Mac) Lee Collection)

Fishing activity is clearly evident as men proceed to the fishing grounds in their boats. Schooners can be seen in the background. (Martin R. (Mac) Lee Collection)

Fishermen "dipping" codfish from the codtrap at Boone Esperance, Labrador. Captain W.H. Whiteley, Bonne Esperance, is credited with having invented the codtrap in 1866. By the end of the century it was being widely used. (Captain George C. Whiteley, Jr. Collection)

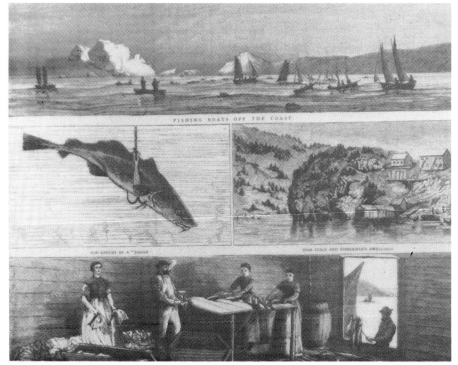

The Newfoundland fishery in the 1870s showing fishing boats, a codfish caught on a jigger, fish stage and fishermen's dwellings, and the processing operation below. The principal ways in which this operation differs from the operation depicted in Herman Moll's map (see above) are as follows: men are fishing from boats not from the side of the ship, people are living in dwelling houses on shore, and women are engaged in processing the fish. (From **Graphic***, December 19, 1874)*

Fishermen at Bonne Esperance returning from the fishing grounds. Note the boats loaded with fish in the foreground. (Captain George C. Whiteley, Jr. Collection)

Codfish being gutted, headed and split. The "splitter" in the foreground is removing the "soundbone." (Captain George C. Whiteley, Jr. Collection)

After the soundbone is removed the fish is washed and salted — layers of fish alternating with layers of salt. Heavily salted fish is usually left in saltbulk for twenty-one days. (Shannon Ryan, 1975)

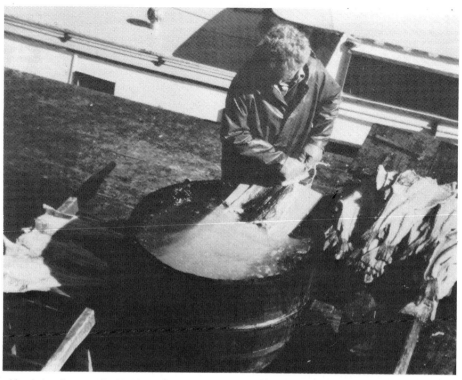

After it is taken out of saltbulk the fish is washed thoroughly. (Hal Andrews, 1975).

Fishermen at Smokey, Labrador, bringing their fish out to spread it on the bawn. (Shannon Ryan, 1975).

Fish is put in "pile" periodically while drying. The weight of the pile forced the moisture out of the fish. During inclement weather fish was piled and repiled in an effort to aid the curing process. In the nineteenth century piles were covered by tree rinds to keep off the rain. (Shannon Ryan, 1975).

This crew at Bonne Esperance is working at the fish pile. Note the hand-flakes in the background. (Captain George C. Whiteley, Jr. Collection)

Culling fish in Ferryland. The fish has been brought to the site on a horse-drawn cart. (PANL Collection)

*Two men in Bay Bulls rest their handbarrow of fish on top of an unused "bark pot" or "tan pot" (see **DNE**). The cast iron bark pot was a feature of most larger fishing rooms. It was used to boil the buds and rinds which made the bark. Nets and twine were soaked in the bark to help preserve them. (Captain George C. Whiteley, Jr. Collection)*

Two men place their handbarrow of fish on the weigh scales. Most likely, these two men are selling their fish while the third man is weighing it on behalf of the firm. (Captain George C. Whiteley, Jr. Collection)

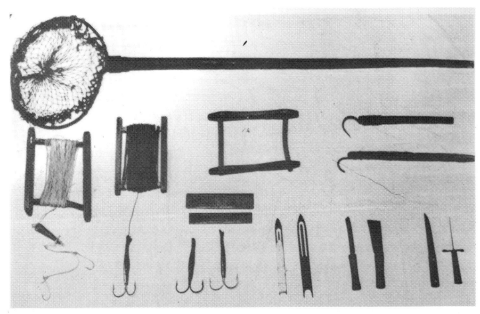

Equipment used in the cod fishery. Dip net, hand line, jiggers, an empty reel, flat wooden boards for determining the mesh size of nets, needles for knitting nets, splitting knives, and cut-throat knives. (Jack Martin, MUN, 1975)

The cooperage of Mr. John R. Harvey, St. John's, c.1908. Coopers and cooperages were an integral part of the saltfish industry as fish exported to the West Indies was packed in casks and fish exported to Brazil was packed in drums and half-drums. (Rev. Don Harvey Collection)

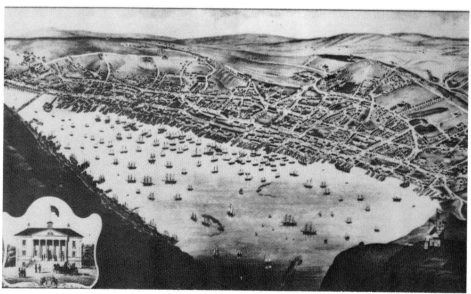

The capital city, St. John's, in the 1870s. (Martin R. (Mac) Lee Collection)

Harbour Grace, the leading outport in the seal and Labrador cod fisheries in the 1870s. (Martin R. (Mac) Lee Collection)

J.W. Hiscock's premises, Smokey, Labrador. The bawn on which the fish was dried can be seen in the foreground. This bawn was made over the course of many decades by vessels being required to off load their ballast [stones] on what was flat marshy ground. (Shannon Ryan, 1975)

Battle Harbour, Labrador, c.1900. One of the most important centres of the Labrador cod fishery, Battle Harbour was established by the Slades (merchants from Poole, Dorset) in the latter 1700s. The Slades brought fishermen and their familes from Poole and a substantial community developed. During the nineteenth century fishermen from the island of Newfoundland began to migrate annually to Battle Harbour to participate in the rich fishery. In the latter 1800s the Slades sold out to Baine, Johnston & Co., which firm in turn sold out to Fred and Guy Earle, Carbonear, in 1955. (Baine Johnston & Co. Ltd. Collection)

Many Newfoundland communities were built around small coves. (Gordon King Collection)

Eastern Tickle, Fogo, c.1900. (MHA, MUN Collection)

Harbour Buffett, c.1900. This was a centre for an inshore fishery and a bank fishery. On the left can be seen part of the Chambers premises and on the right the Wakley premises. Alberto Wareham succeeded Chambers and W.W. Wareham succeeded Wakely. (Dr. Wilfred Wareham Collection)

Burin, c.1900, was noted for its deep-sea, or bank fishing fleet. (MHG, MUN Collection)

English Harbour West, Fortune Bay, a south coast centre for the bank fishery and the inshore fishery. (Michael Harrington, photographed from the premises of J. Petite & Sons, Ltd.)

The French fishery at Cape Rouge, c.1900. This fishing station on the east side of the Great Northern Peninsula was one of the many on the French Shore that was occupied on a seasonal basis by the fishermen from France. Although such fishing rooms were used annually through most of the period from 1713 to 1904, they retained a temporary appearance because they were occupied only during the summer months. (From Prowse, **History of Newfoundland** *(London: 1895), p. 548.)*

The French island of St. Pierre, off Newfoundland's south coast, was the site of a French Shore Fishery and the main bait supply depot for the French Grand Bank fleet. In the 1890s Newfoundland government regulations prohibited the exportation of bait to St. Pierre and in the early twentieth century the French Grand Bank fleet began to change over to steam trawlers. St. Pierre declined as its importance to the French Grand Bank fishery dwindled. (PANL Collection, identified by Mrs. Shirley Scarlett)

Fishermen often built their houses in awkward locations in order to live near good fishing grounds. (Martin R. (Mac) Lee Collection)

The first attempt to reduce Newfoundland's dependence on the fisheries occurred in the 1880s when the government decided that the colony's prosperity would be enhanced by building a railway. In 1883 the first line connected St. John's with Harbour Grace (in the background). Many Conception Bay fishermen decided that employment on the construction and maintenance of the railway was preferable to the uncertainty of the problem-ridden fisheries of the 1880s and 1890s. (Mrs. Frank Ryan Collection)